D1033454

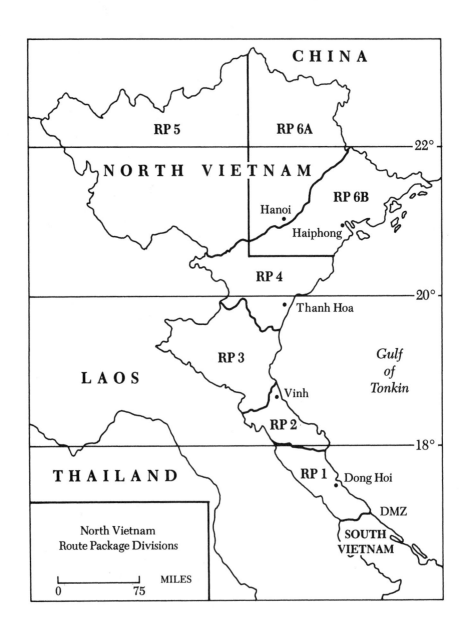

CHINA

RP 5   RP 6A

22°

NORTH VIETNAM

RP 6B

Hanoi

Haiphong

RP 4

20°

Thanh Hoa

LAOS

RP 3

Gulf
of
Tonkin

Vinh

RP 2

18°

THAILAND

RP 1   Dong Hoi

DMZ

North Vietnam
Route Package Divisions

SOUTH
VIETNAM

MILES

0   75

THE LIMITS OF
AIR POWER

——— • ———

The American Bombing of
North Vietnam

MARK CLODFELTER

With a new introduction by the author

UNIVERSITY OF NEBRASKA PRESS • LINCOLN

Chapter 8 originally appeared as "Air Power Versus Asymmetric Enemies: A Frame-work for Evaluating Effectiveness" in *Aerospace Power Journal* (Fall, 2002).

Library of Congress Cataloging-in-Publication Data
Clodfelter, Mark.
The limits of air power: the American bombing of North Vietnam / Mark Clodfelter;
with a new introduction by the author.—1st Nebraska paperback printing.
p. cm.
Includes bibliographical references and index.
ISBN-13: 978-0-8032-6454-0 (pbk.: alk. paper)
ISBN-10: 0-8032-6454-2 (pbk.: alk. paper)
1. Vietnamese Conflict, 1961–1975—Aerial operations, American.   2. United States.
Air Force—History—Vietnamese Conflict, 1961–1975.   3. Air power—United
States—History.   I. Title.
DS558.8.C56   2006
959.704'348—dc22   2005035597

TO
WALTER A. CLODFELTER, JR.
Corporal, 20th Air Force, USAAF, 1945–1946

AND

JOHN R. ALLEN
Captain, 8th Air Force, USAF, 1972–1973

Contents

——•——

	Introduction	ix
	Preface and Acknowledgments	xiii
I	From Unconditional Surrender to Flexible Response	1
II	The Genesis of Graduated Thunder	39
III	An Extended Application of Force	73
IV	Restraints and Results, 1965–68	117
V	Nixon Turns to Air Power	147
VI	Persuading Enemy and Ally: The Christmas Bombings	177
VII	Assessment	203
VIII	Epilogue	211
	Notes	225
	Bibliography	277
	Index	299

Introduction

———— • ————

In the 16 years since the initial publication of *The Limits of Air Power*, I have continued to study the use of American air power as a political instrument. The compilation of my thoughts from teaching air power courses at the Air Force Academy, the School of Advanced Airpower Studies (SAAS), the University of North Carolina, and the National War College resulted in the framework for evaluating air power effectiveness that now appears as this book's epilogue. In presenting that framework I provide more detailed explanations of "positive" and "negative" political objectives than I did in the original edition; plus, I examine key variables that affect whether air power can succeed as a political tool. The reader may find the additional chapter helpful in understanding my analysis of the American air campaigns against North Vietnam.

The new chapter refers to several uses of American air power since the Vietnam War. Indeed, the United States has relied on air power as a vital instrument of military force in all of its post-Vietnam conflicts, particularly those of the last decade and a half. Air power alone challenged the Iraqis for the first 38 days of the 42-day 1991 Persian Gulf War, and America contributed only air power as a military means to thwart aggression in Bosnia and Kosovo. To wreck Taliban rule in Afghanistan, the United States committed a handful of Special Forces troops and large doses of air power, and an aerial display of "shock and awe" triggered the start of Operation Iraqi Freedom. In many respects Presidents George H. W. Bush, William Clinton, and George W. Bush have mirrored the emphasis on air power shown by Presidents Lyndon Johnson and Richard Nixon. Both Johnson and Nixon believed that bombing would end a difficult war in Vietnam without a significant commitment of American ground forces, although the situation each man faced was certainly different—Johnson hoped to preclude a ground build-up, while Nixon sought to remove troops from a war the bulk of the American people no longer supported. In both cases air power, with its promise of a cheap and speedy victory, seemed to offer the solution to a thorny predicament.

Air power's siren song has only grown louder in the aftermath of Nixon's Linebacker bombing campaigns, where dramatic episodes of bombing with "smart" munitions set the tone for much of what has followed. The seemingly impregnable Dragon's Jaw Bridge over the Song Ma River, which had survived more than 700 attacks during Johnson's Rolling Thunder air offensive, fell on Linebacker's fourth day when several laser-guided bombs slammed into a single span of the bridge. The images of bombs traveling down airshafts during Desert Storm intensified the conviction of American leaders that they could pristinely destroy targets at a minimum cost to civilian lives and property. Additionally, the precision capability of smart munitions, especially when combined with stealth technology, enabled pilots to drop their bombs from relatively safe standoff distances. Cruise missiles further provided accuracy with impunity. Yet the ordnance that counted most in 1991 may well have been the conventional "dumb" munitions dropped on Iraqi frontline positions in Kuwait. Roughly 100,000 Iraqis surrendered to coalition forces before General Norman Schwarzkopf's ground offensive began, and many cited the impact of the bombing as a key reason for their defection.

Nonetheless, the seed planted by the smart bombs of Linebacker grew fertile in the ground tilled by Desert Storm. America had only 148 servicemen and women killed in combat during the 42-day war, though it proved incapable of stopping Iraqi air power in the form of mobile Scud missiles that accounted for 28 of those deaths. In both the Bosnia and Kosovo conflicts the percentage of smart munitions greatly increased, while the number of deaths suffered by American combatants fell to zero. The precision attacks also caused very few civilian casualties given the amount of bombs dropped. Nevertheless, an incredibly precise bombing capability did not guarantee zero civilian deaths. As the attacks on the al Firdos bunker in Baghdad and the Chinese embassy in Belgrade revealed, precision bombing demands precision intelligence. With media outlets instantly beaming bombing results to the world community, mistakes have assumed a much greater impact, especially since American political and military leaders have stressed air power's accuracy.

Still, those leaders have remained convinced that air power provides the best way to thwart an enemy at a minimum cost to both attackers and defenders. Besides relying on bombing to resolve the crises in Bosnia and Kosovo, President Clinton also used it as a political instrument on other occasions. He responded to the August 1998 attacks on American embassies in Kenya and Tanzania with cruise missiles aimed at one of Osama bin Laden's terrorist camps in Afghanistan and a pharmaceutical plant in Sudan. In December of that year Clinton launched Operation Desert Fox, sending aircraft and cruise missiles against Iraqi targets in response to Saddam Hussein's continued refusal to permit UN weapons inspections. President Clinton's successor, George W. Bush, further exhibited a significant reliance on air power, counting on it to help destroy the Taliban regime in Afghanistan in 2001 and Saddam Hussein's regime in Iraq in 2003. These air efforts were against enemies who waged conventional war similar to that fought by the North Vietnamese Army in 1972 when opposed by Nixon's Linebacker air campaigns. Today, the wars in Afghanistan and Iraq resemble that encountered by Johnson in Vietnam—an intensely motivated but sporadically waged insurgency employing guerrilla warfare methods and receiving resilient assistance from outside sources. Of course, major differences exist between Vietnam and these latter conflicts: for example, ethnic, religious, and tribal divisions cause distinctive problems in Afghanistan and Iraq that were not paramount concerns in Southeast Asia.

Yet from an air power perspective, the positive political goal of creating a stable, democratic Iraq parallels the difficulty of achieving a stable, non-Communist South Vietnam. Achieving the positive objective in Iraq demands the application of military force, but negative objectives again lurk in the background, and American leaders can achieve them only by limiting the amount of force used. Key among those negative goals is the desire to win "hearts and minds"—not only of members of the Iraqi populace but also of the worldwide Muslim community. In the same way that Lyndon Johnson's Cold War concerns with China and the Soviet Union gave him pause before he sanctioned bombing raids on North Vietnam, President Bush must be mindful of how air strikes in Iraq might bolster al Qaeda in the broader war against global terror.

Unfortunately, precision bombing may not be the answer. Despite being several technological generations ahead of the capability displayed in Vietnam, smart munitions still do not guarantee zero collateral damage. Many of the precision air attacks against insurgent leaders have produced claims by insurgents—as well as by Iraqis who do not support the insurgency—that Iraqi civilians have been killed in the raids. Whether true or not, such accusations grab headlines in the Islamic press and on Al Jazeera, providing the *perception* among many in the Muslim world that such attacks display a callous disregard for Muslim civilian lives. In the type of war that America now faces, those perceptions have become reality to many opposing the United States. In such conflicts, even with such advantages as Predator drones and Hellfire missiles, the long-term harm of applying lethal air power is likely to eclipse its short-term benefit. As long as negative political goals remain substantial, the limits of air power displayed in Vietnam will continue to restrict its utility in the twenty-first century.

Preface and Acknowledgments

———— • ————

On April 10, 1988, Richard M. Nixon told NBC's *Meet the Press* that his greatest mistake as President was not Watergate but his failure to bomb and mine North Vietnam early in 1969 as he later did in 1972. "If we had done that then," he said, "I think we would've ended the war in 1969 rather than in 1973."

The former President's sentiments are not unique. Indeed, most of the war's high-ranking air commanders share them. The conviction that massive bombing of the North could have won the war in 1969—or 1965—has permeated today's Air Force and reinforces a doctrine that emphasizes victory through strategic bombing. The signing of the peace treaty less than a month after Nixon's "Linebacker II" bombing offensive, in which B-52s and fighter aircraft dropped 20,000 tons of bombs on North Vietnam's heartland in eleven days, indicates to many that air power alone ended the conflict. An excerpt from a staff sergeant's 17 March 1988 letter in *Stars and Stripes* typifies the current Air Force perception of the December 1972 air campaign: "In retrospect, Linebacker II erased all doubts that the Vietnam War could have been won. Unfortunately, there was nothing done in 1972 that could not have been done in 1965."

The President and the staff sergeant both ignore the essence of why bombing "worked" in 1972—because it was the *proper* instrument to apply, given Nixon's specific *goals* and the political and military situation that *then* existed. The President had two aims in 1972, and both were limited: an American withdrawal that did not abandon South Vietnam to an imminent Communist takeover and, after October, convincing South Vietnamese President Nguyen Van Thieu that the United States would back the South if the North resumed hostilities. Having received a free hand in Vietnam from the Chinese and Soviets, Nixon could apply air power without many of the restraints plaguing his predecessor. Moreover, for the first time since America's full-fledged involvement in 1965, Hanoi's leaders decided to wage a sustained conventional war, an effort requiring vast logistical support that was vulnerable to air attack. This specific combination of goals and conditions was not present until 1972.

Air commanders, however, remained convinced throughout the war that bombing would ultimately compel the North Vietnamese to stop fighting. The air chiefs' conviction stemmed from World War II strategic air campaigns, which they believed demonstrated that air power could wreck an enemy's capability to resist, and from the air doctrine emerging after the perceived "aberration" of Korea, which contended that the strategic principles suitable for a war against the Soviet military machine could be adapted to any level of conflict. From mid-1964 on, air commanders advised political leaders to launch a Linebacker II-type assault on North Vietnam. They failed to consider whether massive bombing suited the nature of the war, which was primarily a guerrilla struggle before March 1972 (with the notable exception of the 1968 Tet Offensive), or whether it suited American war aims. Nurtured by a deep-rooted tradition stressing battlefield annihilation, most commanders never fully comprehended the civilian leadership's desire to keep the war limited. Many air chiefs also failed to realize that American objectives in Vietnam changed after Tet.

American political leaders likewise did not thoroughly consider whether bombing was an appropriate instrument in Vietnam. Concerned about Soviet or Chinese intervention and unwilling to focus attention away from his Great Society programs, President Lyndon Johnson believed in February 1965 that the threat of destruction presented by limited bombing would deter North Vietnam from supporting the Viet Cong. The President and his advisers had seen the Soviet Union retreat in Cuba from the threat of American air power, and they could not imagine the North Vietnamese withstanding a similar display of resolve. After almost five months of air strikes, however, Johnson had a change of heart. In July 1965, he concluded that the bombing could not stop Northern participation in the war and that strengthening South Vietnam had higher priority. Still, his decision was not final, and for the remainder of his presidency his view of bombing's utility vacillated between a means to restrict Northern backing of the Viet Cong and a means to win the war. Four years later, Nixon used air power to guarantee an American withdrawal by thwarting the 1972 Easter Offensive and to persuade both North and South Vietnam to sign a cease-fire agreement. Although his bombing was more fruitful than Johnson's, Nixon's recent comments imply that his successful application of air power owed more to happenstance than to sound reasoning.

In the final analysis, the supreme test of bombing's efficacy is its contribution to a nation's war aims. Clausewitz's definition of war as "a continuation of political activity by other means" provides the only true measure for evaluating air power's effectiveness. My goal is to provide such a Clausewitzian appraisal of the air war against North Vietnam. I have attempted to do so by evaluating the three air campaigns against the North—Rolling Thunder (2 March 1965–31 October 1968), Linebacker I (10 May 1972–23 October 1972), and Linebacker II (18–29 December 1972)—in terms of how effectively they supported American war aims. I have also tried to place the air war in its broadest possible historical setting by briefly analyzing the U.S. air campaigns in World War II and Korea, as well as the doctrine emerging from them. Those earlier efforts helped mold the air power convictions of American civilian and military leaders during Vietnam.

Evaluating the political efficacy of the three air offensives required first identifying the specific war aims guiding each. The goals were disparate; not only did they vary from campaign to campaign, but many of them *restricted* the application of air power. These latter goals, achievable only by *limiting* military force, are termed "negative" objectives. "Positive" objectives are those that were attainable only by *applying* military power. For example, President Johnson's positive political goal in Vietnam was an independent, stable, non-Communist South, but he also pursued the negative aim of avoiding direct intervention by the Chinese or Soviets. Clausewitz asserts that "a preponderantly negative policy will . . . retard the decision" in war, an observation that fits my definition. I maintain that political controls on air power flow directly from negative objectives, and that the respective emphases given to positive and negative aims can affect air power's political efficacy.

Other factors can influence bombing's political effectiveness. In addition to the political controls stemming from negative objectives, military controls—such as doctrine, moral concerns, and administrative arrangements—and operational controls—such as enemy defenses, technology, geography, and weather—can limit an air campaign's prospects for success. Those factors may also serve to *enhance* bombing efficacy, depending on the nature of the war and the specific goals sought. Air Force bombing doctrine was one such chameleon in Vietnam. During Rolling Thunder, the emphasis on destroying the North's means of production and distribution limited bombing effectiveness, because Communist forces in the South needed few external supplies. But during Linebacker I, when the North Vietnamese mounted a large-scale, conventional assault requiring massive logistical support, the doctrine proved sound.

My findings cannot be definitive, because my evidence is not all-inclusive—many American sources remain classified, and American historians do not enjoy access to archives of the North Vietnamese Politburo, the source that would most clearly reveal air power's accomplishments—but to wait until all evidence is available before evaluating it would be a mistake. Enough information is present to determine many of the reasons why bombing failed as a political tool for Lyndon Johnson, and why it succeeded for Nixon. This is not to imply that Nixon's bombing should serve as a blueprint for applying air power, or that Johnson's approach should be avoided. Each man pursued different objectives and faced unique circumstances in Vietnam, and the combination of aims and conditions directly affected bombing efficacy. What I hope emerges from this work is a realization that conventional air power's effectiveness as a political instrument varies according to many diverse factors. Vietnam provides no concrete models for effective bombing. Above all else, the conflict epitomizes Clausewitz's notion that war is a fluid process. Yet many of the elements that influenced the air campaigns against North Vietnam could reappear in future American conflicts, and an awareness of these factors could benefit civilian and military leaders wrestling with the prickly options of air power employment. As the April 1986 attack on Libya demonstrates, the probability is high that the United States will continue to rely on air power as a political tool.

A final point must be made. My focus on how well air power complemented American political objectives highlights the Air Force's role in Vietnam. This emphasis is in no way an attempt to slight the enormous efforts in the air campaigns by the Navy and Marines. Rather, I am endeavoring to portray how the indelible stamp of Air Force strategic bombing doctrine affected the air war against the North, and how doctrinal convictions established long before Vietnam colored air commanders' perceptions of bombing effectiveness.

This work would have been impossible without the assistance of many people. First, I must thank Major John R. Allen, USAF (ret.), a veteran of three Linebacker II missions and my boss in Korea. His recollections of his B-52 flights over Hanoi—remembrances that evoked pride, fear, exhilaration, and above all a profound sense of despair—provided the spark that grew into this book. I dedicate this work in part to him. General John W. Vogt, Jr., USAF (ret.), spent many hours with me discussing both Linebacker and Rolling Thunder, and Lieutenant General Joseph H. Moore, USAF (ret.), sent me a letter answering my many questions about his role in Rolling Thunder. Other Air Force participants in the air war against North Vietnam who granted me interviews were Colonel Clyde E. Bodenheimer, Colonel Robert D. Clark, Colonel Charles Ferguson, USAF Reserve; Lieutenant Colonel William Greenhalgh (ret.) and Major George Thompson (ret.). Major Jim Rash, USAF (ret.), a veteran of three Linebacker II missions, responded to my request for information with a detailed letter. Major Fred Watts, USMC (ret.), sent me a thorough description of the Marine Corps's raids in the Korean War against hydroelectric power plants. Major John R. Scoggins, Jr., USAF, gave me data on North Vietnam's resupply capability.

Four civilian leaders who played influential roles in the air war provided valuable information. Former Secretary of State Dean Rusk, former National Security Adviser Walt W. Rostow, and former State Department Director of Vietnam Affairs Paul M. Kattenburg allowed me to interview them. Former Secretary of Defense Robert S. McNamara patiently answered my questions concerning Rolling Thunder over the telephone.

The staffs at the Air Force Historical Research Center and of three presidential libraries aided me tremendously. Judy Endicott, Pressley Bickerstaff, Margaret C. Claiborn, Lynn O. Gamma, Dr. James H. Kitchens, Nora S. Bledsoe, and Sarah F. Rawlings, all of the Air Force Historical Research Center at Maxwell Air Force Base, Alabama, spent untold hours fulfilling my requests for obscure documents. At the Dwight D. Eisenhower Presidential Library, Herbert Pankratz and Kathy Struss provided assistance, while at the Harry S Truman Library Erwin Mueller, Niel Johnson, Elizabeth Safly, Anita Heavener, and especially Dennis Bilger eagerly responded to my many requests for source material. Dr. David C. Humphrey, Shellynne Eickhoff, Linda Hanson, and Nancy Smith guided my research at the Lyndon Baines Johnson Library, and Dr. Humphrey responded with alacrity to my subsequent requests by mail.

At the Office of Air Force History, Dr. Wayne Thompson, and at the U.S. Army Center for Military History, Colonel John Schlight,

USAF (ret.), answered many questions concerning the air war against North Vietnam.

Colonel Jimmie N. Murphy, Major John L. Hesse, Carol Rose, and John Corcoran of the Air Force Office for Security Review assured a timely return of declassified notes that greatly aided my research.

The University of Alabama Press kindly permitted me to use material from my chapter in *The Foreign and Domestic Dimensions of Modern Warfare: Vietnam, Central America, and Nuclear Strategy,* copyright 1988 by The University of Alabama Press.

For critical comments and suggestions, I am indebted to many people. James R. Leutze, R. Don Higginbotham, Michael H. Hunt, Alex Roland, Peter F. Walker, Samuel R. Williamson, Jr., Guenter Lewy, George C. Herring, Kenneth P. Werrell, and John M. Thompson all provided guidance. Colonel Dennis M. Drew, Director of the Air Power Research Institute at the Air Force's Center for Aerospace Doctrine, Research, and Education (CADRE), and Lieutenant Colonel Price T. Bingham and Major Earl Tilford, also at CADRE, have been most helpful in critiquing my chapters. Dr. Robert F. Futrell provided detailed comments on chapter one. My dad, the most meticulous proofreader I have seen, thoroughly reviewed the entire text. Without the special attention given by two individuals, however, I could not have completed this work to the best of my ability. David MacIsaac and Peter Maslowski offered a multitude of constructive criticisms after reading each chapter. They chided me when I needed it, praised me when they felt I deserved it, and provided me with encouragement when I feared the cause was lost. They are the ideals of whom I think whenever I hear the term "historian."

I must also mention the assistance of colleagues and cadets at the Air Force Academy. Many tough questions in the classroom and casual conversations in the hall have broadened my horizons as much as any specific criticism. Several individuals in particular deserve acknowledgment: Colonel Carl Reddel, Lieutenant Colonel Harry Borowski (ret.); Lieutenant Colonel Phillip Meilinger; Majors "Barney" Ballinger, Brian Nichelson, and Mike Worden; Lieutenant Steve Maffeo, USN Reserve, and Second Lieutenant Robert Renner. The responsibility for all that is written, however, is mine alone, and my work does not necessarily represent the views of the United States Air Force Academy or the United States Air Force.

Finally, I must thank friends and family. Majors Curt Bedke,

Steve Petersen, "Dutch" Remkes, and Dave Gragan, USMC, class-mates and confidants, reassured me throughout the research and writing. Don Winslow of Lincoln, Nebraska, supported the work when it first began in 1982. Karen Clark provided me a place to stay in Kansas City during my research at the Truman Library. My next-door neighbor in North Carolina, Sherry Gates, literally saved chapter one when my computer threatened to erase it, and never once complained of hearing my printer at two in the morning.

Those who deserve the most credit are the three individuals whom I hold most dear: my parents and my wife. Without the values that Mom and Dad have instilled in me, I cannot imagine myself ever undertaking such an effort; without Donna's continual support, I cannot imagine myself satisfied with the result. I owe a special thanks to Dad, who told me countless times of B-29s rolling off the runway at Tinian, brought me model kits of famous World War II bombers, and guaranteed that I saw such movies as *Twelve O'Clock High* and *The War Lover*. I am certain that he planted the seed that grew into my interest in strategic bombing, and I dedicate this book in part to him.

M. C.
Colorado Springs, Colorado
August 1988

The Limits of Air Power

I

From Unconditional Surrender to Flexible Response

It is clear . . . that war is not a mere act of policy but a true political instrument, a continuation of political activity by other means. What remains peculiar to war is simply the peculiar nature of its means. War in general, and the commander in any specific instance, is entitled to require that the trend and designs of policy shall not be inconsistent with these means. That, of course, is no small demand; but however much it may affect political aims in a given case, it will never do more than modify them. The political object is the goal, war is the means of reaching it, and means can never be considered in isolation from their purpose.

CARL VON CLAUSEWITZ[1]

The military forces of the United States can perform their greatest and most economical service in any form of international conflict by providing circumstances in which the United States can exercise a compelling initiative in international affairs.

AIR FORCE MANUAL *1-2*
1 December 1959[2]

The achievement of manned flight in 1903 added a new dimension to the political instrument of war. Visionaries proclaimed that air power would dominate future conflicts, but in the great struggle of 1914–18 the airplane played an innocuous role. Still, the dream persisted. During the interwar period, such prophets as Giulio Douhet, Hugh Trenchard, and William "Billy" Mitchell argued that air power would become the decisive element of military force.

1

They asserted that "strategic" bombing—aimed at a country's war-making potential rather than at its deployed armed forces—could destroy not only the *capability* of an enemy to wage war but also the enemy's *will* to fight. In the United States, strategic bombing proponents stressed these concepts at Maxwell Field's Air Corps Tactical School (ACTS), the training ground of World War II's air commanders.[3] While ACTS officers emphasized air power as a means to demolish war-making potential, the belief that bombing could destroy national will was not ignored. They contended that destroying an enemy's war-making capability through attacks on its economic "vital centers" would disrupt its social fabric and lead to a collapse of morale. Lieutenant Haywood Hansell observed in a 1936 ACTS lecture: "A nation's attacking air force would be at liberty to proceed directly to the ultimate aim in war: overthrow of the enemy will to resist through the destruction of those vital elements upon which modern social life is dependent."[4] The ACTS viewed transportation, steel, iron ore, and electric power facilities as the elements most essential to an industrial nation's economic well-being and hence the most likely objectives for air attack.[5]

To American air theorists during the interwar period, strategic bombing offered the means to accomplish two interrelated objectives. First, by destroying an enemy's capability and will to resist, it could win a war independently of armies and navies. Second, because of its ability to achieve an independent decision, strategic bombing provided a rationale for making the Air Corps a separate service from the Army. The Army's air branch made some strides towards autonomy between the world wars. In 1926, it changed its name from the Air Service to the Air Corps and received special representation on the Army's General Staff; in 1934, it established a General Headquarters (GHQ) Air Force that directed all combat units and stressed strategic bombing as the Air Corps's primary mission; in 1941, it became the Army Air Forces, directed by a commander who served as Deputy Chief of Staff for Air. Boeing's 1935 prototype of a four-engine "heavy" bomber (the XB-17, which could also serve as a passenger airplane) and perfection of the Norden bombsight in that same year provided the Air Corps with the tools to conduct precision raids against essential elements of an enemy's economy.

Strategic bombing advocates refused to proclaim their perceived ability too loudly, however. They instead echoed Mitchell's earlier pronouncements that bombers offered the best means of protecting the United States against invasion.[6] Most Army officers viewed the

Air Corps as a means of infantry support and had little faith that strategic bombing could independently achieve victory. For them, "tactical" bombing—that designed to assist ground forces on the battlefield—was the Air Corps's primary mission. "Air Forces constitute a highly mobile and powerful element which . . . conducts the operations for carrying out the Army mission," the Army's 1935 regulation governing Air Corps combat responsibilities declared.[7] By retaining control of the Air Corps, Army commanders felt that they could guarantee that air power remained responsive to their needs. Strategic bombing proponents chafed under the Army's dominion. "I am confident that no general thinks he can control the Navy or no admiral thinks he can operate an army." Air Service Captain Horace Hickam said, "but some of them think they can operate an air force."[8]

World War II gave American air leaders a chance to vindicate their faith in strategic air power, as they directed huge armadas against Germany and Japan in pursuit of "unconditional surrender." The perceived contribution of strategic bombing to the Allied victory was largely responsible for the creation of the Air Force as a separate service in 1947. Strategic bombing's effect on the war in Korea was less clear-cut. In Korea, Air Force commanders applied air power to help obtain limited political objectives that varied between the securing of South Korean independence and the elimination of Communism from the Korean peninsula. The differences in both the political objectives and the military conduct of the two wars produced ambiguous conclusions for those who analyzed the effectiveness of strategic bombing. Military chiefs tended to view Korea as an aberration. As a result, the air doctrine developed in the decade after the struggle focused on global conflict and slighted limited war. While civilian analysts saw Korea as a model for future wars, they did little to dissuade Air Force commanders from emphasizing large doses of air power as the cure for all military confrontations. The perceived efficacy of bombing as a political tool in World War II and Korea, combined with Air Force doctrinal developments during the post-Korea decade, significantly affected how the United States employed air power during the Vietnam War.

World War II

President Franklin D. Roosevelt believed that the territorial aggrandizements of both Germany and Japan during the 1930s posed direct threats to the security of the United States, its interests abroad, and the entire Western Hemisphere. Pearl Harbor and Hitler's subsequent declaration of war against the United States united American public opinion in the belief that total victory over the Axis was an appropriate goal. Roosevelt had long held the conviction that nothing less than complete conquest would erase the threat of future militarism by Germany and Japan, and he felt that the failure to crush the German regime in World War I spawned the stab-in-the-back theory that facilitated Hitler's rise.[9] The President's January 1943 announcement of "unconditional surrender" as the Allied war aim accomplished a twofold purpose: It notified the Axis that the Anglo-Americans would not negotiate a settlement prior to the total defeat of the Axis powers, and it assured the Soviets and Chinese that the Anglo-Americans intended to crush the enemy. Roosevelt, Winston Churchill, and Joseph Stalin reaffirmed the unconditional surrender idea in a joint declaration at Yalta.[10]

Unconditional surrender was the cornerstone of America's "positive" political objective during World War II. The objective was "positive" in that it could be accomplished only through military force; to achieve unconditional surrender, the Allies had to destroy the Axis nations and their political institutions. "Negative" objectives—those achievable only by restraining military power—were nonexistent. Thus, the United States could direct its unbridled military might against its enemies in devastating fashion.[11] Unconditional surrender remained the Allies' goal throughout America's participation in the war. It committed them to a restructuring of the political institutions of Germany, Italy, and Japan. In the view of Allied leaders, the political revamping could not occur until the Axis military machines suffered complete defeat.

Military cooperation between the Soviets and the Anglo-Americans promised the best method of maintaining an alliance whose members had different thoughts regarding postwar German political structure. To guarantee that the Russians and British survived the German onslaught, Roosevelt committed the United States to a strategy of "Germany first." The American and British Chiefs of Staff confirmed this policy, along with the premise of unconditional surrender, at the Arcadia Conference in January 1942.

One year later, at Casablanca, the Combined Chiefs of Staff announced the start of a "round-the-clock" Anglo-American bomber offensive as an integral part of the total effort to subjugate Germany.

Roosevelt's emphasis on aircraft production combined with Air Corps planning to produce a bombing strategy focusing on mass and precision. The President believed that air power offered a way to employ overwhelming force to obtain unconditional surrender in minimum time, and he placed a high priority on the public's desire to end the war quickly and bring American troops back home. In addition, both Roosevelt and Secretary of War Henry Stimson initially felt bombing would demonstrate the seriousness of the American war effort to Russia and China at a small cost in manpower and money. Air Corps planners, prior to Roosevelt's production increases, had developed an air strategy stressing detailed target selection and precision bombing. With the additional aircraft provided by Roosevelt, the foundations of the strategy set the tone for AWPD-1, the air plan completed in August 1941, which guided the American bombing of Germany.[12]

Designed to facilitate—or obviate—the invasion of Europe, AWPD-1 aimed at crippling German war-making capability through attacks on essential industrial complexes. Moreover, by emphasizing strategic rather than tactical employment of air power, the air planners sought to demonstrate the bomber's unique ability to strike deep behind the battle line, a mission that could, they believed, lead to air force autonomy. The planners selected 154 targets and divided them into four groups: the German electrical power system, transportation system, oil and petroleum industry, and air defense system.[13] At the Casablanca Conference, destruction of the capability and will of the German nation to resist became the announced goals of the Combined Bomber Offensive (CBO). The Americans, through "precision" daylight attacks, trained their portion of the assault against the German war-making capability, while the British designed their nighttime area raids to have maximum effect on the morale of industrial workers. Because of British merchant shipping losses and German air superiority over the Continent, the Combined Chiefs changed specific target priorities at Casablanca to make submarine construction yards and the German aircraft industry the two top objectives. In May 1943 the Luftwaffe took on the number one priority as an "intermediate objective," which, if not defeated, could thwart the projected invasion.[14]

Not until early March 1944, after the arrival of the P-51 Mustang, did the Allied air forces achieve air superiority over the Continent. In that month General Dwight D. Eisenhower took control of the Anglo-American bomber force and directed it against the transportation network of northern France. Oil became the highest priority target on 8 June 1944,[15] but Eisenhower retained control of the bomber fleets until September to prevent the Germans from massing a counterattack against the invasion beachhead. General Carl A. Spaatz, Commander of the U.S. Strategic Air Forces, and Air Chief Marshal Arthur Harris, Commander of RAF Bomber Command, began the concerted effort against oil on 23 September, with rail and waterborne transportation systems assuming second priority.

Although oil remained the highest priority target for the duration of the Combined Bomber Offensive, a 31 January 1945 directive assigned second priority to selected cities in eastern Germany "where heavy attack will cause great confusion in civilian evacuation from the east and hamper reinforcements."[16] The 8th Air Force directed its February raids on Berlin, Leipzig, and Dresden against such military-related targets as railroad marshaling yards. Yet the targets selected were in close proximity to residential areas. The German attack at the Ardennes in December 1944 shocked the Allied High Command and demonstrated that Germany still possessed the capability and will to resist. To facilitate the goal of unconditional surrender, American air commanders ordered raids that they believed would directly affect civilian morale. Two days before the 3 February 1945 attack on Berlin, Lieutenant General James H. Doolittle, the 8th Air Force Commander, wired Spaatz, asking:

> Is Berlin still open to air attack? Do you want priority oil targets hit in preference to Berlin if they definitely become visual? Do you want center of City in Berlin hit or definitely military targets, such as Spandau, on the Western outskirts?[17]

Spaatz's reply was terse. He told Doolittle to "hit oil if visual assured; otherwise, Berlin—center of City."[18] Cloud cover over the primary target forced Doolittle's air crews to attack their secondary objective: government buildings in the heart of downtown Berlin. The attack killed 25,000 people. The Anglo-American assault ten days later against Dresden resulted in the deaths of at least 35,000 civilians.[19] Despite Lieutenant General Ira Eaker's 1943 declaration, "We must never allow the record of this war to convict us of throwing the strategic bomber at the man in the street,"[20] by 1945 the American raids on Germany resembled the RAF's area attacks in their consequences.

In the Pacific, the onslaught of Major General Curtis E. LeMay's B-29s shattered Eaker's expectations. As a lieutenant in the late

1930s, LeMay had served on the staff of the GHQ Air Force and flown as a B-17 navigator. He led the grueling mission against Regensburg as commander of the 305th Bomb Group in World War II's European theater. Before his arrival in the Pacific, the Twentieth Air Force bombed Japan ineffectively from Chinese bases. The unit launched its first raid from the Marianas on 24 November 1944, and until 9 March 1945, the primary objective of the Marianas-based XXI Bomber Command was Japanese aircraft production and repair facilities. The B-29s flew raids against specific targets in much the same manner as did B-17s and B-24s in Europe. These attacks, designed to support the planned invasion of Japan, produced little damage because of the dispersal of the Japanese aircraft industry and the difficulty of bombing from very high altitudes. As a result, LeMay searched for a new method by which to conduct strategic bombing.

While the Japanese had dispersed many of their large industries, they relied heavily on plants employing fewer than 250 workers for subcontracted parts and equipment. Scattered throughout the residential sections of many Japanese cities, the small plants accounted for 50 percent of Tokyo's industrial output.[21] Japanese cities also contained a large number of highly inflammable wooden structures, and much of the American public sought maximum retribution for Pearl Harbor.[22] These combined factors led LeMay to initiate the firebombing of Japan.

LeMay's incendiary assault and the atomic raids that followed revealed a new emphasis in the strategic campaign against Japan: the direct destruction of the enemy's will to resist. American air leaders believed that the loss of war-making capability would cause a corresponding loss of national morale, as a nation's economic collapse would trigger social chaos. With Japanese industry impervious to precision raids, LeMay chose to target the enemy's will directly. His low-level attacks against industry clumped in residential districts produced tremendous civilian losses and led him to believe that the fire assault would ultimately compel a Japanese surrender. President Harry S Truman's decision to use the atomic bomb manifested a similar conviction. Truman believed that the bomb's effects would be no worse than the results of LeMay's fire raids and that a Japanese capitulation without invasion would save an immense number of Allied lives.[23]

Both Roosevelt and Truman firmly directed grand strategy, yet the absence of negative political objectives allowed them to give the

Joint Chiefs an essentially free rein in conducting such combat operations as strategic bombing. Roosevelt frequently overruled the Joint Chiefs on strategic matters. General Henry H. "Hap" Arnold, Commanding General of the Army Air Forces, disagreed with the President's 1942 decisions to invade North Africa and to give General Douglas MacArthur additional material support. The air chief perceived that both policies detracted from the aim of defeating Germany first by transferring scarce bomber resources away from the 8th Air Force's buildup in England. Yet Arnold noted that "once the President of the United States agreed on the general principles [of an operation], he relied upon his Chiefs of Staff to carry them out—to make plans for the consummation of these general ideas." Arnold delegated broad authority to his subordinates LeMay and Spaatz. While Arnold assisted LeMay in some target selection, Spaatz "operated with free hands." The bulk of command restraints on the Strategic Air Forces commander stemmed from Eisenhower.[24]

For all their freedom from political controls, Army Air Forces commanders faced numerous operational restrictions. In addition to the diversion of bombers and crew members to other theaters, the arrival of untrained airmen encumbered the buildup of the 8th Air Force.[25] The absence of a long-range fighter plagued the American campaign against Germany throughout 1943, and following the disastrous October mission to Schweinfurt General Eaker prohibited further unescorted raids against the Reich. Unfavorable weather also restricted the air campaigns in both Europe and the Pacific. To maintain "round-the-clock" pressure on Germany, the Army Air Forces commanders resorted to blind bombing techniques that provided results similar to those achieved by the British area offensive. In the Pacific, Japan remained immune to strategic air attack until the Americans could secure bases within 1,500 miles of the home islands; prior to the conquest of the Marianas, B-29s could not bomb Tokyo.

Not until the latter stages of the war against both Germany and Japan did the brunt of the Allied strategic bombing campaigns occur. The Anglo-American Bomber Commands dropped 1,234,767 tons of bombs—more than 60 percent of the total falling on Axis Europe during the entire war—between July 1944 and April 1945. The Combined Bomber Offensive killed 305,000 German civilians, wounded 780,000, rendered 1,865,000 homeless, forced evacuation of 4,885,000, and deprived 20 million of public utilities. By the third quarter of 1944, the campaign had tied down an estimated 4.5 million workers, nearly 20 percent of the nonagricultural labor force, in air raid–related activities. Bombing had destroyed half the supply of all petroleum products by December 1944, while reserves of aviation gasoline had fallen by 90 percent of their level when the oil campaign began in May. The attack on transportation that began in September 1944 had, in five months, lessened the volume of railroad car loadings by 75 percent.[26]

B-29s dropped 147,000 tons of bombs on Japan during the whole of the Pacific War, but only 7,180 tons fell prior to the first fire raid on 9 March 1945. The 20th Air Force conducted fire assaults against sixty-six Japanese cities, killing 330,000 civilians and rendering 8.5 million homeless. Production hours lost because of bombing rose from 20 percent in 1944 to more than 40 percent in July 1945, by which time industrial production had declined to 35 percent of the Japanese wartime peak.[27]

Destruction of the enemy's war-making capability marked only one of the goals of the Allied bombing offensives; destruction of the enemy's will was an aim of equal importance. Compiled by a team primarily of civilian researchers at the end of World War II, the United States Strategic Bombing Survey (USSBS) concluded that the bombing of Germany "did not stiffen [German] morale."[28] Yet it also revealed that the German populace could withstand the Allied air onslaught:

> The mental reaction of the German people to air attack is significant. Under ruthless control they showed surprising resistance to the terror and hardships of repeated air attack, to the destruction of their homes and belongings, and to the conditions under which they were reduced to live. Their morale, their beliefs in ultimate victory or satisfactory compromise, and their confidence in their leaders declined, but they continued to work efficiently as long as the physical means of production remained. The power of a police state over its people cannot be underestimated.[29]

Against the Japanese, LeMay's fire raids produced an increasing disenchantment with the war. When the incendiary attacks began in March 1945, 19 percent of the Japanese civil populace believed that Japan could not achieve victory; just prior to the surrender in August the total had increased to 68 percent, of which more than one-half of the individuals interviewed credited air attacks, other than the atomic raids, as the principal reason for their beliefs.[30] By the time of Hiroshima, some members of the Japanese Supreme War Council already favored peace. The atomic attacks induced the Emperor to intervene in the usual functioning of the Council to secure an armistice. Thus, the Survey concluded, the atomic bombs "did foreshorten the war and expedite the peace."[31]

The Survey did not claim that strategic bombing achieved victory in either the European or the Pacific theater; however, it surmised that had Allied armies not overrun Germany in 1945, bombing would have halted the nation's armament production by May, resulting in the collapse of German resistance a few months thereafter.[32] Likewise, the Survey asserted that "certainly prior to 31 December 1945, Japan would have surrendered even if the atomic bombs had not been dropped, even if Russia had not entered the war, and even if no land invasion had been planned or contemplated."[33] The Survey further claimed that the application of Allied air power in Europe was "decisive" and implied the same in its summation of the Pacific War. Still, in both cases the study viewed the contribution of strategic bombing as complementing the efforts of ground and naval forces.

In the larger sense, the bombing campaigns complemented the primary goal of unconditional surrender, accomplishing it by a preponderance of effort rather than through surgical precision. The Army Air Forces *hammered* both Germany and Japan, but use of the bludgeon rather than the rapier meshed with the purpose of obliterating the political as well as the military foundations of the Axis nations. Bombing also supported the aim of achieving victory in the shortest time, facilitating the invasion of France and obviating the invasion of Japan. In hastening unconditional surrender, the air offensives prevented untold Allied casualties, especially regarding the projected assault on Japan, although the air campaigns themselves were not cheap in either money or men. The costs of aircraft production and air crew training absorbed a significant chunk of the War Department's budget, and the air war in Europe claimed 63,410 American casualties.[34]

While the Combined Bomber Offensive ultimately wreaked havoc on Germany's war-making capacity, significant results did not appear until the campaign's final seven months, when the bulk of the tonnage dropped fell on the Reich. Hitler had geared the German economy for a short war, and only after Stalingrad did German factories begin the transition to maximum output. This production lag hindered the effectiveness of the CBO during 1943. In the Pacific, the American submarine fleet's isolation of the Japanese home islands from needed raw materials enhanced the effectiveness of LeMay's incendiary onslaught and further demonstrated to the Japanese populace the hopelessness of the war. Yet, despite the massive destruction wrought by the fire raids, only after Hiroshima did the Emperor assert his authority to seek an armistice.

To Army Air Forces commanders, the bombing offensives vindicated their belief that air power would play a vital role in securing victory. General Spaatz, the U.S. Air Force's first Chief of Staff, typified the thoughts of most American air leaders at the end of World War II when he commented: "We might have won the war in Europe without [strategic bombing], but I very much doubt it."[35] The general pointed to the achievement of air superiority and a policy of continuous pressure as the keys to success. LeMay spoke for many air commanders in the Pacific when he offered his opinion on the effectiveness of the atomic bomb: "I think it was anticlimactic in that the verdict was already rendered."[36] Army generals, less certain of strategic bombing's impact, thought that tactical air power missions such as close support and battlefield interdiction made more significant contributions to victory than did the long-range attacks. Nevertheless, air chiefs viewed strategic bombing as successful, and hence a justification for Air Force autonomy.

While believing that conventional bombing had contributed greatly to Allied victory, air leaders viewed the atomic bomb as the supreme weapon to complement the ACTS concept of strategic air power. The bomb's destructive force made real the possibility that a strategic assault at the beginning of a conflict could decide the struggle before the mobilization of armies or navies. The bomb provided a further rationale for service autonomy, as the Army Air Forces possessed the weapon's sole means of delivery. The Air Force achieved independent status in 1947, and the service's doctrine remained structured around ACTS tenets. Those principles guided air strategists as they prepared for conflict with the Soviet Union, which emerged as America's primary threat in the postwar era. Air planners continued to stress attacks on "essential" elements of an enemy's economy, although they realized that atomic raids would destroy far more than the intended industrial targets. Still, they refused to target cities as such and emphasized the effects of destroying an enemy's war-making capability. Colonel Turner C. Rodgers, a member of the Air Staff's Research and Development branch, remarked:

Success in a war of the future will depend more then ever before on the industrial capacity and efficiency of the protagonists, therefore destruction of the enemy's industrial capacity will contribute most toward reduction of his ability to wage war. This fact coupled with the character of the atomic explosion leads to the conclusion that the most profitable target for the atomic bomb will be large industrial centers.[37]

Despite the air planners' willingness to use atomic weapons, both the number of atomic bombs and the number of B-29s capable of delivering them limited the U.S. ability to launch an atomic assault prior to 1950. America's atomic stockpile consisted of two bombs in 1945, nine in 1946, thirteen in 1947, fifty in 1948, and 250 in 1949.[38] In late 1946, only sixteen of forty-six B-29s modified for atomic bombs during World War II were available for combat missions, and none of the B-29s deployed to England during the Berlin blockade were capable of carrying atomic weapons.[39] As a result of this meager atomic capability, most Air Force war plans developed prior to the Korean War stressed conventional operations against Soviet industrial targets.[40]

As an analysis of conventional bombing, the USSBS offered insight for those grappling with the problems of a projected air campaign. Perhaps the Survey's most significant determination for the future application of American air power appeared in the summation concerning the effectiveness of strategic bombing against the Japanese:

> The experience in the Pacific War supports the findings of the Survey in Europe that heavy, sustained and accurate attack against carefully selected targets is required to produce decisive results when attacking an enemy's sustaining resources. It further supports the findings in Germany that no nation can long survive the free exploitation of air weapons over its homeland. For the future it is important fully to grasp the fact that enemy planes enjoying control of the sky over one's head can be as disastrous to one's country as its occupation by physical invasion.[41]

Korea

Unlike in World War II, American political objectives vacillated during the Korean conflict, and the shifts influenced bombing's political efficacy. President Truman viewed the North Korean assault in June 1950 as a threat to American national interests and committed military force to preserve the South Korean government. The forceful restoration of an independent, non-Communist South Korea to its preinvasion territorial status was the United States' positive political objective during the initial four months of the Korean War. Truman considered the North Korean aggression part of a larger Russian plan for world domination and made support for South Korea "a symbol of the strength and determination of the West."[42] Yet he committed American forces only to repel the North Korean attack, for while he acknowledged that "the Reds were probing for weaknesses in our armor," he also concluded that "we had to meet their thrust without getting embroiled in a world-wide war."[43]

The President's desire to avoid a world war was the principal negative objective limiting the employment of American military power. To prevent such a catastrophe, Truman restricted the conflict to the Korean peninsula and strove to forestall Soviet or Chinese intervention. Other negative objectives also restrained America's military involvement. The President and his advisers contended that the North Korean attack was a feint to test the willingness of the United States to confront Communist aggression. They believed that the main Communist assault would come in Europe, and the goal of preserving a non-Communist Western Europe significantly lessened the number of American troops sent to Korea.[44] In addition, Truman and his counselors placed a premium on maintaining the integrity of the United Nations military effort. The British in particular feared that too much force in Korea could lead to Soviet reprisals against Europe, and their call for caution further restricted the intensity of American combat participation. "Great Britain is our greatest ally," Secretary of State Dean Acheson remarked. "We have to go just like pigeons—when one turns, the others do it too. We have to fly wing to wing."[45]

Following the success of the Inchon invasion, Truman revamped America's positive political objective. On 27 September 1950 the President approved NSC 81/1, which allowed General MacArthur to advanced north of the 38th parallel to destroy North Korean forces.[46] The United Nations supported Truman's action. On 7 October the General Assembly recommended that "all appropriate steps be taken to ensure conditions of stability throughout Korea" and called for the creation of a "unified, independent, and democratic government in the Sovereign State of Korea."[47] The positive goal of unifying Korea by military force was contingent upon achieving the unchanged negative objectives. Once the Chinese intervened in November, Truman again modified the positive goal.

For the duration of Truman's presidency, the United States pursued the positive objective of an independent, non-Communist South Korea, with a northern boundary suitable for defense and not substantially below the 38th parallel.[48] After securing an acceptable position in June 1951, the UN Command entered into negotiations to achieve a military settlement based upon the battlefield status quo. The President then added an additional positive goal: a settlement without the forced repatriation of prisoners of war.[49] Negative objectives remained the same, and the Chinese involvement heightened fears on the part of Truman and his advisers that the Russians might intervene as a result of the Sino-Soviet Defense Pact. Although he desired a rapid settlement, the President was unwilling to sacrifice military gains during the negotiations or use the talks to resolve Korean political issues. Having committed the nation's prestige to the defense of South Korea, he demanded an "honorable" accord to achieve American political goals.[50]

Truman's successor also insisted upon an "honorable" agreement, but Dwight Eisenhower did not seek identical political objectives. While no difference existed between the final positive aims desired by Truman and the positive goals sought by Eisenhower, negative objectives varied greatly. In essence, Eisenhower had no objectives that limited his willingness to apply military power. The President did not desire a world war or Soviet intervention in Korea; however, he was willing to risk both to secure America's positive goals. In the spring of 1953 Eisenhower decided that he would have to launch a massive attack against Manchuria to compel the Communists to "accede to an armistice in a reasonable time. . . . To keep the attack from becoming overly costly," he observed, "it was clear that we would have to use atomic weapons."[51] In late May Secretary of State John Foster Dulles communicated this message to India's Prime Minister Jawaharlal Nehru for relay to China. Eisenhower also sent this message to Peking through Chinese officials at Panmunjom.[52]

The general-turned-President had no misgivings about the civilian casualties that would result from an atomic offensive. As *de facto* chief of the Anglo-American bomber force following the Normandy invasion, Eisenhower had approved Operation Thunderclap, a plan to terror-bomb a war-weary German civilian populace into demanding surrender from the Nazi leadership. "Since conditions stated [for the attack] are that military defeat is certain and obvious," he penciled in August 1944, "I agree the project would be a good one. (We would no longer require bombing on strictly military targets.)"[53] President Eisenhower realized that a nuclear "Thunderclap" in Manchuria would have disrupted relations between the United States and many of the United Nations members. Still, he thought that if the offensive was successful "the rifts so caused could, in time, be repaired."[54] The President felt that the Chinese could do little in response to an atomic attack. He also believed that Stalin's death in March 1953 and the confused state of the Russian leadership minimized the chances of Soviet retaliation. "The men in the Kremlin were still in the turmoil of the succession period," he later noted. "For the moment, possibly, they were more anxious about individual survival and position than about Soviet long-term policy and foreign relations."[55]

As American political objectives vacillated during the war, the results sought, by strategic bombing to support those objectives changed as well. Until MacArthur's success at Inchon, the Far East Air Forces (FEAF) attempted to stymie the advance of the North Korean Army. Air commanders employed bombing as a tool to wreck North Korean political and military institutions during the UN effort to unify the peninsula. After the Chinese involvement, the FEAF again attempted to stem the southward movement of Communist forces. With the beginning of negotiations in June 1951 and the stabilization of a front line, the FEAF became the UN's primary force to use against the Communists. General Omar N. Bradley, Chairman of the Joint Chiefs of Staff (JCS), observed in November 1952 that air power "constitutes the most potent means, at present available to the United Nations Command, of maintaining the degree of military pressure which might impel the communists to agree, finally, to acceptable armistice terms."[56]

The leaders of the newly forced U.S. Air Force relied on their training, their combat experience, and the dictates of the Commander-in-Chief, United Nations Command (CINCUNC) to determine specific mission objectives. World War II had demonstrated the need to gain air superiority, and the FEAF quickly destroyed the North Korean Air Force. The FEAF Commanders, Lieutenant General George E. Stratemeyer until June 1951, and General O. P. Weyland for the remainder of the war, then turned to the CINCUNC for targeting guidance. CINCUNC MacArthur depended on the FEAF primarily for interdiction and close air support of ground forces, the Air Force's principal missions (along with maintaining air superiority) during the war's first year. The FEAF also attacked the few industrial complexes in North Korea with B-29s, and by 3 October 1950 North Korean industry "was paralyzed."[57] MacArthur believed that the threat of bombing would keep the Chinese out of the war. Should they decide to intervene, he remarked, "air power would destroy them."[58] After the Chinese assault, he gave Stratemeyer authority to wreck the North Korean cities of Pyongyang, Wonsan, Hamhung, and Hungnam.[59] Stratemeyer singled out the North Korean capital for attack, and B-29s bombed Pyongyang twice in the first week of January 1951. For the duration of MacArthur's tenure as CINCUNC, however, the FEAF devoted its primary efforts to interdiction and the close air support.

Close air support and interdiction dominated FEAF missions during the command of MacArthur's successor, General Matthew Ridgway. In May 1951, the FEAF began the first of two operations known as "Strangle." Culminating shortly after the start of truce negotiations, Strangle I aimed at bringing Communist highway traffic to a standstill in the area between the 39th parallel and the front lines. UN commanders' conviction that the Communists planned to use the negotiations as a respite to prepare for an offensive led to the launching of Strangle II against the North Korean rail system on 18 August 1951.[60] The FEAF geared the campaign "to produce a slow strangulation not necessarily of the enemy Army as such, but rather on his power to take the offensive."[61] By depriving the Communists of an offensive capability, Strangle II sought to convince them that further fighting was fruitless and that they should therefore conclude a settlement.

Continued Communist intransigence at the peace talks led the FEAF staff to reappraise the interdiction strategy. In April 1952 Colonel Richard L. Randolph and Lieutenant Colonel Ben I. Mayo produced a study calling for an "air pressure" campaign aimed, like Strangle II, at compelling the Communists to agree to an armistice. Although supported by Weyland, the campaign was opposed by Ridgway, and not until General Mark Clark replaced Ridgway as CINCUNC in May 1952 did Weyland receive authority to initiate the policy. Rather than refer to the air pressure strategy as a radical shift from the previous interdiction efforts, air commanders termed the new operation a "shift in emphasis" so as "not to arouse further Army desire for increased close support."[62] Aircraft, serviceable airfields, and electric power facilities became the priority targets of the FEAF. The first two objectives indicated the continued emphasis on maintaining air superiority, while the latter revealed the thrust of the new campaign—to inflict maximum possible damage on military-related facilities perceived as essential to the civilian populace's well-being. Brigadier General Jacob Smart, Weyland's deputy for operations, issued the following statement regarding the purpose of the air pressure strategy:

> Whenever possible, attacks will be scheduled against targets of military significance so situated that their destruction will have a deleterious effect upon the morale of the civilian population actively engaged in the logistic support of enemy forces.[63]

While both the interdiction and air pressure strategies had the ultimate goal of forcing the Communists to conclude negotiations on terms acceptable to the United Nations, the two strategies sought to achieve this by different designs. Interdiction struck *directly* at the enemy's *capability* to continue fighting and *indirectly* at his *will*. Air pressure attacked *both* objectives *directly*. Like LeMay's World War II fire raids, the air pressure strategy in Korea stemmed from a realization that bombing aimed specifically at the enemy's war-making capability would not yield the desired results. During the last week of June 1952, FEAF and naval aircraft attacked North Korea's hydroelectric plants for the first time. On 11 July, more than 1,200 UNC aircraft struck military targets in Pyongyang, which had not been bombed for almost a year.[64] Despite the destruction caused by these raids, the Communist negotiators at Panmunjom refused to compromise on the issue of prisoner release.

The air pressure campaign continued into the Eisenhower presidency as air leaders searched for a way to inflict unacceptable damage on the Communist forces. In late March 1953, the FEAF's target intelligence chief proposed a series of raids against the North Korean irrigation dam system to inundate and destroy most of the country's rice crop. He argued that successful attacks on the dams "would cause a serious food shortage in North Korea which could seriously hamper the overall war effort in North Korea and possibly result in an economic slump of serious proportions accompanied by a lowering of morale and possibly will to fight."[65] Weyland was skeptical of both the feasibility and desirability of destroying the dams, and he refused to approve a systematic campaign against them.[66] Clark, however, believed that a massive attack against the dams would persuade the Communists to conclude an agreement. If directed to recess the armistice talks indefinitely because of Communist intransigence, Clark notified the Joint Chiefs on 14 May he would attack the twenty dams irrigating the rice fields in northwest Korea. The breaching of those dams would, the general noted, "inundate about 422,000 acres of land, causing damage or destruction of an estimated one quarter million tons of rice, thereby curtailing the enemy's ability to live off the land and aggravating a reported Chinese rice shortage and logistic problem."[67]

The day before Clark's message, FEAF F-84s bombed the Toksan dam 20 miles north of Pyongyang. Weyland had reluctantly approved this raid, and the FEAF Formal Target Committee had suggested on 12 May that "some mode of deception be utilized so that the enemy will not interpret the attack on the dam as being directed toward a program of subsequent destruction of their rice crops."[68] As a result, the FEAF planners also targeted a rail bridge below the dam to give the impression that the attackers sought to destroy the rail line. The raid washed out five bridges and 6 miles of railroad, in addition to flooding 27 miles of river valley. "Somewhat to my surprise, [it] flooded . . . a hell of a lot of North Korea," Weyland later commented.[69] The success of the strike caused the FEAF Commander to order attacks against two additional dams so situated that their destruction would wash out the remaining rail line leading into Pyongyang. F-84s attacked the Chasan dam on 15 and 16 May, and on 22 and 29 May B-29s bombed the Kuwonga dam. The raids on Chasan breached their objective and caused extensive flooding, but attacks on Kuwonga failed to destroy the dam because the Communists had lowered the reservoir's water level.

Emphasizing that he had not authorized a program of flooding the North Korean rice crop, Weyland approved additional attacks on dams "as interdiction targets."[70] Between 13 and 18 June, FEAF and Marine aircraft struck the Kusong and Toksang dams, northwest of the Communist communication center of Sinanju, four times each. The raids severely weakened the two structures and compelled the Communists to drain both reservoirs. The FEAF Commander stopped the attacks on 20 June in favor of raids against airfields. Yet he was prepared to resume the dam assaults. Brigadier General Don Z. Zimmerman, the FEAF's Deputy Commander for Intelligence, wrote on 8 July to the Air Force Chief of Intelligence in Washington that other dams "have been chosen and targeted for the purpose of inundating the rail system." Zimmerman noted that Weyland had decided to refrain from launching all-out dam attacks pending the outcome of the current armistice negotiations.[71] The truce signed nineteen days later in Panmunjom eliminated the need for further strikes.

Despite the shift in target priorities that characterized the war's last year, political controls stemming from negative objectives limited the air effort throughout the conflict. Interdiction and armed reconnaissance totaled 47.7 percent of all combat sorties,[72] not only because the FEAF attempted to halt two Communist invasions, but also because it could not strike the source of Communist war-making capability. China was a sanctuary for troops, supplies, and airfields, and the north side of the Yalu bridges could not be bombed. Although the National Security Council removed restraints on flights near the Manchurian border once the air pressure campaign began, restrictions on air operations within 12 miles of Soviet territory remained.[73] Those controls continued during the Eisenhower presidency but would have disappeared once the former general decided to launch his atomic offensive. Truman's negative objectives, along with a low supply of nuclear weapons, prevented him from employing atomic devices in the Far East.

Truman and Acheson were especially mindful of British fears that escalation in Korea could lead to world war. Alarmed by the President's December 1950 declaration to use "every weapon" to blunt the Chinese offensive, Prime Minister Clement Atlee flew to Washington, where he received assurance that the United States would use the atomic bomb only if UN forces faced annihilation. The British also complained to the Truman administration about its failure to consult with them before the June 1952 raids against the Yalu River hydroelectric plants. In the fall of 1950 the Joint Chiefs, with the President's concurrence, had prohibited attacks on those facilities, and the restriction had remained until Clark requested its removal in mid-June 1952. The outcry caused the State Department to inform the British prior to further attacks near the Soviet or Manchurian border, and a liaison office was established in General Clark's headquarters to receive such information.[74]

To officers who had fought in World War II with virtually no political guidelines on bombing, the White House controls often caused confusion. Upon learning in December 1950 that he could not attack military installations in Manchuria, Stratemeyer turned to Air Force Chief of Staff Hoyt S. Vandenberg for guidance. "When can we expect basic decisions which will orient us out here as to just what our mission is now that China is our enemy and just what instructions can I expect to receive so that I can inform my people?" the FEAF Commander asked.[75] One disenchanted FEAF officer summarized the restrictive air policy that remained in effect after the start of negotiations as: "Don't employ air power so the enemy will get mad and won't sign the armistice."[76]

Many high-ranking officers understood that the Truman administration sought to avoid a third world war, yet few viewed war with the Soviets as a likely possibility. "I know of not a single senior military commander of the United States forces in the Far East—Army, Navy, or Air Force—who believed the USSR would enter war with the United States because of any action we might have taken relative to Red China," Admiral C. Turner Joy, the chief UNC negotiator at Panmunjom, remarked.[77] General Nathan F. Twining, who replaced Vandenberg as Chief of Staff in May 1953, concurred. "We felt that [attacking Manchuria] would never bring on a war, and if it did, [the Soviets] couldn't pick a better time to jump the United States," Twining recalled. "If they wanted to go to war with us, we might have taken them on then much easier than we could any other time. And we never felt, in the military particularly, that it would bring on a war. They weren't ready to [fight]. They had a bad time in World War II."[78]

Not all controls on the air war emanated from the White House; many stemmed from the theater commanders or the Joint Chiefs of Staff. After the Chinese assault, the Joint Chiefs recommended to MacArthur that he consider destroying the Yalu River hydroelectric plants if the enemy crossed the 38th parallel. Instead of requesting authority to attack the plants, the general noted that "their preservation or destruction is predominantly a political rather than a mil[itary] matter." He added: "The reversal of this decision involves considerations far beyond those of the immed[iate] tactical campaign in Korea."[79] Like MacArthur, Ridgway also refused to bomb the Yalu power facilities. The UNC Commander vetoed Weyland's May 1952 proposal to attack all North Korean hydroelectric plants, although with the exception of the Sui-ho plant on the Yalu Ridgway had authority to order the strikes. Clark had no such misgivings. When he ordered the strikes in June, he secured Truman's approval, through the Joint Chiefs, to bomb the Sui-ho plant as well.[80] The Joint Chiefs and Ridgway both restricted attacks against Pyongyang. The JCS disapproved of attacking the North Korean capital in the summer of 1951 because "to single out Pyongyang as the target for an all-out strike during the time we are holding conferences might in the eyes of the world appear as an attempt to break off negotiations."[81] Ridgway allowed Weyland to bomb the city but limited the areas open to attack.[82] Weyland, however, was reluctant to raid the irrigation dam system, despite his authority to do so at any time during Clark's tenure. Echoing Eaker's "man in the street" statement, the FEAF Commander—who had served as George Patton's tactical air chief in World War II—sanctioned attacks only against those dams which would, if breached, cause floodwaters to wipe out North Korean lines of communication.

Neither Stratemeyer nor Weyland controlled the entire air effort against North Korea, and the lack of command unity obstructed air operations. Navy, Marine, and allied air forces (notably, from Australia, New Zealand, and South Africa) flew against the North, as did the FEAF. While a Formal Target Committee met biweekly to select targets for FEAF's two components, 5th Air Force and Bomber Command, the Air Force made little effort to coordinate with the Navy's 7th Fleet, which operated in the Sea of Japan. After the FEAF Commander approved target recommendations, the committee notified 7th Fleet Headquarters of the selections. The 7th Fleet Commander also directed that naval air chiefs give the FEAF advance notice of independently planned air strikes. This "coordination by mutual agreement" did not always work, and the Navy's first strike against North Korea, in early August 1950, came as a complete surprise to Stratemeyer.[83] Yet the Air Force did not invite a Navy representative to attend the FEAF Target Committee meetings until 22 July 1953, one week before the armistice.[84]

In addition to political and military controls on bombing, other difficulties restricted the air effort. Communist air defenses destroyed 1,041 FEAF aircraft during the war and caused B-29s to fly only at night after October 1951.[85] The limited payload and range of the F-80 jet fighter, together with production lags, forced the use of the F-51 Mustang until January 1953. As in World War II, weather hampered efforts to conduct continuous operations against enemy supply lines. Communist countermeasures also plagued the FEAF's attempts at interdiction. MiG-15 jets, air defense radar, and anti-aircraft artillery guarded lines of communication, which labor crews maintained without the aid of heavy equipment. Supplemented by individuals carrying A-frames, horse-drawn wagons, ox-carts, and pack animals, trucks and trains traveled mostly at night, preventing interception by either F-51s or F-80s. Although the F-51 could locate targets at night, rocket and gunfire blinded its pilot, while the F-80 got poor results trying to strafe at jet speeds.[86] The

Communists also resorted to deception, often removing a section of rail or a bridge span at the end of night activities to give the appearance of unserviceability.[87]

The FEAF dropped 476,000 tons of ordnance during the conflict, the Navy and Marine aircraft together delivered 202,000 tons. Despite the difficulties of conducting interdiction, FEAF's various campaigns destroyed 827 bridges, 116,839 buildings, 869 locomotives, 14,906 railroad cars, and 74,859 vehicles, and halted all but 4 or 5 percent of North Korea's prewar rail traffic. More than 500,000 laborers worked in repair gangs along transportation lines. The attacks against hydroelectric plants in June 1952 rendered eleven of thirteen unserviceable, with the remaining two in doubtful condition, resulting in a complete power blackout over North Korea for more than two weeks. The Communists succeeded in restoring these plants to only 10 percent of their former capacity. In addition to washing out 6 miles of railroad and five bridges, the raid on the Toksan dam destroyed seven hundred buildings and 5 square miles of rice crops. All told, UN aircrews claimed to have killed 184,808 enemy troops; North Korea announced that the 11 July 1952 attack on Pyongyang caused seven thousand casualties.[88]

Although the interdiction and air pressure campaigns inflicted heavy losses, the destruction did not by itself compel the Communists to agree to an armistice. With the halt of Lieutenant General James Van Fleet's offensive in the late spring of 1951, air power became the sole ostensible means of forcing a settlement. Yet the bombing continued to be restricted in scope by both political and military controls. Admiral Joy noted: "United Nations Command negotiators at Kaesong and Panmunjom were not in a position to deal from maximum strength, and well did the Communists know it."[89] With the static front that developed after the truce talks began, enemy troops needed very little sustenance to maintain their position.[90] The Communist negotiators stalled for time, hoping that the UN bargaining position would weaken under the strain of mounting casualties. Eisenhower's advisers observed in April 1953:

Whatever the Communist basic attitude towards an armistice may be, the ability of the Communists to supply and reinforce their troop strength in Korea has unquestionably reinforced their unwillingness to concede in the POW question what is possibly to them an important matter of principle and prestige striking at the roots of their system. They may well consider that agreement to any form of non-forcible repatriation so admits to the right of individual self-determination as to endanger maintenance of their concept of relations between the individual and the state.[91]

Until June 1953, the Communists adamantly refused to accept UN terms on prisoner release as the basis for an armistice. On 25 May UN negotiators announced their commitment to voluntary repatriation as a final stand. The Communists denounced the proposal as unacceptable and requested a recess to prepare an official reply. When negotiations resumed on 4 June the Communists seemed more conciliatory, and on 8 June they signed a prisoner exchange agreement accepting the UN position. South Korean President Syngman Rhee's independent release of Communist prisoners on 18 June delayed an armistice by more than a month, but on 27 July both sides initialed a settlement that differed little from the 8 June terms.

While the May attacks against the dams did not directly produce the Communists' about-face, the raids did, in combination with other factors, contribute to their desire to negotiate seriously. Foremost among their other concerns was Eisenhower's willingness to use atomic weapons and expand the war.[92] Dulles communicated this message to Nehru during a visit to India that began on 22 May, and three days later the Communist negotiators in Penmunjom demanded a recess. The May strikes on the dams—targets previously untouched—began on the 13th and ended on the 29th. The North Koreans could prevent bombing from breaching a dam only by draining its reservoir. This measure had the same effect as breaching the structure, for it denied vital water to the young rice crops planted at the start of the spring season. The attacks all came against dams in the northwest, an area so important for rice production that the North Koreans dispatched troops there each spring to help with the planting.[93] The Communists responded to the Toksan raid by building a special railroad to the dam to carry repair materials. They also mounted their most intense propaganda campaign of the war, denouncing American "imperialists aggressors attempting to destroy the rice crop by denying the farmers the life water necessary to grow rice."[94] In short, the raids threatened massive starvation, and the Communists had no effective means to counter the attacks. Whatever their intent as interdiction measures, the raids appeared to the Communists as direct attacks on the civilian populace. As such, they gave credence to Eisenhower's promise to unleash a nuclear holocaust across the North Korean and Manchurian land-scapes.

In addition to the threat of atomic war, the Communists faced the prospect of continued fighting in a conflict that had already cost them heavily in manpower and equipment. The North Korean industrial and transportation systems were in shambles after three years of war. The attacks against the dams portended destruction of the agricultural system as well. Wrecking North Korea's capability to grow rice threatened its survival as a nation, a prospect that appealed to neither Pyongyang nor Peking. With the increasing devastation of their country, the North Koreans feared that they could not prevent the Chinese from keeping troops permanently below the Yalu. "The North Korean desire to salvage their country was a major factor in obtaining serious negotiations," Dean Rusk, Truman's Assistant Secretary of State for Far Eastern Affairs, recalled.[95] The Chinese, however, had no desire to usurp the polity of their Communist ally. They had intervened specifically to preserve North Korean sovereignty, which they rightly believed threatened by the UN advance in the fall of 1950. A substantially weakened North Korea could not serve as an effective buffer against invasion by UN or South Korean troops. Further, the potential loss of the North Korean rice crop posed a serious problem for Chinese forces on the 38th parallel. While the Communist troops needed little in the way of material to maintain their static positions, they relied heavily on northwest Korea for food. The lack of rice would have affected their capability to continue fighting.

Besides concerns over Eisenhower's threat and North Korean devastation, the Communists also had to face the changed political situation caused by the death of Stalin. The Soviet dictator had approved Premier Kim Il Sung's plan to invade the South and in the fall of 1950 had encouraged Chinese intervention.[96] The new Soviet leadership did not, however, contain a central source of power committed to the Communist struggle in Korea. Soon after Stalin's demise in March, Georgyi Malenkov, Lavrenty Beria, and Nikita Khrushchev began to compete for control, and no clear head of state would emerge for the remainder of the Korean War. If they were to continue the conflict, the Chinese and North Koreans would have to fight without Moscow's firm support.

The American interdiction campaign prevented the Communists from launching a large-scale offensive after the summer of 1951 and guaranteed that UN forces could maintain their positions near the

38th parallel. By restricting rail traffic to 5 percent of its prewar level, the FEAF denied the Communists the logistical support necessary for a massive thrust. Yet the inability of the Chinese and North Koreans to mount an offensive did not necessarily mean that air power was successful in restricting enemy action. After June 1951 the Communists may never have intended to launch another mass attack. Air power removed the option, but the effort may have been wasted.

Despite the failure of air power to secure an armistice independent of other considerations, many in the Air Force believed that bombing made *the* significant contribution toward achieving a truce. The "freedom to target and to use airpower [during 1953] brought the war to an acceptable conclusion," General William W. Momyer, a member of the Air War College faculty during the Korean conflict and 7th Air Force Commander in Vietnam, noted. "Interdiction was the fundamental mission that pressured a settlement."[97] The FEAF unit history for July 1953 observed that "the destructive force of FEAF's air power had broken the stalemate."[98] Most air chiefs held the opinion that bombing would have produced decisive results in far less time had fewer political controls limited the air campaign. Stratemeyer, who was a staff officer for Arnold during World War II, voiced his objections not only to the political controls but also to the limited nature of the United States' war aims:

> It [the American military objective] is contrary to everything
> that every military commander that I have been associated
> with or from all of our history—he has never been in a position
> where he could not win the war he started to win. That is not
> American. That is not American. [*sic*] And who did it—I don't
> know. I know that General MacArthur's hands were tied, I am
> sure, not by the Joint Chiefs of Staff, but by the . . . State
> Department.[99]

Joy agreed, listing his greatest handicap during the negotiations as the "reluctance or inability . . . of Washington to give us firm and minimum positions which would be supported by national policy."[100] He contended that the Communists would respond *only* to massive force, and that Truman's unwillingness to pursue such a policy foredoomed American negotiating efforts prior to the spring of 1953.

Most commanders who criticized the limits on the bombing aimed their barbs at the political leadership and ignored the military's self-imposed restraints. Many generals had, like Stratemeyer, participated in all-out offensives against Nazi Germany and Imperial Japan, and they could see no reason why the Communists in Korea should not be similarly destroyed. LeMay, who observed the conflict from Omaha, Nebraska, as the Commander of Strategic Air Command (SAC), suggested at the start of hostilities that his B-29s blast North Korea's principal cities. "The B-29s were trained to go up there to Manchuria and destroy the enemy's potential to wage war," he reasoned. "The threat of this impending bombardment would, I am confident, have kept the Communist Chinese from revitalizing and protracting the Korean War."[101] The general disapproved of using B-29s for interdiction and argued that the bomber "was never intended to be a tactical weapon."[102] Weyland attempted to use air power as a bludgeon to compel a negotiated settlement. Yet his air pressure strategy was a bludgeon fashioned after Spaatz's daylight campaign in Europe rather than LeMay's fire attacks on Japan. While believing that his policy was in accord with American political objectives and that it had a decisive impact on the Communist decision to quit fighting, Weyland also concluded that his predilection for attacking only military-related targets might prove inappropriate for a future war. He wrote in the fall of 1953:

> If the nation under attack [by the United States] were the primary instigator and supporter of the aggression, or if the ground forces were not committed in the air campaign, or if the air forces were balanced to the concept of completely investing the enemy by air, the systems chosen for attack might be, and quite possibly would be, quite different.[103]

The editors of *Air University Quarterly Review*, the official publication of the Air War College, provided an additional vision of the future. In a 1954 article on the dam raids, they proclaimed: "Modern war mobilizes total national resources. Only warfare that cuts sharply across the entire depth of the enemy's effort can bring the war to an end short of exhaustion and economic collapse for both sides."[104]

The Post-Korea Decade

In October 1954, Paul Nitze told the assembled officers of the Air War College that the principal threat to American security interests

stemmed "from the Kremlin design of world domination." He outlined the Soviet leadership's priorities as "first, the maintenance of
their regime; second, the preservation of their power base in Russia
and its satellites; and third, the objective of world dominance."[105]
Nitze's observations had a special appeal for his audience, for he had
served as vice chairman of the Strategic Bombing Survey and, during the Korean War, as Director of the State Department's Policy
Planning Council. Still, his message was more a confirmation than
a revelation. To Air Force senior officers, the Soviet Union was *the*
enemy. Service doctrine reflected the conviction that the United
States would one day confront the Soviets in general war—a euphe-
mism for global nuclear conflict.

The Eisenhower administration's policy of "massive retaliation,"
combined with the Soviet explosion of the hydrogen bomb, a perceived "bomber gap," and the launching of Sputnik, contributed to
the Air Force's priority on preparing for nuclear war. America's nuclear arsenal jumped from a total of 1,750 weapons in 1954 to
26,500 in 1962, with more than 11,000 added between 1958 and
1960.[106] SAC controlled the vast majority of these arms and planned
to deliver most of them in a massive preemptive bomber assault
against the Soviet Union.[107] "The emphasis of air planners was in
making war fit a weapon—nuclear air power—rather than making
the weapon fit a war," one historian of the period commented.[108]
Nowhere was this emphasis more manifest than in the Air Force's
two chief doctrinal publications of the post-Korea decade, Manuals
1-2 and 1-8.

Air planners produced two versions of Manual 1-2, "Basic Doctrine," in the decade after Korea. Both stressed that American military forces could perform "their greatest and most economical service *in any form* of international conflict" by allowing the United
States to "exercise a compelling initiative in international affairs."[109]
Strategic bombing offered the means to demonstrate "compelling
initiative," and Manual 1-8, "Strategic Air Operations," outlined
how bombing would achieve national goals. Dated 1 May 1954, the
document steered Air Force thinking throughout the post-Korea
decade. Air planners did not revise it until December 1965.

Manual 1-8 drew upon the teachings of the Air Corps Tactical
School and the perceived lessons of World War II strategic bombing. Little guidance emerged from the experience of Korea. The
manual defined *strategic air operations* as attacks "designed to disrupt an enemy nation to the extent that its will and capability to
resist are broken."[110] These operations "are conducted directly

against the nation itself" rather than against its deployed armed forces.[111] Destroying the war-making capacity of a nation would "neutralize" its armies and navies. Such destruction would also lead to the collapse of an enemy's will to fight. Air planners contended:

> Somewhere within the structure of the hostile nation exist
> sensitive elements, the destruction or neutralization of which
> will best create the breakdown and loss of the will of that
> nation to further resist. . . . The fabric of modern nations is
> such a complete interweaving of major single elements that the
> elimination of one element can create widespread influence
> upon the whole. Some of the elements are of such importance
> that the complete elimination of one of them would cause
> collapse of the national structure insofar as integrated effort is
> concerned. Others exert influence which, while not
> immediately evident, is cumulative and transferable, and when
> brought under the effects of air weapons, results in a general
> widespread weakening and eventual collapse.[112]

The authors concluded that destroying petroleum or transportation systems would cause the most damage to a nation's will to resist. Only "weighty and sustained attacks," however, would succeed in wrecking either system.[113]

Eisenhower's budgetary controls facilitated the development of SAC into the offensive force envisioned by Manual 1-8's authors. The perceived threat of nuclear war with the Soviets caused SAC to receive priority funding from an administration committed to fiscal restraint. "We could never support all of the forces . . . that might be required to meet all possible eventualities simultaneously," Secretary of Defense Charles E. Wilson explained in 1957.[114] SAC expanded not only at the expense of the Army and Navy but also to the detriment of the Air Force's Tactical Air Command (TAC), which contained primarily single-seat "fighter" aircraft. To meet financial constraints, the Air Force eliminated several tactical fighter wings in the late 1950s.[115] Former Air Force Secretary Thomas K. Finletter complained: "We are still several billion dollars short of the amount we ought to be spending exclusively for the air power we need to handle the threat from Russia in the NATO area. . . . There is nothing like enough air power in our present United States military force levels to back up our foreign policy in the Far East.[116] The paucity of funds for air missions other than strategic nuclear bombing prompted RAND analyst Bernard Brodie to note, with a large measure of truth, that "strategy wears a dollar sign."[117]

To the Commander-in-Chief of Strategic Air Command (CINC-SAC), a defense policy stressing strategic nuclear air power was more than just a proper emphasis on the Air Force's perceived ability to achieve an independent decision in war. General Curtis LeMay viewed SAC as the premier guardian of American democracy. As CINCSAC from 1948 to 1957, he molded the force into a highly disciplined unit possessing awesome attacking power. SAC's mission "was to serve as deterrent against the enemy—a deterrent against nuclear warfare—a striking force so efficient and so powerful that no enemy could, in justice to his own present and future, attack us—through a sneak assault or any other way," LeMay wrote.[118] The general geared his command to the "worst case" scenarios of a full-scale nuclear exchange. In such a confrontation, SAC would deliver the Air Force's nuclear arsenal against Soviet targets in one massive blow.[119] From 1951 on, LeMay did not submit his annually updated war plans for JCS review, and by 1955 he had gained virtual autonomy in target selection.[120] His influence resulted in CINCSAC's designation in the fall of 1960 as the "Director of Strategic Target Planning," with authority to develop, on behalf of the JCS, a Single Integrated Operational Plan (SIOP) for a potential nuclear war. For all the armed services—particularly for the Air Force—the SIOP became the highest-priority mission and severely curtailed availability for other tasks.[121]

One year after the birth of the SIOP, LeMay became Air Force Chief of Staff. He had served as Vice Chief since 1957, during a period when such Army generals as Ridgway, James Gavin, and Maxwell Taylor had advocated a defense policy based on "flexible response" rather than massive retaliation. Under LeMay's tutelage, however, the Air Force raised the strategic bomber on an even higher pedestal. "He was the one who made the strategic thing everything," Brigadier General Noel F. Parrish, who was in the Pentagon during LeMay's tenure as Chief of Staff, recalled. "He not only channeled a terrific portion of our resources into strategic [forces], but he filled a whole headquarters with strategic Air Force people."[122] After LeMay had served three years as Chief, three-fourths of the highest-ranking Air Force officers in the Pentagon came directly from SAC.[123] To these individuals, strategic bombing *was* the Air Force mission, and Manual 1-8 offered the guidance to accomplish that mission successfully.

Air Force doctrine in the post-Korea decade did not completely disregard the Korean experience. Manual 1-2 acknowledged that limited war might recur. The document distinguished between general and limited conflict, stating that in each military forces sought different objectives. In general war, all American military strength "would be directed to the common purpose of prevailing over the enemy by defeating his offensive forces and denying him the resources with which to continue war." In limited conflict, "the composition of the participating forces, their missions and strategy, would be dictated primarily by the Government's objectives in relation to that particular conflict situation."[124] Air planners realized that government controls would be likely to prohibit limited war operations from approaching the intensity of those in general war. The 1959 edition of 1-2 deleted the 1955 observation that "employment of air forces must be undertaken with the expectation of sustaining the operation until the desired effect is accomplished."[125] Regardless of the anticipated political restraints, planners believed that the Air Force possessed the means to achieve decisive results in limited war. With one eye on Korea, they remarked that the service could conduct effective attacks without having to penetrate a major opponent's sovereign territory.[126] If a limited conflict occurred, the Air Force would apply "precisely measured power directly against specific elements of hostile strength."[127]

Although they conceded the possibility of limited war, air planners made few preparations for it. In March 1954, they published Manual 1-7, "Theater Air Forces in Counter Air, Interdiction and Close Air Support Operations," to guide "tactical" air actions. The document revealed that theater, or tactical, air operations differed from strategic actions in two fundamental ways. First, theater forces conducted operations in a confined geographical area, while strategic actions were global. Second, the objective of theater operations was the destruction or neutralization of an enemy's *military forces*, while strategic efforts sought to defeat the enemy *nation* by destroying "the essential elements of the nation's total organization for waging war . . . as distinct from its deployed military forces."[128] Single-seat fighter aircraft could accomplish strategic tasks. Yet air planners viewed interdiction, with its objective to destroy an enemy's military potential prior to its manifestation on the battlefield, as a tactical function. The TAC Commander was responsible for approving interdiction planned by theater air chiefs and for ordering tactical air forces to accomplish it.[129] Despite the disparity noted in Manuals 1-7 and 1-8 between tactical and strategic operations, both documents stressed planning for general rather than limited war, and both advocated using atomic weapons. "The best preparation for limited war is proper preparation for general war," the authors of Manual 1-2 wrote. "The latter is the more important since there can be no guarantee that a limited war would not spread into general conflict."[130]

To air commanders in the post-Korea decade, theater forces provided a means to complement the massive blows of strategic bombers in general war. Major General Edward J. Timberlake, Commander of TAC's Ninth Air Force, extolled his unit's nuclear capability in May 1956:

> The build-up of theater-type air forces during recent years has been gratifying both from a technical and a combat standpoint. Most important has been the marriage of the atomic bomb with the single-seater jet fighter as well as the light bombardment plane. Of no lesser significance is the tactical guided missile. A single fighter, with a crew of one, now has the destructive power of thousands of World War II bombers loaded with conventional ordnance.
>
> Thus, it can be seen that technological progress, ingenuity, initiative, and imagination have developed the tactical air forces to new and potent heights in all types of air operations.[131]

In response to an "overt act by an aggressor nation," theater forces would, the general announced, "launch an atomic punch aimed . . . at turning the enemy military machine into a relatively innocuous group of men by depriving it of the means of waging war."[132]

Timberlake's fighters formed part of TAC's nuclear Composite Air Strike Force (CASF), developed in mid-1955 with a mission to deploy to any world crisis location. To gain exposure to flying conditions in the most probable wartime operating areas, TAC rotated CASF aircraft to Europe and Alaska for six-month periods.[133] The strike force sported the new F-105 Thunderchief, a fighter designed to drop nuclear bombs and unsuited for air combat. Air planners considered the plane's inability to dogfight irrelevant. They contended that nuclear raids on enemy airfields combined with air superiority missions would guarantee the Thunderchief a safe environment.[134]

Most air commanders accepted the Air Force's priority on nuclear weapons. Manual 1-2 noted that the prerequisite for achieving a military objective was a strategy "as simple and as direct as possible," a requirement readily fulfilled by relying on the atomic bomb.[135] The Air Force's nuclear superiority over the Soviets compensated—air chiefs believed—for Russia's predominance in conventional weaponry.[136] Yet the possibility existed that the United States might never confront the Soviets in a general war. Weyland for one challenged the emphasis on a nuclear engagement. He felt that strong, conventional, theater air forces, backed by an announced willingness to use them, would have prevented the North Koreans from attacking in 1950. "It is obvious to me that we must have adequate tactical air forces in being that are capable of serving as a deterrent to the brush-fire type of war just as SAC is the main deterrent to a global war," he asserted in 1957. "Any fighting that we get into in the foreseeable future will very probably be of the peripheral war type."[137] Most senior officers who doubted the appropriateness of Air Force doctrine kept their misgivings to themselves. The text of Timberlake's 1956 speech to California aviation writers mentioned that present Soviet actions did "not foreshadow a general war," and Timberlake made a notation to omit the statement.[138] After LeMay "SACerized" the Pentagon, most high-ranking officers possessed a sincere faith in the nuclear bomber's ability to decide international conflicts. Those who did not believe lacked the power to make any difference.

While the Air Force's leadership remained committed to the gospel of strategic nuclear attack, others questioned the dogma's propriety. In 1957 two studies concluded that the service needed to devote more attention to limited war preparation. A RAND analyst, Robert Johnson, determined in a May report for Pacific Air Forces (PACAF) Headquarters that the danger of limited hostilities was "the most immediate threat" facing PACAF units. Johnson noted that directives to maintain general war capabilities narrowed the resources available to oppose local aggression. He did not think that those units in excess of the general war "retaliatory" force would suffice, in terms of numbers or competency, to repel attacks by guerrilla troops. "It is felt by many," the analyst reported, "that neither the Tactical Air Forces in being, the Strategic Air Forces, the Air Forces of Allied countries, nor the air components of the Army, Navy, and Marines are particularly well-suited to perform the tasks which may be required of air power in local war." He highlighted the efforts of two RAND projects, dubbed SIERRA and RIOT SQUAD, to determine the Air Force's limited war requirements. Using war-gaming techniques, the SIERRA group had evaluated prospective air campaigns in Southeast Asia, but the group's findings remained "tentative and highly controversial." RIOT SQUAD, examining weapons and support systems required by air forces opposing local aggressions, also produced uncertain conclusions. Johnson pointed out that the group had failed to devote adequate attention to the "mission and *modus operandi*" of air units engaged in limited conflict."[139]

Johnson's counterpart at Air University, Colonel Ephraim M. Hampton, agreed that the Air Force needed to prepare for limited engagements. In his March study "The USAF in Limited War," he stressed what he felt was a major dilemma confronting air planners who molded service doctrine: how to guarantee that the Air Force possessed adequate means to cope with both general and limited conflict. Unlike Johnson, Hampton accepted the heavy commitment of forces to general war preparation. The colonel focused instead on "whether these limited war forces in excess of the hard core total war requirements should be specially developed air task forces." He determined that special units would only interfere with the mission of theater air forces, which already had responsibility for operations in potential trouble spots. Yet Hampton offered no advice on how to organize those theater forces exceeding general war requirements. "Generalizations concerning the type forces which could best be employed become exceedingly difficult," he penned. "Each area where a limited war could possibly occur will present different inherent theater capabilities, base structures, and logistic situations. The geography, target systems, and status of indigenous forces will vary. Political situations will present a variety of problems."[140]

Acknowledging that limited conflict could occur in disparate locales, Air University staff members produced a 1958 study evaluating the Air Force's ability to respond to small-scale conflicts in the Middle East, Southeast Asia, Taiwan, and Korea. Bernard Brodie authored the project's final report. Before discussing political situations in the four areas, he provided general observations on the nature of limited war. Brodie asserted that a nation waging limited conflict must rely on "counterforce" tactics and strategies. This meant that the country would direct its military effort against opposing military forces rather than against "sources of national power." The strategy would cause the struggle to resemble a war of attrition.[141]

In contrast to his initial remarks, Brodie also stated that "the United States must use any weapon in its arsenal, as needed, to protect its national interest."[142] "Any weapon" included the atomic bomb. Should limited war erupt in any of the four areas examined, units from TAC's Composite Air Strike Force, Theater Air Forces, and SAC would probably participate. Brodie described how they could make the greatest impact on an enemy:

> Airpower properly employed permits a graduated or mounting application of force and persuasion in which diplomatic negotiation can be integrated precisely either between separate sorties or at the culmination of achieving major objectives. Thus the Air Force is able to operate in a limited war situation by striking, returning to secure territory, negotiating, striking again as necessary and withdrawing repeatedly without the stigma of retreat ever being an issue.[143]

Brodie argued that such a policy might prove useful in Vietnam. There, Ngo Dinh Diem's Southern regime appeared in danger of falling to Communism. "This indirect threat to US interests must be recognized as a matter of first concern to us in Southeast Asia," he contended, "for no amount of military equipment in weak or undecided hands will guarantee security from community encroachment."[144]

A year after the Air University study, Brodie published *Strategy in the Missile Age*. While focusing on air power's role in deterring—or winning—total war, the work also offered guidance on a proper course for air forces in limited conflict. Brodie now doubted that nuclear weapons were appropriate for local wars. "The conclusion that nuclear weapons *must* be used in limited wars has been reached by too many people, too quickly, on the basis of far too little analysis of the problem," he argued.[145] Those whom the United States sought to defend would be likely to disapprove of salvation based on atomic blasts over their homeland. Equally important, the use of nuclear weapons constituted a vast degree of difference from warfare waged by conventional means. Atomic bombs in a limited conflict would greatly increase the chances of a general war.

Brodie's message went unheeded. In August 1957 National Security Adviser Robert Cutler had urged President Eisenhower to develop a credible policy for limited war. Cutler advised relying on tactical atomic weapons to counter Russian aggression "anywhere against any ally."[146] Eisenhower's support of this proposal sanctioned what was already three-year-old Air Force doctrine. That doctrine would not change—in either written or perceived form—for the next eight years.[147] While John Kennedy's enchantment with guerrilla warfare produced changes in Army doctrine, it had no effect on Air Force policy. LeMay guaranteed that his service would continue to emphasize strategic operations above all else and that theater air forces would perform tasks viewed as secondary. His perspective endured beyond his four-year tenure as Chief of Staff.

In May 1953, an ailing Hoyt Vandenberg made his final address as Air Force Chief of Staff. Speaking to the Air War College's class of senior officers, the general summarized his views on strategic air power:

> Air power must not be applied except against the industrial power of the nation; it must not be applied unless you are going to win the war with it. I don't mean that once you have applied it, that you can't apply it to the other portions of war. But surely, let us not drop an A-bomb until we are ready to drop it on the industrial potential, too, or perhaps first. . . . Air power, if it is to be successful, has got to be launched against the industrial potential in the rear areas of a nation. Air power, without the A-bomb, must be so used. Air power should not be used on the front lines, except as an addition to the principle of destroying the industrial potential of a country. Let us keep our eye on the goal of air power, which is to knock out the ability of a nation to fight.[148]

Vandenberg exhorted his audience to emphasize the value of air power to all who questioned its efficacy:

> You must leave no stone unturned to spread the gospel and to do it in a proper way. Let us not claim that all you need is air power, because that is bunk. What we have to do is to point out where it fits into the overall security of the United States and what we must have as a minimum. . . . It [an appreciation of air power] is only going to come by you people who understand it and preach it and preach it [*sic*] to everybody who comes within contact of it. . . . It's your duty because, by God, . . . the only thing that is going to save the United States, is an understanding of this thing. So I hope that you go out and do it.[149]

The officers listening to Vandenberg did indeed go out and spread the gospel, and LeMay became their high priest. Most air commanders in the post-Korea decade saw strategic bombing as a cure-all for any contingency. Several factors shaped their thinking: the ingrained dogma of the Air Corps Tactical School, the perceived success of strategic bombing in World War II and Korea, and Eisenhower's policy of massive retaliation. To the makers of Air Force doctrine, World War II eclipsed the "aberration" of Korea. The campaigns against Germany and Japan seemed to vindicate the ACTS philosophy of striking a nation's vital centers to destroy its warfighting capability. Korea, while considered a victory for air power, was a success flawed by political controls that prohibited attacks against the source of Communist war-making capacity. The policy of massive retaliation presaged conflicts of unlimited scope, much like that waged during World War II in pursuit of unconditional surrender. Air leaders insisted that future attacks directed against a nation's capability to fight would weaken its will to resist. By destroying a nation's key industries, air power would wreck the social fabric of an enemy nation, and the Air Force now possessed the supreme weapon to devastate industrial capability—the atomic bomb.

In their attempt to discover the key ingredients for successfully applying air power, air planners created a rigid formula for success that eliminated such variables as war aims and the nature of the enemy's military effort. The planners geared doctrine toward a general war with the Soviet Union, and the Air Force's doctrinal tenets were appropriate only for a large-scale conflict against a highly industrialized foe. Manuel 1-8 observed that "the fabric of modern nations is . . . a complete interweaving of major single elements."[150] Most air commanders equated "modern" with "all." Despite realizing that North Korea was not a modern nation like World War II Germany or Japan, they believed that attacks on electric power would help destroy the enemy's social cohesion. They viewed the North not only as an integrated society but also as one treasuring its meager industrial prowess. Yet the heart of North Korea was agriculture. Not until Weyland raided the irrigation dams in May 1953 did bombing prove truly threatening to the Communists. Weyland, however, was reluctant to attack the dams, both because he had personal misgivings about a campaign designed to starve people and because Air Force doctrine shunned direct attacks on enemy morale.

Nonetheless, Weyland's dam raids suited Eisenhower's revamped war aims and the nature of the war envisioned by the President. Occurring within days of Dulles's communication that Eisenhower intended to mount a nuclear offensive, the raids demonstrated that the President meant to remove the war's political controls. With no negative objectives to restrain American military power, Eisenhower could devastate North Korea and Manchuria. Nuclear weapons would destroy populations in addition to military targets. The destruction of people threatened, much like the dam attacks, the existence of North Korea, and neither the Chinese nor the North Koreans would tolerate the country's demise.

American strategic bombing in World War II had also threatened the enemy's national existence and meshed well with American political goals. In targeting industrial capacity, the air campaigns struck both an essential component of the Axis capability to fight and a fundamental aspect of social organization. The industrial areas of Germany and Japan *were* "vital centers" of those nations' welfare. Their destruction threatened much more than the ability to win; it threatened survival. The policy of unconditional surrender, which excluded negative objectives, permitted the Army Air Forces to attack Axis industry relentlessly.

World War II and Korea revealed that American political resolve influenced the effectiveness of air power as a political instrument. The distinctive nature of each conflict, which produced military and operational controls on bombing, further affected air power's political efficacy. The more menacing air power appeared to an enemy's essential concerns, the more effective it was in accomplishing political objectives. Air Force and civilian leaders alike imperfectly understood this link between strategic targeting and national goals. They also failed to realize that bombing effectiveness varied according to a host of circumstances that were unlikely to remain constant. Air commanders showed their lack of understanding in their doctrine; civilian authorities would display it when they tried to apply air power as a political tool in the skies over North Vietnam.

II

The Genesis of
Graduated Thunder

We would have to calculate the effect of such military actions [as bombing North Vietnam] against a specified political objective. That objective, while being cast in terms of eliminating North Vietnamese control and direction of the insurgency, would in practical terms be directed toward collapsing the morale and the self-assurance of the Viet Cong cadres now operating in South Vietnam and bolstering the morale of the Khanh regime. We could not, of course, be sure that our objective could be achieved by any means within the practical range of our options.

ROBERT S. McNAMARA
16 March 1964[1]

Little more than a decade after the Korean War, the United States began fighting another limited conflict on the Asian continent. In many ways, the war in Vietnam paralleled the struggle in Korea: America fought to preserve an independent, non-Communist state; the Soviet Union and China backed the Communist aggressors; and negative objectives limited the application of United States military force. Once more, American political leaders relied on air power as a primary means to stop Communist encroachment. Yet the two wars presented key differences: The geography of the conflicts varied greatly; the United Nations did not fight in Vietnam; the South Vietnamese government lacked the stability of its South Korean counterpart; and the Vietnam War, during the Lyndon Johnson era, was primarily a guerrilla struggle, while the war in Korea was throughout a conventional conflict.[2]

Those differences—and others—produced unique circumstances for civilian leaders wrestling with the Vietnam War. For many

39

Johnson administration officials, the backdrop of Korea colored their views on Vietnam. Several had spent their formative years as junior statesmen during the Korean War, and again they faced the possibility of Chinese (and Soviet) intervention on behalf of a Communist ally. They had also viewed Cold War crises in Berlin, Cuba, and Laos during John Kennedy's administration. Many officials perceived the North Vietnamese–backed insurgency in South Vietnam as part of a larger plan for Communist domination in Southeast Asia. After searching for a means to preserve a non-Communist South Vietnam, Johnson and his principal civilian advisers finally agreed on air power. The decision to bomb the North did not, however, represent a consensus on the air effort's political objectives. The "Rolling Thunder" air campaign was, in many respects, a compromise means to secure a multitude of results.

War Aims in Vietnam

Four days after becoming President, Lyndon Johnson announced in National Security Action Memorandum (NSAM) 273 that

> . . . it remains the central objective of the United States in South Vietnam to assist the people and government of that country to win their contest against the externally directed and supported communist conspiracy. The test of all U.S. decisions and actions in this area should be the effectiveness of their contribution to this purpose.[3]

Four months later, NSAM 288 echoed those sentiments. The memorandum stemmed from a trip to Vietnam by Secretary of Defense Robert S. McNamara and General Maxwell Taylor, Chairman of the Joint Chiefs of Staff. The two examined the new South Vietnamese government of Nguyen Khanh, who had taken power in a coup on 30 January. McNamara concluded that the Khanh regime was in danger of collapsing to the North Vietnamese–backed Viet Cong and recommended that the United States assume an increased role in preserving the Saigon government. Johnson agreed and designated the Defense Secretary's written analysis of the situation as NSAM 288 on 17 March 1964. McNamara's memorandum noted that the United States sought "an independent non-Communist South Vietnam [which] must be free . . . to accept outside assistance as required to maintain its security."[4] This statement would serve as America's positive political objective until the President's decision at the end of March 1968 to curtail Rolling Thunder. McNamara emphasized that achieving this goal would yield not only an independent South Vietnam but also a stable Southern government. In a March 1964 speech, he proclaimed: "When the day comes that we can safely withdraw, we expect to leave an independent and stable South Vietnam, rich with resources and bright with prospects for contributing to the peace and prosperity of Southeast Asia and the world."[5]

Although some advisers, notably Special Assistant for National Security Affairs McGeorge Bundy and Secretary McNamara, eventually abandoned their commitment to the memorandum's goal, the President remained devoted to it. "No matter how much we might *hope* for some things," a disheartened McNamara wrote Johnson two years after penning NSAM 288, "our *commitment* is *not*: . . . to guarantee that the self-chosen government [of South Vietnam] is non-Communist . . . and to insist that the independent South Vietnam remain separate from North Vietnam."[6] The President thought otherwise. He rejected the secretary's suggestion to issue a new NSAM redefining the American positive goal as a compromise peace. Johnson maintained that reneging on the original commitment to South Vietnam would lead to weakened military ties in Europe and the Middle East. American allies "throughout the world would conclude our word was worth little or nothing," he reasoned. "Moscow and Peking could not resist the opportunity to expand their control into the vacuum of power we would leave behind us."[7]

NSAM 288 revealed the fear of Johnson and his principal civilian advisers that an American failure to stop the Communist insurgency in South Vietnam would result in the spread of Communism throughout Southeast Asia. They also believed that the fall of South Vietnam would produce a corresponding loss of American prestige around the world. The memorandum labeled the Vietnam conflict "as a test case of U.S. capacity to help a nation meet a Communist 'war of national liberation.'"[8] McNamara cautioned against overtly applying American military force to support the Southern government. He encouraged instead a program of "pacifying" the South Vietnamese populace with the aid of American military and economic advisers. Yet he acknowledged that direct military pressure against North Vietnam might one day be necessary. "The U.S. at all

levels must continue to make it emphatically clear that we are prepared to furnish assistance and support for as long as it takes to bring
the insurgency under control," he observed.[9]

Numerous rationales blended to "justify" the positive political objective stated in NSAMs 273 and 288. Besides containing Communism and preserving American prestige, South Vietnam's survival
would allow it inhabitants to secure "a destiny independent of Hanoi." Many administration officials said the United States had a
commitment to defend South Vietnam stemming from the Southeast
Asia Treaty Organization (SEATO). Taylor argued that American
complicity in Ngo Dinh Diem's assassination demanded firm action
to uphold South Vietnam. Chester Cooper, the Assistant for Asian
Affairs on Johnson's White House staff, identified a perceived sense
of mission to save the world from Communism as the reason the
United States supported the South. "Who wants to yield to China
and the Soviet Union?" the President asked a Columbia University
history professor. Johnson saw North Vietnam as a client state of the
Communist superpowers, much as Truman had considered North
Korea a nation controlled by Moscow.[10] The President also contended that yielding to the North Vietnamese–directed insurgency
would signal American impotence. "I was sure," Johnson remarked,
"that once we showed how weak we were, Moscow and Peking
would move in a flash to exploit our weakness. And so would begin
World War III." While Johnson and his advisers all pursued the
same positive goal—an independent, stable, non-Communist South
Vietnam—they sought that goal for a multiplicity of reasons. Their
differing concerns affected how each viewed the idea of American
military intervention.[11]

In addition to the positive political objective, negative goals
shaped the United States military effort. Johnson and his civilian
advisers placed an overriding emphasis on preventing Chinese or
Soviet active participation in the conflict. "Above all else, I did not
want to lead this nation and the world into nuclear war or even the
risk of such a war," the President wrote later.[12] After Nikita Khrushchev's ouster in late 1964, the Soviets invited North Vietnamese delegates to Moscow for talks, and in February 1965 they agreed to
strengthen Northern military forces. The Soviets signed an additional agreement for economic and military assistance in July.[13] During this span the Chinese directed the North Vietnamese to refuse
any American offer to negotiate.[14] Johnson thought that North Vietnam had entered into secret treaties with the Chinese and Soviets,

under which increasing force beyond a certain level would trigger Communist superpower involvement.[15] That involvement could in turn lead to nuclear conflict. His fear of nuclear war was "difficult to overestimate," Secretary of State Dean Rusk recalled. "That box [containing the command mechanisms needed to launch nuclear weapons] constantly followed the President and hung like a millstone around his neck."[16]

Rusk and McNamara were both convinced that dramatic moves to expand the war would have the direst consequences. "A commitment in South Vietnam is one thing," Rusk declared during a 22 July 1965 meeting of Johnson's top advisers, "but a commitment to preserve another socialist state is quite another. This is a distinction we must bear in mind."[17] Attempting to occupy North Vietnam with conventional forces, he felt, would have resulted in nuclear war against China.[18] As Assistant Secretary of State for Far Eastern Affairs during the Korean War, he had seen firsthand the effects of miscalculating Chinese intensions. McNamara, too, was sensitive to the prospects of a wider war. Although not a member of the Truman administration, he, like Rusk, had played a key role in resolving the Cuban missile crisis, the world's closest brush with nuclear holocaust.

Preventing Chinese or Soviet intervention—and hence World War III—became a goal equal in importance to that of establishing South Vietnamese independence. Yet the objective was a negative one that limited the application of force throughout Rolling Thunder. Nearly a month after the start of the 1968 Tet Offensive, the President told seamen on the carrier *Constellation* that he could do little to increase pressure on Hanoi. "We don't want a wider war," he declared. "They [the North Vietnamese] have two big brothers that have more weight and people than I have."[19] To assure that the war remained limited, Johnson prohibited military actions that threatened, or that the Chinese or Soviets might perceive as threatening, the survival of North Vietnam. The President and his civilian advisers also made numerous announcements, both public and private, that the United States did not seek to destroy the Hanoi regime.[20]

Along with the desire to avoid a confrontation with the Communist superpowers, other negative objectives restrained the employment of military force. Foremost among them was Johnson's intention to preserve his domestic social programs. The vision of a "Great Society" was a longtime goal, and the President refused to let Vietnam shatter his dream. The war, however, presented him with a disturbing dilemma. He recalled:

> I knew from the start that I was bound to be crucified either way I moved. If I left the woman I really loved—the Great Society—in order to get involved with that bitch of a war on the other side of the world, then I would lose everything at home. . . . But if I left that war and let the Communists take over South Vietnam, then I would be seen as a coward and my nation would be seen as an appeaser and we would both find it impossible to accomplish anything for anybody anywhere on the entire globe.[21]

Johnson feared that a massive increase in American force would advertise the seriousness of the threat to South Vietnam, causing the focus of Congressional and public attention to shift away from the social programs that he cherished. A rapid increase in military pressure would have further repercussions. The President hoped to secure a favorable perception of the United States in Third World nations. Too much force in Vietnam might cause those countries to view the American effort as motivated by imperial ambitions or feelings of racial superiority. Johnson also wished to maintain the support of NATO and other Western allies. The greater the effort in Vietnam, the more allies elsewhere would question the ability of the United States to sustain its many military commitments.

Johnson's negative objectives combined to produce the main principle of American strategy in Vietnam: gradual response. America's political leaders believed that military force was necessary to guarantee the South's existence, yet, because of negative objectives, they could not commit unlimited military power. Johnson and his advisers slowly increased the tempo of America's combat involvement, pausing frequently to examine results in the light of both positive and negative goals. Many individuals, including large numbers of high-ranking officers, viewed the military effort as an uncoordinated series of fits and starts.[22] In fact, the gradually escalating air and ground campaigns were carefully orchestrated attempts to achieve American political objectives. The orchestration lacked harmony, however. The conduct of Rolling Thunder epitomized the discord among the President's civilian counselors over how best to employ air power to achieve the nation's war aims. The group never attained unanimity on Rolling Thunder's purpose. As a result, the air campaign's political goals often varied.

Rationale for an Air Campaign, Spring and Summer 1964

On 20 February 1964, Johnson told his principal civilian and military advisers to speed up contingency planning for operations against North Vietnam. "Particular attention should be given," he announced, "to shaping such pressures so as to produce the maximum credible deterrent effect on Hanoi."[23] With this directive, the President provided the initial political goal of a projected air campaign against North Vietnam. NSAM 288 phrased this objective as "eliminating North Vietnamese control and direction of the insurgency."[24] The memorandum offered two additional aims of a potential air effort: to destroy the morale of Viet Cong cadres and to bolster the morale of the Southern regime. Further objectives emerged during the year preceding Rolling Thunder's initiation: to signal to Hanoi the firmness of American resolve to defend the South, to impose a tax on North Vietnam for supporting the insurgency, "to create conditions for a favorable settlement by demonstrating to the North Vietnamese that the odds are against their winning," and to increase American leverage with the Southern government.[25] None of these goals dominated the collective thinking of Johnson's civilian advisers regarding the merits of a bombing campaign. Military chiefs, meanwhile, viewed the objective of a potential air effort as eliminating North Vietnam's support of the insurgency. This dichotomy caused Assistant Secretary of State for Far Eastern Affairs William Bundy to comment in June 1964 that a need existed for "a clearer definition of just what should be hit and how thoroughly, and above all, for what objective."[26]

In NSAM 288, McNamara directed the Joint Chiefs of Staff (JCS) to develop a program of "graduated overt military pressure" against North Vietnam, including air attacks against military and industrial targets.[27] American and South Vietnamese pilots would jointly conduct these raids, which could begin after a thirty-day notice. The Defense Secretary also proposed a more limited program of retaliatory raids, which could begin after seventy-two hours' notification. The JCS responded to McNamara's request on 17 April 1964 with Operations Plan (OPLAN) 37-64, developed by the Commander-in-Chief, Pacific Command (CINCPAC), Admiral Harry D. Felt. The plan linked retaliatory raids to continuous bombing of gradually increasing intensity, thus allowing a sequential implementation of McNamara's two suggested programs. Felt's plan further assumed that the President would order an air campaign "for the purpose of:

(1) causing the DRV [Democratic Republic of (North) Vietnam] to stop supporting the Viet Cong and Pathet Lao and (2) reducing its capability to renew such support."[28] Targets included airfields, bridges, supply and ammunition depots, petroleum storage facilities, and North Vietnam's "industrial base." American and South Vietnamese forces would also mine North Vietnamese ports. The JCS estimated that by augmenting the South Vietnamese Air Force with American Air Force and Navy air units available in the Western Pacific, infiltration targets such as supply depots and petroleum storage areas could be destroyed in twelve days, and the remaining targets within thirty-four days after that.[29]

In late May, the JCS modified their plan. As part of a "thirty-day Vietnam scenario" developed by the State Department, the Joint Chiefs proposed air strikes beginning on day fifteen against North Vietnam's transportation system. Mining would accompany the effort. Attacks would then occur against targets having "maximum psychological effect on the North's willingness to stop the insurgency—POL [petroleum, oil, and lubricants] storage, selected airfields, barracks/training areas, bridges, railroad yards, port facilities, communications, and industries." The raids would continue, despite expected negotiations, until the United States received evidence that North Vietnam had stopped supporting the insurgency.[30]

None of the President's principal civilian advisers recommended that he immediately execute the plan; instead, they advocated intensive diplomatic efforts at a settlement. McNamara refused to accept the Joint Chiefs' proposal without further information. On 30 May he asked the JCS to obtain CINCPAC's views on a series of questions, among them: "What military actions, in ascending order of gravity, might be taken to impress Hanoi with our intentions to strike North Vietnam? What should be the purpose and pattern of the initial air strike against North Vietnam? . . . How might North Vietnam and Communist China respond to these escalating pressures?"[31]

Two days later, the Joint Chiefs replied that they too suffered from an insufficient knowledge about potential warfare in Vietnam. They also expressed anxiety over the lack of specific military goals in Vietnam. "Their first obligation," they insisted, was "to define a militarily valid objective for Southeast Asia and then advocate a desirable course of action to achieve that objective." As a result of this perceived void, they called for the "destruction of the North Vietnamese will and capabilities as necessary to compel the Democratic Government of Vietnam to cease providing support to the insurgencies in South Vietnam and Laos." They argued that large doses of swiftly applied air power would accomplish the requisite damage. The officers distinguished between destroying North Vietnam's capability to support insurgencies and temporarily halting Northern aggression through limited bombing. Although they conceded that limited attacks could guide initial combat operations, they also maintained that restricted air power would not resolve the crisis.[32] "We recommended what we called a sharp, sudden blow which would have, in our opinion, done much to paralyze the enemy's capability to move his equipment around and supply people in the South," Air Force Chief of Staff General John P. McConnell recalled.[33]

The Honolulu conference, convened in early June to resolve questions about pressuring North Vietnam, showed that neither the Chairman of the Joint Chiefs nor the President's top civilian advisers supported the 2 June JCS proposal. Chairman Maxwell Taylor argued against it in Hawaii. After the conference, he advised McNamara not to limit American options to large-scale air assaults. The future Ambassador to South Vietnam believed that strikes of less intensity than those previously suggested by the Joint Chiefs would persuade North Vietnam to stop supporting the Viet Cong. He further noted that civilian officials would probably prefer "demonstrative strikes" that would permit them to increase intensity if the raids failed.[34]

The Honolulu Conference also revealed the lack of consensus among the President's civilian counselors over the political utility of bombing North Vietnam. Attended by McNamara, Rusk, William Bundy, CIA Director John A. McCone, Ambassador to South Vietnam Henry Cabot Lodge, and William H. Sullivan, chief of the interagency Vietnam Coordinating Committee, as well as Taylor, Admiral Felt, and General William C. Westmoreland, the new Commander of the U.S. Military Assistance Command, Vietnam (MACV), the conference clarified little concerning bombing policy. The discussion of North Vietnam "was limited to assessments of the DRV's military capabilities, particularly its air defenses, and their implications for the feasibility of an air attack. Policy aspects of air operations against the North were not mentioned."[35]

The conferees did not discuss the political goals of a projected air campaign because they could not agree on the objectives of such an effort; the campaign finally began in March 1965 because a majority perceived that bombing would help secure what each individually felt was the unique ingredient necessary for an independent, stable, non-Communist South Vietnam. The President was a part of that majority and, like his advisers, had personal aims that he sought through bombing. He refused to order the campaign until both he and his advisers had faith in its success.

At the time of the Honolulu Conference, most of the President's principal counselors thought that the Viet Cong relied heavily on Northern backing. Despite the U.S. Intelligence Board's contention in late May 1964 that "the major sources of communist strength in South Vietnam are indigenous," the advisers believed that the Viet Cong lacked the capacity to overthrow the South Vietnamese government without Northern support. "The Viet Cong standing alone did not have the capability of seizing South Vietnam—under no circumstances," Rusk commented. Walt W. Rostow, Director of the State Department's Policy Planning Council in 1964, noted that "North Vietnam controlled the VC. We never had any worry about the political power of the Communists in the South." Even Under Secretary of State George W. Ball, a member of the World War II Strategic Bombing Survey who emerged as the administration's chief critic of an air campaign, acknowledged that the North directed the insurgency. In a 5 October memorandum, he observed that an air effort against North Vietnam would cast the United States as "a great power raining destruction on a small power because we accused that small power of instigating what much of the world would quite *wrongly* regard as an indigenous rebellion."[36]

While realizing that the North Vietnamese had increased support to the Viet Cong, Johnson's top advisers did not think that the situation in June 1964 merited continuous bombing.[37] McNamara and Rusk noted Lodge's suggestion that attacking the North would "bolster [Southern] morale and give the population in the South a feeling of unity."[38] They did not, however, wish to begin raids irrespective of the political and military situation in the South. Khanh's government had not demonstrated true stability and continued to lose territory to the Viet Cong. If the military situation dictated the need for air power, both secretaries preferred to apply it against the backdrop of a strong Southern regime. McNamara supported Taylor's recommendation for demonstrative strikes against limited military targets should the North continue increasing support to the insurgents.[39] On 15 June, the President concurred with his advisers' proposal to restrict America military actions unless the Communists resorted to "drastic measures."[40]

North Vietnam's alleged attacks in early August on American destroyers in the Gulf of Tonkin,[41] followed in the same month by the near-collapse of the Khanh government, changed the war's complexion for those charged with upholding U.S. interests in South Vietnam. The Tonkin Gulf incident gave Johnson the opportunity to request a Congressional resolution that would demonstrate the American government's firm resolve to oppose Communist aggression in Southeast Asia. The President considered public backing a prerequisite to applying large doses of military pressure against Hanoi.[42] Despite Congress's sweeping endorsement of the Tonkin Gulf Resolution, however, he refused to begin continuous bombing of the North. His civilian advisers, who supported his decision to retaliate with five air strikes, did not consider the time ripe for a sustained air campaign.

Taylor, now serving as Ambassador to South Vietnam, believed that the United States would eventually have to begin continuous bombing to induce Hanoi to stop supporting the Viet Cong. Johnson had given him overall responsibility for the entire military effort in the South, and the former general provided the State Department with a detailed description of his views on 18 August. Taylor argued against initiating an air campaign before the Saigon government achieved greater stability, which he did not foresee before his "target D-Day" of 1 January 1965. Until then, he called for the United States to develop a posture of "maximum readiness" that would permit a deliberate escalation of pressure against the North. Assuming that Khanh solidified his position and Hanoi continued to support the Viet Cong, "a carefully orchestrated bombing attack on North Vietnam, directed primarily at infiltration and other military targets," should begin with the new year. Prior to 1 January, the United States should attack across the border in Laos to stem the supply flow to the Viet Cong. Taylor acknowledged that he had not carved his ideas in stone: "We must always recognize . . . that events may force [the] U.S. to advance D-Day to a considerably earlier date."[43]

Dean Rusk and William Bundy of the State Department searched for means both to improve Southern morale and to pressure the North. A clash involving Catholics, Buddhists, and Viet Cong resulted in anarchy in Saigon by mid-August. Because of the chaos, the State Department focused on restoring the Southern government before starting "serious systematic pressures" against North Vietnam. "The hope . . . through '64 was that if you had to act you'd be able to act in support of a government that had shown it had a

degree of legitimacy and a mandate," Bundy reflected.[44] Like
Taylor, Bundy and Rusk thought that a continuous air campaign
against the North should not begin before 1 January 1965.

In a cable to the new Ambassador, they suggested conducting covert air and naval operations to foreshadow continual pressures. The
two asserted that the Communist response to such clandestine actions might trigger an air campaign, as might a deteriorating situation in South Vietnam. Yet they believed that covert operations
would accomplish the Department's objectives at the "lowest level
of risk." The risk that most concerned the two was the threat of
Chinese intervention, and they noted that Viet Cong aggression
stemmed from the combined actions of Hanoi and Peking.[45] This
fear of Chinese involvement was a key factor in determining how
the State Department leaders judged the utility of an air campaign.

Walt Rostow examined the efficacy of potential air strikes from a
different perspective. An Eighth Air Force targeting officer during
World War II, Rostow had taught American history at Oxford after
the war. There he befriended Ernest Swinton, the inventor of the
tank who had developed a theory of strategic bombing similar to
that produced by the Air Corps Tactical School.[46] Swinton argued
that attacks on vital elements of an enemy's economy (such as a pile
driver in the building of a bridge) would render enemy armies incapable of fighting. Rostow tried to apply Swinton's theory to Vietnam. In late August 1964, he contended that an escalating air effort
against essential components of North Vietnam's economic and military structure would persuade Hanoi to stop supporting the insurgency. North Vietnamese leaders would see such a campaign, he
maintained, as leading to the destruction of the North's national fabric and the loss of autonomy to China.[47]

McNamara's office contested the logic of the "Rostow thesis." Defense analysts argued that Rostow's approach could succeed only if
the United States convinced North Vietnam of its serious intent to
preserve the Southern government. Unless Hanoi understood that
(1) the United States sought a limited goal through limited action;
(2) its commitment to that goal was total; and (3) a public consensus
backed the policy, the analysts did not believe that Rostow's plan
could bear fruit. In particular, they questioned the administration's
ability to "legitimize" the raids to the American public. "The likelihood and political costs of *failure* of the approach, and the *pressures
for U.S. escalation* if the early moves should fail, require serious
examination," they concluded.[48]

McNamara agreed that rapidly initiating an air campaign might produce unforeseen consequences. On 24 August, the new Chairman of the Joint Chiefs, Army General Earle G. Wheeler, recommended a "sudden, sharp blow" as the most effective means "to bring home . . . the intent of the U.S. to bring about cessation of the DRV's support of insurgency in the South." Wheeler presented McNamara with a revised list of ninety-four targets and proposed a sixteen-day aerial assault against all sites. Despite directing the JCS to plan for raids to follow the sixteen-day effort, McNamara refused to advocate the initial proposal unless Hanoi provided "suitable provocation." He preferred instead to follow the "plan of action" developed by the Assistant Secretary of Defense for International Security Affairs (ISA), John T. McNaughton. McNaughton's design was intended "to create as little risk as possible of the kind of military action which would be difficult to justify to the American public and to preserve where possible the option to have no U.S. military action at all." Like the Joint Chiefs, McNamara sought to eliminate the North's direction of and support to the Southern insurgency. Yet in the absence of more severe efforts by Hanoi, he was reluctant at the end of August 1964 to promote the application of air power to achieve his goal.[49]

The President also had doubts that the time was ripe to initiate an air campaign. On 7 September, he met with his top military and civilian advisers to discuss the crisis in Vietnam. The Joint Chiefs recommended that the United States provoke Hanoi into taking actions that would allow retaliation through the ninety-four-target scheme. Rusk disagreed, arguing for an examination of all means of persuasion short of bombing. Both Taylor and McCone considered an air campaign against the North dangerous because of the Saigon regime's weakness. McNamara too felt that Southern instability ruled out an air effort but suggested that bombing should begin if the Communists widened the war. Johnson was skeptical of bombing's ability to improve the situation and scribbled "Can we really strengthen the government of South Vietnam?" on a note pad. He announced that he "did not wish to enter the patient in a 10-round bout, when he was in no shape to hold out for one round. We should get him ready for three or four rounds at least."[50]

The President refused to sanction the JCS plan, although he approved covert naval operations in the Tonkin Gulf and made provisions to initiate limited air strikes in Laos. He also approved future retaliatory air raids against North Vietnam. "We should be *pre-*

pared," he ordered in NSAM 314, "to respond on a tit-for-tat basis against the DRV in the event of any attack on U.S. units or any special DRV/VC action against South Vietnam. The response for an attack on U.S. units should be along the lines of the Gulf of Tonkin attacks, against specific and related targets. The response for special action against South Vietnam should likewise be aimed at specific and comparable targets."[51]

While refusing to condone a campaign against the North, Johnson planted the seed for air strikes that he could expand into a continuous effort. The justification for such raids no longer had to be *North Vietnamese* actions against *Americans; Viet Cong* attacks on *South Vietnamese* now sufficed as a pretext for United States retaliation. Still, the President refused to take any immediate overt military action to preserve the Saigon government. Johnson "knew [that] the situation [in South Vietnam] wasn't good," William Bundy recalled. "He knew that it could be on his plate right after the election, but he was hoping that it would right itself."[52] The prospects of an improvement were dim. Although the turmoil in Saigon produced a triumvirate of Khanh, Duong Van Minh, and Tran Thien Khiem by the end of August, the group never assumed power. Khanh continued as *de facto* Prime Minister, and rumors of coups persisted.

Rationale for an Air Campaign, Fall 1964

During late September and early October, a feeling gradually emerged among the President's top advisers that the United States would have to subject North Vietnam to an air campaign.[53] This perception was more a mood than a belief, resulting from frustration more than conviction. No consensus had developed that bombing was the answer to the Vietnam problem; advisers continued to pursue individualistic goals that each felt would lead to a stable Southern regime. The worsening situation caused them to consider alternatives other than diplomatic initiatives, advisory support, and covert operations to accomplish their objectives. In reviewing options, their thoughts turned to air power—a means of applying military force with minimal American personnel, a means envisioned in NSAM 288, and a means already applied at the Tonkin Gulf. While Rusk advised against beginning an air effort for the remainder of 1964, he argued that Johnson should not seek a settlement in Vietnam until after having both hurt the North and assured the South of his resolve. McNamara and McNaughton concurred that the President should avoid negotiations until he had damaged North Vietnam.[54] By 5 October, George Ball saw the fundamental questions regarding an air campaign this way: "Should we move toward escalation because of the weakness of the governmental base in Saigon in hope that escalation will tend to restore strength to that base; or can we risk escalation without a secure base and run the risk that our position may at any time be undermined?"[55]

The 1 November Viet Cong attack on the American air base at Bien Hoa dashed Johnson's hopes that tensions would subside in South Vietnam. Despite NSAM 314's provision for retaliatory air strikes and pleas from both Taylor and the Joint Chiefs, the President ordered no military response. Johnson, Rusk, and McNamara feared that a display of force might trigger Chinese involvement, and the President had one eye on the election only days away. His civilian advisers also questioned the appropriateness of another retaliatory raid. "A great many of us felt that the one-shot thing, after you did it a couple of times, conveyed to Hanoi the idea of weakness," William Bundy remembered. "[We felt] that it was far from being useful—if anything, it tended to play itself out very quickly."[56]

Johnson responded to Bien Hoa by organizing a National Security Council (NSC) "Working Group" to analyze alternatives open to the United States in Vietnam. William Bundy chaired the committee, which included representatives from the Departments of State and Defense, the Joint Chiefs, and the CIA. The Working Group was to present its findings to principal NSC members, who would in turn recommend actions to the President. The representatives took three weeks to reach a conclusion.

The group developed three plans of action, labeled Options A, B, and C. Two featured a sustained air effort against North Vietnam. Option A was a continuation of current activity, to include prompt reprisals for major Viet Cong attacks. Option B was a heavy air assault that would continue until Hanoi agreed to quit supporting the insurgency. Option C combined current activities with a milder air campaign that would stop once negotiations began. A negotiated settlement ending Hanoi's support to the Viet Cong was the announced goal of all options, and the lack of American bargaining points caused many representatives to advocate bombing to gain negotiating leverage. Yet not all were certain that an air campaign would deter Hanoi. Bundy noted on 17 November:

We have many indications that the Hanoi leadership is acutely and nervously aware of the extent to which North Vietnam's transportation system and industrial plan is vulnerable to attack. On the other hand, North Vietnam's economy is overwhelmingly agriculture [sic] and, to a large extent, decentralized. . . . Interdiction of imports and extensive destruction of transportation facilities and industrial plants would cripple DRV industry. These actions would also seriously restrict DRV military capabilities, and would degrade, though to a lesser extent, Hanoi's capabilities to support guerrilla warfare in South Vietnam and Laos. . . . We do not believe that attacks on industrial targets would so greatly exacerbate current economic difficulties as to create unmanageable control problems. . . . DRV leaders . . . would probably be willing to suffer some damage to the country in the course of a test of wills with the U.S. over the course of events in South Vietnam.[57]

Some group members observed that implementing Option B would cause the United States to demand "unconditional surrender" from Hanoi.[58] The option specified that air strikes would stop only when the North Vietnamese demonstrated that they had quit supporting the insurgencies in Laos and Vietnam. By insisting that compliance include an end to both Viet Cong terrorism and the resistance to pacification efforts, the alternative required Hanoi to renounce its basic goal of unifying Vietnam. An intensive air campaign might also heighten the risk of war with the Communist superpowers. Vice Admiral Lloyd Mustin, the JCS representative, discounted the possibility of Chinese or Soviet intervention. "To cause the DRV to terminate support of the Southeast Asia insurgencies . . . does not necessarily require that we 'defeat North Vietnam,'" he asserted, "and it certainly does not require that we defeat Communist China. Hence our commitment to SVN [South Vietnam] does not involve a high probability, let alone 'high risk,' of a major conflict in Southeast Asia."[59] Robert Johnson of the State Department's Policy Planning Council added another consideration: "The threat [of an air assault] may be as important as execution . . . in producing desired Communist reactions."[60]

Despite Mustin's efforts to win approval for Option B, the Working Group suggested Option C to the NSC principals on 21 November. The representatives saw little likelihood that Option A could compel an accord. While viewing Option B as having the greatest chance of persuading Hanoi, they rejected it because of possible Chinese intervention. Under C, the group thought "at best . . . the DRV might feign compliance and settle for an opportunity to subvert the South another day." More likely was the possibility that South Vietnam's internal situation would not improve, which would leave the President to grapple with risking escalation that might lead to war with China.[61]

Option C was attractive, however, because it was controllable. An announced willingness to negotiate made the program more appealing than Option B to a majority of group members. Bundy believed that a bombing campaign's objective should be the revival of South Vietnamese morale,[62] a goal supported by any air effort regardless of intensity. McNaughton viewed bombing as a substitute for strengthening the Saigon government. He expected a continued decline in the competency of the Southern regime but thought that air power might cause Hanoi to stem its support to the Viet Cong. "A less active VC can be handled by a less efficient GVN [Government of (South) Vietnam]," he reasoned. Should Option C fail, McNaughton felt it "would leave behind a better odor than Option A" by showing that the United States was "willing to keep promises, be tough, take risks, get bloodied, and hurt the enemy badly."[63]

The NSC principals considered the Working Group's conclusions during the last week of November 1964. They disagreed over whether Option B or C created the greater risk of Communist superpower intervention; Wheeler and McCone argued that B provided less risk while McNamara and Rusk held out for Option C. Taylor joined the group on 27 November and proposed a combination of Options A and C. In contrast to his August recommendations, he suggested initiating an air campaign to help stabilize the Southern government as well as to stop Hanoi's support of the Viet Cong. To stem "the mounting feeling of war weariness and hopelessness which pervade [sic] South Vietnam," the Ambassador recommended intensified covert operations, reprisal bombings, and attacks on supply trails on Laos. Following those actions, the United States would begin a gradually escalating air campaign against suitable targets in North Vietnam. Labeling the raids as anti-infiltration measures would allow strikes on such targets as staging areas, training facilities, and communication centers. The tempo and weight of the assault would vary according to the effects sought. "In its final form, this kind of attack could extend to the destruction of all important fixed targets in North Vietnam and to the interdiction of movement on all lines of communication," Taylor asserted. He advised the principals not to negotiate until North Vietnam was "hurting" and not to permit the North to win unless it "paid a disproportionate price."[64]

Taylor's remarks had a profound effect on the NSC leaders. On 1 December, they recommended to Johnson a two-phase plan mirroring the Ambassador's suggestion. Phase I was a thirty-day extension of current activity supplemented by reprisals and raids in Laos; Phase II, an air campaign against the North of gradually increasing intensity, would begin once the Saigon government showed signs of durability. No negotiations would occur during the first phase. During the second, the United States would demand that Hanoi stop infiltration and compel the Viet Cong to quit fighting.[65]

The President approved Phase I on 1 December but refused to sanction additional action. He also declined to make William Bundy's outline of the two-phase concept a new NSAM. Arguing that a stable Southern government was essential before bombing, Johnson told his advisers: "[There is] no point in hitting the North if the South [is] not together." He informed Taylor that the South Vietnamese must meet "minimum criteria of performance . . . before any new measures against North Vietnam would be either justified or practicable." These prerequisites included a government capable of speaking for its populace and of maintaining law and order in its cities. The President directed his Ambassador to make the requirements clear to Southern leaders.[66]

From Contemplation to Reality, Winter 1964–65

In mid-December, the Saigon government's shaky foundations crumbled further. Supported by high-ranking generals, Khanh attempted to remove the titular head of state, the civilian Premier Tran Van Huong. The turmoil prevented Johnson from responding when the Viet Cong bombed a Saigon hotel on 24 December and killed two Americans. The generals pledged to support Huong on 9 January, but on the 27th they succeeded in removing him from office. Rioting had begun on the 19th in response to increased draft calls. The President remained adamant that he would not start Phase II until the South Vietnamese made a concerted effort to achieve stability. He cabled Taylor that he would then consider retaliatory air strikes, provided they could be conducted jointly by American and South Vietnamese pilots within twenty-four hours of a Viet Cong provocation. Raids would not begin before evacuating American dependents to prevent their future targeting by the Viet Cong. The decision to begin Phase II—assuming a stabilized Saigon government—would "be affected by [American and South Vietnamese] performance in earlier activities."[67] One of those activities was Operation Barrel Roll, the Air Force's armed reconnaissance of supply trails in Laos. The effort had started on 14 December as a part of Phase I.

The deteriorating situation in South Vietnam caused Johnson to dispatch McNaughton and McGeorge Bundy on a fact-finding mission to Saigon in early February. While they were there, the Viet Cong attacked the American air base at Pleiku. The raid strengthened the two emissaries' conviction that the United States had to retaliate with air power against North Vietnam. On 6 February, the day *before* the Pleiku attack, they had drafted a memorandum advocating a "graduated reprisal program" of air strikes. After learning of the Viet Cong foray, they advised an individual raid as "a clear-cut reprisal for a specific atrocity." Thereafter, "reprisal actions would become less and less related to specific VC spectaculars and more and more related to a catalogue of VC outrages in SVN." McNaughton and Bundy doubted that air power would quickly end the insurgency, but they insisted that the situation demanded an urgent display of American resolve. They declared: "The judgment is that a regular program [of air strikes] will probably dampen VC activities *in due course* and will probably inspire the South Vietnamese to more effective efforts. The belief is widespread among the South Vietnamese that the U.S. is on the verge of bugging out."[68]

In a memorandum composed on the return flight to Washington, Bundy elaborated on the need for American firmness. He argued that without a commitment of U.S. military might, defeat in Vietnam was inevitable. "There is one grave weakness in our posture in Vietnam which is within our own power to fix," Bundy proclaimed, "and that is a widespread belief that we do not have the will and force and patience and determination to take the necessary action and stay the course." Air power offered the means to change that perception. While a goal of sustained bombing would be to persuade Hanoi to abandon the insurgency, this was "an important but longer-range purpose." Bundy asserted that "the immediate and

critical targets are in the South—in the minds of the South Vietnamese and in the minds of the Viet Cong cadres." The United States
would not attempt to win an air war over North Vietnam, and the
destruction of Communist air defenses would "in no sense represent
any intent to wage offensive war against the North." Such attacks
would aim only to guarantee the reprisal policy's effectiveness.
Bundy contended that the distinctions between conducting an air
war against North Vietnam and attempting to execute a reprisal
policy should be easy to develop. He further expressed the opinion
that the Saigon government was strong enough to permit a joint air
campaign.[69]

Shortly after learning of Pleiku, Johnson decided to launch retaliatory air strikes. In an NSC meeting on the evening of 6 February,
the President announced that American and South Vietnamese aircraft would, with Saigon's concurrence, attack four targets in the
southern part of North Vietnam. He also ordered the evacuation of
American dependents. The raids occurred on 8 and 9 February under the code name "Flaming Dart." "I thought that perhaps a sudden and effective air strike would convince the leaders in Hanoi that
we were serious in our purpose and also that the North could not
count on continued immunity if they persisted in aggression in the
South," Johnson later asserted. He did not think that the limited
assault would trigger Soviet or Chinese intervention. Despite the
presence of Soviet Premier Alexsei Kosygin in Hanoi, the President
believed that the time had come to demonstrate American resolve
to the North Vietnamese. When William Bundy raised the possibility of negotiations, Johnson dismissed the suggestion. "I just don't
think you can stand still and take this kind of thing," he retorted.[70]

To the President's civilian advisers, Flaming Dart was the signal
for a sustained bombing of the North. "I think that most of us assumed that this was bound to mean . . . that we had to set it [bomb-
ing] up as a policy and do it," Bundy remembered. Taylor cabled
Johnson and expressed his satisfaction over what he thought was the
decision to begin Phase II operations. When the Viet Cong killed
twenty-three Americans in an attack on Qui Nhon two days after
Flaming Dart, the President again ordered air strikes on the North
but did not bill "Flaming Dart II" as a specific response to a particular insurgent assault. The rationale for the air raids was continued
aggression by the Viet Cong, and the White House released a long
list of Viet Cong incidents occurring since 8 February. A joint U.S.–
South Vietnamese statement from Saigon further characterized the

11 February air strikes as part of a continuing effort by terming them "air operations" rather than "retaliatory" raids.[71]

Johnson officially ordered the sustained air campaign known as "Rolling Thunder" on 13 February. His directive meshed well with the desires of his civilian counselors. The Southern government's inability to maintain civil order or stem the tide of Viet Cong aggression—along with Hanoi's increasing support for the insurgents[72]—had caused the momentum for continuous bombing to accelerate since the fall of 1964. The advisers still could not agree, however, on the goals of an air effort. Nor did their individual perceptions of goals remain constant. On 12 February, Taylor advocated an air campaign to break the North Vietnamese will to support the insurgency. He called for "a slow but inexorable barrage of air attacks advancing to the north, capable of convincing the Hanoi government that everything in the Hanoi area was going to be destroyed unless the leaders mended their ways." Taylor now considered boosting South Vietnamese morale a secondary objective, observing that attacks aimed at Northern will would spur Southern morale. A third goal was to limit North Vietnam's physical capability to support the Viet Cong. He suggested a "graduated" air effort at the start to gauge the reactions of Peking and Moscow; if they did not respond, he recommended an intensive assault.[73]

Unlike Taylor, the State Department's William Bundy and Rusk doubted that sustained bombing would deter Hanoi. Bundy wrote that an air campaign would have "some faint hope" of improving the situation in South Vietnam but would "put us in a much stronger position to hold the next line of defense, namely Thailand." Rusk noted that such Asian countries as Thailand, Taiwan, Australia, and the Philippines had a great stake in the security of Southeast Asia. The United States could not negotiate an accord, he contended, until it achieved bargaining leverage. Bombing provided a means to secure that control. "Almost every postwar negotiation . . . has been preceded by some private indication behind the scenes that such a negotiation might be possible. That is missing here," Rusk said in late February.[74]

To McGeorge Bundy and McNaughton, bombing would demonstrate American resolve. As noted in his 7 February memorandum, Bundy thought that air power could provide the lift needed to sustain the South Vietnamese war effort. He also contended that bombing was a cheap method of showing the American commitment. McNaughton believed that an air effort would exhibit the United States' willingness to defend its allies in Southeast Asia. Just before his February trip to Saigon, he pointed out that air strikes would not help South Vietnam much but would have a positive overall effect on America's desire to contain China. McNaughton maintained this perception in early March. He proclaimed that a "progressive squeeze" of North Vietnam would demonstrate "the lengths to which [the] U.S. will go to fulfill commitments," although he did not feel that bombing would improve either the situation in South Vietnam or the American bargaining position.[75]

McNamara's view of bombing resembled Taylor's. The Secretary argued that failure to retaliate after Pleiku would have misled the North Vietnamese and that Flaming Dart communicated American political resolve. The President aimed that message, McNamara insisted, at Hanoi rather than Saigon. The Secretary saw no point in bombing to destroy the North's capability to support the insurgency, because he did not think that air power could accomplish that goal. Instead, he asserted, "we should try to destroy the will of the DRV to continue their political interference and guerrilla activity. We should try to induce them to get out of the war without having their country destroyed and to realize that if they do not get out, their country will be destroyed."[76]

The clamor from Johnson's advisers guaranteed that he would have no dearth of reasons for bombing the North. Besides hearing civilian voices, the President noted the echo from the Joint Chiefs, who continued to recommend their ninety-four-target plan as the best means to eliminate Hanoi's support of the insurgency. The multiple arguments combined with Johnson's negative objectives to prevent him from focusing Rolling Thunder on a single goal. He had intended to use air power to demonstrate American resolve to Hanoi in hopes that the North Vietnamese would shrink before a display of United States military prowess. He had not wished to begin an air campaign without a secure Southern government. Yet to avoid South Vietnam's fall, *some* action was essential, and Rolling Thunder appeared to be a logical step after Flaming Dart. Johnson remarked on 17 February that air strikes might help stabilize the government in South Vietnam.[77] He further reasoned that "if air strikes could destroy enemy supplies and impede the flow of men and weapons coming South, our actions would help save American and South Vietnamese lives."[78]

At the same time, the President remained unconvinced that an air campaign could satisfy his negative political goals. While most

American newspapers supported Flaming Dart, not all did. Both the *St. Louis Post-Dispatch* and the *New York Times* questioned the propriety of the raids.[79] Telegrams to the White House following Flaming Dart I ran 12 to 1 against the operation,[80] and increased bombing could cause the public to focus on Vietnam at the expense of domestic social reform. Most Western nations backed the attacks, but France and Pakistan displayed lukewarm enthusiasm, and many unaligned countries condemned them.[81] The President also had to consider the policy's effect on China and the Soviet Union. Although both had offered restrained responses to Flaming Dart,[82] he had no assurance that they would tolerate continuous bombing. As a result of these negative considerations, Johnson chose not to announce publicly that the United States had embarked on a new path in Vietnam.

Johnson's uncertainty regarding the merits of an air campaign produced second thoughts about launching Rolling Thunder. On 16 February, McGeorge Bundy drafted a memorandum for Taylor outlining Johnson's approval of sustained bombing. Bundy's draft stated that "we have recommended, and the President has concurred in, continuing air and naval action against North Vietnam whenever and wherever necessary." Johnson edited the sentence to read: "We have recommended, and we *think* that the President *will* concur in, continuing air and naval action against North Vietnam whenever and wherever necessary." He scrawled, "We presently plan to present this program to our National Security Council tomorrow" for addition after Bundy's description of the campaign's particulars. Johnson also lined out *against the North* in Bundy's remark, "Careful public statements of the U.S. Government, combined with the fact of continuing air action, are expected to make it clear that military action against the North will continue while aggression continues."[83]

The President's revisions puzzled Bundy. In a memorandum to Johnson on the same day, the National Security Adviser expressed his own and others' misgivings: "I think that some of us . . . have been confusing two questions. One is the firmness of your own decision to order continuing action; the other is the wisdom of a public declaration of that policy by you." He observed that the advisers favoring an air campaign saw its approval as "a major watershed decision." "Precisely because this program represents a major operational change and because we have waited many months to put it in effect," he continued, there is a deep-seated need for assurance that the decision has in fact been taken. When you were out of the room yesterday, Bob McNamara repeatedly stated that he simply has to know what the policy is so that he can make his military plans and give his military orders. This certainty is equally essential if we are to get the necessary political effects in Saigon. If we limit ourselves to reprisals for spectaculars like Pleiku and Qui Nhon, we leave the initiative in the hands of the Communists, and we can expect no good result.

Thus it seems essential to McNamara—and to me too—that there be an absolutely firm and clear internal decision of the U.S. Government and that this decision be known and understood by enough people to permit its orderly execution.[84]

Bundy understood the President's desire to avoid a loud public signal of a major policy change. Announcing the policy shift would, he maintained, compel Hanoi to resist Rolling Thunder to save face. He felt that Rusk could handle any essential public statements, which left "only" the problem of communicating the action to allies. "What we tell them is not likely to stay tightly secret," he acknowledged, "yet I think it is crucial that they not feel left out or uninformed."[85]

Johnson accepted the suggestion to notify allied governments and directed the State Department to produce a White Paper rationalizing the increased bombing. On 18 February he informed his Far Eastern ambassadors that the United States and South Vietnam would begin joint air and naval action against the North. The reason for the military force was North Vietnamese aggression against the South, which the administration planned to detail to the world in the White Paper.[86]

Published on 27 February, the White Paper stressed the material support given to the Viet Cong by Hanoi and belittled the importance of North Vietnamese manpower in the South. The State Department had information on troop infiltration, but CIA Director McCone prevented its public release for fear that it would jeopardize intelligence sources. In addition, different officials produced different segments of the report. "This was one of those damned cases where you put a thing together and nobody looks at it as a whole," William Bundy reflected. "We did a lousy job on the White Paper." Bundy knew from his brother McGeorge of the President's desire not to depict Rolling Thunder as a policy change, and the White Paper reflected a low-key approach to the air campaign. "Really, the policy was making itself and, in effect, declaring itself through our actions. And this was what the President wanted," the Assistant Secretary recalled.[87] While perhaps a "lousy job" from the viewpoint of a State Department bureaucrat, the White Paper admirably accomplished Johnson's intention to minimize Rolling Thunder's distinctiveness. It also demonstrated, to the President's satisfaction, his commitment to an air campaign.

Johnson's moves to begin the campaign were consistent with his desire to prevent attention from focusing on the bombing. On 18 February, more than a week before the White Paper's publication, he ordered the first Rolling Thunder mission for the 20th. An attempted coup by Colonel Pham Ngoc Thao on 19 February produced chaos in Saigon, and Johnson refused to start bombing until the situation stabilized. At the same time, the British and Soviets proposed reopening the 1954 Geneva Conference to resolve the Vietnam crisis. The President had no intention of negotiating a settlement while the Viet Cong held the initiative in the South,[88] but he did not wish to begin Rolling Thunder on the heels of the British–Soviet joint proposal. The political turmoil in South Vietnam continued until the 25th, when Khanh resigned and left the country as an ambassador-at-large. Phan Huy Quat became the new Premier. Meanwhile, the Soviets failed to respond to British suggestions on the conference's format. Khanh's dismissal, combined with the lack of communication between Moscow and London, allowed Johnson to reschedule the first Rolling Thunder strike for 26 February. A violent spring monsoon then prevented any flying until 2 March. On that day, the operation finally commenced, with U.S. Air Force jets bombing the Xom Bay ammunition depot and South Vietnamese aircraft raiding the Quang Khe naval base.

The first attacks set the pattern for the campaign's initial series of strikes. Designated Rolling Thunder 5 because of scheduling delays, the 2 March raids occurred on that day only; Rolling Thunder 6 did not occur until 15 March and was a one-day effort against barracks and ammunition depots in the southern part of North Vietnam. Johnson prohibited reattacks on targets and made participation by the South Vietnamese Air Force mandatory. Taylor bemoaned the limited effort. "I fear to date that Rolling Thunder in [North Vietnamese] eyes has been merely a few isolated thunder claps," he cabled the President on 8 March. Urging a campaign of increasing intensity that advanced steadily northward, the Ambassador suggested a program of several weeks that would convince Hanoi's leaders of the threat to "their sources of power." "Our objective should be to induce in [the] DRV leadership an attitude favorable to U.S. objectives in as short a time as possible in order to avoid a build-up of international pressures to negotiate," he insisted.[89]

The President responded to Taylor's request—which paralleled a Joint Chiefs recommendation—by making Rolling Thunder a weekly effort. The American Embassy in Moscow reported that the Soviets were unlikely to intervene as long as the United States appeared not to threaten North Vietnam's "existence as a socialist state."[90] Johnson believed too that the State Department's White Paper satisfied the public's need for an explanation of the bombing.[91] Beginning on 15 March, he selected targets for the week, allowing air commanders to choose the precise time of raids during that span. The President eliminated the requirement to conduct attacks jointly with the South Vietnamese and permitted air commanders to strike alternate targets without specific approval from Washington. The air effort, he now calculated, would take twelve weeks to produce results.[92] Taylor was to inform Quat that the new measures were aimed at persuading Hanoi that the cost of continuing aggression was "becoming unacceptably high." "At the same time," Rusk explained to the Ambassador, "Quat should understand we continue to seek no enlargement of the struggle and have carefully selected targets with a view to avoiding undesirable provocation." The Secretary added that a "further objective" was to reassure South Vietnam that the United States would keep fighting.[93] Air commanders conducted Rolling Thunder 7 (19–25 March) and 8 (26 March–1 April) in accordance with the new guidelines. Targets remained south of the 20th parallel, except for the Bachlong Island radar station attacked on 26 and 29 March.[94]

Changing Perceptions, Spring and Summer 1965

By the end of March, some of the President's civilian advisers developed doubts that bombing would yield the desired goals. Johnson had placed two Marine battalions in South Vietnam on 8 March to protect American airfields. McNaughton now wondered if the United States could salvage the country without resorting to extreme measures against the North or without deploying large numbers of combat troops. He believed the answer to both questions was no.

The Assistant Secretary of Defense listed "flash point limits, doubts that the DRV will cave," and "doubts that the VC will obey a caving DRV" as reasons why the United States could not conduct "will-breaking" strikes against the North. "French-defeat and [the] Korea syndrome" prevented the President from committing large numbers of combat troops. McGeorge Bundy agreed that the bombing's slow pace was unlikely to change Hanoi's position for some time. He estimated that at best Rolling Thunder would require an additional two to three months before affecting the war. Moreover, as long as the North Vietnamese continued to score successes in the South, Bundy believed, "even a major step up in our air attacks would probably not cause them to become much more reasonable."[95]

The pessimistic evaluations of Rolling Thunder by McNaughton and Bundy stemmed from Hanoi's failure to submit to a limited air campaign. While professing numerous reasons for the offensive, most advisers held the opinion that Hanoi could not withstand a display of American air power.[96] "It seemed inconceivable that the lightly armed and poorly equipped Communist forces could maintain their momentum against, first, increasing amounts of American assistance to the Vietnamese Army, and subsequently, American bombing," Chester A. Cooper remarked.[97] The President's advisers looked to the example of the Cuban missile crisis, in which they had coerced an enemy far more powerful than North Vietnam into backing down from an aggressive posture.[98] Rolling Thunder paralleled the means used to pressure the Soviets. A gradually increasing air campaign threatened North Vietnam's industry in much the same way as America's nuclear arsenal had threatened Soviet urban centers. Rolling Thunder also showed resolve while allowing Johnson to exert the level of force that he considered appropriate. Kennedy's firm stand, demonstrated by a naval quarantine that preserved his freedom of action, had brought rapid results. Given the nature of the opponent in Vietnam, many of the President's counselors expected success there as quickly as in October 1962. Yet at the end of March 1965 Hanoi continued to funnel men and material southward, and South Vietnam's survival remained problematic.

The inability to achieve rapid success with Rolling Thunder prompted McGeorge Bundy to suggest an alternative means to gain American objectives. In a 1 April meeting with Johnson, he stressed his conviction that bombing would not soon end the war. Further, attacks near Hanoi "might substantially raise the odds" of Chinese intervention. Bundy asserted that the United States had to take action in the *South* to stop North Vietnamese aggression. Hanoi would not stop supporting the insurgency, he insisted, until convinced that the Viet Cong could not succeed. Allowing the Marines to begin limited offensive operations would demonstrate America's willingness to fight in the South, although the National Security Adviser expected the initiative to remain with the Communist forces for several months. The President agreed with the proposal, making it NSAM 328 on 6 April. The directive stated that Rolling Thunder strikes would focus on lines of communication at "the present slowly increasing tempo." Concurrently, the mission of the Marine battalions in Vietnam would change to permit a greater involvement in the war, and two additional battalions would bolster the 3,500 Marines already there.[99]

As with the decision to launch Rolling Thunder, Johnson did not want NSAM 328 portrayed as a deviation from previous American efforts in Vietnam. The memorandum concluded with the notation: "The President's desire is that these movements and changes should be understood as being gradual and wholly consistent with existing policy."[100] Nevertheless, NSAM 328 announced a key shift in thinking among many of Johnson's civilian advisers. While the air campaign against the North would continue, the directive established— on the ground and in the South—an American combat effort to secure the same goals as Rolling Thunder. The President's counselors would no longer perceive the air campaign as an independent means to success, as they had prior to NSAM 328. They viewed it instead as a means to support the expanding combat role of American ground forces or as a means to inflict pain on the North while the ground troops demonstrated the Communists' inability to win in South Vietnam.

This change in perceptions was gradual, however, occurring during the spring and early summer of 1965. Rostow argued in a 1 April study that air attacks against North Vietnam's electric power stations would present Hanoi "with an immediate desperate economic, social, and political problem which could not be evaded."[101] McCone believed that NSAM 328 did "not anticipate the type of air operation . . . necessary to force the North Vietnamese to reappraise their policy." He elaborated for the President:

> Specifically, I feel that we must conduct our bombing attacks in a manner that will begin to hurt North Vietnam badly enough to cause the Hanoi regime to seek a political way out

through negotiation rather than expose their economy to increasingly serious levels of destruction. By limiting our attacks to targets like bridges, military installations, and lines of communication, in effect we signal to the Communists that our determination to win is significantly modified by our fear of widening the war.[102]

Despite these criticisms (which mirrored the thoughts of the Joint Chiefs), Johnson used Rolling Thunder to interdict the highways and railroads south of the 20th parallel throughout April and early May. On 7 April, after a month of continuous bombing, he publicly announced his willingness to negotiate if Hanoi stopped supporting the Viet Cong. The North Vietnamese dismissed the offer. From 13 to 17 May, the President halted Rolling Thunder, although he did not believe that Hanoi would reply to the pause by negotiating on American terms. The interlude thus provided the rationale for increased military action.[103] The North Vietnamese did not respond to the pause, and shortly after its conclusion the Viet Cong began heavy attacks on South Vietnamese forces. Devastating several Southern units, the Communist assault was the heaviest to that point, and many American observers predicted a South Vietnamese collapse. Yet the President did not significantly increase the scale of Rolling Thunder. He had ordered nine additional battalions to Vietnam in late April, bringing the total United States troop strength to 82,000.[104] As the fighting progressed, Johnson and his advisers saw that the American ground strategy of securing "enclaves" would not suffice to stem the Viet Cong attacks.

The option to increase bombing remained, and the President's counselors considered it further. On 1 June, Ball cabled Taylor: "We have now reached a point in planning for successive Rolling Thunder operations where we must be clear as to precisely what we are trying to do." He asserted that the United States could follow one of two possible approaches to the struggle in Vietnam. The "major premise" of the first was that the war must be won in the South; the second maintained that action against the North would contribute to the ultimate decision. Ball argued that the proper conduct of Rolling Thunder hinged on how the President chose to achieve success. If Johnson aimed to win in the South, air strikes in the North should be considered ancillary to Southern operations. Rolling Thunder should then attempt to boost Southern morale and harass Northern infiltration efforts while avoiding targets near Hanoi and Haiphong that might trigger Chinese or Soviet intervention. If the President aimed to place greater pressure on the North Vietnamese until they halted the insurgency, then American forces should bomb military installations near Hanoi or Haiphong. "The relevance of all this to the present situation is obvious," Ball concluded. "Action against North Vietnam by US-GVN forces has now reached a critical point."[105]

Taylor and his deputy Alexis Johnson did not agree with Ball's sentiments. They replied that "the air campaign in the North and the anti–Viet Cong campaign in the South . . . are two parts of a single coherent program. The air attacks have as their primary objectives the termination of Hanoi's support for the VC whereas the campaign in South Vietnam has as its primary objective the destruction of the Viet Cong military apparatus within the country." They insisted that each campaign complemented the other, as the reduction of infiltration made the ground effort in the South easier while Viet Cong losses "sapped the will of Hanoi." The two disagreed with Ball that American action had reached a "critical point" and commented that quick results in the South would not occur. "A change in DRV attitudes can probably be brought about only when, along with a sense of mounting pain from the bombings, there is also a conviction on their part that the tide has turned or soon will turn against them in the South," they asserted. Taylor and Johnson called for a maximum air campaign that not only inflicted pain but also heightened the *fear* of increased pain. Targets would primarily consist of lines of communication, varied occasionally to include military installations within the Hanoi-Haiphong area.[106]

As the situation in the South worsened, many of the President's advisers supported increased bombing to raise North Vietnam's level of pain. McGeorge Bundy admitted to the President on 5 June that he was attracted "by the notion of an occasional limited attack inside the Hanoi perimeter."[107] Rusk and McNamara both acknowledged in early June that bombing could help convince Hanoi that it could not win by force.[108] On 7 June Westmoreland notified Johnson that South Vietnam could not survive the Communist thrust unless the United States deployed forty-four combat battalions. Five days later, South Vietnamese officers overthrew the Quat government. Air Force commander Nguyen Cao Ky became the new Premier on the 19th. The President responded by allowing Westmoreland to commit American troops to combat wherever their participation

Packing List for Order #058-3436528-3073320

Shipping to

Norris D. Cash
85 Hillcrest Drive
Orinda, CA 94563
USA

Order Information

Payment Date: 01/08/2007
Buyer Name: Norris D. Cash
Shipping Speed: Standard

Item Details

The Limits of Air Power: The American Bombing of North Vietnam [Paperback] by

ASIN/ISBN: 0803264542
SKU: NP5713
Quantity: 1
Listing ID: 1125B697587
Order-Item ID: 3308054200837
Condition: Used - Very Good
Comments: Clean solid copy that has never been read. Inside is like new and there is very light wear to cover. Remainder mark. Will ship quickly and carefully..

Thank so much!

Seller Information

Shipped by: bestfoundbooks
Seller Email: Bestfoundbooks@neb.rr.com

would, in the general's judgment, prevent a collapse of South Vietnamese forces.

McNamara supported Johnson's action and advocated even stronger measures. The Secretary called for both an increase in ground troop strength to 175,000 and an activation of 100,000 Army reservists. He also urged a substantial increase in Rolling Thunder. "While avoiding . . . population and industrial targets not closely related to the DRV's supply of war material to the VC, we should announce to Hanoi and carry out actions to destroy such supplies and to interdict their flow into and out of NVN," he advised the President on 1 July. McNamara pressed for mining North Vietnam's harbors and for attacks on rail lines to China, POL storage areas, port facilities, power plants, airfields, and surface-to-air missile (SAM) sites. B-52s would accomplish many of the raids. The Secretary quoted a recent CIA study as rationale for his program: "We doubt if the Communists are likely to change their basic strategy in Vietnam unless and until two conditions prevail: (1) They are forced to accept a situation in the South which offers them no prospect of an early victory and no grounds for hope that they can simply outlast the U.S. and (2) North Vietnam itself is under continuing and increasingly damaging punitive attack." Achieving both conditions, McNamara maintained, would cause Hanoi to alter its course of action in South Vietnam.[109]

The Secretary's proposal was too extreme for many of the President's advisers. McGeorge Bundy contended that it had grave limitations. By suggesting heavy air attacks "when the value of air action we have taken is sharply disputed" and failing to examine "the upper limit of U.S. liability," the program was, he said, "rash to the point of folly." Rusk believed that the proposed expansion of Rolling Thunder was "probably broader than necessary." Ball, who prepared an independent analysis of the air effort on 29 June, argued that "the enemy will not be scared into quitting." He thought that increased bombing would only make the North Vietnamese more resolute, and that coolie labor would prevent air power from affecting the Viet Cong's capability to fight.[110]

Although leaning toward a greater military commitment, the President wanted a firsthand assessment of the situation in South Vietnam before making a formal decision. Johnson dispatched McNamara to Saigon on 14 July; when he returned on the 20th he no longer recommended a surge in Rolling Thunder. Dismayed by the

Viet Cong advance, the Secretary now focused almost exclusively on the ground effort in the South. He continued to advocate a 175,000-man American force and called for the President to activate 235,000 reservists. Meanwhile, the air campaign "should increase slowly from the present level of 2,500 sorties a month to 4,000." McNamara omitted the previous requests for mining and for attacks against targets other than lines of communication.[111] The President accepted the suggestion to deploy additional manpower but did not call for the reserves, a move he felt would have caused a greater public awareness of the war. He also agreed to the proposals on Rolling Thunder.

McNamara expounded upon his perception of the air campaign in two memorandums to Johnson at the end of July. On the 28th, the Secretary analyzed what he now considered Rolling Thunder's objectives:

> The purposes of the program of bombing North Vietnam are, I think, being achieved. The purposes, in addition to reprisal (as was the case in the Tonkin Gulf and to a lesser extent after the Pleiku bombing), have been, first, to give us a better bargaining counter across the table from the North Vietnamese and, second, to interdict the flow of men and supplies from the North to the South. The evidence is that the program is valuable in both respects. It seems fairly clear that termination of the bombing program will be worth a good deal to the other side, and we have every reason to believe that the strikes at infiltration routes have at least put a ceiling on what the North Vietnamese can pour into South Vietnam, thereby putting a ceiling on the size of the war that the enemy can wage there. A side effect of the program has been to convey to both North and South Vietnam in unambiguous terms the U.S. commitment to see this thing through. . . . Neither of the purposes I have mentioned have so far required more extended bombing in North Vietnam. As for the value of the program as a bargaining counter in negotiations, that value depends upon there being, at about the same time, an improvement in our situation in the South; I do not believe that even a greatly extended program of bombing could be expected to produce significant North Vietnamese interest in a negotiated solution until they have been disappointed in their hopes for a quick military success in the South.[112]

Two days later, McNamara wrote that "even with hindsight" he felt the decision to launch Rolling Thunder was wise and that the campaign should proceed. Yet his guidance for continued bombing was vague and contradictory. He remarked that the air effort should provide a "credible threat of *future* destruction" while "mak[ing] it politically easy for the DRV to enter negotiations." At the same time, "the program should avoid bombing which runs a high risk of escalation with the Soviets or China."[113] The Secretary's disjointed counsel indicated that he had not settled on an overriding goal for Rolling Thunder, nor did he envision a prevailing objective for the campaign.

McNamara's July perception of Rolling Thunder was a template outlining the views of Johnson's principal civilian advisers. Those views ranged from Rostow's conviction that attacking targets in Hanoi with all means short of using nuclear weapons or inflicting indescriminate civilian casualties was necessary to compel a settlement, to Ball's belief that increased bombing would ultimately cause a confrontation with China or the Soviet Union.[114] Most thought that Rolling Thunder's utility laid somewhere between those two extremes, and by the end of July, virtually all tied the air campaign to the ground effort. As the war continued, their faith in bombing's ability to spur negotiations gradually diminished. Many also came to believe that Rolling Thunder marginally reduced North Vietnam's capacity to infiltrate men and equipment and hence provided minimal assistance to American ground forces. Still, as long as the United States maintained troops in the South, Johnson's advisers had difficulty opposing any measure that supported the ground units.

Although he accepted the bulk of McNamara's July proposals, Johnson had not lost faith in air power. He had, since issuing NSAM 328, lost faith in air power's ability to give him a *quick* victory. The deteriorating situation in the South slowly consumed his attention, until by the late spring he thought that South Vietnam's survival hinged on the large-scale commitment of ground troops. McNamara's Saigon trip and the week of discussions following his return only supported what Johnson had already determined.[115] He could not commit the troops all at once, however, for to do so would have disclosed—like a dramatic increase in Rolling Thunder—the magnitude of the Vietnam crisis. The President realized that the incremental increase of American forces would prolong the war, although by July few of his advisers believed that the war could be rapidly concluded.[116] Until ground troops brought relative stability to South Vietnam, Johnson would see Rolling Thunder primarily as a means to support U.S. Army and Marine infantrymen. That perception of the air campaign was not constant. After American troops helped stall the Communist advance in the autumn of 1965, the President thought Rolling Thunder might tip the scales enough to persuade Hanoi to negotiate a favorable accord. Johnson did not completely give up on the air effort as a means to help secure his positive objective of an independent, stable, non-Communist South Vietnam until March 1968.[117] By then, he was unsure that the goal itself was obtainable.

III
·

An Extended Application
of Force

*The military task confronting us is to make it so expensive
for the North Vietnamese that they will stop their
aggression against South Viet Nam and Laos. If we make it too
expensive for them, they will stop. They don't want to lose
everything they have.*

CURTIS E. LeMAY
July 1965[1]

Like President Johnson's principal civilian advisers, his air chiefs
relied on experience to guide Vietnam planning. In fashioning an
air offensive against North Vietnam, they turned to the perceived
lessons of World War II strategic bombing. Commanders viewed
the "unrestricted" campaigns against Germany and Japan as proper
applications of air power. Most believed that similar bombing
would have produced a swifter end to the Korean War and that an
air effort free of political controls would favorably resolve the Vietnam conflict. While having some understanding of the President's
negative objectives, the air chiefs did not believe that those goals
warranted limitations on Rolling Thunder beyond what they themselves would have applied.[2]

Military planning for Rolling Thunder meshed well with Air
Force strategic bombing doctrine. Preparation for the campaign
drew upon the teachings of the Air Corps Tactical School and the
development of AWPD-1, the plan guiding the Army Air Forces'
bombing of Germany. Air chiefs targeted North Vietnam's economic
and military "vital centers," in the belief that by destroying the
North's war-making capability they would also disrupt its social fabric. Yet as Rolling Thunder would demonstrate, the doctrine
deemed appropriate for general war with the Soviet Union was ill-
suited for a limited conflict with an enemy waging guerrilla war.

Air Commanders' Perceptions of Objectives

Throughout the war, the Joint Chiefs described American political goals by citing NSAM 288: "The objective in Vietnam . . . is a stable and independent noncommunist government."[3] This perception of American war aims among high-ranking officers remained constant during Rolling Thunder's three-year span.[4] Top-level commanders were aware of Johnson's desire not to expand the war, although they did not know all the President's motivations for limiting the conflict. The Joint Chiefs observed that a "basic military task" of American forces was "to deter Communist China from direct intervention."[5] Still, most commanders never considered Chinese or Soviet intervention a serious possibility.[6] Air Force intelligence units in Southeast Asia monitored activity near North Vietnam's China border and noted that the Chinese seldom expanded their airfields or increased their troop strength.[7] Few officers were as broad-minded as Air Force Major General Robert N. Ginsburgh, who served as representative to the National Security Council for Army General Earle G. Wheeler, the Chairman of the Joint Chiefs. "While I personally think we should have done more [bombing] and done is faster," Ginsburgh recalled, "at the same time I'm very conscious that if things hadn't worked out all I could have said was, 'Gee, boss, I'm awful sorry.' But that doesn't help the President very much who still survives in a country in ruins as a result of a Third World War."[8]

Although air leaders at the highest levels possessed a fair knowledge of American objectives in Vietnam, this understanding diminished the more removed an officer was from top command positions. To answer "Why are we fighting?" in April 1965, Commander James B. Stockdale told his pilots simply that "we're here to fight because its in the interest of the United States that we do so."[9] Air Force Chief of Staff John P. McConnell remarked that most Air Force officers did not understand the reasons for the war's political controls.[10] His deputy, Lieutenant General Glen W. Martin, offered a harsh assessment of why they did not: "There was an obfuscation and a confusion and a lack of understanding, a lack of clarity, and a lack of declaration right from the President on down that really created difficulties and set the stage for not only our mistakes but also our eventual defeat."[11] While containing a measure of truth, Martin's evaluation neglected a fundamental factor clouding subordinate air officers' perceptions of the war: the emphasis that top-level commanders gave to the destructive force of air power. Despite comprehending many of Johnson's limited political objectives, air leaders stressed accomplishing the positive goal through an air campaign suited for total war. As a result, field commanders received directives that simultaneously called for restraint and the destruction of the enemy's capacity to fight.

In defining the objectives of an air campaign against North Vietnam, the Joint Chiefs again turned to NSAM 288. In the 2 June 1964 memorandum to Secretary of Defense Robert S. McNamara, they described the purpose of a potential air effort this way: "to accomplish destruction of the North Vietnamese will and capabilities as necessary to compel the Democratic Government of [North] Vietnam to cease providing support to the insurgencies in South Vietnam and Laos."[12] This statement blended the Joint Chief's perception of the campaign's political objective, "to compel the Democratic Government of Vietnam to cease providing support to the insurgencies in South Vietnam and Laos," with their vision of the military objective to be achieved by air power: destroying North Vietnamese "will and capabilities." Administration officials did not challenge these definitions, and the statement guided the military's view of the air offensive for its duration. Lieutenant General Joseph H. Moore, Commander of the Air Force's 2d Air Division through mid-1966, described Rolling Thunder's purpose as "to convince the North Vietnamese that it would be too costly for them to continuing fighting for South Vietnam."[13] Admiral U. S. Grant Sharp, Commander-in-Chief, Pacific Command (CINCPAC) and the operational director of Rolling Thunder, prefaced his campaign orders with the sentence, "[The] objective is to cause the DRV to cease and desist in its support of the insurgency in Southeast Asia."[14]

Sharp's statement of purpose did not reflect a consensus of administration leaders, because Johnson's civilian counselors never agreed on a singular objective for Rolling Thunder. The Joint Chiefs developed their definition in the absence of civilian guidance,[15] and it did not always correspond to the aims of the President and his advisers. Top air leaders realized, however, that multiple goals drove Rolling Thunder. McConnell commented in 1967: "The decision to conduct air operations against North Vietnam is directed toward the attainment of three basic aims: First, to reduce and impede the flow of men and supplies from North Vietnam to South Vietnam; second, to impose a gradually increasing cost on the enemy's campaign of aggression in the south; and third, to convince him that he cannot continue the war of aggression against his neighbor without incurring penalties of still greater severity." He added that "the intent has been to meet our objectives while refraining from the destruction of the North Vietnamese government."[16] Sharp believed in February 1965 that an air campaign would strengthen Saigon's political structure and boost Southern morale.[17] Despite an awareness of Rolling Thunder's multiple aims, air commanders thought that by destroying North Vietnam's capability and will to fight they would achieve all the goals of those advocating an air campaign. In short, air leaders viewed Rolling Thunder as *the* means to secure "a stable and independent noncommunist government" in the South.

Designing a Campaign

In response to the directive in NSAM 288, military chiefs designed a campaign consonant with Air Force doctrine. During the spring and summer of 1964, Air Force Chief of Staff General Curtis LeMay oversaw the Pentagon planning effort, which received assistance from Pacific Command Headquarters.[18] Convinced that destroying the North's capability to fight would also weaken its will to resist, he devised an offensive aimed at wrecking North Vietnam's key sources of military and economic power. His planners selected targets on the basis of three criteria: "(a) reducing North Vietnamese support of communist operations in Laos and South Vietnam, (b) limiting North Vietnamese capabilities to take direct action against Laos and South Vietnam, and finally (c) impairing North Vietnam's capacity to continue as an industrially viable state."[19] The planners calculated that attacks against supply, ammunition, and POL (Petroleum, Oil, and Lubricants) storage sites, plus the armed reconnaissance of highways leading into Laos, would greatly reduce North Vietnamese support to the insurgents. Meanwhile, attacks against airfields, railroad and highway bridges, depots, and POL storage areas in Hanoi and Haiphong would restrict Northern "capability to take direct action." Industrial targets included chemical plants and the nation's only steel mill. By mid-August 1964, LeMay's planners had developed a list of ninety-four targets, consisting of eighty-two fixed sites and twelve lines of communication, that they considered the essential components of the North's war-making capacity.[20] Through a "severe" application of air power, they estimated, American and South Vietnamese forces could destroy all targets in sixteen days.[21]

On 26 August, LeMay recommended immediate attacks on the ninety-four targets to McNamara. The general noted that "only significantly stronger military pressures" on Hanoi would provide the "relief and psychological boost" needed for governmental stability in the South. He added:

> While a U.S. program as discussed above [the ninety-four target scheme] will not necessarily provide decisive end results, the Joint Chiefs of Staff advocate its adoption and implementation at once. Anything less could be interpreted as a lack of resolve on the part of the United States. The military course of action which offers the best chance of success remains the destruction of the DRV will and capabilities as necessary to compel the DRV to cease providing support to the insurgencies in South Vietnam and Laos.[22]

In his memoirs, LeMay remarked that he could have bombed the North Vietnamese "back into the Stone Age" by destroying the ninety-four targets.[23] The plan did not, however, target civilian populations. LeMay's "Stone Age" was exactly what its name implied— the absence of the perceived technological essentials of modern life. In equating economic well-being to industrial strength, the ninety-four-target scheme embodied the essence of American strategic bombing doctrine. Air planners designed it to destroy North Vietnam's ability to wage modern war. After that capacity was eliminated, they believed, Hanoi would have to stop its aggression.[24]

Wheeler agreed with the idea of using air power to destroy North Vietnam's war-making capability,[25] and the Joint Chiefs worked throughout the fall of 1964 to implement some form of the ninety-four-target plan. At a 7 September meeting with Johnson and his principal civilian advisers, Wheeler urged the President to provoke the North Vietnamese into some action that would permit sustained bombing. Johnson turned down the proposal. After the 1 November Viet Cong attack on Bien Hoa, the Joint Chiefs recommended a B-52 strike on Hanoi's Phuc Yen airfield, its primary MiG fighter base. Following the B-52 raid, Air Force and Navy fighter would attack other airfields and the POL storage areas in Hanoi and Haiphong.[26]

The President's rejection of this advice led to more subdued proposals. On 18 November, in the midst of deliberations by William Bundy's NSC Working Group, the Joint Chiefs suggested a "controlled program of systematically increased military pressures" against North Vietnam in coordination with "appropriate political pressures." Air attacks of increasing intensity would reduce North-ern aid to the Viet Cong by killing men and destroying matériel, which would in turn compel Hanoi to divert war resources to home-land defense. Wrecking bridges, staging complexes, and transport, as well as "selected fixed targets," would, the chiefs believed, further limit North Vietnam's capacity to assist the Viet Cong.[27]

The Joint Chiefs criticized the NSC Working Group's three Viet-nam options and provided five alternatives of their own. Option 5, offered in contrast to the Working Group's Option B, called for a controlled program of intense military pressures that would have a major military and psychological impact on the North. If necessary, the attacks' intensity would reach "the full limit of what military actions can contribute toward national objectives," although the early achievement of political goals would end the campaign short of those limits. Option 3 reflected the Joint Chiefs' frustration over their lack of guidance from civilian authorities. It consisted of a gradual air campaign that could begin "without necessarily deter-mining . . . to what degree we will commit ourselves to achieve our objectives, or at what point we might stop to negotiate, or what our negotiating objectives might be." The chiefs contended that this alternative paralleled the NSC's Option C, which they denounced because it did not possess "a clear determination to see things through in full."[28]

Despite the Joint Chief's arguments for an intensive air campaign, their representative to the Working Group, Vice Admiral Lloyd Mustin, acknowledged that the air effort did not have to be severe to produce acceptable results. As long as the campaign struck North Vietnam's capability to support the insurgency, he asserted, it might produce a satisfactory effect. "The actual U.S. requirement with respect to the DRV is reduction of the *rate of delivery* of support to the VC to levels below their minimum necessary sustaining level," Mustin quoted a JCS assessment. "In the present unstable situation something far less than total destruction may be all that is required to accomplish the above. A very modest change in the [South Viet-namese] government's favor . . . *may* be enough to turn the tide and lead to a successful solution." Given the Southern government's uncertain foundations, Mustin—and the others among the JCS agencies—thought that "a program of progressively increasing squeeze" might tip the scales sufficiently in Saigon's behalf to over-whelm the Viet Cong.[29]

Until the Viet Cong's February 1965 attack on Pleiku, the Joint

Chiefs received no real indications that Johnson would support a sustained air effort. The backing that they then obtained was not for the intensive effort envisioned in the ninety-four-target program. On the day following the Pleiku attack, the President ordered the first Flaming Dart reprisal strike, and McNamara requested plans for an eight-week air campaign against the North. American and South Vietnamese air forces would jointly conduct the operation, which would focus on transportation targets south of the 19th parallel. On 11 February, the Joint Chiefs proposed attacking four fixed targets a week along North Vietnam's Route 7 to "demonstrate to the DRV that continuation of its direction and support of insurgencies will lead to progressively more serious punishment."[30] They also called for the deployment of 325 aircraft, including B-52 bombers, to the Western Pacific for use in the offensive. Johnson approved the aircraft transfer, but not the eight-week program.

On 13 February, the day the President ordered the start of Rolling Thunder, the Joint Chiefs briefed McNamara that the rail lines south of the 20th parallel formed "an attractive, vulnerable, and remunerative target system which would hurt the North Vietnamese psychologically, economically, and militarily." The chiefs reasoned that by destroying five bridges, plus the railroad marshaling yard at Vinh, they could "place a stricture" on the North's infiltration of men and equipment.[31] The Secretary asked them to develop a detailed program for attacking the southern end of the North Vietnamese rail system. Contrary to their advice to attack the six major targets simultaneously, he requested a plan permitting incremental raids on individual targets.

While supporting the February JCS recommendations, McConnell did not think that the suggested programs would severely damage Hanoi's capability to support the insurgency. He proposed a twenty-eight-day campaign to destroy all ninety-four targets on the Joint Chiefs' target list, with strikes beginning in the southern part of North Vietnam and moving gradually northward to Hanoi.[32] Wheeler, however, backed the rail plan.[33] Believing that three American divisions might deploy to Vietnam, he wanted to destroy first that portion of the North's war-making capacity that might directly affect a confrontation with American ground forces. Army Chief of Staff Harold K. Johnson also supported the rail plan, which received further backing in a proposal by Admiral Sharp.

On 27 February, Sharp suggested beginning an "eight week pressure program" that would "make it as difficult and as costly as possi-

ble for the DRV to support the VC in South Vietnam." Scoffing at
intelligence estimates that air power could have only marginal effects on resupply activities, he recommended an unrelenting campaign against sixteen targets, consisting of supply depots, barracks,
and transportation facilities, south of the 19th parallel. Armed reconnaissance of roads and railroads would supplement the attention
on fixed targets. Rather than attempt to persuade Hanoi's leaders
that the bombing portended destruction of the North, the effort
would call into question their ability to back the Viet Cong. "Ho
Chi Minh has never doubted ultimate victory," Sharp observed. "To
raise such a doubt would be our aim."[34]

Sharp's proposal affected the Joint Chief's planning for a rail
campaign and caused McConnell to withdraw his suggestion for a
twenty-eight-day offensive. The chiefs did, however, give consideration to the Air Force representative's proposal. In late March, they
submitted to McNamara plans for a four-phase, twelve-week bombing program that merged their original idea with those of Sharp and
McConnell. The chiefs considered that the weekly effort started on 15
March sufficed for the first two weeks of their planned campaign.
They limited the initial phase of the remaining ten weeks to inter-
dicting lines of communication south of the 20th parallel. With this
effort, the chiefs sought to "bring home to the [Northern] population
the effects of air strikes since consumer goods will be competing with
military supplies for limited transport." Interdiction north of the
20th parallel would occur during weeks six through eight to disrupt
overland supply routes to China. In week nine, aircraft would bomb
port facilities and mine harbors; during week ten, ammunition and
supply depots would serve as primary targets. The offensive would
conclude with two weeks of strikes against industrial targets outside
of populated zones, "leading up to a situation where the enemy must
realize that the Hanoi and Haiphong areas will be the next logical
targets." McNamara had prohibited raids on targets in urban areas
or against North Vietnamese air defenses, and the JCS plan complied with these restrictions. The Joint Chiefs urged the President to
begin their plan with phase one on 2 April, although they could not
agree on whether he should approve the remainder of the program.
As a result, Wheeler notified McNamara that the chiefs were considering alternatives for a subsequent program of air strikes.[35]

The Secretary of Defense refused to endorse the three-week proposal, but the April Rolling Thunder raids resembled those in the
Joint Chiefs' program. Sharp at first expected the limited interdiction effort to yield dividends. On 4 April he cabled the Joint Chiefs:

The damage inflicted by these attacks on LOCs [lines of communication] and military installations in North Vietnam *will* cause a diminution of the support being rendered to the Viet Cong. Successful strikes on bridges *will* degrade the transportation system with an attendant reduction in its capability to transport food and materials from production to shortage areas. Manpower and supplies *will* undoubtedly have to be diverted toward recovery and rebuilding processes. While the effect may not be felt immediately by the Viet Cong, this increased pressure *will* demonstrate our strength of purpose [and] at the same time make support of the VC as onerous as possible.[36]

Sharp added that more lucrative targets would present themselves as the attacks moved northward. Wheeler, however, was uncertain of Rolling Thunder's effectiveness. In an evaluation of all raids since 7 February (including Flaming Dart), he determined that the air strikes had not reduced the North's military capabilities "in any major way." He further concluded that the raids had minimal economic effects. Yet he also thought that the recent attacks against the Thanh Hoa and Dong Phuong railroad bridges provided the chance "to apply a serious stricture to the DRV logistical support to the South."[37]

The campaign's progression through April at the same level of intensity caused Sharp and other officers concern. President Johnson's decision in NSAM 328 to allow American offensive ground operations, combined with his refusal to increase Rolling Thunder, led some commanders to question the air effort's intent. On 20 April, McNamara convened a conference in Honolulu to guarantee that principal military and civilian leaders in the Pacific understood the President's perception of the war. Wheeler, Westmoreland, Sharp, Ambassador Maxwell Taylor, Assistant Secretary of State for Far Eastern Affairs William Bundy, and Assistant Secretary of Defense for International Security Affairs John T. McNaughton participated in the conference, along with McNamara. The Secretary's report of the meeting stated that none of those present expected a Communist capitulation in less than six months, and that all agreed that Rolling Thunder's current tempo was "about right." According to McNamara, Taylor presented a "majority view" that the air campaign should not strike Hanoi or Haiphong, for to do so would "kill the hostage." The participants' "strategy for 'victory,'" McNamara wrote, "is to break the will of the DRV/VC by denying them victory." American forces would negotiate Communist success through ground combat in the *South*, and "it was agreed that tasks within *South* Vietnam should have first call on air assets."[38]

The authors of the *Pentagon Papers* later commented that "Honolulu marked the relative downgrading of pressures against the North, in favor of more intensive activity in the South. . . . It seems logical that, with the decision to begin a major U.S. ground force commitment, the air campaign should have been reduced in rank to second billing."[39] Such a conclusion presumes that McNamara's report was an accurate reflection of the participants' attitudes. While it may have presented the current convictions of Westmoreland, Wheeler, and the civilian officials, it did not convey the feelings of Rolling Thunder's operational commander. Sharp subsequently called it "a distortion of the view that I took at that conference."[40] With the exception of a brief span in early April, the admiral remained convinced throughout his tenure as CINCPAC that intensive bombing was necessary to spur a settlement. He did not think that Hanoi would consider halting the aggression until Rolling Thunder affected—or threatened to affect—North Vietnam's capability to continue the struggle. McConnell and most Air Force officers concurred. McNamara himself argued on 1 July for a large increase in bombing.[41] By the time American ground forces had helped stop the Communist advance in the fall of 1965, the Secretary was taking the position that bombing might persuade the North Vietnamese to negotiate.[42] His memorandum of 21 April 1965 was more an expression of his own concern with a deteriorating military and political situation at the moment than the report of an enduring consensus of conference participants.

Sharp continued to argue for heavier raids and maintained that Rolling Thunder had hampered the North Vietnamese war effort. He declared on 12 May that commanders were more likely to minimize than exaggerate the campaign's effects: "Air attacks have disrupted road and rail movements in North Vietnam [and] they have, in a few short weeks, completely changed the pattern of logistic support into Laos." Sharp conceded that interdiction could not stop the North's resupply of the Viet Cong altogether, but increased raids would demonstrate American resolve to Hanoi and generate "a feeling of helplessness among the military and general frustration, anxiety, and fear among the people." The raids would eventually cause Hanoi's attention to focus on internal problems rather than on outside aggression, he wrote. The more intense the bombing, the greater its effect would be in changing the views of Northern leaders. "We should hammer home the main theme of our intent to destroy their military capacity and our determination to continue until the military leave their cousins in peace," the admiral contended.[43]

Sharp's call for heavier attacks came at the start of a five-day bombing pause, and the air campaign's intensity did not significantly increase after the pause ended. Despite the beginning of large-scale Communist assaults in the South, bombing remained below the 20th parallel during May and June. McConnell objected to the campaign's low intensity and again called for attacks on all ninety-four targets, especially industrial sites.[44] The Joint Chiefs backed McNamara's 1 July recommendation for more bombing, although they wanted a campaign focused on interdiction. The chiefs suggested mining Northern ports, attacking major bridges along the routes from Hanoi to China, bombing POL storage areas, and raiding airfields and SAM batteries.[45] The President decided against increasing Rolling Thunder's severity and chose instead to enlarge America's combat role on the ground in the South. On 28 July 1965, he announced that 50,000 men would go to Vietnam immediately, and 50,000 more would follow by the end of the year. The scale of Rolling Thunder attacks was to remain the same.

Although Johnson's emphasis on ground combat did not indicate a lack of faith in air power,[46] the air leaders' calls for increased bombing during the late spring and early summer of 1965 showed a divergence of views about what Rolling Thunder could accomplish. Sharp, McConnell, and Wheeler all considered bombing the North necessary to compel Hanoi to drop its role in the insurgency. They also agreed, by mid-1965, that damaging the North's capability to fight was essential to weakening the enemy's will to resist. They did not agree, however, on what part of the capability should be destroyed to produce the *maximum* impact on the North's capacity, and willingness, to support the Viet Cong.

McConnell, like LeMay before him, insisted the North Vietnamese would not accept the destruction of their industry as a price for continuing the war. In addition, wrecking industry would devastate the North's economy, and the threat of economic collapse would persuade Hanoi to yield. Wheeler saw Rolling Thunder as a means to limit the North's infiltration of men and equipment to the South. Restricting the Communist resupply capability would ultimately guarantee that the growing American and South Vietnamese ground forces could defeat any enemy attempt to overthrow the Southern government. The Communists' inability to win in the South, combined with a large American ground offensive, Wheeler said, would induce Hanoi to stop aiding the insurgency.[47] Increased bombing, along with mining, would further restrict the North's infiltration capability and thereby hasten Hanoi's realization that it could not win. Sharp's perception of Rolling Thunder combined the views of McConnell and Wheeler. The air campaign could restrict Hanoi's capability to back the Viet Cong, he said, but some destruction of the North's economy would be necessary before Hanoi would stop supporting the insurgency.

Rolling Thunder thus became a compromise for military chiefs, but a compromise different from that reached by civilian officials. Whereas civilian leaders in the winter of 1964–65 had seen Rolling Thunder as an appropriate means to accomplish disparate goals, military chiefs in the summer of 1965 agreed on the ends sought by bombing. McConnell, Wheeler, and Sharp differed over how best to employ air power to achieve the common objective of destroying the North's capability to fight. By the end of July, the three concurred that the air campaign had placed a cap on North Vietnam's infiltration capacity,[48] although both McConnell and Sharp regarded this as insufficient to deter Hanoi, and Wheeler held that heavier bombing would produce results faster. Still, the three agreed that Rolling Thunder curtailed the North's capacity to support the Viet Cong. McNamara shared their conviction. "We have every reason to believe that the strikes at infiltration routes have at least put a ceiling on what the North Vietnamese can pour into South Vietnam, thereby putting a ceiling on the size of the war that the enemy can wage there," he wrote on 28 July.[49] Rolling Thunder's perceived effect on infiltration became one of the few mutual assumptions of civilian and military leaders regarding the air campaign for much of its duration. The notion did not completely disappear until the 1968 Tet Offensive exposed it as a myth.

The Target Selection Process

Despite air leaders' pleas for heavier bombing, Johnson and his principal civilian advisers tightly controlled the target selection process. The President's perception of Rolling Thunder's military objective differed from that of his air commanders. Although he wanted to reduce the North's capability to fight, he refused to let bombing threaten his negative objectives, which prevented a rapid extension of the air campaign. Final target approval occurred at Johnson's Tuesday White House luncheons, attended by McNamara, Secretary of State Dean Rusk, National Security Adviser McGeorge Bundy (until his replacement by Walt Rostow), and Press Secretary Bill Moyers (until his resignation). Not until late October 1967, when General Wheeler began attending, did those sessions include a military representative.[50] Geography drove target selection, and almost all targets picked before August 1965 were south of the 20th parallel.

Because of his negative objectives, the President advanced the bomb line northward slowly. He did not authorize attacks against areas near Hanoi or Haiphong until June 1966. The cities themselves became "prohibited areas" that pilots could not overfly without specific permission from Johnson. To avoid provoking the Russians and Chinese, he forbade attacks on North Vietnamese airfields and SAM sites while under construction. The President feared that casualties among advisers from the Communist superpowers might trigger intervention.[51] "The decision to hit or not hit [a target]," McNamara remarked, "is a function of three primary elements: the value of the target, the risk of U.S. pilot loss, and the risk of widening the war, and it depends on the balance among those elements as to whether we should or should not hit."[52] Johnson thought that bombing civilians also might prompt the Soviets or Chinese to "widen the war" and was likely to result in an international outcry. "The concern for the lives of the civilian populace is overriding in almost everything up there," Major General Ginsburgh observed.[53] Occasionally this concern led the Tuesday lunch group to select routes of flight for attacking aircraft.[54]

Johnson's personal control of the air war limited options for the air commanders implementing Rolling Thunder. The Tuesday lunch group at first assigned targets in "packages" of one a week, then changed to packages of three every two weeks by September 1965. The group members also allocated a specific number of sorties against selected targets to achieve an 80 percent rate of destruction. Until accomplishing that amount of damage, aircrews repeatedly attacked the same targets for the one- or two-week period. Losses increased as the North Vietnamese realized that the constraints would allow them to mass their defenses for extended periods around a small number of targets. Weather further hampered the effort, because aircrews could fly the assigned sorties only during the one or two weeks allowed. At the end of a package's alloted time, the unflown sorties were lost unless Johnson and his advisers reinstated the same target in a subsequent package. When targets received a greater sortie allocation than air commanders considered appropriate, the full number of sorties assigned were still flown anyway. "Obviously, if you do not fly [the allocated sorties], you can make a case that you did not really need them anyway," Major General Gilbert L. Meyers, 7th Air Force Deputy Commander, explained. "We wanted to be sure there would be no loss of future sorties on the basis that we had not flown them in the past period."[55]

The President's tight control over the bombing did not mean that the Joint Chiefs played no role in planning the air offensive. On the contrary, they consistently urged Johnson to increase Rolling Thunder's intensity. The chiefs submitted numerous proposals through McNamara for systematic air campaigns along the lines of the original ninety-four-target plan. Yet Johnson's personal direction on a weekly basis compelled the JCS Chairman to improvise a more expeditious means for providing targeting suggestions than the formal recommendation process. "The White House wanted to tightly control and approve each individual target, each piece of real estate that was authorized for strike. For this reason and in the interest of time, in seven days you just couldn't sit down and work a JCS paper and get joint agreement across the board," Colonel Henry H. Edelen, an Air Staff officer involved in North Vietnam contingency planning, recalled. In March 1965, Wheeler organized a "Rolling Thunder Team" of two officers, one Army and one Navy, in the Pacific Division of the Joint Staff. Neither individual was a pilot; however, together they reviewed the targeting proposals coming from Sharp's headquarters and made their suggestions to Wheeler, who in turn provided target recommendations to McNamara before the Tuesday lunches. "*If time permitted*, the Chairman would call the proposals to the attention of the Joint Chiefs of Staff and then go forward with them," commented Edelen. "Nowhere in this pattern did the Air Force really play a role."[56]

The workload involved in preparing the packages, the lack of experienced personnel, and the displeasure expressed by McConnell because no Air Force officer appeared in the decision-making process led Wheeler to expand the Rolling Thunder Team to five members in May 1965. Colonel Edelen became the single Air Force representative and was joined by officers from the Marine Corps and Navy. Before the air campaign ended in 1968, an Army officer and another Air Force officer increased the team total to seven.[57]

After expanding the Rolling Thunder Team in May, Wheeler attempted to include the service chiefs in the planning process. Before advocating a substantial shift in target priorities, he discussed his ideas with his colleagues during one of their weekly meetings. He could then modify individual package proposals to reflect those opinions that he accepted. "I would not necessarily submit the smaller programs to the other members of the Joint Chiefs of Staff," Wheeler recalled, "because I knew their views on the broader programs."[58] The service chiefs received word of Wheeler's weekly (or bi-weekly) target proposals from action officers assigned to monitor the Rolling Thunder Team's progress. After the team members made their initial target selections, they advised the action officers of the choices. These officers briefed their respective service chiefs on the targets and remained alert for changes in the team's proposals. The officers also notified the chiefs on Friday mornings of last-minute alterations, which allowed the service heads to voice disagreement to the Chairman during their weekly meetings on Friday afternoons.[59]

If any of the chiefs opposed the target proposals on Friday, Wheeler's team had little time to make changes. The Secretary of Defense requested a copy of the proposals before his weekly discussion of the bombing with Rusk, which occurred in McNamara's office on Saturday or Sunday.[60] McNamara had originally asked Wheeler to provide the White House and State Department with copies of the target proposals prior to the Tuesday lunch. In October 1965, the Secretary advised the Chairman to forward the advance copies for the White House and State Department to him. He then decided whether to provide those offices with early copies.[61]

McNamara dominated the targeting process for much of Rolling Thunder. Edelen remembered:

> Initially, the guiding light in establishing the weight of effort authorized was the Secretary of Defense. He attempted to keep sortie allocations at a low level for reasons best known to himself. There were a whole series of instances when we'd run out of sorties. In other words, there were targets available but no strike sorties available to CINCPAC to put on the targets. Then CINCPAC would send in a message and we'd have to get the approval. The approval came in all cases from the Secretary of Defense.[62]

Unlike most of Johnson's civilian advisers, McNamara frequently proposed targets at the Tuesday lunches, and his proposals did not always come from the list prepared by Wheeler's Rolling Thunder

Team. During periods when the Tuesday lunch group did not meet, when the President did not feel that the proposed target list needed his personal endorsement, the Secretary had authority to approve targets.[63]

Interdiction Dominates, August–December 1965

After Johnson expanded the ground war in July 1965, the Joint Chiefs redoubled their efforts to intensify Rolling Thunder. On 27 August, they gave McNamara two memorandums calling for increased bombing through an eight-week program. Unlike their March twelve-week proposal, the eight-week plan did not advocate a gradual expansion of Rolling Thunder. The scheme first called for attacks on military installations in Haiphong and Hon Gay, the mining of ports, and raids on roads and rail lines north of Hanoi. After this effort, Air Force and Navy aircraft would strike airfields, SAM sites, and other military facilities in Hanoi. Next would come attacks on POL storage areas and electric power stations, followed by raids on Hanoi and Haiphong industry. Heavy interdiction of major supply routes would supplement all phases of the campaign.[64]

The Joint Chiefs referred to their plan as an "accelerated interdiction" program to make the North Vietnamese stop the war or to make them ineffective if they pursued it. Yet the proposal was much more than a program to limit support to the Viet Cong. The plan reflected the combined ideas of Wheeler, McConnell, and Sharp, and an intent to meet the goals of all three air commanders. "Stepped-up interdiction efforts against the DRV target system would significantly affect industrial and commercial activity in the DRV and place in serious jeopardy the viability of the nonagricultural sector of the North Vietnamese economy," the Joint Chiefs remarked. The impact of intensified interdiction on the North's economy, the chiefs declared, could compel Hanoi to choose between supporting Communist forces in the South and fulfilling "the increasing domestic needs" of the Northern populace.[65]

The Joint Chiefs warned that the current air campaign could not completely eliminate adequate logistical support to the enemy. They blamed controls on both targeting and weight of effort, along with the small amounts of aid required by current Viet Cong and North Vietnamese operations, for Rolling Thunder's failure to affect the supply flow. To curtail that movement, air power not only would have to interdict supplies going south but also would have to reduce the amount of goods entering North Vietnam. In addition, American and South Vietnamese ground forces would have to raise "the intensity of combat to that level where VC/DRV consumption rates of heavy items, principally ammunition, could not be sustained by present [resupply] efforts." If American ground forces did not expand combat operations and Rolling Thunder's scope remained limited, the chiefs warned, Johnson would ultimately face what he sought most to avoid: superpower intervention. "Our strategy for Vietnam should not allow the communists to keep pace with or more than match our military efforts," the chiefs reasoned. "A program of slowly rising intensity with both sides in step carries with it the danger that it will lead to less flexibility of choice, creeping intervention by the Soviets and Chinese, first with material and later with troops, and the eventual engulfing of both camps unwillingly into an expanded war."[66]

McNamara refused to back the Joint Chiefs' proposal, although the monthly Rolling Thunder sortie total increased from 2,879 in August to 3,553 in September. In September American pilots began the interdiction of rail and highway routes in northwestern North Vietnam; in October they attacked bridges on the Northeast Railroad from Hanoi to China. By the end of October, they had struck 126 of the 240 targets on the Joint Chiefs' expanded target list. Of those remaining, seventy-five were in the "off-limits" areas of Hanoi, Haiphong, and the 30-mile zone near the Chinese border. Most of the others were in the "northeast quadrant," an area bounded by 20 degrees 40 minutes latitude and 105 degrees 20 minutes longitude and containing Hanoi, Haiphong, and the territory north of both cities. Because of the quadrant's concentration of population and industry, Johnson was reluctant to approve attacks in it. Yet, if he planned to continue gradually increasing air pressure on the North, he had little alternative to striking targets in the North Vietnamese heartland.[67]

McNamara perceived a need for attacks in the northeast quadrant as a prelude to introducing more ground troops in the South. Westmoreland had devised a three-phase plan to defeat the Communist forces, and to accomplish each phase's objective required added manpower. The Secretary felt that additional bombing was necessary prior to starting Phase II deployments.[68] On 3 November, he advised the President to adopt an "evolving" Rolling Thunder program that would gradually permit attacks on targets in the heartland. The effort would span five months, concluding with raids on POL storage areas and the mining of Haiphong harbor. Following the program, Johnson could begin Phase II deployments. "I favor 'evolution' of Rolling Thunder before Phase II deployments because . . . I believe that there is a finite chance that added pressure on the North, without Phase II deployments, may be enough to bring the DRV/VC to terms," McNamara asserted. He maintained that the public would be more likely to approve Phase II deployments if the administration first conducted his evolving Rolling Thunder program.[69]

Besides asking Johnson to expand the air campaign, the Secretary recommended that the President first halt Rolling Thunder for four weeks. McNamara argued that a bombing pause would offer the North Vietnamese a chance to move toward a settlement. A pause would also reduce the dangers of intervention in response to his planned raids on the heartland, he argued, and would demonstrate that American attempts to end the war were genuine. Finally, it would set the stage for another pause, possibly in late 1966, that might produce a settlement. McNamara suggested that the pause should be a "hard-line" effort in which the administration firmly committed itself to a bombing resumption unless Hanoi began to stop its support to the Viet Cong.[70]

Shortly after McNamara's proposal, the Joint Chiefs reiterated their belief that Rolling Thunder was having a minimal impact on the North Vietnamese war-making capacity. The chiefs claimed that bombing had not weakened the Communist armed forces except to limit their capability for overt aggression. While infiltration was more difficult, they noted, it continued at the level needed to support the enemy's combat activity in the South. Further, the strikes had not brought Hanoi's leaders any closer to abandoning the insurgency. Once more the chiefs blamed political controls for the paucity of results: "The establishment and observance of de facto sanctuaries within the DRV, coupled with a denial of operations against the most important military and war-supporting targets, precludes complete attainment of the objectives of the air campaign." They called for a "dramatic" change in Rolling Thunder "which will leave no doubt that the U.S. intends to win and achieve a level of destruction which [the North Vietnamese] will not be able to overcome." Primary targets for such an effort were POL storage areas and power plants, followed by airfields, supply routes, and port facilities.[71] A 20 November message from Sharp echoed the chiefs' arguments, although the admiral listed POL and port facilities as the most important targets in the North.[72]

Johnson pondered the proposals from McNamara and the Joint Chiefs during the late fall of 1965. On 18 December, Soviet Ambassador Anatoly Dobrynin told McGeorge Bundy that if the bombing stopped for a three-week span, the Soviets would attempt to persuade Hanoi to negotiate a settlement.[73] McNamara, Rusk, William Bundy, and Under Secretary of State George Ball urged the President to order a bombing halt. Rusk, William Bundy, and Ball held the view that a diplomatic move might yield success, but McNamara still considered the pause in the light of stronger measures to come. Johnson harbored reservations, deeming the likelihood of failure as "the most dangerous aspect" of a pause.[74] He accorded a bombing halt little chance of producing a settlement, and in his view its failure to secure peace would bring increased demand from Republicans in Congress to end American involvement. The President persisted in the opinion that the lack of unified congressional support for the war would cause public attention to focus on Vietnam rather than on his domestic social programs. Much like the Joint Chiefs' eight-week bombing proposal, an extended pause marked an extreme change in the conduct of the war that could not escape the public's notice. Moreover, the small but articulate group of antiwar protesters who had emerged since the beginning of Rolling Thunder made bombing the focal point of their outcry, and to suspend the campaign and then restart it would elicit a barrage of condemnation from them. The Joint Chiefs voiced a final concern: Wheeler had met with the President on 17 December and argued that a pause would relieve, rather than spur, pressure on the North to negotiate.[75]

Despite these considerations, on 27 December Johnson acceded to the pleas of his top civilian advisers and ordered an extension to the bombing pause that was part of a limited Christmas truce. The President originally intended the extension to last for twenty-four to thirty-six hours, but on the 29th he refused to resume Rolling Thunder. The Soviets had dispatched a Polish diplomat, Jerzy Michalski, to Hanoi to attempt a settlement, and Johnson awaited results. Hanoi did not respond quickly. By the middle of January, the Joint Chiefs' requests for renewed bombing had become a clamor, yet the President persisted in waiting for a signal from the North. It finally arrived in Rome at the end of the month. The Pope received a letter from Ho Chi Minh bluntly stating the North's commitment to pursue the war to victory and denouncing the pause of a "sham peace trick." Rusk summarized the frustration felt by administration officials in a meeting on the 29th: "The enormous effort made in the last 34 days has produced nothing—no runs, no hits, no errors." Johnson's advisers now unanimously agreed that he should restart Rolling Thunder.[76]

The Emphasis Shifts to Oil, January–August 1966

The pause's failure to produce a settlement had a profound effect on Johnson. Despite recommendations from his civilian advisers that a pause would benefit the American war effort, he had maintained doubts about the measure's utility throughout its thirty-seven-day span. Ho Chi Minh's response only confirmed the President's conviction that "he had been talked into doing something that was essentially a sucker's move."[77] Ho's reply also gave Johnson a greater appreciation for the North's determination. The American Army's fall defeat of Communist forces in the Ia Drang Valley and the dropping of 40,000 tons of bombs on the North had not weakened Hanoi's willingness to fight. The perceived failure of civilian leaders to provide him with sound advice and the North's show of resolve caused the President to listen more intently to his military chiefs' call for "dramatic" air raids.

The 31 January resumption of Rolling Thunder was a murmur rather than a roar, however. Although intending to launch heavy strikes against the North, Johnson calculated that a strong display of force immediately after the pause would cause many people to consider the cessation an insincere effort to achieve peace.[78] Upon restarting Rolling Thunder, he prohibited attacks against fixed targets and restricted interdiction to areas south of the 21st parallel. Targets within a 30-mile radius from the center of Hanoi and within a 10-mile radius from the center of Haiphong were off limits. These controls remained until 1 April, when the President announced his intention to strike the North's oil storage facilities.[79]

In November 1965, the Joint Chiefs determined that oil was a vital ingredient of the North's infiltration capability. With five North Vietnamese Army regiments in the South, Hanoi had expanded its truck fleet to resupply its troops. The vulnerability of rail lines to interdiction increased the trucks' value as a logistical tool. By destroying the North's oil supply, the chiefs believed they could render the trucks useless and strain Hanoi's capacity to equip its growing forces in the South. They pointed out that the North possessed no oil fields or refineries and had imported 170,000 metric tons of POL in 1965. Most imports arrived at Haiphong, the only port capable of conveniently handling the bulk supplies carried by large tankers. Prior to distribution, the North Vietnamese stored the oil entering Haiphong at tank farms 2 miles from the city. The chiefs considered those storage sites, with a holding capacity of 72,000 metric tons, the most vulnerable part of the POL target system. They insisted that the facilities' destruction, followed by raids on the eight remaining major storage areas, would "be more damaging to the DRV capability to move war-supporting resources . . . than attacks against any other target system." The chiefs estimated that dismantling the North's oil storage capacity would require 416 aircraft sorties and cause forty-four civilian casualties.[80] Sharp, who independently examined the merits of striking POL, reached a stronger conclusion than the Joint Chiefs about the value of the oil storage areas. In the midst of the January bombing pause, he argued that the destruction of POL storage sites, combined with intensified interdiction in the northeast quadrant and mining, "*will* bring the enemy to the conference table or cause the insurgency to wither from lack of support."[81]

Intelligence estimates differed on the effect that attacking POL would have on the North's capability to continue the war. In November 1965, Defense Intelligence Agency (DIA) analysts reported that the North possessed a total POL storage capacity of 179,000 metric tons while requiring only 32,000 metric tons a year to sustain current combat operations. Yet they also stated that attacks on the Haiphong storage area would reduce the Communists' capacity to move larger units or heavy equipment.[82] Central Intelligence Agency (CIA) evaluators asserted at the end of December that raids on the Haiphong sites would have minimal impact on the war in the South. The loss of the storage facilities would slow the Communists' logistical flow, but the enemy needed a daily average of only 12 tons of external supplies, and that amount "would continue to move by one means or another." The CIA analysts predicted that destroying the Haiphong sites would cause the North Vietnamese to import oil overland. As most oil came from the Soviet Union, the loss of Haiphong's storage facilities would create political problems for the Russians, who would have to send it south over Chinese railroads. Hanoi's economy would suffer as well, the analysts surmised, because the disruption of normal rail traffic would limit the North's industrial output and complicate the internal distribution of goods.[83] In January 1966, the DIA further contended that destroying both the Haiphong storage area and dispersed POL sites would produce local oil shortages and transportation bottlenecks.[84]

Defense Department officials hesitated at first to endorse POL attacks, although they believed that Rolling Thunder should continue. In mid-January, Assistant Secretary of Defense John T. McNaughton named the destruction of POL third on his list of essentials for an effective interdiction program. He considered intensive, around-the-clock armed reconnaissance the primary requirement, followed by the destruction of untargeted transportation facilities. Yet McNaughton doubted that any interdiction could stymie the Communist supply flow. He remarked that enemy forces needed 80 tons of supply a day to sustain light combat and that the expected infiltration of men during 1966 would raise that amount to only 140 tons, less than three-quarters of the current monthly average arriving in the South. McNaughton still regarded intensive bombing was necessary, however, if for no other reason than to make the Chinese increase their aid to the North Vietnamese. Such assistance might threaten to "smother" North Vietnam, causing Hanoi to call off the insurgency rather than risk a loss of independence to its superpower neighbor.[85]

Instead of continued interdiction, the Assistant Secretary proposed raids against locks and dams. His rationale was similar to that of Air Force planners seeking to pressure the North Koreans and Chinese thirteen years earlier. "Such destruction does not kill or drown people," McNaughton wrote. "By shallow-flooding the rice, it leads after time to widespread starvation (more than a million?) unless food is provided—which we could offer to do 'at the conference table.'" Because dam attacks would not directly target the civilian populace, he insisted that they would not provoke the Chinese or Soviets. Still, McNaughton questioned bombing's ability to produce a settlement. A long as the Viet Cong maintained the initiative in the South, he did not believe Rolling Thunder could end the war.[86]

McNamara, too, suggested increased bombing at the end of January. He advised the President to raise the number of strike sorties to 4000 a month, a monthly increase of roughly 500 over the totals for late 1965. The Secretary doubted that additional bombing could place a "tight ceiling" on the Communist effort in the South. Yet he noted that Rolling Thunder had heightened infiltration's cost and had forced the North Vietnamese to divert manpower to air defense activities and repair work. Continued bombing might, Mc-Namara commented, "condition" Hanoi "toward negotiations and an acceptable end to the war." In addition, he thought that it would help maintain South Vietnamese morale.[87]

By March 1966, McNamara and Johnson both felt that the time was ripe to subject the North to sterner measures. On the 10th, the Joint Chiefs reasserted their conviction that destroying major oil storage areas would significantly damage Hanoi's capability to sustain Communist forces in the South.[88] McNamara asked the President to order attacks on seven oil storage sites, including the Haiphong storage area.[89] He further recommended raids on the Haiphong cement plant and supply routes in the northeast quadrant. The cement plant furnished 50 percent of the North's cement, and McNamara and the chiefs thought its destruction would hamper road and bridge construction.[90] Johnson was receptive to the proposals. He told Bromley Smith, the executive secretary to the National Security Council (NSC), that he desired a "maximum effort" against infiltration during the next two months.[91] On 1 April, the President gave Sharp permission to strike four bridges in the northeast quadrant and to interdict nine main supply routes in the heartland. The admiral also received orders to plan for April raids against the seven POL storage areas and the cement plant.[92]

Domestic turmoil in South Vietnam dashed Johnson's hopes to attack oil in April. On 12 March, Premier Nguyen Cao Ky removed his primary political opponent, the popular general Nguyen Chanh Thi, from command of I Corps. Thi's dismissal caused Buddhist monks to begin anti-Ky demonstrations in Da Nang and Hué. Dissidents joined the protest, not only condemning the Ky regime but also denouncing the American presence in Vietnam and calling for negotiations with the Viet Cong. Newsmen gave wide coverage to the unrest to the United States. In Congress, both Democrats and Republicans questioned the propriety of American involvement to save a people who appeared not to want assistance. More than 10,000 Buddhists demonstrated in Saigon on the 31st, and similar demonstrations occurred in other cities the following week. Johnson had been reluctant to begin Rolling Thunder in February 1965 in the wake of Southern political turbulence, and he was unwilling a year later to increase the air campaign's intensity until Ky restored order.[93] Calm did not return until early May, when Ky dispatched one thousand South Vietnamese Marines to Da Nang to quell the protests.

In the meantime, international efforts to start negotiations further delayed the POL raids. Early in April, United Nations Secretary General U Thant proposed a bombing halt as a prerequisite to negotiations; on 29 April, Canada's Prime Minister Lester Pearson suggested a cease-fire to start talks and a gradual troop withdrawal once discussions began. In May, officials from the Netherlands, Guinea, and Algeria called for a bombing halt as the initial step toward peace in Vietnam. The publicity of those attempts prevented Johnson from ordering the strikes against POL, as any increase in the air campaign could be seen as "worsening the atmosphere" of the peace efforts.[94] The continued delay also caused the President to have second thoughts about the raids' necessity.

Johnson's counselors argued against any cessation of the bombing and urged him to order the oil attacks. Maxwell Taylor, serving as special military adviser after his July 1965 return from Vietnam, told the President: "If we gave up bombing in order to start discussions, we would not have the coins necessary to pay for all the concessions required for a satisfactory settlement."[95] William Bundy advised not to quit bombing unless the North Vietnamese stopped infiltration and reduced military operations in the South.[96] Walt Rostow, who had replaced McGeorge Bundy as National Security Adviser, argued that Johnson should attack POL as soon as conditions permitted. Referring to the raids on German oil during World War II, he asserted that attacking North Vietnam's major reserves could severely damage Hanoi's capability to fight. "Oil moves in various logistical channels from central sources," he maintained. "When the central sources began to dry up the effects proved fairly prompt and widespread. What look like reserves statistically are rather inflexible commitments to logistical pipelines."[97]

At the end of May, Johnson allowed strikes against six small POL storage facilities in unpopulated areas, but he refused to order raids against the major sites.[98] The Canadian Ambassador, Chester Ronning, planned a mid-June trip to Hanoi to determine the Communists' negotiating attitude, and Rusk wanted the main POL strikes delayed until Ronning's return. On 17 June, after Ronning's mission had failed, Johnson told NSC members that he was still uncertain about initiating the POL attacks.[99] He remained hesitant five days later. At an NSC meeting on the 22nd, McNamara, Wheeler, Taylor, William Bundy, and CIA Director William Rayborn argued strongly for the raids' immediate start. The following exchange between Wheeler and the President typified the intensity of the discussions:

WHEELER: A POL strike will not stop infiltration, but it will establish another ceiling on what they can support. There are three divisions there with another ready to move.

JOHNSON: Suppose your dreams are fulfilled. What are the results?

WHEELER: Over the next 60 to 90 days, this will start to affect the total infiltration effort. It will cost them more. In a very real sense, this is a war of attrition.

JOHNSON: You have no qualification, no doubt that this is in the national interest?

WHEELER: None whatsoever.

JOHNSON: People tell me what not to do, what I do wrong. I don't get any alternatives. What might I be asked next? Destroy industry, disregard human life? Suppose I say no, what else would you recommend?

WHEELER: Mining Haiphong harbor.

JOHNSON: Do you think this will involve the Chinese Communists and the Soviets?

WHEELER: No sir.

JOHNSON: Are you more sure than MacArthur was?[100]

The consensus from his military and civilian advisers that oil attacks were necessary finally persuaded Johnson to begin the raids. After the meeting, he ordered strikes on the Hanoi and Haiphong oil storage areas for dawn on 24 June. Attacks on the remaining five facilities would follow. The President believed the raids would persuade Northern leaders to negotiate. "I thought that if we could seriously affect their POL supplies, and we could make it much more difficult for this infiltration to succeed, that they'd look at their hole card and say, well, what's the use, maybe we ought to try to work out some agreement," he recalled.[101] To ensure that the attacks would not disturb world public opinion or provoke the Chinese or Soviets, Johnson went to great lengths to avoid civilian casualties. Hand-picked crews would fly the missions, and they would not attack under marginal weather conditions. If poor weather delayed the strikes, the President ordered that they *not* begin on 26 June, a Sunday.[102]

Poor weather caused two postponements, and on 24 June the *Wall Street Journal* published details of the prospective attacks on Haiphong's POL. Appalled by the security leak, Johnson canceled the raids the next day, but with no intention of stopping them permanently. Military preparations for the strikes continued. On the 28th, Sharp notified Wheeler that his forces were ready and that the weather was favorable. The President rescinded the cancellation, and on the 29th the attacks commenced.

Both military and civilian leaders regarded the initial raids as a success. The Haiphong storage area appeared 80 percent destroyed, and the Hanoi site, containing 34,000 metric tons of POL, was completely demolished. To General Meyers, the operation was "the most significant, the most important strike of the war." McNamara sent a congratulatory message to the field commanders who had planned and executed the attacks. At Honolulu on 8 July, the Secretary told Sharp that the President wanted a complete "strangulation" of the North's POL system. Monthly strike sortie allocations jumped from 8,100 to 10,100, and McNamara told the admiral not to observe any sortie limitations in attacking oil. A new directive for the air campaign reflected the emphasis on POL. Designated Rolling Thunder 51, it announced that concentrated strikes on the POL system would serve as "an essential element of the program to cause [the North Vietnamese] to cease supporting, controlling, and directing insurgencies in Southeast Asia." General John D. Ryan, Commander of Pacific Air Forces, informed his units that the oil effort was necessary to reduce the North's war-making capability.[103]

The American public strongly backed the initial raids, although the response from U.S. allies was less favorable. In early July, the President's rating in a Harris opinion poll on his conduct of the war had risen 12 points, from a pre-bombing low of 42 percent in June to a post-bombing score of 54. The poll also showed that Americans approved the attacks on the storage sites by better than five to one. The reason most cited for that approval was "a desire to get the war over with."[104] The raids received less acclaim in Europe, where several leaders questioned their wisdom. Prime Minister Harold Wilson publicly dissociated himself from the attacks, whereupon Johnson began to view British statements on Vietnam with a jaundiced eye. "There's no doubt that in the President's mind this established Wilson . . . as a man not to go to the well with," William Bundy recalled.[105]

The POL strikes continued throughout July and August. At the end of July, the DIA determined that bombing had reduced the North's POL storage capacity to 75,000 metric tons, a total more than sufficient to meet requirements. Two-thirds of this amount remained in storage sites at Phuc Yen and Kep airfields, two of the main areas originally targeted by the Joint Chiefs in November 1965. Johnson denied Sharp's July request to attack the two facilities because of possible civilian casualties. As the raids progressed, however, DIA analysts concluded that destroying the airfield sites would not seriously affect the Northern war effort. They maintained that the North Vietnamese possessed enough dispersed storage areas to offset the bombing losses. Rather than continue the attack against the small depots scattered throughout the North, the President directed Rolling Thunder's emphasis back to interdiction. On 4 September, Sharp announced the air campaign's new priorities as the "attrition of men, supplies, and equipment."[106]

The euphoria initially experienced by civilian and military leaders over the POL raids vanished in the wake of a new analysis of Rolling Thunder. The Jason Summer Study, a group of forty-seven top scientists briefed on the war by administration officials, produced a 30 August report on the effects of bombing North Vietnam. The group's evaluation of the POL attacks was more pessimistic than the DIA assessment; the study estimated that only 5 percent of the North's POL requirements were necessary to support infiltration by truck and that plenty of oil remained to support those operations. The Soviets could provide additional POL in easily dispersed drums. "North Vietnam has basically a subsistence agricultural economy that presents a difficult and unrewarding target system for air attack," the study concluded.[107]

The Jason Summer Study's observations, combined with the POL effort's failure to produce decisive results, shook McNamara and caused him to question Rolling Thunder's utility. Never again did he recommend an intensification of the air war. After a mid-October trip to South Vietnam, the Secretary returned to Washington convinced that Johnson should end the struggle through diplomacy rather than military force. He now viewed the war in the South as a stalemate and rejected Sharp's request for a 140,000-man increase in ground troops. McNamara advised only a 40,000-man increase to Johnson, which would give the United States a total force of 470,000. The Secretary suggested that ten thousand to twenty thousand of these troops could construct and maintain an infiltration barrier of wire, mines, and sensors along South Vietnam's northern borders, while the remainder defeated the Communists inside the South. His scheme called for Rolling Thunder aircraft to interdict areas adjacent to the barrier. "I recommend, as a minimum, against increasing the level of bombing of North Vietnam and against increasing the intensity of operations by changing the areas or kinds of targets," McNamara urged the President. He also advised Johnson to stop bombing the North indefinitely and to pursue covert peace efforts.[108]

Major General Ginsburgh's assessment of the Jason Summer Study findings typified air commanders' perceptions of Rolling Thunder in September 1966. "The report is very difficult to refute conclusively," he observed, "because it involves many judgments which can not [sic] be proven wrong unless an expanded program is authorized." The "expanded program" that the general envisioned was one with minimal political controls. Having bombed the North for a year and a half under the President's stringent guidelines, air chiefs continued to believe the Rolling Thunder could have a telling impact on the war only if they received a free hand. Systematic campaigns against the enemy's economic assets, many air leaders thought, would ultimately strike the target essential to the North's war-making capability, which would in turn collapse the insurgency and cause Hanoi to sue for peace. Johnson's controls did not allow thorough campaigns against North Vietnamese target "systems." Nevertheless, by the fall of 1966, air commanders no longer believed that the transportation or POL systems were the "vital centers" of the North's capacity to fight. They hesitated to suggest, however, that the essential component of Northern war-making capability might be other than a modern element of an industrial state. They were also loath to admit that a year and a half of Rolling Thunder had had no appreciable impact on the enemy. Ginsburgh reasoned: "The bombing of the North *must* have some effect on the war in the South and the punitive effects in the North *must* have some influence in measuring the course of the war in the South against the costs in the North."[109]

Ginsburgh's comment indicated the depth of the air leaders' conviction that their bombing doctrine suited the nature of the war. In fact, air commanders had molded the war to suit their doctrine.

Most air chiefs viewed the war as a conventional conflict in which the enemy required essential logistical support, not as an infrequently waged guerrilla struggle. Those few who perceived Vietnam as a "people's war" thought that the North attached great value to its nascent industrial establishment, which included the transportation and POL systems. In like fashion, the air chiefs' emphasis on destroying the "modern" elements of the Northern state obscured Johnson's negative goals and caused many commanders to dismiss the President's fears of Chinese or Soviet intervention. Air leaders thus proceeded in Vietnam much as their predecessors had in World War II—they aimed to wreck the enemy economy to produce a prostrate foe. They seldom paused to consider whether or not their perception of the war was correct, or if it conformed to that of their political leaders.

Johnson and his advisers contributed to the intensity of the air commanders' beliefs by failing to clarify how bombing the North would help achieve the positive aim of an independent, stable, non-Communist South Vietnam. Each of the President's advisers had a unique perception of what bombing needed to accomplish to help produce a free South, and Johnson himself could not decide whether air power was more effective as a measure to support American ground forces or as a way to hurt the North. Moreover, the President and his advisers never really considered whether bombing was a *viable* political instrument, given the conflicting nature of American war aims. A combination of experience and faith persuaded political leaders that they could achieve their goals in Vietnam through restrained military power. Yet the goal of an independent, stable, non-Communist South Vietnam required more than simply bombing the North or advancing on the ground in the South. Civilian leaders realized too late that air power—served in either gradual doses or large gulps—could not turn the tide.

Johnson's failure to articulate specific objectives, his lingering hope that bombing would eventually cause Hanoi to end the war, and his reluctance to halt Rolling Thunder while American forces battled in the South combined with his air chiefs' assurances to generate the impetus for continuing the air campaign. The air commanders' perception of Rolling Thunder's military objective—to destroy North Vietnam's capability and will to fight—remained unchallenged by the political leadership. Accordingly, after the POL strikes failed to reduce the North's war-making capability, the air chiefs again relied on their doctrine to yield targets that would disrupt the Northern economy. This time, though, they proposed raids that would directly affect war-making capability *and* the will to resist.

The Shift to Industry and Electric Power, October 1966–May 1967

The Joint Chiefs adamantly disagreed with McNamara's bleak view of the war in the fall of 1966. In response to his call for a bombing halt to induce negotiations, they proposed attacks on power plants, industry, port facilities, and locks and dams. "The Joint Chiefs of Staff believe that the war has reached a stage at which decisions taken over the next sixty days can determine the outcome of the war," they declared to Johnson in mid-October 1966.[110] The chiefs condemned McNamara's barrier concept and argued that Rolling Thunder had prevented the Communists from mounting a major offensive. With Congressional elections on the horizon, the President was lukewarm to the chiefs' suggestion to expand the bombing. Several "peace candidates" challenged the administration's commitment to the war, and Johnson did not wish to give them encouragement by ordering heavy raids before the voting.

On 8 November, the Joint Chiefs elaborated on Rolling Thunder 52, their proposed directive for increased bombing. The program showed their continuing desire to destroy the North's war-making capacity. Yet unlike their previous bombing proposals, Rolling Thunder 52 showed that they had decided to attack North Vietnamese will directly. The chiefs targeted eight major power plants "to affect to a major degree both military and civilian support to the war effort." They contended that the power plants' destruction would not only reduce the operating efficiency of railway shops and the Haiphong shipyards but also disrupt the daily regimen of the inhabitants of Hanoi and Haiphong. Attacks on four locks controlling water levels on supply canals would "exert desirable psychological pressures on both leaders and population" by making them think that raids on the Red River dikes were imminent. Strikes on port facilities would demonstrate American willingness to attack harbor installations regardless of the shipping present.[111]

The air commanders' plan to mount direct attacks on North Vietnamese morale while also striking war-making capability was consistent with the conduct of past American air campaigns. Such an air pressure strategy paralleled LeMay's World War II fire raids and the attacks on hydroelectric plants and irrigation dams in Korea. Against both the Japanese in World War II and the Communists in Korea, air chiefs had first concentrated on destroying the enemy's capability to fight, believing that wrecking that capacity would lead to a collapse of morale. After finding that bombing aimed specifically at an enemy's war-making capability would not soon yield victory, air commanders had next focused their attacks on both the capability and willingness to resist. Although not stated in the directive, Rolling Thunder 52 was an admission that continued raids on the North's capacity to support the insurgency were insufficient to produce the desired results. Wheeler knew that the public, both in the United States and around the world, would discern the significance of raids on power plants, locks, and port facilities. When asked by the President in June 1966 to explain the difference between attacks on POL storage areas and power plants, he had replied that "POL is recognized as a legitimate military target."[112] The Joint Chiefs sought to drive home precisely that point to Hanoi— that the United States was now willing to strike targets not universally perceived as military fixtures. Rolling Thunder's implied threat to destroy the most valuable economic components of the North Vietnamese nation would once again guide the air effort, but commanders now intended to give that threat some teeth.

The Joint Chiefs' suggestion to expand Rolling Thunder mirrored the recommendation that Johnson had received from Westmoreland at the Manila Conference in late October.[113] The President returned to Washington on 2 November and left for his Texas ranch two days later.[114] There, in the aftermath of an election that produced sizable Republican gains in Congress, he looked over the chiefs' 8 November proposal. McNamara had forwarded the plan without comment so that the President could "receive it as promptly as possible,"[115] and Johnson liked what he saw. On 12 November, he authorized Rolling Thunder 52, which increased the number of monthly attack sorties in North Vietnam and Laos to 13,200 and allowed strikes on two power plants, the Haiphong cement plant, and the Thai Nguyen steel factory.[116] Several of the targets were inside the Hanoi prohibited area, requiring specific approval from the President before pilots could attack them. Still, Johnson, in relative isolation from his military and civilian advisers, accepted his military leaders' recommendation to increase pressure through air power.[117]

Shortly after the authorization of Rolling Thunder 52, Hanoi seemingly indicated a desire to begin negotiations. In response to an initiative by the Polish diplomat Januscz Lewandowski, Johnson had proposed a "Phase A–Phase B" plan in which he would stop Rolling Thunder (Phase A) *provided* that Hanoi agreed in advance to halt infiltration in key areas (Phase B).[118] In late November, the North Vietnamese suggested to the Poles that they would meet with American representatives in Warsaw on 6 December. They failed to show after American aircraft struck a rail yard near Hanoi on 2 December and a vehicle depot on the 4th. Although Johnson suspected that the Northern desire for an accord was "phony" and had ignored advice to refrain from bombing Hanoi, he was furious that the North Vietnamese chose not to meet.[119] Yet, because of the Polish announcement that the raids—and those that followed on 13–14 December—had sabotaged the talks, and the Northern outcry that the attacks had killed civilians, the President on 21 December curtailed Rolling Thunder 52. He suspended strikes within 10 miles of Hanoi, prohibited aircraft from traversing the 10-mile ring, and limited attacks to no more than three new targets a week.[120] He had no intention, however, of stopping the air campaign. "I was convinced that the North Vietnamese were not ready to talk with us," he later commented. "The Poles had not only put the cart before the horse, when the time of reckoning came, they had no horse."[121]

On 28 January 1967, North Vietnamese Foreign Minister Nguyen Duy Trinh publicly announced that Hanoi would not agree to peace talks until the "unconditional cessation" of air strikes against the North.[122] Johnson also revamped his November proposal. He maintained his stringent controls on Rolling Thunder until early February, when he stopped the campaign on the 8th for the Tet holiday truce. He then used the lull to write Ho Chi Minh secretly that he would make the pause permanent and freeze the number of American troops in Vietnam once assured that infiltration into the South "has stopped."[123] The appearance of three North Vietnamese divisions massed near the 17th parallel caused the President to discard his Phase A–Phase B plan. He feared that if he suggested the phased proposal, Ho would agree to it and quickly send the troops into the South before a bombing halt.

During the Tet truce, Soviet Premier Aleksei Kosygin visited Prime Minister Wilson, and the two attempted to mediate a settlement to the war. When Kosygin proposed talks in exchange for a bombing halt, Wilson responded by suggesting the Phase A—Phase B plan. Since the Prime Minister's refusal to support the oil raids,

Johnson had hesitated to send him secret information on Vietnam, and Wilson's latest word from the President did not mention the terms proposed to Ho.[124] Wilson was irate when informed of his mistake but amended his proposal. Premier Kosygin left London on the 12th, and Johnson extended the bombing pause until the Soviet leader arrived in Moscow on the 13th. No further communication came from Kosygin. On the 15th, Ho answered the President's letter. He called Johnson's offer unacceptable, stating that peace talks could not begin until the bombing stopped "definitively and unconditionally."[125]

Ho's blunt refusal to stop infiltration, the war's slow progress in the South, and the American public's overall support for the air campaign caused Johnson to order many of the attacks originally approved in Rolling Thunder 52. Westmoreland had launched Operation Cedar Falls, the largest American ground offensive of the war, in January against Communist units in the Iron Triangle near Saigon. Despite killing almost a thousand enemy soldiers, the assault had little impact on the fighting. "Even though the North Vietnamese and their Viet Cong followers were suffering one defeat after another," Johnson recalled, "they showed no evidence that they were ready to pull back."[126] On 13 February, the day the President resumed the bombing, a Harris poll showed that 67 percent of the American public supported Rolling Thunder.[127] After a 21 February review of Vietnam policy options by his civilian advisers, Johnson ordered raids on industrial targets that included the Thai Nguyen steel factory, the Haiphong cement plant, and all thermal power plants except those in Hanoi and Haiphong. He also approved the mining of rivers and estuaries south of the 20th parallel. Ironically, after finally receiving authority to attack many of the North's industrial targets, air commanders found their goal of a systematic campaign foiled by weather. Not until 10 March did aircraft bomb the Thai Nguyen steel complex, and by 21 March monsoons had canceled all but four of fifty-one strikes scheduled on the facility.[128]

On 21 March, Hanoi published the letters exchanged between Johnson and Ho Chi Minh during the Tet truce. By revealing its communication with the United States, Hanoi thus assumed some responsibility for the failure of the peace effort. In addition, the tone of Johnson's letter was more compromising than Ho's. The President saw the letters' publication as an opportunity to heighten Rolling Thunder's intensity. In January 1967, Sharp had prepared a study outlining what he felt were the North's six basic target systems: electric power, war-supporting industry, transportation support facilities, military complexes, petroleum storage, and air defense.[129] Following on the heels of the December outcry against the bombing, the admiral's plea that Johnson approve unlimited attacks on all components of a target system fell on deaf ears. After the announcement of the secret correspondence, the President reexamined Sharp's proposal. On 22 March he approved strikes on Haiphong's two thermal power plants, the facilities that Sharp had listed first for attack. The admiral's target list drove Johnson's target selection for much of 1967,[130] although Sharp's priorities differed little from those of the Joint Chiefs.

Since his November 1966 authorization of Rolling Thunder 52, Johnson, much like his military leaders, had begun to see the air campaign as a means to break the North's will to fight. He told NSC members on 8 February 1967 that the bombing would continue "until we get something from the North Vietnamese."[131] In mid-March, he informed the Tennessee legislature that two objectives of Rolling Thunder were to deny the enemy a sanctuary and to exact a penalty for the North's violations of the Geneva Accords.[132] Yet the President still sought to break Hanoi's will without sacrificing his negative objectives. His desire to portray America as a nation working for peace prevented him from ordering heavy assaults in the aftermath of the aborted Warsaw Conference and while Wilson and Kosygin were trying to produce acceptable negotiating terms.

Rolling Thunder's gradually increasing pace dismayed many members of Congress. Senator John Stennis, Chairman of the Preparedness Investigating Subcommittee of the Senate Armed Service Committee, announced his intention to launch hearings on the conduct of the air war. Knowing that Stennis was sympathetic to the air commanders' desire for a campaign free of political controls, Johnson worked to reduce the conflict between civilian and military leaders. Hanoi's publication of the letters permitted the President to accede to many of his air chiefs' demands. He believed that increased bombing would demonstrate his resolve to fight, and he hoped it would also weaken Northern morale sufficiently to achieve a favorable peace.

Johnson approved raids on Hanoi's central power station on 8 April. On the 20th, after several weather delays, aircraft attacked Haiphong's thermal power plants. The President also ordered, for the first time in the war, attacks on MiG airfields. American forces struck the Kep and Hoa Lac MiG bases on 24 April, but poor weather prevented the attack on Hanoi's power facility until 19 May. Although pleased with Johnson's expanded targeting, the Joint Chiefs retracted their earlier assertion that raids on power plants would affect "both military and civilian support to the war effort."[133] Wheeler notified the President on 5 May: "The objective of our attacks on the thermal power system in North Vietnam was not . . . to turn the lights off in major population centers, but were [sic] designed to deprive the enemy of a basic power source needed to operate certain war-supporting facilities and industries."[134]

The Chairman's memo contradicted the chiefs' original purpose for the raids. Air commanders *had* decided that direct attacks against both the North's capability and its will were necessary. After finally conducting the strikes, Wheeler had second thoughts about admitting their complete objective. His pronouncement mirrored that of the Korean War's General O. P. Weyland, who referred to the raids on North Korean irrigation dams as interdiction efforts to wash out rail embankments. Despite his Army background, Wheeler knew that Air Force doctrine did not condone direct raids on civilians. Further, the doctrine taught that destroying a vital part of the enemy's economy *would* weaken morale. Yet just as Weyland had difficulty accepting the need to attack North Korean rice, Wheeler had trouble justifying the raids on electric power except in terms of their strict military value. Only with supreme difficulty could he advocate attacks aimed at disrupting morale, and once these attacks occurred, he could critique them only in regards to their effect on combat operations.

For the moment, Johnson resolved Wheeler's dilemma. The 19 May strike on the Hanoi power plant was the last attack of the spring offensive against industry and electric power.

The Objective Wavers, May 1967–March 1968

The May raid on the Hanoi power station occurred in the midst of a vigorous policy debate over the future conduct of the war. In late April, the Joint Chiefs had backed Westmoreland's request for 200,000 additional troops, called for ground assaults into Laos and Cambodia, and urged the President to mine North Vietnamese ports. William Bundy, Rostow, McNaughton, and McNamara opposed such extensions of the war. Bundy argued strongly against mining and recommended no further attacks against "sensitive" targets in the heartland. Rostow, McNaughton, and McNamara proposed a cessation of raids north of the 20th parallel. They argued that Rolling Thunder had destroyed the bulk of important fixed targets and that interdiction would be most effective if confined to the supply flow through the "neck" of the North's logistical funnel.[135]

Unlike Johnson and the Joint Chiefs, the President's principal civilian advisers no longer perceived Rolling Thunder as a primary means to weaken Northern morale. "Its basic objective," William Bundy declared on 9 May, "[is] to make the total infiltration and supply operation more costly and difficult."[136] McNamara could see little value in the air campaign either as an interdiction measure or as a hammer to persuade Hanoi to quit fighting. Yet he also felt that confining Rolling Thunder below the 20th parallel would impose the lowest possible ceiling on infiltration. Frustrated by the lack of American success in Vietnam, he advised Johnson to seek a compromise peace, and he thought a bombing cutback would help obtain that goal. "The war in Vietnam is acquiring a momentum of its own that must be stopped," he asserted. "Dramatic increases in U.S. troop deployments, in attacks on the North, or in ground actions in Laos and Cambodia are not necessary and are not the answer."[137]

Because of the division between his civilian and military counselors, the President ordered a thorough analysis of Vietnam options. Yielding to his civilian advisers' suggestions, he prohibited further attacks within 10 miles of Hanoi. Raids on airfields in the heartland continued, however. The outbreak of the six-day Arab-Israeli War in early June diverted attention from Vietnam, and for the remainder of the month Johnson focused on his meeting with Kosygin in Glassboro, New Jersey.[138] On 20 July, the President finally announced new directives for combat operations. McNamara had visited Westmoreland to determine the general's exact troop requirements and found that a 200,000-man increase was not essential. As a result, Johnson ordered only 50,000 additional troops to Vietnam.

When considering Rolling Thunder, the President examined three options: to increase bombing in the Northern heartland, to restrict attacks to below the 20th parallel, and to maintain the campaign's current level of intensity. He chose the last. The new Rolling Thunder directive, number 57, allowed raids on sixteen fixed targets in the northeast quadrant as well as extensive interdiction. The prohibition on attacks within 10 miles of Hanoi remained, despite cries from Sharp and the Joint Chiefs. Johnson's directive satisfied neither his civilian nor his military advisers; in effect, it was "a decision to postpone the issue."[139] With Stennis's committee scheduled to meet in August and almost 500,000 troops in Vietnam, he could not justify a significant decrease in the bombing. His negative objectives prevented more extensive attacks, and he was now faced with a growing antiwar protest that was extremely visible and articulate. In April nearly 100,000 people in New York and San Francisco had demonstrated against the war. While the middle road prevented him from exerting the desired amount of pressure against Hanoi, it helped to assure that he would maintain the support necessary from both his civilian advisers and the American people to prosecute the war.

Air commanders exploited the publicity surrounding the Stennis hearings to press their requests for increased bombing. In early August, the Joint Chiefs combined their target list with Sharp's to create an "Operating Target List" of 427 fixed targets.[140] Of these, aircraft had attacked 259, and the President had prohibited strikes against 138. On 9 August, the opening day of the hearings, the chiefs recommended attacks on seventy of the restricted targets. Johnson knew that such commanders as Sharp and McConnell would use the hearings to vent their displeasure over the air campaign's political controls, and he responded to the chiefs' request by expanding Rolling Thunder 57 authorizations. He approved attacks on sixteen additional fixed targets, six within the 10-mile Hanoi circle and nine on the Northeast Railroad inside the Chinese buffer zone. The President continued to remove restrictions, and by mid-September aircraft had struck forty of the suggested targets.[141] Speaking of the freedom given to 7th Air Force to attack the Northeast Railroad, Lieutenant Colonel William H. Greenhalgh observed that "we were finally given carte blanche."[142] That autonomy resulted in the realization of one of Johnson's great fears. Two fighters raiding the railroad strayed across the Chinese border on 21 August, and Chinese MiG's shot down both of them.[143]

The China overflight contributed to the President's decision to prohibit further strikes within Hanoi's 10-mile perimeter. Although the Chinese did not increase their military aid to the North, Johnson worried that another incident might trigger direct involvement. In addition, the President had dispatched Dr. Henry A. Kissinger to Paris in response to French indications that the North Vietnamese might negotiate, and Johnson did not want Rolling Thunder to undermine the possibility. Kissinger proposed an end to the bombing if the cessation would "promptly lead" to "productive discussions."[144] The offer differed from the previous November's Phase A–Phase B overture, for Kissinger stated that the bombing halt would last as long as the North did not "take advantage" of it. Normal military activity in South Vietnam, including resupply, would be allowed to continue until a cease-fire occurred.[145] On 29 September, Johnson publicly announced the terms in a speech to the National Legislative Conference in San Antonio. Four days later, North Vietnam's Communist Party newspaper described the proposal as a "faked desire for peace."[146] French intermediaries confirmed that Hanoi no longer appeared willing to talk. "The channel was dead," the President recalled. "The door was closed and locked."[147]

Kissinger's failure to bring about negotiations led to the intensification of Rolling Thunder. Johnson approved raids on five targets in or near Haiphong on 6 October, and on the 23d aircraft attacked inside the Hanoi perimeter for the first time in two months. On the 25th they struck Phuc Yen airfield, the primary MiG-21 fighter base and a target frequently recommended by Sharp and the Joint Chiefs. The Phuc Yen raid showed that Johnson's desire to batter Northern morale had begun to override his negative objectives. Three weeks before the attack, he had pointed out that an assault on the airfield would kill two hundred Soviet technicians. He had also expressed his concern over the lack of public support for his handling of the war, which had plummeted to a 28 percent approval rate by October in light of draft calls exceeding 13,000 per month and his recommended 10 percent surtax to cover the war's increasing costs.[148] Yet the Phuc Yen raid came only four days after 50,000 antiwar protesters staged a dramatic march on the Pentagon.

While they approved of the President's expansion of Rolling Thunder, air commanders argued that it was not enough. "North Vietnam is paying heavily for its aggression and has lost the initiative in the South," the Joint Chiefs informed McNamara, but "at our present pace, termination of North Vietnam's military effort is not expected to occur in the near future."[149] On 27 October, the chiefs urged Johnson to reduce the Hanoi "no fly" zone to a 3-mile radius. A month later, they asked the President to initiate a four-month campaign against twenty-four restricted targets. Mining would supplement the effort, and the combination of air and sea interdiction would, the chiefs maintained, increase the hardships imposed on the North. In proposing the four-month program, they asked the President to accept an expected increase in civilian casualties as "justifiable and necessary."[150] McConnell questioned the restrictions on attacking the Northern rice crop, which he saw as a target that would affect the Communists' war-making capacity as well as their will to fight. "My experience is limited to World War II and Korea," he testified. "In neither of those was there any attempt to preserve the agricultural base, if the targets were required from the standpoint of suppression of [the enemy's] ability to wage war."[151]

McNamara advised Johnson not to expand Rolling Thunder, but the Secretary made little headway against the military's arguments for increased bombing. Since the oil raids in mid-1966, he had questioned the air campaign's military effectiveness, and since the spring of 1967 he had doubted that the United States could accomplish its original political objectives through force. The President, however, remained committed to the goals espoused in NSAM 288, and the vision of an independent, non-Communist South Vietnam still guided the military's planning. Wheeler became a regular member of the Tuesday lunch group in October 1967, ensuring that the President would receive the Joint Chiefs' views firsthand on a weekly basis. Moreover, Westmoreland reported a lack of Communist activity in the South. The general's optimism buoyed Johnson's hopes that the North Vietnamese were finally starting to feel the effects of military pressure. The President brought Westmoreland to the United States in November to defend the administration's conduct of the war to an increasingly skeptical American public. Johnson received additional support for his management of the war from a special senior advisory group. Consisting of such former officials as Dean Acheson, Robert Murphy, and Douglas Dillon, the group informed the President that continued military force *would* pressure the North into a favorable settlement.[152] McNamara could not accept that conclusion. Faced with growing isolation from the mainstream of administration thinking, he decided in November to resign as Secretary of Defense.[153]

Johnson's approval of ten of the Joint Chiefs' twenty-four recommended targets on 16 December revealed not only McNamara's inability to influence military policy but also the President's disdain for the Jason Summer Study's second evaluation of Rolling Thunder. Completed at McNamara's request by many of the scientists who participated in the 1966 review, the December 1967 report concluded that North Vietnam's war-fighting capacity had *increased* because of the bombing. The scientists asserted that Rolling Thunder had caused the North Vietnamese to enhance their transportation system by making it more redundant and eliminating choke points. As long as Hanoi's capability to support Communist forces in the South remained, the study insisted, bombing could not affect the North's will to fight. The scientists reported further that they could not devise an air campaign that would reduce the amount of men and goods flowing south.[154] Sharp countered the study's findings with his own evaluation of the air effort: "Although men and material needed for the level of combat now prevailing in South Vietnam continue to flow despite our attacks on LOCs, we have made it very costly to the enemy in terms of material, manpower, management, and distribution."[155] Sharp, the Joint Chiefs, and the President all believed that the high cost inflicted by air power, combined with the Communists' inability to win in the South, would ultimately cause Hanoi to yield to American terms.

By mid-December 1967, Johnson knew that the enemy planned to launch an offensive in the South, and he felt confident that American forces could parry the blow. "The view in the White House was optimistic," Major General Ginsburgh recalled. "We speculated that this might be a go-for-broke campaign and that before the campaign terminated there would be a real possibility for entering into negotiations."[156] The President considered North Vietnamese Foreign Minister Trinh's public statement on 29 December further proof that conditions were ripe for settlement. Trinh stated that the North *would* begin discussions with the United States once the bombing stopped, which was a change from his previous comment that talks *could* begin if the bombing ended.[157] Johnson prohibited raids within 5 miles of Hanoi on 3 January 1968, and in his State of the Union address on the 17th he encouraged Hanoi to accept his "San Antonio formula" as the basis for peace talks.

On 30 January, one day after the start of the cease-fire for the Tet holiday, the North Vietnamese and Viet Cong began their offensive. The assault caught Johnson and his civilian advisers off guard. "We were very surprised when it came during the Tet holidays, which both sides had traditionally reserved as a stand-down period," Rusk remembered.[158] The attack's magnitude stunned air commanders. An estimated total of 70,000 troops struck thirty-six of the South's forty-four provincial capitals and five of its six autonomous cities.[159] Air leaders had consistently maintained that Rolling Thunder limited the scale of Communist ground operations, and the Tet Offensive shattered that conviction. The assault also demonstrated that bombing had not dampened the North's will to fight.

As a result of Rolling Thunder's failure to suppress the enemy's war-making capability, air commanders sought to intensity the attack on Northern morale. The ferocity of the enemy offensive caused Wheeler to overcome his misgivings about striking targets that might produce civilian casualties. At the Tuesday lunch on 6 February, he pleaded with Johnson for permission to attack all targets outside of a 3.5-mile radius from the center of Hanoi and a 1.5-mile radius from the center of Haiphong. The general noted that the North Vietnamese possessed an excellent air raid warning system that would help keep civilian casualties to a minimum. He told the President that he was not bothered by civilian losses when measured against the Communists' "organized death and butchery" in the South.[160] Johnson removed the 5-mile radius limit around Hanoi and approved attacks on fourteen previously restricted targets, but he did not give Wheeler authority to attack additional targets without his approval. The Chairman continued to press for raids to weaken Northern will. On 19 March, he proposed striking the Haiphong docks, located near a large concentration of the city's inhabitants.[161] The President rejected the suggestion. By this time, he had grave doubts that military pressure against the North would achieve his goals in Vietnam.

At the end of February, Johnson had asked Clark M. Clifford, his new Secretary of Defense, to review Vietnam policy options. Clifford started the analysis convinced that increased force was the proper response to the Tet Offensive. The conviction proved transitory. Westmoreland had requested 206,000 more men to thwart the Communist assault, but the Joint Chiefs could not give Clifford a precise time when the attrition of enemy forces would become "unbearable."[162] In addition, Clifford and his assistants determined that a significant increase in bombing could not affect the North's war-making capability. They observed that the only purpose of intensifying Rolling Thunder "would be to endeavor to break the will of the North Vietnamese leaders," a prospect they thought had little chance of success even if the United States attempted deliberate strikes on population centers or the Red River dikes. Besides failing to destroy Northern morale, such measures would, they contended, alienate allied and domestic support for the war and heighten the risk of superpower intervention.[163] The dismal prospects for military success either on the ground or through the air caused Clifford to reconvene the senior policy advisers who had counseled Johnson in November 1967. Meeting at the White House on 25 and 26 March, most of the officials now advocated a withdrawal from Vietnam.[164] Clifford concurred.

The second "wise men" meeting closely followed domestic and political crises for the President that had a major impact on his ability to intensify the war. On 10 March, the *New York Times* reported Westmoreland's request for 206,000 more troops, adding to the popular outcry against the war fueled by the Tet Offensive. Three days later, Johnson narrowly defeated Democratic peace candidate Eugene McCarthy in the New Hampshire primary. On the 16th, Senator Robert Kennedy, Johnson's primary political foe, announced his candidacy in the Presidential race. The events of March 1968 starkly demonstrated that Johnson's nagging fear had become a reality—he had lost the public support necessary to prosecute the war. Clifford's about-face and the senior advisers' consensus helped tip the scales against applying additional military force in Vietnam.[165] Rusk also contributed to the growing clamor for de-escalation. On 4 March he advised Johnson simply to stop bombing above the 20th parallel and see how Hanoi reacted. The President could then set conditions for a complete halt, such as the withdrawal of North Vietnamese forces from South Vietnam's two northernmost provinces and a restoration of the DMZ.[166] In a 31 March television address, Johnson announced that he would indeed de-escalate the war. Aircraft would no longer bomb the North, except in the area directly north of the 17th parallel where enemy buildups threatened American and South Vietnamese troops. To help assure that the unilateral action led to negotiations, he stated that he would devote his remaining time in office to peace efforts and that he would not seek re-election.

The trauma of March 1968, combined with the shock of the Tet Offensive, caused Johnson to abandon his attempt to create an independent, stable, non-Communist South Vietnam by applying a military power against the North. His hope for a non-Communist South remained, but, as one historian has noted, "the circumstances in which the March decisions were made and the conciliatory tone of Johnson's speech made it difficult, if not impossible, for him to change course."[167] The President understood that he could not obtain a free South Vietnam without backing from the American public. "My biggest worry was not Vietnam itself; it was the divisiveness and pessimism at home," he later wrote regarding the aftermath of his 31 March address.[168] He could not overcome that divisiveness. For the remainder of his presidency, Johnson never achieved better than a 2–1 negative response from the American public in polls evaluating his efforts in Vietnam.[169] The lack of public support for the war finally forced him to include American withdrawal as part of his positive political goal in Vietnam.

Johnson thus provided his successor with a dilemma, and that dilemma formed the basis of America's revised war aims. On the one hand, the public's failure to support the war compelled the President to remove American forces from Vietnam. On the other hand, he still sought to preserve a non-Communist South. Fittingly, Johnson provided the label for these twin goals at the conclusion of his 31 March address. "Let men everywhere know," he proclaimed, "that a strong, a confident, and a vigilant America stands ready tonight to achieve an honorable peace."[170]

In attempting to achieve "peace with honor," Richard M. Nixon would place a large measure of faith in air power.

IV

Restraints and Results, 1965–68

We are considering air action against the North as the means to a limited objective—the improvement of our bargaining position with the North Vietnamese. At the same time we are sending signals to the North Vietnamese that our limited purpose is to persuade them to stop harassing their neighbors, that we do not seek to bring down the Hanoi regime or to interfere with the independence of Hanoi.

GEORGE W. BALL
5 October 1964[1]

It is within our power to give much more drastic warnings to Hanoi than any we have yet given. If General Eisenhower is right in his belief that it was the prospect of nuclear attack which brought an armistice in Korea, we should at least consider what realistic threat of larger action is available to us for communication to Hanoi.

MCGEORGE BUNDY
30 June 1965[2]

A variety of controls limited the bombing of North Vietnam. While President Lyndon Johnson's much-publicized political restrictions were the most obvious limitation on the campaign, military and operational restrictions also confined the air effort. Those controls reduced bombing's military effectiveness, and hence its efficacy as a political instrument. The air campaign did not significantly lessen the North's capability to fight, nor did it weaken Hanoi's willingness to continue the war.

Rolling Thunder's failure to achieve decisive results did not stem entirely from the controls placed on it. Of equal importance was the failure of civilian and military leaders to appreciate the type of warfare waged by the enemy. Despite frequently *stating* that the Communists were conducting guerrilla warfare, both groups assumed that the destruction of resources necessary for *conventional* conflict would weaken the enemy's capability and will to fight unconventionally. The United States had never opposed a guerrilla foe in the nuclear era, and memories of unconventional conflicts in the Philippines and Latin America had faded in the aftershock of Hiroshima. America had also fought only one limited war in the atomic age. Air commanders in the early 1960s considered Korea an aberration and prepared for global conflict with the Soviet Union. Meanwhile, civilian leaders witnessed the Soviet retreat in Cuba from the threat of American air power. The absence of limited war experience in an unconventional environment, combined with smug self-assurance, led to a misplaced faith in Rolling Thunder. Instead of facilitating victory, the air power convictions of civilian and military chiefs served as blinders obscuring the true image of the Vietnam War.

Controls on Rolling Thunder

Johnson's controls on the air campaign flowed from his negative political objectives. The goals of avoiding Soviet or Chinese intervention, preserving the Great Society, securing a favorable American image overseas, and maintaining the support of Western allies caused him to keep a tight rein on Rolling Thunder. Although he periodically relaxed his controls, the President remained constantly alert for signs that Rolling Thunder threatened his negative aims. By restricting weaponry, targets, and sortie rates, he tried to fashion an air campaign that would hurt North Vietnam without provoking external observers.

Armament limitations included both a ban on nuclear weapons and the restricted employment of B-52 bombers. Neither Johnson nor the Joint Chiefs seriously considered using the atomic bomb against the North. To do so would have invited the nuclear exchange that the President feared; further, air leaders found no targets worthy of atomic ordnance. They proposed sending B-52s with 30-ton loads of conventional "iron" bombs against marshaling yards and airfields.[3] Johnson dispatched additional bombers to the Pacific in early 1965 but hesitated to send them across the 17th parallel. He believed that B-52 attacks on the North would appear too provocative, and he wanted to avoid losses to a major component of America's nuclear deterrent.[4] In mid-June 1965 he permitted bomber raids in the South. The "Arc Light" campaign of B-52 close air support soon became a regular feature of the Southern war. Not until 1966 did Johnson order the bombers northward. They flew only 141 Rolling Thunder missions, and most occurred near the demilitarized zone.[5]

Controls on targets also limited the air effort. American jets did not attack the enemy heartland north of the 20th parallel until late 1965. Johnson restricted raids against Hanoi, Haiphong, and targets adjacent to the Chinese border, although the limitations varied in severity. Unless they secured the President's approval through the Joint Chiefs, air commanders could not attack targets within a 30-mile radius from the center of Hanoi, a 10-mile radius from the center of Haiphong, and within 30 miles of China. Those "restricted area" controls remained in effect for the duration of Rolling Thunder. In December 1966, Johnson established "prohibited areas" around Hanoi and Haiphong. These were zones where no attacks or overflights were permitted. The prohibited area restrictions fluctuated according to Johnson's temperament and the seriousness of American negotiating efforts. For most of 1967, the zones were a 10-mile circle around the center of Hanoi and a 4-mile circle around Haiphong.[6]

Besides determining *where* his pilots could attack, the President decided *how often* they could do so. By assigning targets in weekly or biweekly increments, he assured that the campaign would intensify gradually. Johnson also stopped Rolling Thunder completely on eight occasions between March 1965 and March 1968. His reasons for the cessations varied. In May 1965, he halted the campaign for six days as "a propaganda effort" to demonstrate that he sought a peaceful solution to the war.[7] The attempt to negotiate was not genuine, unlike bids made in December 1965 and February 1967 in connection with bombing pauses of thirty-seven days and six days, respectively. Johnson stopped Rolling Thunder briefly during both Christmas and New Year's in 1966 and 1967, and for twenty-four hours on Buddha's birthday in May 1967.

Conditions in South Vietnam further affected the tempo of the air campaign. The President refused to start bombing in December 1964 or February 1965 while coups immobilized the Saigon government. Likewise, he hesitated to attack oil storage facilities while Buddhist protesters challenged Premier Nguyen Cao Ky's authority in the spring of 1966. Johnson had initially intended Rolling Thunder to be a joint operation by American and South Vietnamese air forces. The difficulty of coordinating with Southern leaders,[8] the lack of sophisticated South Vietnamese aircraft, and a shortage of highly trained pilots caused him in March 1965 to drop the requirement for Southern participation. The qualification restricted operations during Rolling Thunder's first two weeks, the period when the President's civilian advisers had the most faith in its success.

In addition to announced bombing controls, Johnson and his civilian counselors limited Rolling Thunder indirectly. Concerns other than Vietnam reduced the attention that civilian leaders could devote to the air campaign, and Tuesday lunch decision-making sometimes blurred the intentions of the President and his advisers. At the end of April 1965, an attempted coup in the Dominican Republic compelled Johnson to focus on the Caribbean when Rolling Thunder was less than two months old. Determined to forestall the establishment of a second Communist regime in the Western Hemisphere, he dispatched 22,000 troops to the country. The Dominican crisis continued until early June and prevented Johnson from giving careful thought to his May decision to stop Rolling Thunder temporarily.[9] The Arab–Israeli War in June 1967, followed by the Glassboro summit later that month, also diverted the President's attention from Vietnam. After having asked for a review of Vietnam policy options in May 1967, he delayed his response to bombing proposals until late July. The North Korean capture of the American intelligence ship *Pueblo* on 23 January 1968—seven days prior to the Tet Offensive—distracted Johnson and his advisers from Vietnam and heightened the surprise of the Communist assault. Instead of sending reserve ground and air units to Southeast Asia to oppose the attack, he ordered reserves to Korea to bolster American forces there.

The President made many of his foreign policy decisions, including those concerning Rolling Thunder, during his Tuesday White House luncheons. The lunch group met roughly 160 times between 1964 and 1968, although the frequency of meetings was erratic. After a 9 March 1965 session, Johnson convened Tuesday lunches for eleven consecutive weeks, and he relied on them often in August and September. In the first twenty weeks of 1966, the lunch group met only six times, but after December 1966 the luncheons occurred an average of four out of every five weeks.[10] Johnson preferred the lunch sessions to NSC meetings because they lessened the chance that secret material might leak to the press. "In effect, the Tuesday luncheons were NSC meetings—the key participants of the NSC were present," Secretary of State Dean Rusk later explained. "The luncheon format allowed complete candor; there was nobody sitting in chairs along the wall. We knew what was said wouldn't be in the *Washington Post* the next day."[11]

While permitting candor, the luncheons did not guarantee clarity. Only Johnson's principal advisers attended the gatherings, and they did not publish the sessions' results.[12] William Bundy, Assistant Secretary of State for East Asian Affairs, described the Tuesday lunch as "an abomination."[13] He recalled that after a luncheon he would telephone his counterpart at the Defense Department, Assistant Secretary John T. McNaughton, to discuss what each thought were the decisions made at the session. Different perceptions were frequent. Benjamin Read, the State Department's executive secretary, noted that occasionally after talking with Rusk and National Security Adviser Walt W. Rostow, "you would think that they had attended separate lunches."[14]

The information that air chiefs received from the Tuesday luncheons was sometimes incorrect and often caused confusion. Secretary of Defense Robert S. McNamara informed Admiral U. S. Grant Sharp, Rolling Thunder's operational commander, on 10 May 1965 that the bombing would stop for several days "in order to observe [the] reaction of DRV rail and road transportation systems."[15] The Secretary did not mention that Johnson intended the interlude as a ploy to demonstrate his willingness to negotiate. When the bombing resumed, the lunch group produced a definition of "acceptable" interdiction targets that baffled air commanders. Pilots learned that they had authority to strike moving targets such as convoys and troops, but could not attack highways, railroads, or bridges with no moving traffic on them.[16] Moreover, the precise meaning of "moving targets" was unclear to those executing Rolling Thunder. A wing commander in Thailand expressed his confusion over permissible interdiction targets to 2d Air Division Headquarters in Saigon:

What is a military convoy? How many vehicles constitute a convoy? When a specified number of vehicles covers what length of road is it a convoy? Is a single vehicle travelling by itself an authorized target? . . . Targets on a "truckable ancillary road" are listed as a target. How far off of a specified route are we authorized to follow a truckable ancillary road? "Troops" are listed as targets. The difficulty of recognizing groups of civilians on the ground from troops is readily apparent. I recognize this as my problem but believe that it can be better defined.[17]

The air commanders' failure to receive precise information from the Tuesday lunch group stemmed partly from its lack of a military representative. Until late 1967, Chairman of the Joint Chiefs of Staff Earle G. Wheeler did not regularly participate in the sessions. General Wheeler had the impression that the President harbored suspicions of military parochialism, which at first prevented Johnson from inviting him to the Tuesday lunches.[18] Whatever the reason, the President omitted him not only from the Tuesday sessions but also from other decision-making forums. Wheeler did not attend the three Cabinet Room Meetings in December 1965 at which Johnson and his civilian advisers discussed the merits of a bombing halt.[19] In January 1967, the President formed a special committee to examine Vietnam planning. Its members gathered on Thursdays and often evaluated Rolling Thunder. Air Force Major General Robert N. Ginsburgh, Wheeler's representative to the NSC, soon learned of the meetings but "was specifically prohibited from informing the Chairman of the Joint Chiefs of their existence." Wheeler remained unaware of the committee for two months before Johnson finally allowed him to participate in it.[20]

Until the spring of 1967, the President relied extensively on his civilian advisers in Rolling Thunder decision-making. Uncertain of himself in foreign affairs, he trusted the judgments of those possessing strong foreign policy credentials. He retained this faith in his counselors during the target selection process. McNamara, Rusk, and respective National Security Advisers McGeorge Bundy and Rostow formed the core of Johnson's brain trust. Their targeting suggestions did not always conform to the Joint Chiefs' proposals. Major General Gilbert L. Meyers, 7th Air Force Deputy Commander, noted that many of the targets assigned during 1966 were abandoned complexes built by the French.[21] Lieutenant Colonel William H. Greenhalgh, Deputy Director of Targets for 7th Air Force Intelligence, recalled that a message arrived from Washington in late 1966 asking why 7th Air Force had not attacked a missile propellant storage area near Hanoi. The intelligence officers responded that they knew of no such facility, and received word that the building appeared on film taken during a particular photographic reconnaissance mission. The officers scrutinized the film, failed to find the structure, and reported that fact. They were directed to examine specific coordinates on a single frame of the film. They enlarged the frame and found only a small village, typical of others in the area, with a long storage building. No roads, railroads, or waterways led to the hamlet, Greenhalgh recalled, "so we could not figure out how anyone could have thought there was any significant military target in the village." Greenhalgh briefed General John D. Ryan, the Commander of Pacific Air Forces, who was in Saigon on an inspection. Ryan took the briefing calmly and replied only, "Bomb it." Seventh Air Force fighters were sent to attack the structure, "but the pilots could not pick out which village they were to bomb and laid their bombs on the best they could figure out. From the bomb damage assessment photographs we were able to show the pilots which village they *were* to bomb, and the next mission wiped it out. There was no sign of missile propellant or anything else of military value."[22] During the whole of 1966, Johnson approved only twenty-two of the Joint Chiefs' recommended targets.[23]

The strained relationship between the Secretary of Defense and the Chairman of the Joint Chiefs was a further indirect control on Rolling Thunder. To guarantee that Johnson received the Joint Chiefs' views, Wheeler often sent McNamara memorandums with a request to forward the correspondence to the President. The Secretary complied with the Chairman's appeals,[24] but he did not always forcefully present the chiefs' views during meetings with Johnson. McNamara told the President that the military's opposition to a December 1965 bombing pause was "baloney" and stated that he could "take on the chiefs."[25] He rarely notified military leaders before arguing against the suggestions they sent to Johnson.[26] Such behavior led Wheeler to write at the end of his November 1966 proposal for Rolling Thunder 52: "I recommend the following: (a) that President Johnson be briefed in the immediate future on RT 52 so that his early approval on the program can be obtained; and (b) that I be present in order to explain the photography and RT 52 and to respond to any questions the President might have."[27]

By the fall of 1966, Wheeler knew that McNamara had lost faith in Rolling Thunder. Yet the Chairman continued to present his case for increased bombing through the Secretary rather than by going directly to Johnson. In his capacity as top military adviser, Wheeler had the right to express his views firsthand to the President. He chose instead to tender his opinions strictly within the confines of the chain of command.[28] Wheeler and his counterparts were pleased, however, when Johnson made him a regular member of the Tuesday lunch group. "The JCS was much more comfortable in having their case made by their own colleague," recalled Rostow, who helped persuade the President to add the general to the sessions.[29]

As the war progressed, Johnson's civilian advisers became less able to provide him with sound recommendations. The demands of the conflict became a grim routine that tended to stifle original thought. Chester Cooper, a White House staff member, observed:

> The problem was that there was no time or opportunity for quiet conversation or even for quiet contemplation. Exhausted, harassed, besieged men found it necessary to concentrate on tactics rather than strategy, on micro-problems rather than macro-solutions, on today's crises rather than tomorrow's opportunities. New bombing target "packages" rather than diplomatic or political initiatives tended to be the typical menu for the President's "Tuesday Lunch." Someone once said as he watched the Secretary of State dashing off to the White House, "If you told him right now of a sure-fire way to defeat the Viet Cong and to get out of Vietnam, he would groan that he was too busy to worry about that now; he had to discuss next week's bombing targets."[30]

Although Johnson's reliance on his civilian advisers ebbed during Rolling Thunder, he never completely disregarded their recommendations. The intimate atmosphere of the Tuesday lunch heightened the counselors' influence on Johnson. After the December 1965 pause suggested by his advisers failed to produce peace, the President listened less to their proposals.[31] Still, he refused to order the oil storage attacks in mid-1966 until a consensus of *both* civilian and military leaders recommended the strikes. McNamara's influence waned once he lost faith in America's ability to win the war. Johnson then frequently turned to Rostow,[32] who shared the President's belief in early 1967 that more bombing would pay dividends. Gradually, however, other advisers joined McNamara. By March 1968, Johnson found that most of his counselors no longer supported the war. Despite the Joint Chiefs' call for more extensive air attacks, the President needed more than the backing of his military leaders to expand the conflict. Without his civilian advisers' endorsement, he doubted that he could win in Vietnam.

In the final analysis, Johnson was himself an indirect control on

Rolling Thunder. His frequent absences from Washington hampered both civilian and military chiefs who sought to implement new bombing policies. In early October 1965, he entered Bethesda Naval Hospital for gall bladder surgery, remained there two weeks, and then spent eight of the year's remaining ten weeks at his Texas ranch. While in Texas, he ordered the December bombing pause on the night of the 27th without any prior notice.[33] The President spent most of November and December 1966 at the ranch, where in mid-November he approved the Joint Chiefs' proposal for Rolling Thunder 52. William Bundy considered the Texas trips "a *significant* impediment in the way of government" because they prevented Johnson's advisers from meeting with him face to face.[34] The absences disrupted the Tuesday lunch targeting process, which sometimes resulted in the failure to update the approved list of targets.

While significant, Johnson's departures from Washington were not his most telling control on the air campaign. Perhaps more than any other factor, the President's ego limited Rolling Thunder. He saw himself in the image of Franklin Roosevelt[35]—a leader who could provide the nation with guns and butter. Unlike Roosevelt, Johnson could not do both, yet he was unwilling to surrender either goal. His commitment to the Great Society clashed with his determination not to be the first President to lose a war. The conflicting desires stymied his ability to make a hard decision about either concern. "No President, at least not this President, makes a decision until he publicly announces that decision and acts upon it," he reflected.[36] Throughout the three years of Rolling Thunder, Johnson's major declaration of bombing objectives came on 31 March 1968, when he voiced his intention to curtail the campaign to induce negotiations.

Although less obvious than political restraints, military controls limited Rolling Thunder's effectiveness. Foremost among the military limitations was Air Force strategic bombing doctrine. As a result of Air Corps Tactical School instruction, World War II experience, and postwar planning, that doctrine stressed destroying an enemy's capability to fight through attacks on its economic vital centers. Most air chiefs equated economic viability with industrial prowess, assuming that the destruction of production centers and their means of distribution would *guarantee* the loss of war-fighting capacity. The emphasis on industry stemmed from several factors: The major belligerents in World War II had relied extensively on their industrial might to wage war; the Soviet Union, the expected enemy of the next war, was an industrial power; and—perhaps most important—air leaders knew the value of industry to their own nation's war-fighting capability. Moreover, they knew that the manufacture and distribution of goods were essential elements of American society. They assumed that any opponent would place a high premium on preserving what they perceived not only as necessary components for modern war but also as fundamental features of twentieth-century social order.[37]

Largely because of those beliefs, air planners designed a campaign to wreck North Vietnam's industrial capacity. They realized that the North possessed a meager industrial base heavily supplemented by imports. Yet, in their eyes, the overall lack of technological sophistication increased the value of the North's minuscule industry. They contended that its destruction would disrupt the Northern economy to such a degree that Hanoi could no longer support the Viet Cong. "Stepped-up interdiction efforts against DRV target systems would significantly affect industrial and commercial activity in the DRV and place in serious jeopardy the viability of the nonagricultural sector of the North Vietnamese economy," the Joint Chiefs informed McNamara at the end of August 1965.[38] This perception endured until the 1968 Tet Offensive. It caused the chiefs to argue for attacks on oil storage facilities, cement and steel factories, and electric power plants in addition to raids on the transportation system.

The air leaders' conviction that industrial targets were the proper objectives for an air campaign caused them to shun attacks on irrigation dams and the Red River dikes. North Vietnam possessed ninety-one waterway locks and dams, but the Joint Chiefs targeted only eight.[39] The chiefs suggested attacking the eight to disrupt traffic on inland waterways, although in November 1966 Wheeler noted that raids on four locks would also "exert desirable psychological pressures on both leaders and population."[40] The chiefs never formally proposed attacks on the Red River dikes, which Lieutenant Colonel Greenhalgh considered the North's most lucrative targets.[41] The North Vietnamese had built extensive dikes along the river's banks to prevent it from flooding and to channel water to rice crops. Bisected by the river, Hanoi lay 20 feet below its surface during monsoon seasons.[42] Other cities in the delta were similarly vulnerable to flooding. While Air Force Chief of Staff John P. McConnell later commented that attacks against the dikes would have been "a pretty fruitless operation," Ginsburgh maintained that B-52 raids during high-water periods would have destroyed the structures.[43] Wheeler provided an additional reason why air leaders never recommended attacking the dikes. "We tried to be sensible men," he remarked in 1969.[44]

The desire to conduct a "sensible" air campaign complemented the accepted tenets of strategic bombing doctrine and further limited Rolling Thunder. General Ira Eaker's 1943 admonition against "throwing the strategic bomber at the man in the street" lingered in the minds of air commanders.[45] Besides demonstrating the efficacy of air power, they hoped to show that bombing could be effective without being wanton. The Joint Chiefs' ninety-four-target scheme aimed to destroy Northern industrial assets with a brief display of selective bombing; the raids would shock Hanoi's leaders not by killing civilians but by rapidly eliminating the means to fight. "We advocated, militarily, that we should undertake the most sizable effort that we could against remunerative targets, exluding populations for targets. None of us believed in that at all," Wheeler reflected.[46] The Chairman was especially sensitive to the prospect of civilian casualties. While advocating strikes against electric power plants, he pressed for the raids only after attacks against "strictly military" targets had produced marginal results.[47]

The air leaders' concern for civilian casualties resembled that displayed in previous American air campaigns. In both World War II and Korea, bombing began against targets that were, for the most part, removed from populated areas. As fighting continued without signs that the enemy would yield, air leaders reluctantly ordered direct strikes on war-making capability *and* civilian morale. Such was the case in Vietnam. Air chiefs realized by August 1965 that Johnson was not going to implement the ninety-four-target plan. They then advocated attacks on the transportation system and oil storage facilities, the two industrial components that they perceived as most important to the Northern war effort. Not until after the oil attacks did air leaders clamor for raids against electric power plants. Their entreaties indicated a changing perception of how Rolling Thunder could best accomplish its military objectives. From late 1966 on, they intended to make the North's civilian populace wince from the destruction of military targets. Air leaders adopted this aim hesitantly, however. Wheeler's assessment of the attacks on electric power betrayed the uncertainty that many felt about attacking morale.[48] The fury of the Tet Offensive caused air chiefs to overcome their misgivings about striking near populated areas. Still, they refused to advocate direct attacks on North Vietnamese civilians.

To some extent, the shift in bombing emphasis from transportation to oil to electric power resulted from the Joint Chiefs' efforts to propose targets acceptable to Johnson. "The fact that we were able to sell the POL (Petroleum, Oil, and Lubricants) system made us feel that perhaps the next thing would be to sell the thermal power system," Colonel Henry H. Edelen, a member of Wheeler's staff who reviewed target suggestions, recalled.[49] Yet the changing priorities were much more than alternatives randomly selected after attacks against a particular target system proved inconclusive. The chiefs' proposals revealed their twin desires to destroy the North's industrial base and to cause minimal loss of life to its civilian population. Those goals prevented them from suggesting raids on targets like dams that would have had a more telling effect on the North's capability to fight.

Besides doctrinal and moral considerations, the military's organizational arrangements for Rolling Thunder limited the air campaign. Wheeler proposed targets to McNamara after a "Rolling Thunder Team" of seven officers reviewed recommendations arriving from Admiral Sharp's Pacific Command (PACOM) headquarters. Before May 1965, this team comprised two individuals, and neither was a pilot or an Air Force officer.[50] Despite serving as Rolling Thunder's operational commander, Admiral Sharp exercised little overall control from his Honolulu office. He allowed his chief subordinates, the Commander of Pacific Fleet (PACFLT) and the Commander of Pacific Air Forces (PACAF), to direct the air units of their respective services.

The absence of a single air commander produced chaos. The 2d Air Division in Saigon, the Air Force headquarters with direct control over fighter wings participating in the campaign, received guidance not only from PACOM and PACAF, but also from 13th Air Force in the Philippines. Meanwhile, the Navy's Carrier Task Force (CTF) 77 in the Tonkin Gulf received supervision from PACOM and PACFLT. To simplify the multilayer Air Force command arrangement, PACAF changed the 2d Air Division to the 7th Air Force in early 1966. The confusion then increased, however. Instead of providing the 7th Air Force with complete control over the 2d Air Division assets, PACAF gave the 7th Air Force "operational" direction over the fighter wings, while the 13th Air Force retained "administrative" control.[51] The ultimate result of this bizarre arrangement was the creation of the 7/13th Air Force in Thailand, which then assumed *administrative* control of the fighters! "Command arrangements were a mess," a 7th Air Force staff officer recalled. "There was only one person that you could say was in command, and that was the President."

The lack of a single air commander further prevented military chiefs from integrating Rolling Thunder with other air efforts in Southeast Asia. Besides bombing North Vietnam, American fighter squadrons raided the Ho Chi Minh Trail in southern Laos in Operation Steel Tiger. In Operation Barrel Roll, they provided close air support for Laotian government forces battling the Pathet Lao and North Vietnamese in northern Laos. Pilots flew by far the largest number of sorties in support of friendly ground troops in South Vietnam. American aircraft dropped 2.2 million tons of bombs on the South between 1965 and 1968, as against 643,000 tons dropped on the North.[52]

A dearth of interservice cooperation also constrained Rolling Thunder. Navy air units vied with Air Force squadrons for higher sortie totals against the North. "Putting it bluntly, it was a competition," 2d Air Division Commander Lieutenant General Joseph H. Moore recounted. Moore objected to efforts to divide North Vietnam into specific zones for separate Air Force and Navy attacks. "I resisted this quite bitterly for a long time," he explained "because it ended up with us [the Air Force] going to be up around the highly defended areas, and I thought we ought to share that privilege with the Navy."[53] In November 1965, an Air Force–Navy Coordinating Committee established six "route packages," or target zones, over the North. The 2d Air Division obtained a weekly responsibility for conducting attacks in three packages, then alternated zones with CTF 77. Committee members soon agreed to make the exchange monthly to reduce confusion.[54]

On 1 April 1966, Sharp overruled Moore's protests and made the route package assignments permanent. He also divided the zone in the Northeast quadrant to create a seventh route package. The Air Force received responsibility for attacks in Route Packages 5 and 6A, the two northernmost zones containing Hanoi and the Northwest Railroad. The Navy had responsibility for Route Packages 2, 3, 4, and 6B, which together extended from the 18th parallel to China and included Haiphong and part of the Northeast Railroad. General William C. Westmoreland, the Commander of U.S. Military Assistance Command, Vietnam (COMUSMACV), received authority to schedule strikes in Route Package 1, located immediately north of the DMZ.

Although policy allowed the Air Force to attack targets in the Navy's zones and vice versa, such raids occurred infrequently. Seventh Air Force could attack Navy targets only with that service's prior permission, and the Air Force's permission was likewise required for the carrier group to make strikes in Air Force zones.[55] Johnson's numerical limitations on sorties fueled the rivalry between the services to secure missions, resulting in raids during poor weather and missions with decreased bomb loads during the 1966 munitions shortage.[56] "There is nothing more demoralizing," a frustrated Air Force pilot wrote in 1966, "than the sight of an F-4 taxiing out with nothing but a pair of bombs nestled among its ejector racks. However, it looks much better for the commander and the service concerned to show 200 sorties on paper, even when 40 or 50 would do the same job."[57]

In addition to interservice competition, the military's intelligence efforts hampered Rolling Thunder's effectiveness. The Defense Intelligence Agency (DIA), comprising intelligence specialists from the four services, was the primary source of the Joint Chiefs' information for Rolling Thunder. The agency paid little attention to what Hanoi said on the radio and dismissed Northern broadcasts as propaganda.[58] Instead of trying to determine Hanoi's strategy, the DIA focused on quantifying the destruction caused by Rolling Thunder. This emphasis led air commanders to judge the campaign's results in numerical terms. Wheeler told the President that in 1966 Rolling Thunder had "destroyed over 4,600 trucks and damaged over 4,600 trucks; destroyed over 4,700 logistic water craft and damaged an additional 8,700 water craft; destroyed over 800 items of railroad rolling stock and damaged nearly 1,700; and destroyed 16 locomotives and damaged an additional 15."[59] The DIA evaluated the raids on power plants by estimating the percentage of the North's generating capacity destroyed; it did not further assess whether remaining facilities would adequately supply the enemy's needs. The amounts of destruction given were also suspect. "When a pilot reported a burned-out truck you didn't know whether it was empty or full or, in fact, whether it was a truck that had already been counted by somebody else," Colonel Edelen explained.[60] The agency could not accurately calculate how many tons of supplies the North Vietnamese shipped, how many tons the Americans destroyed, or how many tons arrived in the South.

Seventh Air Force intelligence operations highlighted the difficulties of acquiring valid bombing results. Between 1965 and 1966, the intelligence staff was never fully manned. Some officers at the Saigon headquarters began their day preparing for the commander's 0600 morning intelligence briefing and worked until 2100. To determine the results of raids, Brigadier General Rockly Trantafellu, the Chief of 7th Air Force Intelligence, demanded that reconnaissance units obtain as many poststrike target photographs as possible. This requirement yielded a massive influx of photographs into the headquarters. "So many pictures came in that the photo interpreters were swamped," Lieutenant Colonel Greenhalgh remembered. "We had far too many to process them all."[61] Copies of the processed photographs went to intelligence officers assigned to fighter units, yet pilots did not always see them. Greenhalgh recalled visiting strike squadrons and finding reconnaissance photographs stacked in a corner.[62] The problem was not a dereliction of duty, but that some of the officers sent to field units were too inexperienced to know the material's value. Many of the most capable intelligence officers had security restrictions preventing their assignment away from Saigon. This limitation caused 7th Air Force Headquarters to dispatch some individuals with inadequate intelligence backgrounds to fighter squadrons.[63]

To pilots, operational controls were the most ominous limitation on the air campaign. While political and military constraints reduced Rolling Thunder's effectiveness by limiting its scope, operational controls hindered the accomplishment of approved missions. Chief among those obstructions were enemy defenses. MiG fighters downed their first American aircraft in April 1965. Three months later, the first American jet fell to a surface-to-air missile (SAM). By August 1967, the North possessed roughly two hundred SAM sites, seven thousand anti-aircraft guns, a sophisticated ground-controlled intercept (GCI) radar system, and eighty MiG fighters, ranging in types from the MiG-15 to the formidable MiG-21.[64] The array caused Colonel Jack Broughton, Deputy Commander of the 355th Tactical Fighter Wing, to describe North Vietnam as "the center of hell with Hanoi as its hub."[65] Hanoi gained the reputation as the world's most heavily defended city, contributing to the decision not to commit B-52s against its installations. The toll of aircraft lost over the North rose from 171 in 1965 to 280 in 1966, then to 326 in 1967, although the loss *rate* declined during the campaign.[66]

Passive defenses also hindered Rolling Thunder. North Vietnamese General Van Tien Dung proclaimed that the "central task of all the party and people" was to assure the southward movement of men and supplies. To accomplish that goal, Hanoi mobilized its manpower to thwart interdiction. An estimated total of 500,000 laborers repaired rail lines, roads, and bridges. Pilots frequently wrecked the Kep Rail Yard on the Northeast Railroad, only to find the facility operational on the day following a strike. The North Vietnamese maintained heaps of steel rails and railroad ties at regular intervals along important routes to speed repair. Construction crews usually began working immediately after a strike and posted one or two individuals to watch unexploded bombs for signs that they might detonate. If a line break stalled a train, bicycle brigades unloaded its cargo and traveled beyond the break to where a second train arrived. They then reloaded the goods while repair crews continued to mend the track.[67]

The Communists exerted similar efforts to maintain roads and bridges. Most highways were tar-surfaced over clay, allowing repair by shovel brigades. The North Vietnamese built miles of by-pass roads around choke points to make the highway system redundant. The journalist David Schoenbrun reported that a 65-mile trip from Hanoi to Nam Dinh took five hours in August 1967 because the highway

> . . . virtually does not exist as a road. A few miles out of
> Hanoi it becomes a crater-filled obstacle course. One does not
> drive down it, one bounces along over ruts and rocks. Within
> ten miles it runs out completely, and the Route detours across a
> river and on to a dike.[68]

The North Vietnamese replaced destroyed bridges with fords, ferries, and pontoons. They constructed some bridges just below the water's surface, which prevented aerial observation of the structures.[69]

The Communists also restricted travel times and dispersed oil reserves. Men and supplies moved only during darkness or poor weather. Beginning in mid-1965, the North Vietnamese placed oil storage tanks holding between 2,200 and 3,300 gallons near major highways. They supplemented those tanks with 55-gallon drums, which they deposited along roads and in cities, towns, and rice paddies. They placed large quantities near dikes as well, figuring that American raids against the structures were unlikely.[70]

Geography and weather provided additional limitations on Rolling Thunder. North Vietnam's lush terrain was ideal for camouflage, and the enemy frequently resorted to deception. Hanoi also exploited the proximity of Laos and Cambodia. Snaking through the eastern areas of both countries, the Ho Chi Minh Trail was a primary route to the South.[71] Weather was one of the air campaign's most significant operational controls. From September to April, the dense clouds of the winter monsoons made continuous bombing impossible. The monsoons prevented Rolling Thunder from starting in late February 1965 and canceled numerous missions in March. Poor weather also delayed the 1966 oil raids and the 1967 strikes against the Thai Nguyen steel complex and electric power plants. Most of the raids scheduled during the monsoon season against fixed targets became interdiction strikes because clouds obscured the primary objective. In 1966, only 1 percent of the year's 81,000 sorties flew against JCS-proposed fixed targets,[72] and weather was a key reason for the low total. Moreover, the prospect of monsoons during spring 1968 contributed to Johnson's 31 March decision to curtail the campaign.[73]

Three aircraft types performed most Rolling Thunder air strikes, and none were well suited to the forbidding environment of North Vietnam. The Air Force relied on the Republic F-105 Thunderchief and the McDonnell-Douglas F-4 Phantom, while the Navy employed the F-4 and the McDonnell-Douglas A-4 Skyhawk. Designed during the 1950s as a nuclear-attack fighter, the F-105 flew more than 75 percent of all Rolling Thunder strike sorties.[74] The massive single-seat fighter weighed more than 50,000 pounds fully loaded and had difficulty turning in dogfights. Despite a reputation for sustaining damage, the F-105 was especially vulnerable to anti-aircraft artillery. Maintenance problems also plagued the Thunderchief, which gained the nickname "Thud" from its pilots. The Navy developed the F-4 as a high-altitude interceptor. The Air Force acquired the dual-seat fighter in 1962 and modified it for ground attack. Capable of carrying 8 tons of bombs, the Phantom suffered from a vulnerability to ground fire, poor rear cockpit visibility, and engines that emitted a heavy black smoke, revealing its location. In addition, the Air Force version of the F-4 lacked an internal cannon for defense.[75] The Skyhawk, a diminutive single-seat fighter that carried a 4-ton bomb load, flew more bombing missions than any other naval aircraft in Vietnam.[76] The F-105, the F-4, and the A-4 could not bomb in poor weather. With the B-52's virtual exclusion from Rolling Thunder, only the A-6 Intruder flown by the Navy and Marines possessed an all-weather capability, and only two A-6 squadrons (thirty-two aircraft) normally operated with CTF 77.

The combination of political, military, and operational controls produced a further operational limitation on Rolling Thunder: low pilot morale. Lieutenant Eliot Tozer III, an A-4 pilot, gave vent in his diary to the bitterness many of his comrades felt over the campaign:

> The frustration comes on all levels. We fly a limited aircraft, drop limited ordnance, on rare targets in a severely limited amount of time. Worst of all, we do all this in a limited and highly unpopular war. . . . All theories aside, what I've got is personal pride pushing against a tangled web of frustration.[77]

While the multiple controls did not diminish courage or competence, they did produce disillusionment. The tremendous psychological strain on those who flew the air campaign cannot be quantified, but it must be included in the final assessment of Rolling Thunder's limitations.[78]

Bombing Results

The 643,000 tons of bombs that fell during Rolling Thunder destroyed 65 percent of the North's oil storage capacity, 59 percent of its power plants, 55 percent of its major bridges, 9,821 vehicles and 1,966 railroad cars.[79] Yet the numerical results of Rolling Thunder gave little indication of the campaign's true impact, and the price of inflicting any destruction was high. Besides the loss of men and aircraft, the campaign cost the United States $6.60 to render $1.00 worth of damage in 1965, and $9.60 a year later.[80]

Almost 90 percent of Rolling Thunder's weight struck transportation-related targets.[81] Although bombing hindered the movement of men and supplies, it did not significantly affect infiltration. Two factors limited interdiction's effectiveness: the nature of the war in the South, and the North's excess resupply capability. The war in South Vietnam was a guerrilla conflict. Hanoi had only 55,000 North Vietnamese Army troops in the South by August 1967; the remaining 245,000 Communist soldiers were Viet Cong.[82] None of these forces engaged in frequent combat, and the Viet Cong intermingled with the Southern populace. As a result, Communist supply needs were minimal. Enemy battalions fought an average of one day in thirty and had a total daily supply requirement of roughly 380 tons. Of this amount, the Communists needed only 34 tons a day from sources outside the South.[83] Seven 2½-ton trucks could transport the requirement,[84] which was *less than 1 percent* of the daily tonnage imported into North Vietnam. Sea, road, and rail imports averaged 5,700 tons a day, yet Hanoi possessed the *capacity* to import 17,200 tons. Defense Department analysts estimated in February 1967 that an unrestrained air offensive against resupply facilities, accompanied by the mining of Northern harbors, would only reduce the import capacity to 7,200 tons.[85] The amount of goods that the Communists shipped south "is primarily a function of their own choosing," the Joint Chiefs remarked in August 1965.[86] Their appraisal remained valid throughout Rolling Thunder.

Instead of limiting North Vietnamese imports, the air campaign fostered their growth. Hanoi's leaders pointed to the bombing to extract greater support from the Chinese and Soviets. "In the fight against the war of destruction," General Van Tien Dung announced, "we must rely mainly on our own strength, and, at the same time, strive for international assistance, especially the assistance of all countries in the socialist camp."[87] With the help of Chinese laborers, the North Vietnamese modified the narrow-gauge rails of the Northeast and Northwest railroads so that Chinese standard-gauge cars could move onto North Vietnamese tracks. An average of 1,000 tons of supplies arrived daily by the Northeast railroad.[88] The combined value of Chinese and Soviet imports totaled between $250 and $400 million in 1965 alone, producing a 6 percent *increase* in the North's Gross National Product. By January 1968, Hanoi had received almost $600 million in economic aid and $1 billion in military assistance.[89] The Soviets had virtually suspended aid during the three years prior to Rolling Thunder, but with the initiation of the air campaign Soviet support rapidly eclipsed the Chinese. The Russians did not wish to appear unwilling to help a sister Communist state, nor did they want the war to heighten Chinese influence in Southeast Asia.[90]

Like interdiction, the attacks on oil storage areas and electric power plants had a marginal effect on Hanoi's war effort. Although North Vietnamese Defense Minister General Vo Nguyen Giap called the POL strikes the "most serious" intensification of the air war,[91] the raids did not reduce infiltration capacity. Northern trains ran on coal or wood rather than oil. Hanoi required 32,000 tons of oil per year to operate its economy, and it possessed more than 60,000 tons in dispersed sites by the end of 1966. To fuel the trucks on the Ho Chi Minh Trail, the North Vietnamese needed less than 1,600 tons of oil a year.[92] Meager requirements resulted in a similar excess of generating capacity. The 189,000 kilowatts produced by power plants were not essential to the North's economy. More than two thousand portable generators compensated for the power stations destroyed in the spring of 1967.[93] Two of the facilities attacked were 1,000-kilowatt plants near the Chinese border. The North's largest power station had a capacity of 32,500 kilowatts, which equaled the capacity of an American plant supporting 25,000 people in a lightly industrial town.[94] "To a Western, so-called developed society, cutting our electricity means something," Oliver Todd commented after visiting Hanoi. "It doesn't mean very much in Vietnam. The Vietnamese for years and years have been used to living by candlelight or oil lamps."[95]

Contrary to Admiral Sharp's contention that the air campaign "was very costly to the enemy in terms of material, manpower, management, and distribution,"[96] most North Vietnamese civilians did not suffer from the bombing. Rolling Thunder's political and military controls helped keep the civilian death toll low for a campaign of its magnitude. The CIA estimated that the 200,000 tons of bombs dropped by 1967 had caused 29,600 civilian casualties.[97] By comparison, the United States dropped 147,000 tons of ordnance on Japan during the last six months of World War II and *killed* 330,000 noncombatants.[98] Harrison Salisbury, who visited Hanoi during December 1966, remarked that the casualty figures he received for the 13 December raid on a vehicle depot "were not impressive." North Vietnamese authorities told him that the attack had killed nine persons and injured twenty-one, yet Hanoi Radio proclaimed that American pilots had blatantly raided civilian structures and caused substantial casualties.[99] For the three and a half years of Rolling Thunder, bombing killed an estimated total of 52,000 civilians out of a population of 18 million.[100]

Evacuations contributed to keeping the number of civilian casualties down, but neither Hanoi nor Haiphong was devoid of people. Salisbury described the capital as a "vibrant, pulsating city" and observed that its inhabitants thronged to beer parlors and bars each afternoon. North Vietnamese leaders issued their first order to evacuate Hanoi on 28 February 1965. Only 50,000 persons had left by the end of the year, and many drifted back because the city appeared safer than the countryside. During 1965, the Northern government encouraged people in the frequently bombed southern panhandle to settle in areas north of Hanoi. While traveling, they could stay in the capital for two weeks to buy necessities and settle their affairs. Rolling Thunder's intensification in mid-1966 produced a corresponding increase in evacuation. By late 1967, the city's population had shrunk from 600,000 to less than 400,000. Thirty thousand children remained, despite orders for their mandatory removal, and Todd thought that Hanoi was "still a fairly lively place." Haiphong's population fell from 400,000 to 250,000 by mid-1967.[101]

For the typical North Vietnamese, Rolling Thunder was a nuisance rather than a danger. Few consumer goods other than food arrived in the North. While the average daily intake of calories fell from 1,910 in 1963 to 1,880 in 1967, the total was more than sufficient to sustain the population. The North Vietnamese produced a yearly average of 4.4 million tons of rice, but the combination of too much spring rain and a fall drought in 1966 reduced that year's total to 4 million tons. China provided more than 600,000 tons in 1967 to offset the deficiency. Hanoi's use of 500,000 individuals to repair lines of communication had no effect on rice production. The North Vietnamese farmed their rice fields inefficiently, employing more manpower than necessary. Farmers also worked erratic schedules. During the 1965–66 spring rice season in Nam Ha province, they spent an average of 29.1 days in the rice fields during January and stayed in the fields only 1.3 days in April. Hanoi further relied on a rapid population growth and evacuees to supplement air defense and repair activities. "Fight and produce at the same time!" was the slogan guiding the homefront's struggle against Rolling Thunder. The vast amount of available manpower guaranteed that the Communists could simultaneously accomplish both tasks with ease.[102]

Although Rolling Thunder was a surprise to the North Vietnamese, they quickly displayed a stoic determination to resist the bombing. Premier Pham Van Dong commented that the first raids created a "crisis" because of the disorganized movement of men and supplies to the South and the lack of sophisticated air defense weaponry.[103] By early April 1965, however, Northern leaders felt confident that they could withstand the aerial onslaught. Dong announced a "Four-Point Program" for peace in Vietnam and proclaimed that its terms were the only basis for a settlement. The program's key features were the withdrawal of American forces from Vietnam and the acceptance of a Communist government in the South. Hanoi soon added a fifth prerequisite: an unconditional bombing halt. North Vietnamese leaders knew that Johnson had no intention of unleashing unrestricted air power against their country. On 24 February 1965, the American Ambassador to Poland gave China's Ambassador Wang Kuo-chuan a letter stating that the United States had no desire to destroy North Vietnam. Blair Seaborn, a Canadian emissary, repeated this message in a March visit to Hanoi, and American officials echoed the pronouncement.[104] North Vietnamese leaders understood many of the reasons for the restraint. "The U.S. imperialists must restrict the U.S. forces participating in a local war because otherwise their global strategy would be hampered and their influence throughout the world would diminish," General Giap remarked in 1967. "They must restrict their participation in order to avoid upsetting the political, economic, and social life of the United States."[105]

Realizing that Rolling Thunder would not produce unacceptable damage, Northern leaders used the air offensive to create popular support for the war. "In Churchillian style, the [Hanoi] Politburo portrayed the North as a set-upon David fighting a bullyboy Goliath, the United States, and thereby was able to rally the North Vietnamese into grimly determined war efforts," Air Force Major General Edward Lansdale observed.[106] Hanoi responded to the small number of air attacks in 1965 by dispersing its oil and ordering the evacuation of urban centers. Although those measures stirred some resentment in the populace, they tended to confirm the Strategic Bombing Survey's assertion that a police state could maintain effective control over national will in the wake of bombing. Rolling Thunder's gradually increasing severity acclimated the North Vietnamese to the campaign, further solidifying Hanoi's control over its people. "In terms of its morale effects," the RAND analyst Oleg Hoeffding argued in 1966, "the U.S. campaign may have presented the [North Vietnamese] regime with a near-ideal mix of intended restraint and accidental gore."[107]

For Northern leaders, a strong popular resolve was crucial to achieving the goal of a unified Vietnam. They never acknowledged the South Vietnamese government as legal, and they viewed the Viet Cong insurgency as a just movement to overthrow a tyrannical regime. Consequently, Northern leaders regarded Rolling Thunder and other efforts supporting the Saigon government as unlawful actions. To Hanoi, Johnson's proposals to stop the bombing were tantamount to demands for unconditional surrender. In exchange for a bombing halt, he called for an end to both infiltration and Communist attacks in the South. Meanwhile, American and South Vietnamese ground forces would continue fighting. Northern leaders could never respond to an American bombing halt by reducing insurgent support, for to do so would give Rolling Thunder, and hence the Saigon government, a measure of legitimacy. By late 1967, the President had relaxed his preconditions for ending the campaign. Yet he still demanded that the Communists "not take advantage" of a bombing halt. Northern leaders shunned the offer. Their decision in early April 1968 to begin negotiations signified not acquiescence but necessity.

Although the 1968 Tet Offensive was a psychological defeat for the United States, it was a military disaster for the North Vietnamese. Almost 40,000 Viet Cong, the core of the insurgent leadership, died in the assault.[108] The brutality exhibited by many Communist units—the Viet Cong executed 2,800 South Vietnamese in Hué and buried them in mass graves[109]—caused many who had backed the Communists to transfer their allegiance to Saigon. In short, the Tet Offensive destroyed the Viet Cong's combat effectiveness.[110] To continue the war, Hanoi had to rely on its regular army, and Northern troops could not sustain the massive assault in the South. North Vietnam's leaders thus decided to begin negotiations. Observing the Tet Offensive's impact on the American public, they believed that protracted peace talks, accompanied by small-unit harassing attacks in the South, might force the United States to abandon its ally.[111] Further, Northern leaders felt confident that the American reaction to Tet would trigger a withdrawal of some United States ground troops, increasing the likelihood of Communist victory in a future offensive. When they launched their final assault against the South, Hanoi's officials did not want Americans to stand in the way.

Rolling Thunder made a meager contribution toward achieving Johnson's positive political goal of an independent, stable, non-Communist South Vietnam. Despite the bombing, the North Vietnamese did not abandon the Southern insurgency. Civilian leaders and air commanders alike miscalculated the effect that the campaign would have on the North. Both groups thought that the North's industrial apparatus was vulnerable to air attack and that its vulnerability offered a means to end the war. Civilian leaders— and, initially, some air chiefs[112]—believed that the *threat* of industrial devastation would compel Hanoi to end the conflict. By July 1965, air commanders unanimously maintained that the *destruction* of essential industries was necessary before the North would stop fighting. The only industrial component vital to the North's war-making capacity was its transportation system, and it did not have to operate at peak efficiency to be effective. A glut of imports and the Communists' limited needs rendered the remainder of the North's industrial establishment superfluous. Air commanders grossly miscalculated the value of oil to the Northern war effort. They also thought that the destruction of the steel and electric power industries would disrupt the North's economic and social welfare. Perceptions in Hanoi differed from those in Washington and Honolulu. Northern leaders had no qualms about sacrificing their "high-value" industries. "Depending on the concrete situation, sometimes we regard destroying the enemy as the main task and sometimes we regard defending targets from the enemy as the main task," Giap asserted. "Yet normally the principle of positively destroying the enemy is the most basic and decisive one in our efforts."[113]

Besides overestimating the importance of Northern industry, American leaders underestimated their enemy's determination. "I have a feeling that the other side is not that tough," Rusk told Johnson in December 1965.[114] The Joint Chiefs shared that notion. In January 1966, they contended that McNamara exaggerated the "will of the Hanoi leaders to continue a struggle which they realize they cannot win in the face of progressively greater destruction of their country."[115] Ambassador Maxwell Taylor recalled that American civilian and military chiefs knew little about the North's leaders and virtually nothing about their intentions.[116] Nevertheless, Johnson was certain that the North Vietnamese had their price, and he believed that air power would help him find it. Neither he nor his political advisers and air commanders imagined that their Third World enemy could withstand even a limited bombing campaign. When events proved them wrong, it came as a great shock to all of them.

To be effective, bombing had to eliminate the prospect of Communist victory in the South. It could not do so. Political and military controls prevented attacks against the only two targets that would have affected Northern war-making capacity: people and food. Yet raids against population centers and the Red River dikes would have had a minimal impact on the war in the South, where Communist forces held the initiative as to the locale, duration, and frequency of combat. As long as they chose to fight sparingly, they had little to fear from Rolling Thunder. "We have no basis for assuming that the Viet Cong will fight a war on our terms when they can continue to fight the kind of war they fought so well against both the French and the GVN [Government of (South) Vietnam]," Under Secretary of State George Ball warned in June 1965.[117] The Joint Chiefs ignored the caution. They searched in vain for a way to bring the Communists to battle, believing that increased combat would produce increased supply requirements, which in turn would make interdiction effective. General Dung labeled the air campaign "the product of defeat on the Southern battlefield" and insisted that it would never affect the Communists' initiative in the South.[118] Giap concurred, exclaiming that the "great power of the people's war" would overcome the "so-called superiority of the U.S. Air Force."[119] Propaganda aside, the two generals' assertions contained a large measure of truth.

The Tet Offensive provided the most graphic illustration of Rolling Thunder's failure to affect the Southern war. Hanoi completed planning for the attack in mid-1967.[120] By September, American intelligence units were receiving inklings of the assault.[121] The advanced notice was of little value to the air chiefs, however, for the Communists had already stockpiled much of the necessary material through normal infiltration. To launch the offensive, Communist field commanders needed only to know when and where attacks should occur. Rolling Thunder had no effect on the enemy's capability, or willingness, to start the assault.

The air campaign *did* boost South Vietnamese morale. In March 1965, it probably contributed as much to the stability of the Southern regime as any measure could have. Rolling Thunder took Northern leaders by surprise and demonstrated American resolve. Yet it could not *sustain* Southern morale at a high level. As the bombing continued, the South Vietnamese began accepting it as the status quo. "In a sense, South Vietnam is now 'addicted' to the program," McNamara remarked on 30 July 1965. "A permanent abandonment of the program would have a distinct depressing effect on morale in South Vietnam."[122] Continued raids increased the United States' commitment to Saigon. Finally, in March 1968 Johnson determined that the cost of the undertaking had become too great.

While failing to achieve the President's positive goal, Rolling Thunder also hindered the attainment of many negative objectives. The campaign did not cause the Soviets or the Chinese to intervene actively in the war, but it stimulated Soviet assistance to the North. The Soviet Union and China competed for Hanoi's favor, which enabled the North Vietnamese to act independently of the guidance of either. Although Johnson and his advisers were aware of the animosity between the Communist superpowers, they could not exploit it.[123] The President hesitated to mine Northern ports, not only because he doubted mining's effectiveness in reducing imports but also because he felt that it would provoke the Soviets. All Soviet imports arrived by sea, and the Chinese were unlikely to permit the transfer of Russian goods across Chinese territory.[124] Moreover, mining could humiliate the Soviets by reminding them of the 1962 naval quarantine around Cuba. Johnson thus believed that a disruption of Soviet shipping would compel the Russians to fight, a conviction shared by Llewellyn Thompson, his Ambassador to Moscow.[125] By influencing the Soviets to support Hanoi, Rolling Thunder intensified the President's fear that Vietnam might trigger a nuclear holocaust.

Besides increasing Johnson's apprehension over a third world war, Rolling Thunder helped to create an unfavorable impression of America abroad and to wreck the President's designs for a Great Society at home. Instead of viewing the air campaign as a U.S. effort to support an ally, many nations saw it as an exercise of American aggression. France, Britain, and India officially denounced the 1966 raids on oil storage areas in Hanoi and Haiphong. The spring 1967 raids on power plants drew similar responses. In the United States, student protesters castigated Rolling Thunder, and in October 1967 thirty Congressmen sent Johnson an open letter urging him to stop the bombing. Yet to most Americans the air offensive was a source of confused anger. Baffled by the bombing restrictions, they called for heavier raids on the North. The 1966 oil attacks boosted the President's sagging popularity.[126] In July 1967, a Harris poll revealed that 72 percent of the public favored continued bombing and that 40 percent wanted *increased* military pressure on Hanoi.[127] Rolling Thunder satisfied neither "hawks" nor "doves," but its salience caused both groups to divert their attention from Johnson's domestic programs to Vietnam. The war turned the President's plans for a Great Society to ashes, and bombing helped obliterate his dream.

Those who directed Rolling Thunder had difficulty evaluating its effectiveness, and bias tainted most appraisals. To Johnson and his political advisers, the campaign was a qualified success; to air commanders, it was a qualified failure. "I was always convinced that bombing was less important to a successful outcome in Vietnam than what was done militarily on the gound in the South," the President recounted.[128] He thought that Rolling Thunder significantly reduced the amount of men and matériel available to the Communists in South Vietnam and that bombing demonstrated American resolve. He was uncertain, however, that Rolling Thunder affected the North's willingness to fight. Despite later stating that he never expected air power to assure victory, he thought that the attacks on oil and electric power might persuade the Communists to end the war.[129] Rolling Thunder's failure to induce negotiations left the President ambivalent over the campaign's results. He felt that it had benefited the quest for an independent, non-Communist South Vietnam but noted that the objective still remained out of reach.

Rusk and Taylor believed that Rolling Thunder slowed Hanoi's drive to subdue the South. "We never thought we could suffocate North Vietnamese supplies by bombing," the Secretary of State remembered. "We could cause *some* effect; perhaps with Rolling Thunder it took two months instead of two weeks for a given amount of supplies to arrive in the South." He also asserted, however, that the campaign was not worth the cost in men and planes, and that it had a meager effect on Northern morale. "Possibly we should have tried saturation bombing," he conjectured.[130] Taylor contended that Rolling Thunder raised Southern morale and made infiltration more difficult. Like Rusk, the former Ambassador speculated that a massive air attack might have paid dividends. "We could have flattened everything in and around Hanoi," he later maintained. "That doesn't mean it would stop the war, but it would certainly have made it extremely difficult to continue it effectively." He insisted that heavy bombing would have disrupted the North's centralized government and produced chaos. Still, although he deplored the bombing restrictions, he considered Johnson's tight control of the campaign appropriate. "The bombing of North Vietnam was the use of a military tool for political purposes. . . . The fact that the control came from [Washington] was entirely justified."[131]

National Security Adviser Walt W. Rostow agreed that Rolling Thunder supported American goals in Vietnam. He argued that bombing imposed a tax on Hanoi's logistical flow and forced a large amount of Northern manpower to participate in air defense activities. "Why do you think they kept saying 'Stop the bombing' and brought forth every device of diplomacy they could think of?" he asked. "Of course [bombing] was painful. But it was not painful enough *by itself.*" Rostow declared that the United States could have won a military victory only by cutting the Ho Chi Minh Trail with American ground troops. He claimed that the Communists' supply needs far exceeded intelligence estimates and that severing the Laotian route would have dealt the enemy a fatal blow.[132]

Despite his opposition to Rolling Thunder, McNamara thought it was successful when "weighed against its stated objectives." The Secretary maintained that bombing had raised Southern morale, forced the North Vietnamese to pay a price for continuing aggression, and made infiltration more difficult. "There can be no question that the bombing campaign has and is hurting North Vietnam's war-making capability," he said in August 1967.[133] Yet McNamara believed that bombing could accomplish nothing more. He stated that the Communists' minimal logistical requirements prevented interdiction from affecting the scale of their combat operations. He further insisted that no campaign, except one targeting the Northern population, would independently force Hanoi to end the war. Unlike most of his air commanders, McNamara recognized a fundamental flaw nullifying Rolling Thunder's utility as a persuasive instrument. "The agrarian nature of the economy precludes an economic collapse as a result of the bombing," he declared.[134] As long as Hanoi chose to wage guerrilla warfare, his contention that air power would have a meager effect on the conflict remained valid.

In contrast to Johnson and most of his political advisers, air commanders considered Rolling Thunder a failure. They blamed its lack of success on the President's political controls. "We should lift these restrictions and we would then get results," General McConnell told Johnson in 1966.[135] Air leaders repeated his pronouncement after the campaign ended. Major General Ginsburgh argued that the Joint Chiefs' ninety-four-target scheme could have produced victory at any time during 1965 and 1966.[136] Admiral Sharp remarked that such an effort after the Tet Offensive would have won the war.[137] Yet the "victory" pursued by air commanders differed from that envisioned by the President. By destroying the vital elements of Northern industry, air leaders hoped to gain the unconditional triumph promised by Air Force strategic bombing doctrine. Bombing would, they maintained, wreck the Northern economy and compel Hanoi to end the war. Johnson's aims in Vietnam did not include a North prostrated by air power. For him, "victory" was an independent, non-Communist South and a North that accepted that condition as the status quo. While attempting to stop Hanoi's aggression, he sought other goals that limited his use of force. Those negative objectives led to Rolling Thunder's political controls. Most air commanders never fully understood the President's negative aims. Accordingly, they could not fathom the controls that contradicted the main tenets of strategic bombing doctrine. In their eyes, the restrictions did little to obscure bombing's grim realities. Sharp commented: "The application of military, war-making power is an ugly thing—stark, harsh, and demanding—and it cannot be made nicer by pussy-footing around with it."[138]

Johnson's controls produced a profound sense of despair among air leaders. At the end of a 1967 briefing on Rolling Thunder, General McConnell held his head in his hands and lamented, "I can't tell you how I feel . . . I'm so sick of it . . . I have never been so goddamned frustrated by it all."[139] Two years later, after announcing his retirement, McConnell received a letter from 7th Air Force Commander General William W. Momyer, whose comments epitomized the air chiefs' disillusionment:

> It has been a privilege to serve as a member of your team. My regret is we didn't win the war. We had the force, skill, and intelligence, but our civilian betters wouldn't turn us loose. Surely our Air Force has lived up to all expectations within the restraints that have been put on it. If there is one lesson to come out of this war, it must be a reaffirmation of the axiom— don't get in a fight unless you are prepared to do whatever is necessary to win. This axiom is as old as military forces, and I don't see that modern weapons have changed it. I suppose a military man will always be in the dilemma of supporting policy even though he knows it surely restricts the capacity of military forces to produce the desired effect. One has no alternative but to support the policy and take the knocks that inevitably follow when military forces don't produce the desired effects within the constraints of the policy.[140]

Air leaders viewed Momyer's axiom, which paraphrased Douglas MacArthur's evaluation of the Korean War, as the overriding lesson of Rolling Thunder. Sharp, Wheeler, and Moore echoed the remark in their assessments of the air campaign.[141] Their statements leave no doubt as to the air chiefs' conviction that they would have gained victory had Johnson given them a free hand. Their assumption lacked substance, however. The nature of the war—plus the air commanders' own controls—argued strongly that Rolling Thunder could never provide more than token support to Johnson's political objectives. Air leaders like Sharp, who pointed to the 1972 air campaigns as examples that Rolling Thunder could have achieved American goals earlier, failed to notice that neither the war nor the American objectives were the same in 1972 as they were in 1965. They also failed to observe that the result of the 1972 campaigns was not the total victory they had aimed to achieve.

V

Nixon Turns to Air Power

What really matters now is how it all comes out. Both Haldeman and Henry seem to have an idea—which I think is mistaken—that even if we fail in Vietnam we can still survive politically. I have no illusions whatever on that score, however. The U.S. will not have a credible policy if we fail, and I will have to assume responsibility for that development.

RICHARD M. NIXON
diary entry, April 1972[1]

On 20 April 1969, President Richard M. Nixon announced that he would withdraw 150,000 men from Vietnam during the next year. The decision conformed to the Vietnam policy outlined almost a year earlier by his predecessor: The United States would rely on negotiations and an improved Southern army, supported by decreasing amounts of American military power, to end its Vietnam involvement. Lyndon Johnson had halted all bombing of the North in October 1968 in exchange for Hanoi's "agreement" to negotiate seriously and stop certain military activities.[2] Rolling Thunder officially ended, and the air effort devoted to it was shifted to the Ho Chi Minh Trail. Except for infrequent "protective reaction strikes" in response to violations of the October accord, the North was a refuge from American bombs from November 1968 to April 1972.[3]

After ten months of no progress in the public negotiations begun in Paris by the Johnson administration, Nixon dispatched Henry A. Kissinger, his Assistant for National Security Affairs, to meet secretly with North Vietnamese representatives in August 1969. Kissinger met with delegates Le Duc Tho and Xuan Thuy twelve times before the North Vietnamese abruptly halted the connection in October 1971. He achieved no more than the deadlocked public talks paralleling his unannounced sessions. Nixon became convinced that Hanoi had no intention of settling the war at the conference table, a

147

supposition confirmed by the North's massive invasion of South Vietnam in March 1972. When the Southern army threatened to collapse before the onslaught, the President turned to air power to help achieve his vision of an honorable peace.

In certain respects, Nixon's "Linebacker" campaign against North Vietnam differed little from Johnson's Rolling Thunder. Air Force strategic bombing doctrine guided both offensives, and pilots attacked many of the same targets in Linebacker as they had earlier. Both campaigns were also political instruments. Yet the peace that Nixon sought was not the same as that pursued by Johnson, and the campaigns differed greatly in their utility as political tools. Because of revamped American political objectives and the North's decision to wage conventional war, Linebacker proved more effective than Rolling Thunder in furthering U.S. goals in Vietnam.

War Aims

In October 1971, South Vietnam's President Nguyen Van Thieu agreed to a new American peace proposal.[4] Nixon's offer provided for the withdrawal of all American forces from the South in six months, a prisoner exchange by both sides, and a cease-fire throughout Indochina.[5] Thieu also agreed to an internationally supervised election in the South, before which he and Vice President Tran Van Huong would resign to assure to all candidates an equal opportunity for selection.

Nixon's proposal underscored his war aims. Although Kissinger's negotiations did not involve the South Vietnamese, the President equated "peace with honor" to an American withdrawal that did not abandon the South to an imminent Communist takeover. This objective—much more limited than Johnson's aim of an independent, stable, non-Communist South—was Nixon's positive political goal. To achieve it, Nixon applied military force in concert with his twin policies of negotiation and Vietnamization. "We were going to continue fighting until the Communists agreed to negotiate a fair and honorable peace or until the South Vietnamese were able to defend themselves on their own—whichever came first," he reflected. "The pace of withdrawal would be linked to the progress of Vietnamization, the level of enemy activity, and developments on the negotiating front."[6]

Relying on world opinion to compel Hanoi to negotiate, Nixon broadcast his October proposal in a television address on 25 January 1972. Concurrently, he publicized Kissinger's secret negotiating record. The President stressed that the United States would conclude either an agreement on military and political issues or one that would "settle only the military issues and leave the political issues to the Vietnamese alone." He repeated his pledge not to abandon South Vietnam, stating that he would not agree to a settlement that threatened the existence of a non-Communist South. His call for a return to negotiations ended with a warning: "If the enemy's answer to our peace offer is to step up their military attacks, I shall fully meet my responsibility as Commander-in-Chief of our Armed Forces to protect our remaining troops."[7]

While the goal of an "honorable" withdrawal compelled the President to apply increased force if Hanoi challenged his commitment to the South, the objective also limited the amount of force available. By January 1972, only 139,000 Americans remained in Vietnam, and the number fell to 69,000 in April. American departure thus became for Nixon the primary negative political objective as well as a positive political goal. The public's dissatisfaction with the war after the 1968 Tet Offensive necessitated the steady withdrawal of troops; Americans had responded sharply to Nixon's original plan to increase manpower slightly in the spring of 1969. To oppose Northern aggression, the President had to rely on air and naval power. Unlike Johnson, however, he had few negative objectives limiting the application of those resources.

In 1971 Nixon took steps to isolate Hanoi from its chief benefactors. Tensions between the Chinese and Soviets had accelerated sharply since the Johnson presidency. Throughout 1969, the two superpowers had fought a series of savage engagements along their mutual border. State Department officials noted that the Soviets had completed plans for conventional air raids against Chinese nuclear production facilities and then had moved missiles near Manchuria for possible retaliation if the Chinese responded to the attacks by firing nuclear weapons.[8] By 1971, the Soviets had forty-four divisions poised on their border with Mongolia, and Chinese troops stood ready to give battle.[9] Both nations looked to America as a counterweight in a potential conflict. Moreover, both had individualistic needs that only the United States could satisfy. Shunned by the Soviets, the Chinese required American support to end the isola-

tion aggravated by their Cultural Revolution. Meanwhile, the Soviets desired an agreement on strategic nuclear weapons, and they
desperately needed American grain.[10]

Nixon resolved to make the changing international climate work
for him in Vietnam. Kissinger secretly visited China in early July
1971, and on the 15th Nixon proclaimed that he would visit the
country in February the following year. Three months after that
disclosure, he and Soviet leader Leonid Brezhnev jointly announced
that Nixon would travel to Moscow in May 1972 for a summit. Although neither the Chinese nor the Soviets were eager to forsake
Hanoi, the goal of détente ultimately prevailed over their commitment to a Northern victory. The President gambled that the needs of
both powers would prevent them from interfering with his military
actions in Vietnam, and his intuition proved correct. Except for ver-
bal protests, neither nation responded to Nixon's application of air
and naval power in 1972. "At last we had a free hand to use all our
force to end the war," a Kissinger aide later recalled.[11] With some
exaggeration, his observation reflected reality.

Besides the freedom of action stemming from his diplomatic
coups, Nixon's willingness to use force was not limited by conflicting
concerns over domestic programs. The President desired public support for the war, and most Americans backed the May 1972 decision
to initiate the Linebacker campaign. Unlike Viet Cong attacks inside the South, Hanoi's twelve-division assault crashed across clearly
defined borders and was a blatant display of aggression. The majority of American ground troops had left Vietnam, causing the press
to focus on whether bombing and mining would cancel the Moscow
summit. The Soviets' mild response, followed by the summit's re-
sounding success, assured Nixon of popular support for an air campaign. A Harris poll in September showed that 55 percent of the
public approved heavy bombing of the North.[12]

The public's enthusiasm for military pressure was not, however,
shared by many members of Congress. Congressional moves to end
the war intensified during Linebacker. On 24 July, an amendment
insisting on an American withdrawal in return for a prisoner release
passed the Senate by five votes before failing in the House. Nixon
realized that the Congress elected in November might establish
terms for withdrawal less favorable than those sought in Paris. To
preclude such an occurrence, he resolved to end the war prior to
January 1973.

Nixon's desire to end the war rapidly was matched by his desire to preserve an adequate base of support for an "honorable" accord. Those were the two primary negative objectives limiting the application of air power. On the one hand, he had to conclude the war while he possessed the necessary backing to secure a favorable agreement. On the other hand, applying too much force might cause his support to vanish. "I was prepared to step up the bombing after the election," the President later commented, "but there was no way of knowing whether that would make [the North Vietnamese] adopt a more reasonable position before the American public's patience ran out, before the bombing began to create serious problems with the Chinese and Soviets or before Congress just voted us out of the war."[13] While the goal of American withdrawal had little impact on the air campaign, the dual objectives of a quick end to the war and the preservation of support for it limited both the duration and the intensity of the Linebacker offensive.

Rationale for an Air Campaign, December 1971–May 1972

As Hanoi's 1972 offensive would demonstrate, Vietnamization had not yet produced a Southern army capable of independently stopping Northern aggression. Nixon suspected that the South would need American support when the attack came, and he decided to pursue a policy of combined diplomatic and military pressure to achieve his goal of an honorable peace. After learning in late 1971 of vast Communist stockpiles near the DMZ, the President began to implement his design to preserve the Southern regime. When the North Vietnamese shelled Saigon in December, violating the terms of the 1968 bombing halt "agreement," he responded. Seventh Air Force fighters flew more than a thousand sorties between 26 and 30 December in Operation Proud Deep Alpha, attacking supply targets south of the 20th parallel.[14] Nixon hoped that the bombing would dissuade Hanoi from mounting an invasion, which American military chiefs predicted for February 1972.

On 26 January 1972, the day following his announcement of Kissinger's negotiations, the President notified the Chinese and Soviets that he would oppose a Northern attack with strong military countermeasures. China assumed a "posture of indifference" in response to the message.[15] Because of the small amount of matériel supplied by China to North Vietnam, Nixon was content with the Chinese reply. Moscow expressed a tepid approval of Hanoi's actions, and the glut of Soviet goods reaching the North appeared to indicate that the Soviets would support an invasion. To limit Moscow's potential contribution, Kissinger informed Soviet Ambassador Anatoly Dobrynin that a Northern offensive would jeopardize the Moscow summit. Nixon visited Peking during late February, and in that month American air forces conducted twenty-seven protective reaction strikes against the continuing buildup north of the DMZ. The President did not intend for Hanoi to embarrass him with an offensive before his trip to China.[16]

Prior to departing for Peking, Nixon bolstered American air units in Southeast Asia. At a 2 February National Security Council meeting, he declared: "In the final analysis we cannot expect the enemy to negotiate seriously with us until he is convinced nothing can be gained by continuing the war. This will require an all-out effort on our part during the coming dry season."[17] Eighteen Air Force F-4D fighters, which began deploying from Clark Air Base in the Philippines on 29 December, completed their transfer to South Vietnam and Thailand on 8 February. More significant was the deployment of thirty-seven B-52s under Operation Bullet Shot. Eight of the bombers arrived at U-Tapao Royal Thai Air Force Base on 5 February, while the remainder went to Andersen Air Force Base, Guam, two days later. The dispatch of B-52s raised the total number of bombers in-theater to eighty-four, with fifty-three at U-Tapao and thirty-one at Andersen.[18]

Hanoi responded to Nixon's 25 January appeal for renewed negotiations on 14 February, proposing any time after 15 March as an acceptable date for talks. The President suggested 20 March, and Hanoi accepted his offer on 29 February. Two weeks before the negotiations, the North Vietnamese announced that 20 March was no longer acceptable and demanded a postponement until 15 April. "Had we reflected," Kissinger later noted, "we might have concluded that Hanoi was gearing the resumption of negotiations to the timing of its forthcoming offensive. It wanted to have the talks take place under conditions of maximum pressure and discomfiture for us."[19]

General Vo Nguyen Giap, the North Vietnamese Defense Minister, finally unleashed his attack on 30 March, the Thursday before Easter. Despite knowing of the impending invasion, American civil and military officials underestimated its magnitude. Giap sent three divisions, backed by two hundred tanks and 130-mm heavy artillery, smashing across the DMZ into South Vietnam's Military Region I. This assault was the first of a three-pronged attack, and it signaled the movement of nine other divisions to staging areas in Laos and Cambodia. In early April, three divisions struck Military Region III from Cambodia. They surrounded An Loc, located on the highway leading south to Saigon, on 13 April. The remaining Northern troops moved west of Kontum, causing Southern commanders to brace for an assault against the Central Highlands.

Giap's Easter Offensive strengthened Nixon's resolve to preserve South Vietnam as an independent political entity. The President considered the attack a desperate move to forestall Vietnamization. He further viewed it as offering an opportunity to end the war. Nixon believed that by defeating the assault and launching a massive counterblow against the enemy homeland, he could compel Hanoi to sign a favorable accord. Kissinger concurred with the President's assessment, telling Nixon on 3 April that the United States "would get no awards for losing with moderation."[20] The National Security Adviser felt that the timing of the attack revealed much about North Vietnamese intentions. He perceived Hanoi's strike, coming seven months prior to the Presidential election, as an attempt at battlefield victory while political pressures prevented Nixon from interfering decisively. The blatant nature of the assault, however, provided Nixon with the public support necessary to retaliate.

To blunt the offensive, the President turned to air power. American combat troops remaining in the South received orders not to engage the enemy. Nixon intended the withdrawal of ground forces to proceed on schedule regardless of the invasion. In contrast, he ordered additional aircraft to Southeast Asia. Operation Constant Guard increased the total of F-4s in-theater from 185 on 30 March to 374 by 13 May. Many pilots flew missions within seventy-two hours after they were alerted at their bases in the United States. Between 4 April and 23 May, Bullet Shot deployments resulted in the arrival of 124 B-52s at Andersen, which brought the combined total of bombers in Guam and Thailand to 210—more than half the B-52s in SAC. Noting the influx of bombers swamping Andersen's taxiways, one member of the 8th Air Force planning staff at Guam observed: "We kept waiting for the northern end of the island to sink." Nixon did not limit the aircraft increases to Air Force units In April, he dispatched the carriers *Constellation* and *Kitty Hawk* to join the *Coral Sea* and *Hancock* in the Tonkin Gulf. By July, the carriers *Midway* and *Saratoga* had joined this force, giving the Navy the greatest concentration of firepower it would enjoy during the war.[21]

Nixon intended this array to thwart the enemy assault and to carry the war to North Vietnam proper. Air units began Operation Freedom Train against Northern supply concentrations south of the 18th parallel on 5 April. They also attacked the large number of SAM sites defending supply stockpiles north of the DMZ. "Although the United States effort was substantial," an Air Force study observed, "the flow of personnel, supplies, and material did not diminish."[22] To achieve "the necessary military impact," Nixon concluded that raids would have to strike near Hanoi and Haiphong.[23] He reasoned that strikes by B-52s, with their enormous 30-ton bomb loads, would prove more effective against supply depots in the heartland than would attacks by fighters. In addition, sending the bombers north was, in Kissinger's words, "a warning that things might get out of hand if the offensive did not stop."[24] B-52s had never before flown against the North's two largest cities. On 16 April, 20 bombers from the 307th Strategic Wing at U-Tapao attacked Haiphong's oil storage facilities in Operation Freedom Porch Bravo. B-52s flew five missions against the North during April, but they did not attack Hanoi.

At the end of the month, Nixon approved raids on targets south of 20 degrees 25 minutes North Latitude. Kissinger called the application of such force necessary "for the political goal of bringing matters to a head and overawing outside intervention." He elaborated: "If we wanted to force a diplomatic solution, we had to create an impression of implacable determination to prevail; only this would bring about either active Soviet assistance in settling the war or else Soviet acquiescence in our mounting military pressures, on which we were determined should diplomacy fail."[25]

The Soviets responded to the American aerial assault, and Nixon's accompanying refusal to continue public negotiations, by inviting Kissinger to Moscow to discuss the war's escalation. Dobrynin had extended this invitation on 10 April, but Moscow did not withdraw the offer after the 16 April raid on Haiphong accidentally hit four Soviet ships. Kissinger thought that the Soviets' enthusiasm for the summit would persuade them to restrain Hanoi and direct their ally to negotiate. Nixon went farther in his estimation of the summit's importance to the Soviets, directing Kissinger not to discuss it until Moscow pledged to help end the war. Both agreed that military pressure on the North was necessary while applying diplomatic pressure on the Soviets, and bombing continued during Kissinger's 20–24 April visit. In Moscow, Kissinger clarified an ambiguity of his secret talks with Northern representatives—he announced that the North Vietnamese could keep troops in the South after a negotiated settlement, provided that they agreed to withdraw the soldiers who had entered since the start of the invasion.[26] Brezhnev passed this message to Hanoi but refused to ask the North Vietnamese to end their offensive. Still, he assisted in reestablishing Kissinger's negotiations. The National Security Adviser agreed that American delegates would attend a public negotiating session on 27 April, provided that Le Duc Tho met with him for secret talks on 2 May. To Kissinger, the importance of his April trip was that "the USSR engaged itself in the [negotiating] process in a manner that worked to our advantage."[27]

Despite Kissinger's Moscow journey, Le Duc Tho appeared to hold the upper hand at the 2 May meeting. Brezhnev's assistance in renewing the talks, plus Kissinger's 22 April pledge that aircraft would not strike Hanoi and Haiphong pending the session, indicated that serious negotiations might result. Nixon had refused to renew discussions until after the Soviets had made clear their position. He also wanted to avoid giving the North Vietnamese a chance to negotiate from strength. On 24 April, however, Giap attacked Kontum in the third phase of his offensive. A subsequent assault against Military Region I led to the panicking of many South Vietnamese units, and on 1 May the North Vietnamese captured Quang Tri, their first provincial capital in the South.

Although impressive, Hanoi's battlefield achievements could not persuade Nixon to cancel the 2 May meeting. Such a move conflicted with his basic strategy of balancing diplomacy and military force. Nixon planned to counter the North's latest attacks with air power—on 30 April he sent Kissinger a memorandum ordering a three-day series of B-52 strikes against Hanoi and Haiphong beginning 5 May[28]—but he would not apply greater force until *after* Le Duc Tho had proved intransigent at the bargaining table. The President wanted America's need to retaliate perceived as obvious, especially by the Soviets. Kissinger had warned Brezhnev that the United States would answer militarily should the 2 May session fail. Nixon told his adviser to "be brutally frank" with the North Vietnamese delegation, "particularly in tone." He further directed: "In a nutshell you should tell them that they have violated all understandings, they [have] stepped up the war, they have refused to negotiate seriously. As a result, the President has had enough and now you have only one message to give them—Settle or else!"[29]

At the 2 May meeting, Le Duc Tho and Foreign Minister Xuan Thuy refused to respond to Nixon's 25 January peace proposal or Kissinger's Moscow offer. Spending much of the session reading Hanoi's publicly announced war aims, the Northern delegates called for the immediate resignation of President Thieu and a halt to Vietnamization. Kissinger's attempt to determine whether Hanoi would accept a military settlement, as opposed to a combined military-political accord, ended in failure. "What the 2 May meeting revealed," Kissinger later commented, "was Hanoi's conviction that it was so close to victory that it no longer needed even the pretense of a negotiation."[30] The talks adjourned after three hours, making them one of the briefest sessions held between Kissinger and Tho.

After returning from Paris, the National Security Adviser met with the President to decide on a proper response to Hanoi's intransigence. Both agreed that only a massive shock could deter the North Vietnamese from their goal of total victory. Kissinger felt that the "one-shot" character of Nixon's desired B-52 raids would not dissuade Hanoi; further, the attacks might produce severe domestic criticism. Major General Alexander Haig, Kissinger's military assistant, had submitted a plan that the National Security Adviser thought was a suitable means of retaliation. Haig's design called for the bombing of all Northern military targets except those bordering China and for the mining of ports. The proposal relied on fighter interdiction to close the enemy's overland supply routes. Nixon supported the scheme, and on 4 May Chairman of the Joint Chiefs of Staff Admiral Thomas Moorer began drafting the orders that resulted in Operation Linebacker I.

The President announced the escalation in a television address on 8 May, the earliest date Moorer had given for the initiation of mining. He stated:

> There are only two issues left for us in this war. First, in the
> face of a massive invasion do we stand by, jeopardize the lives
> of 60,000 Americans, and leave the South Vietnamese to a long
> night of terror? This will not happen. We shall do whatever is
> required to safeguard American lives and American honor.
>
>   Second, in the face of complete intransigence at the
> conference table do we join with our enemy to install a

Communist government in South Vietnam? This, too, will not happen. We will not cross the line from generosity to treachery.[31]

Nixon eschewed the options of immediate American withdrawal and continued negotiations. The former course would remove bargaining leverage needed for the return of American prisoners, while the second would allow the enemy offensive to go unchecked. "I therefore concluded," he remarked, "that Hanoi must be denied the weapons and supplies it needs to continue the aggression."[32] Aircraft would mine Northern ports and interdict lines of communication until Northern leaders agreed to release American prisoners and to support an internationally supervised cease-fire. Once Hanoi fulfilled these conditions, a complete American withdrawal from Vietnam would occur within four months. Nixon made no mention that a withdrawal of Northern troops was required to end the bombing.

While certain of the need to escalate, the President worried that his decision might provoke the Soviets. Nixon sent a personal letter to Brezhnev explaining his action prior to the public announcement, and on 8 May he reiterated that "these actions are not directed against any other nation."[33] The President and his advisers thought the Soviets would not intervene, yet many officials believed that they would express their disapproval by canceling the summit. Kissinger received Dobrynin's official protest on 10 May, but the low-key statement contained no word of the conference. Taken aback, Kissinger asked the Ambassador if planning for the meeting should continue. Dobrynin answered that the summit was not an issue, observing, "You have handled a difficult situation uncommonly well."[34] Soviet merchant ships docked at Haiphong remained there, and those en route to the port turned back. Nixon's gamble that the Soviets' desire for détente would outweigh their zeal for Northern victory had succeeded.

Having received Soviet acquiescence, Nixon was eager to punish the North Vietnamese. "I intend to stop at nothing to bring the enemy to his knees," the President informed Kissinger. Nixon urged his military chiefs to "recommend *action* which is very *strong, threatening, and effective*," although Kissinger acknowledged that curtailing Northern supplies would require time. Still, the National Security Adviser believed that increased military pressure, together with the decreasing commitment from Moscow, might compel Hanoi to accept the 8 May peace proposal. By sending massive doses of air power against the Northern heartland, Nixon gave substance to his claim that he would not abandon Saigon. Moreover, the attacks demonstrated that he was no longer willing to engage in inconclusive negotiations.[35]

In response to Nixon's directive, air chiefs designed a campaign having the same initial aim as Rolling Thunder: to destroy the North's war-making capability. Admiral Moorer announced that Linebacker's threefold objective was to: "(a) destroy war material already in North Vietnam, (b) to the extent possible, prevent the flow of war material already in Vietnam, and (c) interdict the flow of troops and material from the north into combat areas, South Vietnam, Laos and Cambodia." As in Rolling Thunder, the Joint Chiefs targeted what they considered the vital components of the North's industrial apparatus, and once more they emphasized the transportation system. Targets included rail lines and road networks, bridges, railroad yards, equipment repair facilities, petroleum, oil, and lubricants (POL) storage areas, and thermal power plants. Unlike Rolling Thunder, however, the chiefs received authority to attack the various targets simultaneously. They could also approve strikes on enemy defenses.[36]

Code-named Pocket Money, the Navy's mining operation complemented the air campaign's assault on the North's overland supply routes. With mining, air commanders believed, Linebacker could halt Hanoi's logistical flow. They concurred with Kissinger's speculation that their efforts would take time to erode Northern resources. Air strikes and mining could limit the amount of matériel entering North Vietnam, but the nation had stockpiled goods for more than three years virtually unhindered. Kissinger observed: "The President had gained some maneuvering room with his bold decision to bomb and mine, but if it did not bring results fairly quickly, it would be increasingly attacked as a 'failure.' The demands for 'political' alternatives would mount."[37]

Campaign Overview

On the morning of 10 May, the initial strike of the new bombing campaign occurred under the designation "Rolling Thunder Alpha"; the name "Linebacker" had not yet reached field units. Thirty-two F-4s from Thai bases attacked one of Rolling Thunder's most frequently bombed targets, Hanoi's Paul Doumer Bridge. They also struck the city's Yen Vien Railroad Yard. Pilots dropped twenty-nine laser- and electro-optically guided "smart" bombs on the bridge and eighty-four conventional bombs on the marshaling yard, heavily damaging both targets. Fifty-eight additional aircraft supported the raid by performing reconnaissance, SAM suppression, escort, and electronic countermeasures (ECM).[38]

Linebacker's first raid typified attacks during the next three months. Large numbers of support aircraft accompanied a relatively small number of strike aircraft to the target, with the strike/support ratio varying according to the severity of enemy defenses. The type of target determined the number of strike aircraft required. Against area targets such as railroad yards and storage facilities, where the risk of civilian casualties was minimal, fighters dropped conventional "iron" bombs. These raids required a much higher strike sortie rate to assure success than did attacks on precision targets. Precision targets demanded fewer strike sorties because of a technological advance perfected after Rolling Thunder—the "smart" bomb. Using laser or electro-optical guidance, these bombs could hit targets in heavily populated areas with remarkable accuracy. On 26 May, a single flight of F-4s dropped laser-guided bombs that destroyed the Son Tay warehouse and storage area. The three buildings attacked measured 300 × 260 feet, 260 × 145 feet, and 210 × 65 feet. The F-4s dropped only three bombs, and all hit their respective targets. "Laser-guided bombs . . . revolutionized tactical bombing," Air Force Major General Eugene L. Hudson, 7th Air Force Director of Intelligence, asserted. Since most Linebacker targets required precision ordnance, the number of strike aircraft per mission remained low. Until August, a raid's strike force averaged eight to ten aircraft.[39]

While Air Force and Navy fighters flew most Linebacker missions, B-52s also participated in the campaign. Kissinger dissuaded Nixon from sending large numbers of bombers northward. The National Security Adviser believed that large-scale B-52 raids might cause a domestic outcry and that in any case such attacks were unnecessary. B-52s struck Northern targets near the DMZ in their first Linebacker mission on 8 June, and they averaged thirty sorties a day over the North through October. Targets included storage areas and lines of communication. As during Rolling Thunder, most bomber missions occurred over the South in support of ground forces.[40]

By early June, Giap's offensive had begun to sputter, and Kissinger judged that the time was ripe for renewed negotiations. "The war had to be ended," he wrote, "by a demonstration that our government was in control of events, and this required maintaining the diplomatic initiative."[41] Hanoi accepted the proposal for private talks to reconvene on 19 July. This time Nixon did not curtail bombing, as he had before the 2 May meeting. He asserted: "It has always been my theory that in dealing with these very pragmatic men . . . who lead Communist nations, that they respect strength—not belligerence but strength—and at least that is the way I am always going to approach it, and I think it is going to be successful in the end."[42]

Despite sanctioning negotiations, the President was less than enthusiastic about returning to the bargaining table. With the growing certainty of reelection, he had little domestic reason to resume the talks. Kissinger felt that as reelection became more obvious, Nixon could induce Hanoi to settle before receiving a renewed mandate. Yet, according to the National Security Adviser, the President feared that the North Vietnamese *would* accept his 8 May peace proposal. Nixon believed that Hanoi's acceptance would erode the conservative Republican support that he felt was necessary for a successful presidency. "Nixon saw no possibility of progress until *after* the election and probably did not even desire it" Kissinger remarked. "Even then, he preferred another escalation before sitting down to negotiate."[43]

Kissinger met with Le Duc Tho three times between 19 July and 14 August. The insolent tone that Tho presented at the 2 May meeting had disappeared, and he conceded points that had highlighted his negotiating position since the start of talks. He relinquished his call for President Thieu's immediate removal. He also abandoned the demand for an unconditional deadline on the withdrawal of American forces. Kissinger meanwhile had announced in Moscow that the United States would support a tripartite electoral commission—consisting of members from Thieu's government, the Viet Cong, and neutralists—in South Vietnam after the cease-fire.[44] Still, Tho continued to press for a coalition government, with substantial Communist representation, in the South. Nixon was discouraged by the sessions, writing on Kissinger's report of the 14 August meeting that he did not believe successful negotiations could occur until after the election. "We have reached the stage where the mere *fact* of private talks helps us very little—if at all," he concluded.[45] Nevertheless, he assented to Kissinger's scheduling of the next round of negotiations for 15 September, after the National Security Adviser met with Thieu in Saigon.

In the midst of Kissinger's renewed talks, Nixon enlarged the air campaign. On 8 August, the Commander-in-Chief, Pacific Command (CINCPAC), Admiral John S. McCain, Jr., notified his subordinate commanders that Linebacker would begin to hit the North harder:

> There is growing concern here and in Washington that insufficient effort is being applied against the North Vietnamese heartland. . . . To signal Hanoi in the strongest way possible that our air presence over their country will not diminish, I wish to intensify the air campaign in Northern NVN [North Vietnam].[46]

The admiral ordered three of the six carriers in the Tonkin Gulf to devote all of their sorties to Linebacker. Half of those missions would occur in Route Package 6B, the Navy's northernmost zone of operations.[47] McCain directed the Air Force to schedule a minimum of forty-eight strike sorties a day in its two northern areas of responsibility, Route Packages 5 and 6A. He also called for periodic B-52 strikes into northern North Vietnam, although this was a request to the Commander-in-Chief, Strategic Air Command (CINCSAC), rather than an order, as McCain had no operational control over SAC bombers.

From 9 August until 16 October, Air Force planners scheduled forty-eight strike sorties a day into Route Packages 5 and 6A. Because of the excellent results achieved with smart bombs, commanders attempted to conduct as many precision raids as possible. A shortage of guidance pods for laser-guided bombs prevented many precision attacks, however, and often one-third of the strike force carried conventional ordnance. Foul weather further hampered attacks, allowing only sixteen missions to fly in August. In September the weather improved. Compared with Linebacker's previous months, four times as many strike aircraft flew in September, making it the most productive month of the campaign. Seventh Air Force flew 111 laser-guided bomb sorties, and most attacks destroyed their targets. Pilots perfected LORAN (Long Range Navigation) bomb delivery techniques, allowing them to fly missions normally weather-canceled. The 25 September arrival of forty-eight F-111s in Thailand provided air commanders with an additional means of striking the enemy. Capable of flying supersonically at tree-top level in darkness and poor weather, F-111s attacked in increasing numbers until by 13 October they accounted for half the Air Force's strikes in the heartland. "The mere presence of 24 sorties a night striking at random and without warning throughout North Vietnam must have caused considerable consternation," Major General Hudson surmised. One of the few F-111 pilots shot down remembered that a guard approached him, declaring, "You F-111." He then made a flat, sweeping motion with his hand, and in an awed tone said, "Woosh!"[48]

Interdiction remained the thrust of the air offensive during its final two months. The new CINCPAC, Admiral Noel A. M. Gayler, issued a 7 October statement of bombing objectives that mirrored Admiral Moorer's May declaration. Targets associated with resupply from China, such as rail lines and truck routes, and the electric power system received the highest priority. In mid-October Gayler initiated joint Air Force/Navy strikes against the interior area bounded by the vital Northeast and Northwest Railroads. His attempt to eliminate the inefficiency stemming from the route package system had little chance for success, however. On 23 October, Nixon ended Linebacker and halted all bombing north of the 20th parallel.[49]

Kissinger's progress during the September and October rounds of negotiations resulted in the President's decision to curtail bombing. The breakthrough occurred on 8 October, when Tho dropped the demand for a Southern coalition government and agreed to an in-place cease-fire followed by the withdrawal of American troops. The National Security Adviser had long believed that the best prospects for settlement lay in separating military from political issues to achieve a strictly military accord like that gained in Korea. "After four years of implacable insistence that we dismantle the political structure of our ally and replace it with a coalition government," he observed, "Hanoi had now essentially given up its political demands."[50]

Yet Kissinger had also made concessions. Besides permitting Northern troops to remain in the South, he had accepted Le Duc Tho's suggestion of a tripartite "National Council of Reconciliation and Concord" that would monitor Southern elections and comprise the three segments Kissinger had proposed for the tripartite electoral commission. The council would operate on the principle of unanimity and would have no governmental authority. Thieu, who had not learned of Kissinger's stance on the electoral commission until late August, complained that it held the potential to become a coalition government. Despite the Southern President's protest, Kissinger, with Nixon's concurrence, presented the commission proposal formally to Tho on 26 September. Tho responded by suggesting the National Council of Reconciliation and Concord. Not until 19 October did Thieu see the draft peace agreement that included provisions for the National Council and for Northern troops to stay in the South.[51]

Although the negotiations appeared on the verge of producing a settlement, Linebacker's fury continued. Kissinger had notified Tho that bombing would decrease during the final phase of talks. On 13 October Nixon reduced the number of daily attack sorties to two hundred and restricted the scope of B-52 operations, but that move produced no reduction of Air Force sorties sent against the Northern heartland. Three days later, as Kissinger journeyed from Washington for a "final" negotiating session, Nixon cut the number of daily strikes to 150. This measure reduced Air Force strike sorties against Route Packages 5 and 6A by only ten. After meeting with Xuan Thuy on the 17th, Kissinger flew to Saigon to obtain President Thieu's concurrence on the settlement. Thieu's bitter opposition to certain parts of the agreement, notably the National Council of Reconciliation and Concord and the provision allowing Northern troops to remain in the South, caused Nixon to request one more meeting between Tho and Kissinger. "As a token of good will," the President suspended attacks above the 20th parallel. "But," he announced, "there was to be no bombing *halt* until the agreement was signed. I was not going to be taken in by the mere prospect of an agreement as Johnson had been in 1968."[52]

Controls on Linebacker

In terms of political controls, the campaign ending on 23 October differed in many respects from Rolling Thunder. Like Rolling Thunder, however, Linebacker's political controls flowed from the President's negative goals. Nixon initially prohibited raids within 30 miles of the Chinese border and within 10 miles of Hanoi and Haiphong. Moscow's low-key response to the President's May escalation lessened the extent of those restrictions. By 8 June air strikes had occurred 15 miles from China, and geographical restrictions on attacks near Hanoi and Haiphong vanished. An Air Force report noted that "the prevailing authority to strike almost any valid military target during LINEBACKER was in sharp contrast to the extensive and vacillating restrictions in existence during ROLLING THUNDER." Nixon and the Joint Chiefs approved a master target list from which subordinates designed individual attacks. Rarely did the Joint Chiefs direct strikes against specific targets, and field commanders received authority to conduct raids systematically rather than piecemeal. Seventh Air Force Commander General John W. Vogt, Jr., later confirmed that he had the authority to direct the Air Force portion of Linebacker effectively.[53]

Nixon prohibited attacks threatening civilian casualties, and this restriction conformed with his air commanders' own wishes. The original Linebacker directive stated: "It is essential that strike forces exercise care in weapons selection to minimize civilian casualties and avoid third country shipping, known or suspected PW [Prisoner of War] camps, hospitals, and religious shrines." While similar limitations prevailed during Rolling Thunder, the use of smart bombs during Linebacker greatly increased number of permissible targets. Nixon forebade the bombing of dams "because the results in terms of civilian casualties would be extraordinary"; using guided ordnance, a flight of F-4s destroyed the generator of the Lang Chi Hydroelectric Plant, leaving the dam 50 feet away untouched. Vogt was proud of 7th Air Force's efforts to avoid civilian losses and remarked that his pilots were always conscious of that goal.[54]

Many command and control problems unresolved from the time of Rolling Thunder hindered Linebacker. Because of the parochial concerns of Air Force and Navy leaders, Nixon named no overall air commander, and CINCPAC retained the route package system. "Despite repeated efforts to fully integrate the U.S. effort against North Vietnam," an Air Force study commented, "U.S. air resources conducted relatively independent air operations against separate geographical sections of North Vietnam." The tremendous number of Air Force sorties flying over the Tonkin Gulf led to oversaturated airspace, resulting in a joint Air Force/Navy conference in July. Participants established altitude blocks separating the two services' flights, although time separation between strikes remained an *informal* agreement. The campaign ended before Admiral Gayler's attempt to integrate flights could bear fruit. Still, Vogt did not object to the route package system, believing that it "saved . . . a great deal of detailed coordination." He did oppose Linebacker's overlapping chain of command. Vogt reported in turn to the Commander-in-Chief, Pacific Air Forces (CINCPACAF) and CINCPAC, and he received added guidance from the Chief of Staff of the Air Force and the Chairman of the Joint Chiefs. To employ B-52s, he had to coordinate with either the Joint Chiefs or CINCPAC, who sometimes received targeting authority for the bombers, and with CINC-SAC, who retained control of the time and weight of B-52 strikes. "I would much have preferred," he later declared, "to have control of the whole air situation myself."[55]

Northern air defenses provided the most obvious operational control on the campaign. MiG fighter totals in May 1972 had increased to 204, of which ninety-three were MiG-21s. SAM sites numbered three hundred. Enemy defenses claimed forty-four Air Force aircraft during Linebacker, and in June MiGs downed seven Air Force fighters while losing only two of their own. Despite those losses, air commanders did not launch a systematic effort against the MiGs. The reason for this decision, an air chief commented, was "simply that we have been given objectives of far greater priority and we are gaining these objectives without significant hindrance by the North Vietnamese fighters." He noted with satisfaction that MiGs "have not been able to prevent our strike aircraft from reaching their targets in a single instance." Yet he was probably unaware that SAC's directives for B-52s "provided for breaking off or diverting a mission if the anticipated or encountered threat became severe enough."[56]

The Air Force did take action to thwart enemy defenses. At the end of July, the "Teaball" Weapons Control Center at Nakhon Phanom, Thailand, began operations, providing pilots over the North with a combination of radar and intelligence information. Teaball negated the MiGs' ground radar advantage and helped produce an Air Force-to-MiG kill ratio of 5 to 19 from 1 August through 15 October, as against an 18 to 24 ratio from 1 February through 31 July. The Air Force also devised hunter–killer teams comprising two F-105 "hunters" and two F-4 "killers" to find and destroy enemy radars. The effectiveness of both Teaball and the hunter–killer teams reduced the number of support aircraft needed for strike defense, which in turn allowed many support aircraft to become attackers after the August increase in strike sorties.[57]

Pilot inexperience led to many losses during Linebacker's first three months. Because of the three-year ban on flights north of the 20th parallel, few pilots had previously flown in Route Packages 5 and 6A. To increase an awareness of enemy tactics, mission critique conferences began on 10 July at 7th Air Force Headquarters, and the minutes of those sessions went to all field units. Vogt ordered specific squadrons to specialize in particular tasks to achieve the maximum efficiency of his fighter force. As a result, the 8th Tactical Fighter Wing became the exclusive users of laser-guided ordnance.[58]

Passive defenses also hampered Linebacker. The Communists employed anti-interdiction techniques developed during Rolling Thunder, although the conventional nature of the Easter Offensive produced much higher supply needs than before. Pilots stymied rail traffic from China, forcing the enemy to rely on truck convoys. The North Vietnamese constructed a pipeline, from China through Laos to South Vietnam, that supplied nearly 50,000 metric tons of oil a month. The redundancy of both the road network and the oil pipeline made the two targets difficult to attack successfully. Hanoi countered efforts to destroy its thermal power capability by using thousands of portable generators to operate war machinery and radars. Passive measures proved especially effective during the early phase of Linebacker, when the South appeared near collapse. Air commanders diverted many missions to fly close air support for Southern ground troops and did not possess the necessary aircraft to conduct heavy interdiction of the North as well. Even with the August bombing increases, passive defenses continued to frustrate Linebacker.[59]

Weather was an additional operational control, and overcast skies prevented smart bomb delivery. While the Navy's A-6 Intruder and the increasing use of B-52s permitted some bombing during adverse weather, commanders searched for other means to overcome this limitation. General Vogt's summer requirement for pilots to gain familiarity with LORAN bombing techniques paid dividends when monsoons appeared in August. Beginning in that month, Air Force planners scheduled two separate Linebacker missions daily, and each had the option of guided or unguided munitions. This planning procedure eliminated many maintenance problems caused by poor weather. The F-111's arrival in late September offered another boost to Linebacker's all-weather bombing capability.

Bombing Results

From April through October 1972, 155,548 tons of bombs fell on North Vietnam, one-fourth the tonnage dropped during Rolling

Thunder. "More damage was done to the North Vietnamese lines of communication during Linebacker than during all our previous efforts," Vogt acknowledged. Smart bombs inflicted most of the destruction, and the Northeast and Northwest Railroads each experienced an average of fifteen wrecked bridges throughout the campaign. Interdiction reduced overland imports from 160,000 tons to 30,000 tons a month, while mining decreased seaborne imports from more than 250,000 tons a month to near zero. The Chinese heightened the effectiveness of both efforts. For three weeks following the mining of Northern ports, they refused to ship *any* goods to North Vietnam, and they denied the transport of Soviet goods across their territory for three *months*. "This was just to let the North Vietnamese know who lived on their border," commented Walt W. Rostow, who remained in contact with Kissinger after serving as Johnson's National Security Adviser.[60]

The conventional nature of the Easter Offensive gave rise to matériel needs that far exceeded those previously required by Communist forces. For the first time in the war, the North Vietnamese employed large numbers of tanks and heavy cannon in an assault resembling the blitzkrieg of World War II. Vast amounts of ammunition and oil were essential to the success of the invasion, and the transport and storage of such goods were especially vulnerable to air attack. "You cannot refuel T-54 tanks with gasoline out of water bottles carried on bicycles," the British military authority Sir Robert Thompson observed. In addition, Communist troops could not obtain necessary foodstuffs from the South, and a poor rice harvest affected food supplies throughout the North. After the reopening of Haiphong in 1973, the North imported 1 million tons of grain—a three-month supply of their current ration.[61]

By the end of Linebacker, aircraft had destroyed almost all fixed oil storage facilities and 70 percent of the electric power generating capacity. Hanoi's portable generators provided current only to military facilities. A correspondent in the capital noted that "the industrial power plant for the city has been destroyed, and the electric current that emanates from the remaining power plant is feeble and subject to repeated failure." The attacks disrupted the lives of Hanoi's inhabitants, causing between 20 and 40 percent of the city's populace to evacuate. Those who remained found little occasion to gather socially. All theaters and museums closed, and Catholic priests conducted mass at 4:30 A.M. Perhaps the greatest indicator of how bombing affected civilians came from Hanoi's national radio.

Typical broadcast topics during Linebacker included: "How to Achieve High Yield in Rice Cultivation Despite the Bombing" and "How Young People in the Country Should Receive City Children Being Evacuated."[62]

Although Linebacker failed to produce a settlement, its damage helped persuade Northern leaders to abandon their goal of an immediate military takeover and contributed to their concessions at the bargaining table. The six men constituting North Vietnam's Politburo, First Secretary Le Duan, National Assembly Chairman Truong Chinh, Prime Minister Pham Van Dong, Defense Minister Vo Nguyen Giap, and Secretariat members Pham Hung and Le Duc Tho, had committed themselves to unifying a country that they considered arbitrarily divided. The six viewed elimination of the South Vietnamese government as a prerequisite for unification, yet they did not agree on the method to achieve the fusion. Truong Chinh stressed political measures, emphasizing a protracted war in the South to accomplish the goal. Le Duan advocated large-scale military action, arguing that after the Southern defeat political unification could occur at leisure. Following the 1968 Tet Offensive's failure, the Politburo heeded Truong Chinh's policy of protracted war and strengthened the Northern Army. By late 1970, Hanoi felt that its rear areas were secure, and Le Duan's call for an invasion met with approval.[63]

Northern leaders found many reasons to justify an assault. A strategy of protracted war risked both manpower shortages and economic stagnation. The Northern army suffered from low morale, and the Laotian invasion early in 1971 indicated that Vietnamization had bolstered Southern combat capability. The continuing withdrawal of American troops increased the chances of Nixon's reelection, which Northern leaders thought would give him greater freedom of action in Vietnam. They also believed that a successful invasion while some Americans remained would not only discredit Vietnamization but also serve as a defeat for the United States. The capture of additional Americans would provide negotiating leverage, although the offensive's goal was complete victory. Despite endorsing Northern editor Hong Chuong's boast that "we are ready to fight [the United States] for a century," Communist leaders hoped for success in less time. All were over sixty and had pursued the goal of unification for most of their lives. The prospect of dying with the dream unfulfilled, as had Ho Chi Minh, loomed before them. Consequently, Robert Thompson remarked, they were "old men in a hurry."[64]

Throughout 1971, North Vietnam prepared for the assault. Le Duan visited Moscow in the spring to secure weaponry and transport, and in the summer the Politburo issued the invasion order. Having committed themselves to the offensive, Northern leaders turned down Nixon's offer for secret negotiations and denounced the President's October proposal. Hguyen Van Tien, one of Hanoi's delegates to the public talks in Paris, told California Representative Robert L. Leggett on 26 February 1972 that no proposal was reasonable as long as the Thieu government remained in power. Tien demanded the formation of a coalition government, followed by general elections, after which a cease-fire could occur. Without the simultaneous settlement of military and political questions, Tien argued, a lasting peace in South Vietnam was impossible.[65]

Kissinger was made aware of Hanoi's resolve when the secret negotiations finally resumed on 2 May. "Even if pressed by Moscow," he later asserted, "Hanoi would want to play to the end its current offensive, to which it was fully committed, to improve its bargaining position."[66] The Politburo considered negotiation Nixon's primary recourse in the face of the assault. A Communist Party journal announced in April:

> Because of its ignominious defeats the United States does not
> dare re-escalate the war no matter how disastrous the
> consequences of this offensive and how great the danger of
> collapse will be for the puppet [South Vietnamese] army. . . .
> We will force the enemy to acknowledge his defeat and accept
> a political settlement on our terms.[67]

Moscow's role in reinitiating Kissinger's secret talks indicated that the Soviets would provide little additional aid to Hanoi. At this juncture, however, the North Vietnamese had stockpiled enough goods to support their drive south. Seemingly on the brink of victory, Le Duc Tho exuded the confidence of Hanoi's leadership by curtly dismissing Kissinger's proposals.

Nixon's massive application of air and sea power shocked Northern leaders. Moreover, Linebacker and the tactical air campaign in the South combined with the increasing resistance of the Southern Army to negate any chance for the Easter Offensive to produce victory. American intelligence experts estimated that air power alone had cost the North Vietnamese 120,000 casualties by August, and Giap had sent every division save one to fight in the South.[68] "As the summer wore on, our losses had become prodigious, and we began to see that many of the territorial advances could not be sustained,"

Truong Nhu Tang, Minister of Justice in the Viet Cong's Provisional Revolutionary Government, recalled.[69] The President's decision to bomb and mine stood unopposed by both Moscow and Peking. The summit gained him the public support that the Politburo had hoped to undermine with its invasion, and that support virtually assured his reelection over the foundering Democratic Party candidate, George McGovern. The disastrous offensive and the prospect of Nixon's success at the polls caused Northern leaders to reconsider their emphasis on a military takeover. Pham Hung's mid-September directive to Communist cadres, "that an effort would be made to 'force' Nixon to settle the war before election day,"[70] indicated that the Politburo had given negotiated settlement first priority.

As Hanoi moved toward negotiations, American and South Vietnamese military pressure increased. Nixon answered Hanoi's concessions during the July and August rounds of talks with added bombing. On 15 September, three Southern divisions pushed six Northern divisions out of Quang Tri, and the one-time besiegers of An Loc found themselves hard pressed to avoid annihilation. While Hanoi worked for an accord prior to November, the military situation dictated that it obtain a cessation of hostilities *as soon as possible*. Thompson asserted: "For the first time in the Indochina wars the communist side was being compelled to negotiate in order to forestall the possibility of defeat."[71]

Hanoi had four objectives at the bargaining table. Its first was to remove the American Air Force and Navy from the war, which would prevent defeat and allow the North Vietnamese Army to rebuild for later operations. Second, Northern leaders aimed at restricting future United States military activity in the South. Third, they wanted to retain Northern units in the South; in this regard Nixon's 8 May 1972 proposal stressing an in-place cease-fire offered a chance to secure some military gain from the Easter Offensive. Finally, Hanoi desired the removal of Thieu and the establishment of a coalition government in the South. Speaking for the Politburo, Le Duc Tho stated that Thieu was the predominant obstruction to a unified nation and that his government would collapse once the Americans withdrew support.[72] Although Northern leaders desired these objectives at the cost of minimum concessions, a rapid curtailment of American military pressure was paramount. "The overriding aim was to get the United States out of Vietnam on the best basis possible, and keep her out," Truong recounted.[73] Ideally, Hanoi hoped that election stresses would force Nixon to sign an imprecise agreement dealing with general principles and ending American involvement in Vietnam.[74]

During the September and October negotiations, Le Duc Tho displayed a sense of urgency to end the war. He produced a schedule on 26 September for a settlement within one month, yet he continued to demand Thieu's removal before signing an agreement. At the decisive 8 October session, Tho suggested that the United States and North Vietnam sign an accord focusing on military issues. Accepting Nixon's proposal for a cease-fire, Tho dropped the requirements for a coalition government and for Thieu's resignation. By 12 October only two substantive issues remained: prisoner release and continued American military assistance to Saigon. Kissinger left Paris to brief Thieu on 18 October, sending Hanoi a proposal for the disputed points and stating that an additional negotiating session would probably be required. The next day, in Saigon, Kissinger received a message from Hanoi accepting verbatim the text that he had submitted.

Of all the concessions made by Hanoi, surrendering the demand for a political settlement proved the most difficult. By removing their demand for Thieu's dismissal, Northern leaders accorded his government a measure of legitimacy that ran counter to their aim of unification. In mid-1969, during the early stages of the Paris peace talks, a Northern negotiator privately confided to South Vietnamese Vice President Nguyen Cao Ky that Thieu was the primary obstacle to a settlement.[75] Hanoi's opposition to the Southern leader remained firm three years later. When asked by a member of the French Communist Party in May 1972 if the North Vietnamese could deal with Thieu, Le Duc Tho replied:

Impossible; he is responsible for Vietnamization. Without him, [the Saigon government] will fall apart immediately. He has become—necessarily—our number one enemy: his departure is imperative. In addition this [struggle at the negotiating table] is a test for us against the Americans. Through our demands, we come to know how much longer Nixon will support him; as soon as he drops him, we will have won. We can, therefore, go slowly . . . without letting up.[76]

Communist leaders understood the importance Nixon placed on the Thieu government's survival. Le Duc Tho's 8 October concessions did not sacrifice the North's war aim, but they revealed that Hanoi had temporarily abandoned a major principle of its policy. In accepting the in-place cease-fire, Tho managed a degree of face-saving by refusing to acknowledge the presence of "foreign" North Vietnamese soldiers in the South. Additionally, he gained Kissinger's support for a National Council of Reconciliation and Concord, which would provide a sanctioned Communist presence in South Vietnam. Yet Hanoi's 8 October concessions resulted in only negligible bombing decreases on 13 and 16 October.

To obtain a substantial bombing reduction, the Politburo on 19 October accepted Kissinger's proposals resolving the issues of prisoner exchange and matériel support for the South. Kissinger had informed Northern leaders that he would travel to Hanoi to initial an agreement, and his message of the 18th stated: "With the text of the agreement completed [the United States] would stop bombing the North altogether twenty-four hours before my arrival in Hanoi."[77] The Politburo's latest concessions were additional violations of principle and betrayed its desperation to curtail American involvement. Hanoi shunned its Viet Cong ally by accepting the release of all prisoners except Viet Cong cadres in Southern jails. More importantly, the Communists permitted the United States to resupply the South following American withdrawal. In consenting to a military accord the Politburo assured the retention of the Thieu government; by permitting that government to receive military aid, the Communists helped to guarantee its survival. Nixon notified North Vietnam's Prime Minister Pham Van Dong "that the agreement could now be considered complete,"[78] although he also called for a one-day delay in Tho's 26 September schedule to resolve unilateral declarations concerning Laos and Cambodia. Hanoi accepted the American position on the declarations on 21 October. Two days later, Nixon suspended bombing above the 20th parallel, ending Linebacker I.

Linebacker's effectiveness in helping to wring concessions from Hanoi stemmed from a number of factors absent during Johnson's application of air power. Both the Chinese and the Soviets placed a priority on détente with the United States, and their emphasis obviated the primary negative objective that had restricted Rolling Thunder. Nixon's diplomatic initiatives to Peking and Moscow allowed him to increase attacks in August without fear of a reprisal by the Communist superpowers. The success of the trips to China and the Soviet Union further provided the President with the public support necessary to conduct an extensive air offensive. Hanoi acknowledged the impact of Nixon's diplomacy. On 17 August, the Party newspaper Nhan Dan published a bitter condemnation of the

Chinese and Soviet détente with the United States. The editorial described the Communist superpowers' actions as "throwing a life-buoy to a drowning pirate . . . in order to serve one's narrow national interests. . . . This is a harmful compromise," it concluded, "advantageous to the enemy, and disadvantageous to the Revolution."[79]

Another key to Linebacker's success was the conventional character of the war in 1972. Rolling Thunder had caused minimal damage to the Southern insurgency because Viet Cong operations required few external resources. In contrast to the guerrilla war waged during Johnson's presidency, the Easter Offensive, a massive conventional attack supported by tanks and heavy artillery, was tailor-made to suit the Air Force's bombing doctrine. Although targets were essentially the same ones attacked in Rolling Thunder, Northern forces during Linebacker demanded frequent resupply, and mining negated Hanoi's primary source of matériel. With no possibility of provisioning by sea, the North turned to stockpiled goods and overland transportation. Both sources were vulnerable to air power, the latter especially because of technological improvements in ordnance. Linebacker, together with mining, tactical air support in the South, and stiffening Southern resistance, wrecked Hanoi's capacity to conduct offensive warfare. Moreover, the bombing and mining restricted *all* Northern imports, and the Politburo found its populace in danger of starving.

Without corresponding successes in the South, Linebacker could not have secured gains in the North. Nixon noted in early May 1972: "All the air power in the world and strikes on Hanoi–Haiphong aren't going to save South Vietnam if the South Vietnamese aren't able to hold on the ground."[80] After a shaky initial performance, the Southern army, backed by large doses of close air support, blunted the Northern onslaught. By June Giap's offensive was spent, and the morale of Southern units climbed as they anticipated a counterattack. The 15 September recapture of Quang Tri by three fewer divisions than the Communists had defending the city signaled the Politburo that its army faced ruin.

Kissinger's skill at the bargaining table also increased Linebacker's impact. His two years of previous negotiations had given him an understanding of Northern perceptions that served him well in 1972. He heightened the urgency for Tho to conclude an accord by granting concessions while the bombing intensified, and he promised that the attacks would decrease as soon as Tho accepted the American terms. Having gained the respect of his diplomatic adversaries, Kissinger knew that they would not lightly regard any statement outlining conditions for a cessation of military activity.

A final ingredient in Linebacker's success was that Nixon employed it in support of very limited objectives. Unlike Johnson, who used air power to help establish an independent, stable, non-Communist South Vietnam, Nixon applied air power only to guarantee America's continued withdrawal and to assure that the South did not face imminent collapse after the United States' departure. Those goals were easier to achieve through bombing than Johnson's, especially in light of Nixon's and Kissinger's diplomatic initiatives and the conventional nature of the Easter Offensive. In short, Nixon sought an interlude in which the South could build without facing a mortal threat from the North, and air power helped buy him that time.

Although Linebacker was not solely responsible for Hanoi's negotiating reversal, Nixon could not have gained Communist concessions without it. With overland routes to China left open, mining would have served no purpose and the resupply of the Northern army would have posed little problem. Giap's conventional offensive made North Vietnam susceptible to the type of air campaign espoused by air leaders throughout Rolling Thunder, one aimed at production centers and their means of distribution. Nixon assured Linebacker's consistency, an essential factor if the operation was to hurt Hanoi. He granted Vogt and the Joint Chiefs considerable authority to direct the campaign, and the general used his control to conduct systematic assaults on Northern resources. The North Vietnamese did not feel the full effects of bombing until after they had depleted their stockpiles. Once supplies dwindled, the campaign had a telling impact.

While it contributed to Hanoi's negotiating concessions, Linebacker did not achieve the "honorable peace" desired by Nixon. Paradoxically, while the campaign contributed to Hanoi's willingness to settle on Nixon's terms, it also stiffened Thieu's opposition to an agreement by convincing him that he could gain total victory. Viewing the concessions that Linebacker helped extract from Hanoi, the South Vietnamese President reasoned that continued strikes could win the war, and he was skeptical that Kissinger's accord could produce a lasting peace. He told the National Security Adviser that an agreement had to define the DMZ as a formal boundary between North and South Vietnam, remove Northern troops from the South, and guarantee that the National Council of Reconciliation and Concord did not become a coalition government. Those demands, Kissinger later remarked, were a façade. He stated: "We failed early enough to grasp that Thieu's real objection was not to terms but to the fact of *any* compromise. Conflict between us and Thieu was built into the termination of the war on any terms less than Hanoi's total surrender."[81]

While seeking victory, Thieu also perceived that agreeing to Kissinger's October settlement might well lead to Southern defeat. An American withdrawal matched by a cease-fire in-place committed Thieu to a political struggle against the disciplined organization of the Communists, and Thieu was unwilling to risk his demise either politically or militarily. Hanoi grasped the point of his opposition. Northern leaders understood—as did Thieu—that Nixon's commitment to "honor" prevented him from a unilateral settlement. Having obtained a bombing curtailment permitting receipt of overland supplies, Northern officials had no intention of granting Thieu added stature. On 26 October, Hanoi Radio broadcast the previously secret record of the Kissinger–Tho negotiations, including the text of the draft peace agreement. North Vietnam condemned "the Nixon Administration's lack of good will and seriousness" and called for a signing of the accord on 31 October, the date originally scheduled.[82]

To counter Hanoi's charges, Kissinger conducted a press conference on 26 October that produced his declaration, "We believe peace is at hand." He commented that "what remains to be done [to secure an agreement] can be settled in one more negotiating session with the North Vietnamese negotiators lasting . . . no more than three or four days." Yet he also cautioned:

> Saigon is . . . entitled to participate in the settlement of a war fought on its territory. . . . We will not be stampeded into an agreement until its provisions are right. We will not be deflected from an agreement when its provisions are right. And with this attitude, and with some cooperation from the other side, we believe that we can restore both peace and unity to America very soon.[83]

Nixon, Kissinger, and most American military chiefs believed that Linebacker helped force Hanoi to make the negotiating concessions that led to a draft agreement. Air Force operational reports reflected that perception. A 1975 study stated that "interdiction operations were a primary factor in the decision of NVN leaders to abandon their hope for an outright military victory and to step up their diplomatic efforts in order to achieve their goals through political means."[84] Many commanders contrasted Linebacker with Rolling Thunder and concluded that reduced political controls made Linebacker effective. Army General William C. Westmoreland attributed the campaign's success to its intensity. He commented: "When President Nixon decided to use our available military power in a manner that truly hurt North Vietnam, negotiations began to move in a substantive way."[85] Perhaps the military's most representative assertion concerning Linebacker's impact came from one of the men responsible for its implementation. Speaking in 1978, General Vogt acknowledged that "after Linebacker I, the enemy was suing for peace. They were hurt real bad. Most of the major targets had been obliterated in the North . . . , and they were ready to conclude an agreement." He also thought that Nixon had halted Linebacker prematurely:

> Kissinger and Le Duc Tho got together and then indications were that the agreement was imminent. Kissinger then informed me that he was going to order the bombing stopped in the Hanoi area as a gesture of good will to speed up the signing of the agreement. This was . . . in October 1972. I protested and said, "You know our history with Communists is of having to keep the heat on them in order to get them to do anything. If you take the heat off them, they may never sign."[86]

Even though it did not produce a settlement, Linebacker increased South Vietnam's chances for survival. The campaign helped wreck the North's military capability, ensuring that Hanoi could not soon launch another offensive. Linebacker also helped wring the concessions from Hanoi that Nixon considered essential to an "honorable peace." Still, the bombing did not end the war. The President would gear the next round of Linebacker toward compelling both his ally and his enemy to accomplish that goal.

VI

Persuading Enemy and Ally: The Christmas Bombings

I think, sir, any time you conduct a military operation like this the objective is quite clear in military terms. Of course, you can go on to say that war is an instrument of policy and what we are all trying to do is to bring this war to a close so we can release the prisoners and cease U.S. participation.

ADMIRAL THOMAS H. MOORER
9 January 1973[1]

On the eve of the 1972 election, President Richard M. Nixon faced a dilemma over Vietnam. Nixon had severed Hanoi from its allies and crushed its bid for military victory, resulting in its acceptance of his 8 May peace proposal. South Vietnam's President Nguyen Van Thieu then refused to endorse the agreement. Thieu insisted on modifications that were unacceptable to the North Vietnamese, who demanded that Nixon sign the accord negotiated in October by National Security Adviser Henry Kissinger. Thus, Nixon found both Hanoi and Saigon blocking his goal of an "honorable" disengagement.

To achieve that aim, Nixon once more relied on the combination of diplomatic and military pressure. After another round of negotiations failed to produce a settlement, the President again applied air power against the North. The December 1972 Linebacker campaign, however, differed from its namesake in *how* it was to attain "peace with honor." Nixon had intended Linebacker I to accomplish his objective by wrecking North Vietnam's war-making capacity; he intended Linebacker II to destroy the North's will to fight while demonstrating to Thieu that America would remain committed to Southern independence.

177

War Aims

Nixon's goals in Vietnam in November 1972 differed in two key respects from those articulated prior to Hanoi's Easter Offensive. Although he still sought an American withdrawal that did not abandon South Vietnam to an imminent Communist takeover, he also aimed to convince Thieu that the U.S. commitment to Southern independence would continue after the departure of American troops. Those objectives formed Nixon's positive political goals. A significant feature of the President's negative objectives also changed following his reelection. Nixon was certain that Congress would stop the war when it met in January. As that deadline neared, he became more willing to risk the loss of public support through increased military pressure in Vietnam. While realizing that the December bombings would be likely to trigger an outcry, he believed there was little he could do to dissuade Congress from ending Vietnam funding. By far, the January 1973 time limit was the President's greatest restraint on applying military force after his reelection.

Nixon's commitment to "honor" prevented him from completely ignoring Thieu's proposed changes to the October draft accord. Kissinger maintained that a settlement had to incorporate at least some of Thieu's demands. "If we could not bring about a single change requested by Saigon," the National Security Adviser recalled, "it would be tantamount to wrecking the South Vietnamese government."[2] Still, both Nixon and Kissinger wanted an agreement falling within the October accord's basic framework. The President brusquely dismissed the plea for a Northern troop withdrawal, noting that Thieu had accepted a proposed cease-fire since October 1971. "We could not agree with our allies in South Vietnam when they added conditions to the established positions after an agreement had been reached that reflected these established positions," Kissinger explained.[3] Nor would the United States continue the war to gain a Southern victory. Nixon included a minimum number of Thieu's proposals in a bargaining position that he felt gave Saigon the means to prevail against the Communists inside Southern borders.

To guarantee that the South survived a future military onslaught, the President pledged to defend the Thieu government. General Alexander Haig, Kissinger's military assistant, conveyed Nixon's assurances to Thieu on 9 November. Haig emphasized that Nixon considered the October agreement excellent but would attempt to incorporate some of Thieu's changes into a final accord. When Thieu condemned the President for disregarding many additions, Nixon answered that attaining all of the modifications was "unrealistic." He added: "But far more important than what we say in the agreement . . . is what we do in the event the enemy renews its aggression. You have my absolute assurance that if Hanoi fails to abide by the terms of this agreement it is my intention to take swift and severe retaliatory action."[4] Nixon expected the Southern leader ultimately to agree to a settlement, yet he worried about the timing of Thieu's acquiescence. Haig informed Thieu of the danger in stalling, and Nixon told both Haig and Kissinger that 8 December was the final date for an accord that would allow its completion prior to Congress's return. "If Thieu could not be convinced to come along by then," the President later remarked, "I could be reluctantly prepared to reach a separate agreement."[5]

Rationale for an Air Campaign, November–December 1972

Nixon's eagerness for a November settlement matched that displayed by Le Duc Tho the preceding month. The President increased military pressure to induce Hanoi's return to the bargaining table. B-52s began attacking north of the DMZ on 2 November, and two days later the North Vietnamese agreed to a mid-November meeting. Believing that Linebacker had contributed to Hanoi's October concessions, Nixon thought additional bombing would provide similar results should the North again prove intransigent. He advised Kissinger on 24 November to suspend talks for a week if no progress occurred, during which time he would authorize a massive air attack on North Vietnam.[6]

Negotiations resumed on 20 November. Kissinger noted that his adversary was not the same Le Duc Tho of late summer who relentlessly pushed toward a settlement. The National Security Adviser contributed to Tho's foot-dragging by submitting all sixty-nine of Thieu's suggested changes for consideration.[7] Tho responded to this gesture with his own modifications, one of which linked the release of American prisoners to Saigon's release of jailed Viet Cong. On the 22d, Kissinger dropped many of Thieu's demands. Tho in turn granted concessions, although the prisoner release proposal remained. The next day he offered to remove "some" troops from the northern areas of South Vietnam in exchange for a release of Viet Cong political prisoners.

With the U.S. Presidential election over, Kissinger thought the North lacked the incentive to negotiate seriously. Nixon differed, contending that an absence of military pressure prevented a settlement. Both agreed that Hanoi delayed an accord in hopes that Congress would terminate American involvement. Kissinger considered this threat significant as he observed Tho's attempts to widen the split between Washington and Saigon. On the 25th, the National Security Adviser asked for a recess until 4 December, and Le Duc Tho approved.[8]

Nixon cabled Hanoi on 27 November that the United States would return to the talks for a final session. At Kissinger's suggestion, the President uncharacteristically reduced bombing 25 percent to demonstrate his desire to settle. He did not, however, have faith that the negotiations would bear fruit. Kissinger outlined two options if the talks stalemated: First, Nixon could resume bombing north of the 20th parallel; second, he could accept the minimal concessions made by Tho in November and demand their incorporation into the October agreement. Neither Nixon nor Kissinger felt that Saigon would approve the second option. The National Security Adviser thought additional talks were necessary, while the President leaned toward the "massive bombing" alternative. Yet Nixon believed, as he had in April, that increased military pressure could only follow a breakdown in negotiations stemming conspicuously from Hanoi. "It was my firm conviction," he later declared, "that we must not be responsible—or be portrayed as being responsible—for the breakdown of the talks." The President met with the Joint Chiefs on 30 November to discuss an appropriate military response should the negotiations fail. The chiefs had completed two plans, one for a three-day and the other for a six-day series of strikes involving B-52s against the Northern heartland.[9]

Departing for Paris on 3 December, Kissinger hoped to settle the remaining issues in two days. Le Duc Tho soon disabused him of the thought. On the 4th, Tho withdrew nine of his twelve concessions from November while maintaining all his demands for changes. The only option he presented Kissinger was acceptance of the original October accord. Two days later Hanoi's position remained unchanged. Nixon informed Kissinger that if the next meeting did not produce a breakthrough, he would begin heavy bombing. The National Security Adviser arrived at the 7 December session prepared to offer a "rock-bottom position," but Tho prevented that by advancing concessions. The Northern delegate agreed to six of the nine changes that he had denounced on the 4th and dropped the demand for a Viet Cong prisoner release. At the same time, he objected to the previously accepted stipulation respecting the DMZ as a provisional boundary between North and South Vietnam. "This was precisely where Le Duc Tho wanted us," Kissinger recalled, "tantalizingly close enough to an agreement to keep us going and prevent us from using military force, but far enough away to maintain the pressure that might yet at the last moment achieve Hanoi's objectives of disintegrating the political structure in Saigon."[10]

With the danger of Congressional action less than a month away, Kissinger offered concessions to obtain an immediate agreement. By 9 December only the DMZ issue remained, and Kissinger planned to concede it. The settlement *would* include *some* of Thieu's demands. Still, the National Security Adviser reasoned, "we can anticipate no lasting peace in the wake of a consumated agreement. . . . We will probably have little chance of maintaining the agreement without evident hair-trigger readiness . . . to enforce its provisions."[11] Nixon concurred that the time was ripe for an accord. "It would be painful if Thieu refused to go along," the President reflected, "but there was no question that we had done everything possible to help him and that now we had to look to our own interests and conclude an agreement if the terms were acceptable."[12]

Le Duc Tho refused to accede to Kissinger's design. On 11 December, the Communist delegate rejected the agreed-upon signing procedures and demanded withdrawal of American civilian technicians from the South. Kissinger concluded that Tho was stalling to deter *either* a suspension of negotiations *or* an agreement. Announcing on 12 December that he would depart for Hanoi in two days to confer with the Politburo, Tho offered to return to Paris, although he stated that messages could resolve the remaining issues. Kissinger agreed and cabled Nixon that the North Vietnamese "have reduced the issues to a point where a settlement can be reached with one exchange of telegrams." "However," he added, "I do not think that they will send this telegram . . . in the absence of strong pressures."[13]

The National Security Adviser termed the 13 December session as "the day that finally exploded the negotiation."[14] When American linguistic experts met with Hanoi's, they found that the North Vietnamese had inserted seventeen changes into the completed portion of the agreement's text. Tho proved inflexible regarding the additions. Reluctantly, Kissinger decided that future talks were pointless. After the meeting he advised Nixon

> . . . to turn hard on Hanoi and increase pressure enormously through bombing and other means. . . . This would make clear that [the North Vietnamese] paid something for these past ten days. Concurrently . . . pressures on Saigon would be essential so that Thieu does not think he has faced us down, and we can demonstrate that we will not put up with our ally's intransigence any more than we will do so with our enemy.[15]

Nixon too believed that the time had come to apply military force. "We had now reached the point," he remembered, "where only the strongest action would have any effect in convincing Hanoi that negotiating a fair settlement with us was a better option for them than continuing the war." He decided to use air power, but the question of how much to employ remained. When the President met with Kissinger and Haig on the 14th, the National Security Adviser suggested a return to October's Linebacker operations, while the general argued for large-scale B-52 strikes north of the 20th parallel. Nixon agreed with Haig; anything less than bomber raids, he said, "will only make the enemy contemptuous."[16]

Unlike Linebacker I, the President aimed the December bombing directly at the North's will. The President desired a maximum psychological impact on the North Vietnamese to demonstrate that he would not stand for an indefinite delay in the negotiations. His objective fitted the pattern of America's previous strategic bombing campaigns. Linebacker I, like the initial air offensives against Germany, Japan, and North Korea—as well as the first year and a half of Rolling Thunder—had attempted to destroy enemy morale by wrecking the capability to fight. After finding that bombing aimed specifically at an enemy's war-making capacity would not accomplish American objectives, air commanders had focused their attacks on *both* the capability and willingness to resist. They would do likewise in Linebacker II.[17]

The B-52, with its massive conventional bomb load and all-weather capability, was air power's best tool to disrupt an enemy psychologically. Viet Cong Minister of Justice Truong Nhu Tang recalled: "The first few times I experienced a B-52 attack it seemed, as I strained to press myself into the bunker floor, that I had been caught in the Apocalypse. The terror was complete. One lost control of bodily functions as the mind screamed incomprehensible orders to get out."[18] Attacking at altitudes over 30,000 feet, the bomber could be neither seen nor heard by those on the ground. Moreover, B-52 raids against the North's well-defended heartland, by placing aircraft essential to the nation's nuclear capability at risk, would display the depth of American resolve. Nixon hoped that Thieu, as well as the North Vietnamese, would note this determination. Since an agreement would rest on America's air power deterrent, Nixon counted on the bombing to demonstrate continued support for Saigon. On the afternoon of the 14th, he ordered a three-day series of raids against Hanoi beginning on 18 December.[19]

The President refused to announce the escalation. Kissinger thought that Nixon should make a television address similar to the one in May to declare why bombing was necessary and to outline requirements for its cessation. The President believed that such a proclamation would delay talks by appearing as an ultimatum and making their resumption a matter of prestige. Instead, he directed Kissinger to conduct a press conference on 16 December explaining that the stalemated discussions stemmed from Communist intransigence. At the conference, the National Security Adviser hinted that the United States might resort to sterner measures to spur the talks. "I expect that we [Kissinger and Le Duc Tho] will meet again," he said, "but we will have to meet in an atmosphere that is worthy of the seriousness of our endeavor." Nixon cued the North's public negotiators in Paris with equal subtlety. In a message sent less than twelve hours prior to the first B-52's arrival over Hanoi, he asserted that the North Vietnamese "were deliberately and frivolously delaying the talks." The President proposed a return to the agreement's November text with the addition of one or two subsequently negotiated changes. "On this basis," he contended, "we would be prepared to meet again any time after December 26 to conclude an agreement."[20]

While refusing to give Hanoi an ultimatum, Nixon presented one to Thieu. The President dispatched Haig to Saigon on 18 December, handing the general a personal letter for the Southern leader. Nixon stated his intention to settle if Hanoi accepted his latest proposal, warning that an increase in military pressure did not indicate a willingness to continue the war. He concluded:

General Haig's mission now represents my final effort to point out to you the necessity for joint action and convey my irrevocable intention to proceed, preferably with your cooperation, but, if necessary, alone. . . . I have asked General Haig to obtain your answer to this absolutely final offer on my part for us to work together in seeking a settlement along the lines I have approved or to go our separate ways.[21]

Campaign Overview

Having decided on escalation, Nixon turned to his military chiefs to ensure that they would apply a large-scale effort to the air campaign dubbed "Linebacker II." He told Admiral Thomas H. Moorer, the Chairman of the Joint Chiefs: "This is your chance to use military power effectively to win this war and if you don't I'll consider you personally responsible." The operation's contingency plan called for three days of all-weather, around-the-clock attacks on essentially the same targets raided during Linebacker I. The President's emphasis on bombers led air commanders to modify the plan significantly to include heavy B-52 participation. SAC Headquarters at Offutt Air Force Base, Nebraska, rewrote the operations order and forwarded it to the Joint Chiefs for approval. On 14 December, Moorer notified SAC's commander, General John C. Meyer, of Nixon's decision to implement Linebacker II. Meyer in turn advised the 8th Air Force Commander, Lieutenant General Gerald W. Johnson, whose B-52s at Andersen and U-Tapao constituted the brunt of the strike force. Johnson received this word on the 15th because of the time differential between Nebraska and Guam.[22]

The final Linebacker II plan stressed a maximum effort in minimum time against "the most lucrative and valuable targets in North Vietnam." Many of the targets matched ones raided in Linebacker I, but Linebacker II was no interdiction campaign. While seeking to avoid civilian casualties, air chiefs complied with Nixon's desires and designed Linebacker II to inflict the utmost civilian distress. "I want the people of Hanoi to hear the bombs," Moorer told Meyer, "but minimize damage to the civilian populace." B-52s would attack rail yards, storage areas, power plants, communication centers, and airfields located on Hanoi's periphery. Meanwhile, 7th Air Force and Navy fighters would strike objectives in populated areas with smart bombs. Most targets were within 10 nautical miles of Hanoi, forcing its inhabitants to respond to each attack, and B-52s would strike throughout the night to prevent its populace from sleeping.

The night raids would also reduce the MiG threat, although air chiefs did not devise Linebacker II to achieve air superiority. The time constraints attached to the campaign dictated an immediate assault, and continual pressure was necessary to secure favorable results. SAC planners estimated that they would lose 3 percent of attacking B-52s to enemy defenses. Nixon understood that the bomber force would not emerge unscathed, as his diary showed: "We simply have to take losses if we are going to accomplish our objectives."[23]

As the Linebacker II operational order began to arrive at Andersen, General Johnson grew increasingly annoyed. In August 1972, SAC Headquarters had directed the 8th Air Force to prepare a plan for striking major targets in North Vietnam with B-52s. Johnson's staff had complied and submitted their proposal to SAC. The Linebacker II order bore little resemblance to the plan developed at Andersen. "As far as we were concerned," one member of the 8th Air Force staff recalled, "it was a new plan." Johnson was irate about the lack of versatility in routing his bombers to target. "General Johnson just blew his cork when [SAC] wouldn't change the axes of attack," an officer in the headquarters remembered. The general's staff estimated that the repetitive routing would result in losses considerably higher than SAC's 3 percent prediction. One staff officer recollected: "When I saw the map [showing the flight path to target], I realized two things: that the weight of effort would be very large, and that it was not going to be a turkey shoot—unless you were on the ground up there."[24]

Despite SAC's planning, much work remained for the 8th Air Force staff. SAC determined targets and weight of effort, subject to approval by the Joint Chiefs, as well as axes of attack and flight routes in the high-threat area north of the 20th parallel. For Andersen-based aircraft, SAC's preparation covered only two to three hours of the fourteen-hour mission. Eighth Air Force planned the remainder, consulting with the KC-135 tanker wing at Kadena Air Base, Okinawa, to arrange in-flight refueling and with 7th Air Force for fighter support packages similar to those in Linebacker I. Finally, Johnson's staff combined its planning with SAC's into a single directive that enabled aircrews to fly the mission.[25]

On Monday afternoon, 18 December, the crews of 129 B-52s learned that they would finally attack North Vietnam's capital city. Most greeted the news with disbelief followed by some amount of apprehension. U-Tapao's Captain E. A. Petersen remarked, "It was just kind of amazing that we were actually going to do it . . . I almost thought it was a joke at first."[26] Major Robert D. Clark, who would soon lead the third wave from Andersen, recalled that "everybody got cranked up. I was ready to do it; my nav [navigator] was just absolutely terrified; my gunner was a hawk. My EW [electric warfare officer] was horribly curious about whether his equipment was going to work—he was excited but scared."[27] Premission briefers gave scant attention to targets. Captain John R. Allen, who would fly three Linebacker II missions, noted that the absence of target information mattered little:

> There wasn't a whole lot of time devoted during the briefing to the intelligence aspect as to what your target was. All you knew was that you were going "Downtown," and that you might not be coming home. If they had told you that the world was made of green cheese, you wouldn't even have heard it— all you were thinking about was were you going to make it back or were you not . . . , and what about the guy sitting next to you. They [the briefers] didn't belabor the point of what the targets were because it didn't make any difference— you were committed and you were going.[28]

At 1945 hours on the 18th, the forty-eight B-52s constituting the first of three waves struck the Kinh No storage complex, the Yen Vien Rail Yard, and three airfields on the outskirts of Hanoi. Thirty-nine support aircraft accompanied the bombers. The B-52s flew near the northern border of North Vietnam from west to east, turning southeast to make their bomb runs. Attacking in a trail formation of three-ship "cells," they dropped bombs with up to ten minutes' separation between formations. Because accuracy and assured destruction were primary considerations, pilots stabilized flight for approximately four minutes prior to bomb release. The B-52s turned west after the bomb run to escape SAM coverage and head for base. Striking at midnight and 0500, waves two and three conformed to the first wave's flight pattern. Although 94 percent of the bombers hit their targets, Northern defenders also claimed a measure of success. SAMs downed three B-52s and severely damaged two others.[29]

Linebacker's second and third days paralleled its first in both weight of effort and route of flight. While concerned over the losses on the 18th, General Meyer considered them acceptable. Moreover, the need to complete SAC mission planning forty-two hours prior to initial takeoff precluded routing changes for day two. On the night of the 19th, ninety-three B-52s attacked the Thai Nguyen Thermal Power Plant and Yen Vien Rail Yard in three separate waves. SAMs damaged two bombers, but the defenses scored no kills. SAC planners took the results of the 19th's mission as vindication of their routing. This interpretation, combined with the lead time required between planning and execution, persuaded Meyer to use the same attack plan for the 20th. Ninety-nine B-52s in three waves struck the Yen Vien Rail Yard, Thai Nguyen Thermal Power Plant, and the Kinh No and Hanoi oil storage areas. Against this force the North Vietnamese achieved their greatest triumph of the campaign, destroying six B-52s and damaging a seventh.[30]

The losses infuriated Nixon, who "raised holy hell about the fact that [B-52s] kept going over the same targets at the same times." He had extended Linebacker II indefinitely on 19 December, but that action guaranteed continued raids by only B-52s, F-111s, and Navy A-6s. Poor weather prevented the bulk of the 7th Air Force's daylight sorties and transformed the campaign into an almost exclusive bomber effort. A heavy loss of B-52s—America's mightiest warplanes—would create the antithesis of the psychological impact that Nixon desired. Hanoi's delegate to the public talks in Paris, Nguyen Minh Vy, terminated the 21 December session "as a protest to the war escalation and the about-face of the United States in negotiations." Although he recognized the propaganda intent of such utterances, Nixon reasoned that Hanoi would not bargain seriously until the bombers accomplished a high level of destruction at minimum cost.[31]

Agreeing that the 6 percent losses on 20 December were unacceptable, Meyer revamped Linebacker. He reduced the B-52 sortie rate to thirty aircraft a day, a total that U-Tapao alone could handle. Logistical considerations favored conducting strikes from only one base, and U-Tapao's four-hour missions eliminated the need for air refueling. To protect his bombers, Meyer targeted SAM storage facilities; intelligence showed that Northern gunners possessed no spare missiles at their firing sites. He also prohibited attacks in the immediate vicinity of Hanoi after the raid on the 21st produced the loss of two more B-52s. The bombers flew against Haiphong on the 22d and struck rail yards, storage facilities, and SAM sites in northeastern North Vietnam the next two days. Routing on these missions varied considerably. Escorted by Navy fighters, B-52s traveled over the Tonkin Gulf on the 22d, feinting an attack on Hanoi before turning north to strike Haiphong. On the 23d, the bombers again approached over water but flew through the Chinese buffer zone to reach their targets. B-52s on the 24th traveled overland from west to east before turning south for their bomb run. No B-52s were lost from the 22d to the 24th, and only one bomber received damage. Following the mission on the 24th, Nixon directed a thirty-six-hour bombing pause for Christmas.[32]

Although hoping that the North Vietnamese would respond to the respite with an offer to negotiate, the President had no intention of halting attacks before receiving such a commitment. He cabled Hanoi on 22 December and requested a meeting for 3 January. If Northern leaders agreed, Nixon declared, he would stop bombing north of the 20th parallel on 31 December for the duration of the talks. Hanoi did not respond, and the President ordered a massive raid against both Hanoi and Haiphong for the 26th.

The 26 December assault was Linebacker II's most ambitious, with both Andersen and U-Tapao contributing large numbers of aircraft. Instead of attacking throughout the night, as had bombers on the first three days, 120 B-52s struck ten different targets in fifteen minutes. Four waves totalling seventy-two aircraft simultaneously attacked Hanoi from four directions. Concurrently, two waves of fifteen bombers each struck Haiphong from the east and south, and eighteen B-52s raided the Thai Nguyen Rail Yard north of Hanoi. A multitude of SAMs streaked through the dark sky, revealing that Hanoi's defenders had used the five-day intermission to bolster their armaments. One crewmember counted twenty-six missiles launched at his aircraft before losing track because of the rapidity of fire. Nevertheless, SAMs claimed only two bombers, a loss rate of 1.66 percent.[33]

On the morning of the 27th, Hanoi notified Nixon that talks could resume in Paris on 8 January.[34] The North Vietnamese contended that Le Duc Tho's ill health had prevented earlier discussions. The Communists confirmed their "constantly serious negotiating attitude" and "willingness to settle the remaining questions with the U.S. side." To Nixon, the message signaled that Hanoi had had enough. Before he replied, Hanoi forwarded another message expressing a desire to resume technical talks after the cessation of bombing and emphasizing that Le Duc Tho would meet Kissinger on 8 January. The President responded on the 27th that discussions between Kissinger and Tho's experts must begin on 2 January. Formal negotiations would start on the 8th, with a time limit attached, and the North Vietnamese would not deliberate on matters covered by the basic agreement. Acceptance of these procedures would result in an end to bombing north of the 20th parallel within thirty-six hours.[35]

Despite the North's apparent willingness to negotiate, Nixon did not curtail Linebacker. Sixty B-52s, thirty each from U-Tapao and Andersen, raided targets surrounding Hanoi, plus the Lang Dang Rail Yard near the Chinese border, on 27 December. Except for Haiphong's deletion, the attack was a small-scale version of the previous night's assault. Haiphong's absence from the strike list was symptomatic of a new problem for Air Force planners: a lack of suitable targets. B-52s had achieved sufficient destruction of Haiphong's oil storage center, power transformer, and rail yards to exempt the port city from further attacks. Located on the northeast rail line to China, the Lang Dang complex was an interdiction target raided during Linebacker I. The North Vietnamese fired more SAMs on the 27th than the night before, although aircrews found the gunners less accurate. Still, SAMs downed two bombers, the campaign's final losses.[36]

Sixty bombers flew on both 28 and 29 December, concentrating on SAM storage sites around Hanoi and on the Lang Dang Rail Yard. Varied approaches to the targets continued. Major Clark, who flew three Linebacker missions, felt that by the 29th B-52 tactics were solid.[37] The bombers encountered feeble resistance on the 28th and 29th from enemy defenses. "By the tenth day," Captain Allen remembered, "there were no missiles, there were no MiGs, there was no AAA [antiaircraft artillery]—there was no threat. It was easy pickings."[38] As many crews expectantly prepared for a knockout blow, General Johnson received notification that the 29 December mission was Linebacker's last.

Hanoi's answer to Nixon's proposal had arrived in Washington on 28 December. Northern leaders accepted the President's provisions, stressing their desire to negotiate seriously. Nixon halted all bombing north of the 20th parallel at 1900 hours Washington time on the 29th. The following day he announced the resumption of talks. He also informed Hanoi that the United States approached the coming negotiations "with great seriousness":

The U.S. side wants to again affirm that it will make one final major effort to see whether a settlement within the October framework can be worked out. The U.S. side wants to point out that Dr. Kissinger will not be able to spend more than four days in Paris on this occasion. . . . The decision must be made now whether it is possible to move from a period of hostility to one of normalization.[39]

Controls on Linebacker II

Nixon's reliance on B-52s to produce a rapid settlement contributed to Linebacker II's unique political, military, and operational restrictions. "I fear that . . . in the past . . . our political objectives have not been achieved because of too much caution on the military side," the President wrote early in the campaign. He told Moorer: "I don't want any more of this crap about the fact we couldn't hit this target or that one." To attain higher levels of destruction, Nixon permitted B-52s to attack certain storage facilities raided by fighters during Linebacker I. While most bomber targets lay on Hanoi's outskirts, the President sanctioned strikes against the Bac Mai communication center and storage area in the capital's heart. B-52s also raided Hanoi's commercial airfield, which served as a MiG-21 base. The Lang Dang Rail Yard, a target on four missions, was inside the Chinese buffer zone. Although he controlled the campaign's pace, Nixon offered only general guidance regarding targets. The Joint Chiefs, in contrast, sometimes provided Meyer with specific objectives. Meyer submitted all targets to the chiefs for validation, yet the SAC commander retained a free hand in selecting tactics. Moorer asserted shortly after Linebacker II's conclusion: "The commander of the Strategic Air Command and his staff . . . were not told how to do the job; they were told what to do."[40]

General Meyer's tactical deployment resulted from the continued concern for civilian casualties. Nixon felt that indiscriminate raids might disrupt détente and persuade the Soviets and Chinese to increase support to the North. As no B-52 had flown over Hanoi before 18 December, Meyer demanded routes and formations for the first days that minimized the chances of collateral damage. Major George Thompson, Director of Targets for 8th Air Force Intelligence, later observed that "we were not allowed to bomb many targets much more lucrative because of [possible] civilian casualties." Using smart bombs during a rare period of good weather, 7th Air Force F-4s attacked Thompson's choice for the North's most important target, the Hanoi Rail Yard. F-4s also destroyed Hanoi's SAM assembly plant. The Joint Chiefs prohibited Meyer from striking the complex, claiming that B-52s would kill 24,000 civilians with their misses. Eighth Air Force briefers instructed radar navigators to bring their bombs back unless they were 100 percent sure of their aiming point. All B-52 target maps contained the locations of schools, hospitals, and POW camps, and briefers cautioned crews when bomb runs neared such facilities.[41]

Despite efforts to restrict casualties, Nixon realized that his use of B-52s signaled an escalation in the war that would not go unnoticed by the public. He underestimated, however, the intensity of the reaction to the raids. Kissinger's declaration "peace is at hand," followed by the resumption of talks, led many Americans to speculate that the war would end by Christmas. Instead, as the holiday season neared, Kissinger announced little progress in Paris, and Nixon, without explanation, unleashed the war's greatest aerial assault. "How did we get in a few short weeks from a prospect for peace that 'you can bank on,'" a 28 December *Washington Post* editorial asked, "to the most savage and senseless act of war ever visited, over a scant ten days, by one sovereign people upon another?" The *New York Times*'s Tom Wicker labeled the raids "Shame on Earth." Much of the world press concurred with these viewpoints. The London *Times* noted that Nixon's action was "not the conduct of a man who wants peace very badly," while Hamburg's *Die Zeit* concluded that "even allies must call this a crime against humanity."[42]

The surge of domestic criticism dismayed both military and civil leadership. "I cannot understand why it is that people in this country are so quick to accuse their own country of taking these kinds of actions [obliteration bombing] when they simply are not true," Admiral Moorer lamented in January 1973. Nixon perceived the uproar as the media's first opportunity to strike out against his reelection. Yet both refused to answer the charges leveled at them during Linebacker: Announcing that most B-52 targets lay on Hanoi's periphery would, Moorer feared, allow the Communists to mass SAMs for maximum effect, and the President believed that any hint of the attacks' purpose would appear as an ultimatum and that the North Vietnamese would delay their response to save face.[43] Still, he could not ignore the public outcry. The clamor reinforced his belief that the campaign was his last chance to end the war "honorably."

Congress confirmed Nixon's conviction by echoing the public uproar. Senator Edward Kennedy stated that the raids "should outrage the conscience of all Americans." Senator William Saxbe of Ohio contended that Nixon had "taken leave of his senses." Vowing to force an end to the war, Senate Majority Leader Mike Mansfield termed the bombing "a Stone Age tactic." Democratic Representatives expressed like sentiments. On 2 January 1973, the day before Congress convened, the House Democratic Caucus voted 154 to 75 to cut off all funds for Southeast Asian military operations, contingent upon a prisoner release and the safe withdrawal of American troops. Two days later the Senate Democratic Caucus passed a similar measure, 36 to 12. Nixon approved Kissinger's plan to threaten future Linebacker-type air raids if the Communists again proved intransigent in Paris. Yet he warned Kissinger that "as far as our internal planning is concerned we cannot consider this to be a viable option."[44]

SAC's large-scale participation in Linebacker II produced distinctive command and control problems that further limited the air campaign. Brigadier General Harry Cordes, SAC's Deputy Chief of Staff for Intelligence, noted that 7th Air Force Commander General John W. Vogt "was furious that the B-52s had taken over the primary role and that SAC was selecting its own targets." Cordes added that Navy air commanders shared Vogt's attitude. The Joint Chiefs assigned 7th Air Force and Navy Task-Force 77, located in the Tonkin Gulf, to escort the bombers. Vogt complained to Meyer on 24 December that the delay in receiving essential SAC information prevented the 7th Air Force from providing proper escort. He demanded notice of targets, routes, axes of attack and cell call signs a minimum of eighteen hours prior to bomb release. Eighth Air Force planners also desired a quicker receipt of strike information. On 25 December, Meyer gave the 8th Air Force authority to select axes of attack and withdrawal routes, yet he retained control over target selection. Major Thompson recalled that the preliminary target list once arrived from Offutt three and a half hours prior to takeoff, requiring the 8th Air Force staff to plan the mission in minimum time. Crews were waiting in their aircraft when they received their target packages.[45]

Many crewmen cast barbs in SAC Headquarters' direction, although for all members of Strategic Air Command Linebacker II was a new experience. Planners designed the campaign based on the five B-52 raids over the North in April that had produced no losses. Aside from those attacks, crews had minimal experience flying in a hostile environment. Major Clyde E. Bodenheimer, an 8th Air Force staff officer, recalled that the routine missions over South Vietnam without a threat "were not very exciting." In contrast, the first three days of Linebacker II were a shock. The number of daily sick call patients at Andersen's clinic rose from a precampaign average of between thirty and forty to between fifty-five and sixty. After 19 December crews at both Andersen and U-Tapao questioned aircraft routing at premission briefings. The Andersen Officers' Club was perhaps the best indicator of Linebacker's effect on crews. Major Clark described the club's atmosphere as "uninteresting" and "desultory" before the raids. "By the second day [of Linebacker II]," Clark reflected, "you would walk in there and you could smell the fear. Guys were hanging on each other and just revalidating the fact that they're still alive, and they were getting all that fear out in the open."[46]

As in Linebacker I, enemy defenses were Linebacker II's most significant operational restriction. Whereas MiGs provided a great threat during the earlier Linebacker, thirty-two operational SAM sites furnished the Northern defensive punch in the "Eleven-Day War." The Communists fired approximately one thousand SA-2 missiles, claiming all fifteen B-52s lost and forcing the Air Force to change tactics. SAC Headquarters designed the simultaneous attacks on 26 December to saturate the North's command and control net plus minimize exposure to enemy fire. To guarantee that crews did not sacrifice the mutual ECM (electronic countermeasures) capability inherent in a three-ship cell formation, Colonel James M. McCarthy, Andersen's 43d Strategic Wing Commander, threatened to court-martial any pilot who broke formation to evade SAMs. General Meyer reiterated this warning during his trip to Andersen shortly after Linebacker II ended. Still, some pilots continued evasive maneuvers, and Captain Allen recalled that "there were some of the goddamnedest gyrations I have ever seen done with B-52s to avoid the SAMs." In descending to evade the missiles, pilots risked being hit by AAA, although flak damaged only one bomber. Northern fighters played an almost passive role during Linebacker II. Bomber crews reported few MiG attacks, none of which caused damage, while B-52 tail gunners downed two enemy aircraft. The North Vietnamese used MiGs as scouts, sending them aloft to report the bombers' heading, altitude, and air speed to SAM sites. A Russian trawler off Guam provided Hanoi with a seven-hour warning prior to missions from Andersen.[47]

In addition to tactical variations, the Air Force adopted other methods to counter enemy defenses. An average of eighty-five support aircraft, performing hunter-killer, escort, and ECM duties, accompanied the bombers each night. On 23 December B-52s began striking SAM sites, and on the 28th they initiated raids against missile storage areas. During the latter stages of Linebacker, General Johnson restricted missions in high-threat zones to his D-model bombers possessing the latest ECM gear to deflect SAMs. The campaign started before the modification of many G-models, which suffered six of the eleven losses in the first four days. To assure an adequate number of fresh crews at U-Tapao, Johnson transferred twenty-two D-model crews there from Andersen after the Thai base received the brunt of the campaign on the 22d. Because of the shorter missions, many U-Tapao crews had previously flown every night of Linebacker. Seventh Air Force reinitiated its program of daily mission critiques on 20 December. Representatives from both 7th and 8th Air Force attended the conferences, focusing on coordination between bombers and fighters as well as tactical countermeasures.[48]

Weather proved almost as great an operational restraint as enemy defenses. Nixon ordered the assault in the midst of the winter monsoon season. While the adverse conditions had no effect on the all-weather B-52s, the monsoons severely limited bombing by fighters. The eleven-day span produced only twelve daylight hours acceptable for precision attacks, occurring on the afternoons of 21, 27, and 28 December. F-111s supplemented hunter-killer strikes in poor weather, and B-52s raided some targets normally requiring precision ordnance. An Air Force study concluded that the "attempts to use all-weather systems against small area or point targets proved valueless. . . . These efforts . . . in retrospect should have been applied to area targets for maximum effect."[49]

Bombing Results

From 18 to 29 December 1972, B-52s flew 729 sorties against thirty-four targets north of the 20th parallel and dropped 15,237 tons of bombs. Combining for 1,216 sorties, Air Force and Navy fighters delivered roughly 5,000 tons of ordnance. Rail centers and storage areas received the bulk of the B-52 effort. Bombers destroyed 383 pieces of rolling stock and inflicted 500 cuts in rail lines, completely disrupting rail traffic within 10 miles of Hanoi. Aircraft also demolished 191 storage warehouses. Electric power generating capacity fell from 115,000 to 29,000 kilowatts, and the raids reduced POL supplies by one-fourth. In targeting only three bridges, air chiefs showed that Linebacker II was more than an interdiction campaign. They relied on interdiction during the previous Linebacker, as well as continued mining, to complement the December bombing's effect on resupply activities.[50]

Considering the damage inflicted, Linebacker II caused few civilian casualties, but it did unsettle the North's urban populace. Hanoi's mayor claimed 1,318 civilians killed and 1,216 wounded, while Haiphong reported 305 dead. The low toll resulted from both B-52 targeting and evacuations. Acknowledging the raids' accuracy, the journalist Tammy Arbuckle observed during a trip to Hanoi in March 1973: "Pictures and some press reports had given a visitor the impression Hanoi had suffered badly in the war—but in fact the city is hardly touched." Evacuations from the capital occurred throughout Linebacker II. Michael Allen, a writer who was in Hanoi with Telford Taylor on Christmas day, watched numerous buses evacuate people to the countryside. Individuals remaining in Hanoi received only an hour or two of sleep a night, their nerves strained by the continual attacks. Foreigners in the Gia Lam airport discovered workers wandering around completely disoriented following a strike. American prisoners witnessed a more graphic consequence of Linebacker II. Commander James B. Stockdale, a prisoner for more than seven years, recalled that

> . . . when the ground shook, and the plaster fell from the ceiling . . . the guards cowered in the lee of the walls, cheeks so ashen you could detect it even from the light of the fiery sky. . . . By day, interrogators and guards would inquire about our needs solicitously. The center of Hanoi was dead—even though like our prisons, thousands of yards from the drop zone. We knew the bombers knew where we were, and felt not only ecstatically happy, but confident. The North Vietnamese didn't. . . . They knew they lived through last night, but they also knew that if our forces moved their bomb line over a few thousand yards they wouldn't live through tonight.[51]

Less than one month after Linebacker II, Secretary of State William P. Rogers signed what Nixon called "an honorable agreement."[52] The campaign contributed substantially to both Hanoi's and Saigon's acceptance of an accord. The "Eleven-Day War" was not the only reason for a settlement, but it was a primary one. Nixon's threat of another Linebacker if the North refused to settle helped persuade the Politburo to accept terms that included some of Thieu's provisions.[53] His promise of a future Linebacker should Hanoi violate the agreement, combined with the Congressional furor stemming from the raids, finally gained Thieu's support.

After Linebacker II, circumstances argued strongly that Hanoi should work to prevent additional bombing. Détente prevented the North from receiving increased Soviet assistance, and Hanoi had not fully recovered from Linebacker I. Bombing continued unabated against Northern troops in the South after Linebacker I ended, and Linebacker II destroyed many of the supplies stockpiled above the 20th parallel since 23 October. Having undergone nine months of continual bombing, North Vietnamese General Tran Van Tra, commander of Communist forces in the southern half of South Vietnam, later recalled: "Our cadres and men were fatigued, we had not had time to make up for our losses, all units were in disarray, there was a lack of manpower, and there were shortages of food and ammunition. . . . The troops were no longer capable of fighting."[54] The survival of the Northern army was essential if Hanoi was to maintain control over Southern territory. Linebacker II, combined with mining, threatened to paralyze that force by preventing necessary matériel from flowing to it.

While impressed by Linebacker II's destruction, the North Vietnamese were also impressed by its magnitude. In eleven days aircraft dropped 13 percent of the tonnage delivered during the five months of Linebacker I. Unlike the earlier campaign, Linebacker II continued night after night regardless of weather. Defenses failed to deter the attacks. Only when Hanoi promised to negotiate did the raids stop, and "the threat of renewed and effective bombing," an American negotiator recalled, "was implied in all that we signed with Hanoi." The Politburo could not afford to ignore that threat. Continued bombing would not only further disrupt an already disoriented populace but also endanger its survival. The North lacked sufficient food reserves to endure a sustained air campaign. At the January Paris meetings, Kissinger observed that Le Duc Tho's "mood and businesslike approach was as close to October as we have seen since October. What has brought us to this point," he continued, "is the President's firmness and the North Vietnamese belief that he will not be affected by either congressional or public pressures. Le Duc Tho has repeatedly made these points to me."[55]

The havoc created by Linebacker II prevented Hanoi from achieving an eleventh-hour victory over the United States. After

Linebacker I, the North Vietnamese repaired the rail lines leading to China, which resulted in a matériel influx. Guaranteed a short-term logistical base, Northern leaders then worked to keep Thieu's changes out of an agreement. Saigon's dissatisfaction with the October accord, together with the imminent return of Congress, provided an opportunity to achieve the triumph denied Giap's army. Realizing that Nixon would attempt to modify the October settlement, Le Duc Tho redoubled his efforts to secure the original accord. His renewed confrontation with Kissinger offered the chance to prolong negotiations until Congress reconvened in January, when its members might terminate funds for the war. Such action would not only assure American withdrawal but also halt the flow of American arms to the South. Northern leaders believed that Thieu's government could not survive if abandoned by the United States, and Nixon showed no sign of willingness to let that happen. Surmising that the President might resume Linebacker I to spur talks, they ordered the evacuation of old people, women, and children from Hanoi on 4 December. In the midst of the winter monsoon season, with sufficient matériel, the North Vietnamese felt secure against the resumption of fighter attacks north of the 20th parallel.[56]

Northern leaders did not expect Linebacker II, and its magnitude tempered their response. On the eve of the assault, Radio Hanoi repeated Le Duc Tho's demand that the United States sign the October agreement without further delay. Vice Foreign Minister Nguyen Co Thach, North Vietnam's representative to the technical discussions accompanying Kissinger's private sessions, provided Hanoi's first reaction to the bombing. Kissinger termed Thach's 20 December three-day adjournment of talks "a minimum gesture under the circumstances." Nguyen Minh Vy's 21 December denunciation of the raids at the public discussions also included a promise to renew talks on the 28th. Arriving in Washington on 26 December, Hanoi's call for a resumption of the Kissinger–Tho sessions prompted the National Security Adviser to comment: "We had not heard such a polite tone from the North Vietnamese since the middle of October." Nixon answered on the 27th with his conditions for a return to negotiations. The Politburo's acceptance arrived in Washington in twenty-four hours—"an amazing feat," Kissinger noted, "considering the time needed for transmission to and from Paris and the time differences."[57]

While Hanoi's willingness to negotiate did not necessarily indicate a desire for an agreement, Northern actions in Paris matched Nixon's zeal to end the war. At the 2 January technical session, State Department representative William Sullivan remarked that the Northern delegation "did not comport itself like a victorious outfit which had just defeated the U.S. Strategic Air Force." Le Duc Tho announced after arriving in Paris that he would make a final effort for a rapid settlement, although his meeting with Kissinger on the 8th did not take place in the most cordial atmosphere. Tho bared his true intentions the next day. He told Kissinger that

> . . . in order to prove our seriousness and good will to find a rapid solution, we should adequately take into account each other's attitude. Naturally, there should be mutual concessions and there should be reciprocity. If one keeps one's own stand then no settlement is possible.[58]

To Kissinger, "it quickly became apparent that Tho had come to settle." The Northern delegate accepted the 23 November draft agreement, including the twelve concessions withdrawn in December. Tho agreed to having explicit reference to the DMZ in the treaty, but Kissinger approved its definition as "a provisional and not a political and territorial boundary." Tho also accepted the removal of the phrase "administrative structure" to describe the National Council of Reconciliation and Concord. By 13 January the technical advisers had completed the accord's text, and Nixon scheduled a halt to all bombing for the 15th. Reflecting on Hanoi's January motives, the National Security Adviser concluded: "It was a measure of the extremity in which Hanoi found itself that it felt it could not wait for the almost certain aid cutoff and proceeded with the negotiations."[59] Yet Nixon and Kissinger too were eager to hammer out a settlement, and the January agreement's differences from the October accord were largely cosmetic.

In deciding to settle, Hanoi did not surrender the goal of unifying Vietnam. The Politburo gambled that Nixon's commitment to "honor" prevented him from discarding many of Thieu's demands and that the President's fear of public and Congressional denunciation forestalled a massive military response. The bid failed. Nixon answered Le Duc Tho's stalling with Linebacker II on 18 December. Soon afterward, Hanoi learned of the President's ultimatum to Thieu.[60] By 29 December the North had exhausted its SAM supply, making further defense impossible. Linebacker's pummeling compelled the Politburo to negotiate, the only alternative to continued attacks that Nixon offered. Threatening to renew Linebacker if the

Communists again proved intransigent, the President increased bombing below the 20th parallel. January bomber efforts against Giap's battered army jumped from thirty-five strikes a day to fifty.[61]

Hanoi could ill afford destruction of those forces that provided a base for future activity in the South. A negotiated agreement, however, presented the Politburo with three advantages. First and most important, a settlement would end American involvement, and the North could return to Truong Chinh's protracted war policy without interruption. Meanwhile, Congress might still curtail funding for Saigon. Second, an accord would "legally" permit Hanoi to maintain troops in the South. Finally, an agreement would involve minimal loss of face. Knowing that Nixon planned to settle regardless of Thieu's intentions, Northern leaders felt that they would concede nothing to Saigon by signing an accord. Hanoi's major concessions remained those surrendered to Kissinger in October, and the Politburo rightly perceived that Thieu had minimal impact on the January terms.

At his 24 January news conference, Kissinger voiced approval of the agreement. "It is clear," he said, "there is no legal way by which North Vietnam can use military force against South Vietnam." The National Security Adviser then added: "Now, whether that is due to the fact there are two zones temporarily divided by a provisional demarcation line or because North Vietnam is a foreign country with relation to South Vietnam—that is an issue which we have avoided making explicit in the agreement, and in which ambiguity has its merits."[62] In all likelihood the Politburo concurred.

Besides contributing to Hanoi's acceptance of Nixon's terms, Linebacker II spurred Thieu's endorsement of the January agreement. His approval did not come easily. Asserting that he could not accept Northern troops in the South, Thieu rejected the mid-December ultimatum carried by Haig. Nixon believed that a break with the Southern leader was justifiable, yet he hesitated to take such a step. "I was still reluctant to allow our annoyance with him to lead us to do anything that might bring about Communist domination of South Vietnam," the President later explained. On 5 January he again wrote Thieu, emphasizing that Hanoi's acceptance of the 18 December proposal would produce a settlement. Nixon warned that many Congressmen, angered by Linebacker II, would vote to stop Saigon's funding if Thieu spurned an accord. The President ended by reiterating his November pledge: "Should you decide, as I trust you will, to go with us, you have my assurance of continued assistance in the post-settlement period and that we will respond with full force should the settlement be violated by North Vietnam." Thieu's 7 January reply was noncommittal.[63]

With the agreement's text completed, Nixon sent Haig to Saigon on 14 January in a final attempt to gain Thieu's approval. The general delivered a letter from the President that stated:

> I have . . . irrevocably decided to proceed to initial the Agreement on January 23, 1973 and to sign it on January 27, 1973 in Paris. I will do so, if necessary, alone. In that case I shall have to explain publicly that your Government obstructs peace. The result will be an inevitable and immediate termination of U.S. economic and military assistance which cannot be forestalled by a change of personnel in your government.[64]

Arguing for Thieu's consent, the President again promised to react strongly if the North Vietnamese violated the agreement. On 17 January Thieu requested an additional negotiating session to secure changes. Nixon replied that further changes were impossible and demanded a final response from Thieu by the morning of 20 January. On that day the South Vietnamese President dispatched Foreign Minister Tram Van Lam to Paris to participate in the negotiations. Kissinger deemed this measure "a face-saving formula" indicating consent for the agreement.[65]

Thieu's stalling resulted more from a desire to salvage prestige than from opposition to an accord. He had told his military chiefs in November to prepare for a cease-fire by Christmas. Haig left Saigon in that month convinced Thieu knew that total intransigence would lead to a loss of aid. The Southern leader realized that Nixon would not seek an agreement significantly improved over the October draft, although he also understood that Nixon's commitment to "honor" prevented the President from forsaking Saigon until the last possible moment. Similarly, Thieu's desire to demonstrate independence precluded an early acceptance of Nixon's terms. Linebacker II gave credibility to both the promise of continued American support and Nixon's willingness to use air power to uphold an agreement. The campaign further sparked a Congressional furor to end the war. Regardless of whether Congress would have ended Saigon's funding had Linebacker II not occurred, the uproar caused by the campaign made the termination of funds a virtual certainty if Thieu rejected a negotiated settlement. The Southern leader could not risk losing the backing that he considered essential for survival. Thus, he acquiesced to the accord, but not before Nixon's deadline.[66]

American civilian and military leaders viewed Linebacker II as a successful application of military force. "The bombing had done its job," Nixon later remarked. Kissinger asserted that the air campaign "speeded the end of the war," adding "even in retrospect I can think of no other measure that would have." Many leaders believed that Linebacker II vindicated not only strategic bombing as a political tool but also the tenets of Air Force bombing doctrine. Senator Barry Goldwater declared in February 1973: "Let us hope that the strategic bombing lesson of the 12 days in December does not escape us as we plan for the future. Airpower, specifically strategic airpower, can be decisive when applied against strategic targets—industrial and military—in the heartland of the enemy regardless of the size of the nation." Admiral Moorer concurred, contending that "airpower, given its day in court after almost a decade of frustration, confirmed its effectiveness as an instrument of national power—in just nine and a half flying days." SAC generals Meyer and Johnson shared Moorer's opinion, as did 7th Air Force's General Vogt. Many air commanders likened Linebacker II to the Joint Chiefs' ninety-four-target plan and concluded that such an effort in the spring of 1965 would have won the war.[67]

The conviction that air power played the decisive role in gaining an agreement permeated the Air Force. Commanders cited crew member participation in Linebacker II on officer effectiveness reports. A recommendation from the 474th Tactical Fighter Wing for a Presidential Unit Citation stressed the F-111 wing's contribution to the campaign. The 30 June 1973 request stated: "They [aircrews] attacked vital targets in the enemy heartland, and were subjected to some of the most concentrated anti-aircraft defenses faced by U.S. strike forces. Their efforts have directly assisted in securing peace with honor in Southeast Asia." Major Bodenheimer, who viewed the assault from 8th Air Force Headquarters, maintained that Linebacker II "was *the* single, most important action in the Vietnam campaign which convinced the North Vietnamese that they should negotiate." Major Clark felt that the operation in which he flew "was something that had been long overdue, because in an eleven-day period we brought [North Vietnam's] civilization . . . to a grinding, screeching halt." Clark did not, however, think that Linebacker II gained "peace with honor." "There was no way we could do that," he argued. "The fact that we retreated nullifies the words."[68]

Nixon disagreed with Clark's assessment and pointed to the provisions of the January accord. "I knew that the agreement contained serious weaknesses," the President reflected. "But I believed that on balance it was sound. . . . It was adequate to ensure the survival of South Vietnam—as long as the United States stood ready to enforce its terms."[69] The settlement achieved Nixon's positive political goal of an American withdrawal and gained the return of American prisoners. Meanwhile, the Linebacker campaigns helped provide the South Vietnamese with what the President termed a "decent interval . . . to demonstrate their inherent strength."[70] The bombing improved the South's chances for survival by assuring that Hanoi could not soon attempt a major military operation. It also contributed to Thieu's acceptance of the January accord. By highlighting the Congressional furor created by Linebacker II, Nixon shrewdly used his negative political objective to secure Thieu's support. The Christmas bombings also implied that Nixon's commitment to the South would continue after the departure of American troops.

Nixon's willingness to defend South Vietnam after Linebacker was never tested. When Giap's army crashed across the DMZ in March 1975, Nixon was no longer President, and Congress precluded a military response. The peace that Linebacker helped gain proved but an interval.

VII

Assessment

*The first, the supreme, the most far-reaching act of
judgment that the statesman and commander have to make
is [rightly to understand] the kind of war on which they are
embarking, neither mistaking it for, nor trying to turn it into,
something that is alien to its nature. This is the first of all
strategic questions and the most comprehensive.*

CARL VON CLAUSEWITZ[1]

*Strategic aerospace offense objectives are to neutralize or
destroy an enemy's war-sustaining capabilities or will to fight.
Aerospace forces may conduct strategic aerospace offense
actions, at all levels of conflict, through the systematic
application of force to a selected series of vital targets.*

AIR FORCE MANUAL 1-1
16 March 1984[2]

In his 1842 poem "Locksley Hall," Lord Tennyson foretold of
"airy navies" that "rain'd a ghastly dew" on their enemies. The
ability to annihilate nations through air power is no longer reverie;
Hiroshima has provided the ultimate validation for the theories of
Douhet, Trenchard, and Mitchell. Yet air power's ability to achieve
results through other than nuclear devastation remains uncertain.
The tremendous rush of technology—which has produced gargan-
tuan B-52s and sleek B-1s capable of carrying 30 tons of ordnance,
and supersonic fighters capable of directing laser-guided bombs into
a single warehouse in the heart of a densely populated city—has not
guaranteed military success. What it has done, however, is to create
a modern vision of air power that focuses on the lethality of its
weaponry rather than on that weaponry's effectiveness as a political
instrument. American civilian and military leaders entered Vietnam
convinced that bombing's lethality assured political results. They
never fully realized that air power's political efficacy varies according to many diverse elements, and that no specific formula guaran-

tees success. Indeed, if judged by their reluctance to face up to it, this lesson might prove the most difficult of all for air leaders to learn.

The air campaigns against North Vietnam differed in their effectiveness as political instruments, and the political objectives guiding them contributed to the disparity of results. President Lyndon Johnson turned to air power to help achieve his positive goal of an independent, stable, non-Communist South Vietnam. At the same time, his negative objectives—to prevent a third world war and to keep both domestic and world public attention focused away from Vietnam—limited Rolling Thunder. Johnson believed that carefully controlled bombing would ultimately compel Hanoi to end the war by making it too costly. Yet many of his advisers, who had a significant impact on Rolling Thunder's development, viewed bombing as a compromise means to achieve disparate ends. On the eve of the first Rolling Thunder mission, National Security Adviser McGeorge Bundy argued that bombing would bolster South Vietnamese morale; Ambassador Maxwell Taylor, that it would break Hanoi's will to fight; Secretary of State Dean Rusk, that it would secure bargaining leverage; and Secretary of Defense Robert S. McNamara, that it would convey America's political resolve to Hanoi. Additional reasons for bombing appeared once the campaign began.

President Richard Nixon's objectives in Vietnam differed from his predecessor's. Nixon's positive political goal was an American withdrawal that did not abandon the South to an imminent Communist takeover, and that aim was easier to attain than a stable South capable of independently preserving its existence. Even after he decided to court President Nguyen Van Thieu, Nixon's positive goals remained more limited than Johnson's. Nixon's chief counselor on Vietnam, National Security Adviser Henry Kissinger, agreed that bombing was necessary to secure those objectives, and the President did not allow other advisers to influence the Linebacker campaigns. Negative goals had a marginal impact on Nixon's application of air power. His détente with the Chinese and Soviets removed the threat of an expanded conflict, and the success of the Moscow summit, the continued departure of American ground troops, and the blatant nature of the Easter Offensive assured him of public support for Linebacker I. Although he took pains to keep that backing, he possessed a large measure of freedom to intensify the bombing. By December 1972 one primary negative aim—to end the war before the return of Congress—limited his application of air power, and he made use of that goal to heighten Linebacker II's effect on Thieu.

In the final analysis, Nixon's bombing was more effective than Johnson's because it was more threatening to North Vietnam's vital concerns. The lack of negative objectives allowed Nixon to expand the bombing until it threatened to wreck Hanoi's capability to fight by rendering its army impotent. Yet to assume that a Rolling Thunder unrestrained by political controls would have compelled Hanoi to end the conflict is to misunderstand both the nature of the Vietnam War prior to the 1968 Tet Offensive and the fundamental tenets of American strategic bombing doctrine.

Before the Tet Offensive, the Southern war was a guerrilla conflict. Viet Cong units composed five-sixths of the Communist army and intermingled with the local populace. Together with North Vietnamese troops, they fought an average of one day in thirty. The infrequency of combat produced external supply needs of only 34 tons of matériel daily, and no amount of bombing could stop this meager amount from reaching the South. In truth, Rolling Thunder could have affected Northern war-making capacity only by attacking two targets: people and food. The destruction of either the North's population centers or its agricultural system would have had a minimal impact on the war in the South, however. Whereas the threatened destruction of such targets during the Korean War had helped produce peace in 1953, Vietnam differed significantly from the earlier conflict. President Dwight Eisenhower's threat of nuclear holocaust was effective because it portended defeat for the Communists fighting in Korea; the prospect of North Vietnam's ruin did not guarantee a South Vietnamese victory. *Had* bombing raised the threshold of pain sufficiently so that Hanoi stopped backing the Viet Cong and ordered an end to the insurgency, the Viet Cong could still have refused to comply with Hanoi's wishes. The cessation of Northern support was no guarantee that Saigon could survive against the Viet Cong.

While the absence of negative political aims in 1965 would have generated an air campaign without political controls, the air chiefs' doctrinal and moral beliefs probably would have prevented unrestrained bombing. As a result of Air Corps Tactical School training, World War II experience, and postwar planning, air commanders believed that by attacking an enemy's economic vital centers they could destroy its war-making capability, which would in turn produce the loss of social cohesion and will to fight. The emphasis on wrecking industry persisted throughout Rolling Thunder. Underlying this doctrinal conviction were moral reservations about killing civilians. Although air leaders in World War II and Korea had begun direct attacks on morale, they had done so reluctantly, and only after attacks on capability failed to yield the desired results. In all cases, their attacks on will had come against targets also having a military value. The same was true in Vietnam. Despite the postwar claims of many air chiefs that they would have flattened Hanoi if given the opportunity, such assertions lack credibility. The historian Ronald Schaffer's observation that American air commanders in World War II "based military decisions at least partly on moral concerns" is valid for air leaders in Vietnam as well.[3] In all likelihood, the moral inhibitions of commanders will limit future American air offensives.

Nixon's Linebacker campaigns were effective political instruments not only because they lacked stringent political controls but also because the war's nature changed in 1972. After the decimation of the Viet Cong in the 1968 Tet Offensive, the North Vietnamese Army was the only military force capable of achieving the Politburo's goal of unification. Northern leaders strengthened that force for a massive invasion that they believed would overwhelm the South. In contrast to the stagnant conventional war in Korea from 1951 to 1953, in which bombing was of marginal utility, Hanoi's Easter Offensive was an all-out, conventional assault that made its army vulnerable to air power. For the first time in Vietnam, bombing conformed to Clausewitz's "principle of polarity": It attacked an objective that was essential for a Communist victory. Doctrine and morality, Rolling Thunder's two most significant military controls, now suited the conflict. In addition, laser-guided munitions enhanced bombing efficiency, and the Easter Offensive came just before the peak period of favorable flying weather. As long as Hanoi waged an unrestrained conventional war, Linebacker threatened much more than the North's ability to win; it also threatened the North's ability to defend itself.

Despite the war's transformation from 1965 to 1972, many air chiefs have viewed the conflict as a single entity in which both its nature and American objectives remained constant. When asked in July 1986 if the United States could have won in Vietnam, the retired General Curtis LeMay answered, "In any two-week period you want to mention." He elaborated:

You can remember what went on at the end, when the B-52s finally went up north and started to bomb up there. They bombed for about seven days, and the white flag practically went up. President Nixon stopped it right there to get our people out. Four or five more days would have ended the whole thing, but I think he was so disgusted and fed up with the opposition of the American people that he decided to just get the hell out of there, and that was it.[4]

LeMay's perception of Vietnam mirrors that of Admiral U. S. Grant Sharp and Air Force General William W. Momyer in their postwar examinations of the air campaigns against the North.[5] It also reflects that of Harry G. Summers, Jr., a retired Army colonel, in *On Strategy: A Critical Analysis of the Vietnam War.*[6] Summers asserts that the conflict became a conventional war when the North Vietnamese began sending troops south in 1964 and that the United States should have focused totally on destroying Hanoi's capacity to fight. He writes that the North Vietnamese, not the Viet Cong, were the primary enemy but omits the fact that the overwhelming number of Communist troops in the South prior to 1968 were Viet Cong. His answer to America's failure is that *more* force was necessary *sooner* to wreck Hanoi's war-making capability. While Summers focuses on ground combat, many air commanders accept his view of the war. His book is a text at both the Air Force's Air Command and Staff College and the Air War College.

Reinforcing the conviction that the war was homogeneous is an almost universal Air Force perception that political controls prevented air power from displaying its effectiveness until December 1972. An August 1986 article on Vietnam in *Air Force* magazine, the publication of the Air Force Association, contained the following introduction:

In mid-1964, Air Force and Navy airmen began fighting for approval of a large-scale air campaign against strategic targets in North Vietnam in order to end the war quickly. But timorous military amateurs who were setting policy in Washington both feared unlikely Chinese intervention and believed that close support of ground forces was the way to victory. It was not until eight years, thousands of lives, and billions of dollars later that a major air campaign in the North—Linebacker II—was approved, leading to a cease fire in eleven days.[7]

This commentary implies not only that victory would have resulted from executing the Joint Chiefs' ninety-four-target scheme but that the President *should* have given military leaders free rein to apply air power as they saw fit. Sharp makes precisely this point in his account of the air war: "Our air power did not fail us; it was the decision makers. . . . Just as I believe unequivocally that the civilian authority is supreme under our Constitution, so I hold it reasonable that, once committed, the political leadership should seek, and in the main, heed the advice of the military professionals in the conduct of military operations."[8] Like the majority of Vietnam air chiefs, Sharp had participated in World War II, and that conflict has colored his thoughts—and those of many others—on Vietnam. Many air leaders continue to see unconditional surrender as the proper objective in war. "Once you're in a war, or you've made the decision to use military force to solve your problems, then you ought to use it," LeMay said in 1986.[9] The current edition of Air Force Manual 1-1, Basic Doctrine, stresses the perceived need for unbridled air power by quoting the Italian Air Marshal Giulio Douhet: "The employment of land, sea, and air forces in time of war should be directed towards one single aim: VICTORY. . . . The commander[s] of the Army, Navy, and Air Force should be given the greatest freedom of action in their respective sphere."[10]

Because most air chiefs think political limitations prevented air power from gaining a victory in Vietnam, they have not revamped the fundamentals of strategic bombing doctrine. Their unspoken belief is that since Linebacker II demonstrated bombing effectiveness, political leaders *must* realize that bombing can win limited wars if unhampered by political controls. Yet most air commanders fail to understand that the "Eleven-Day War" was a unique campaign for very limited ends, and its success stemmed from the destruction wrought by the previous Linebacker, the diplomacy of Nixon and Kissinger, and North Vietnamese fears that continued bombing would paralyze the army with which they persisted in waging a conventional war to gain territory. Instead of noting the polarity created by *both* Linebackers, air leaders point to Rolling Thunder as an example of how disregarding such principles of war as mass and surprise can lead to failure. Manual 1-1 states: "Aerospace doctrine flows from these principles and provides mutually accepted and officially sanctioned guidelines to the application of these principles in warfare."[11] Chief among these "guidelines" is the notion that destroying a "selected series of vital targets" *will* result in the loss of an enemy's war-making capacity or will to fight. Vital targets include, according to Manual 1-1, "concentrations of uncommitted elements of enemy armed forces, strategic weapon systems, command centers, communications facilities, manufacturing systems, sources of raw material, critical material stockpiles, power systems, transportation systems, and key agricultural areas."[12] Six of those ten targets are components of a nation's industrial apparatus, while three are components of its military establishment. Although agriculture is listed, past campaigns demonstrate that air chiefs would probably avoid attacks producing widespread starvation. The conviction that the manufacture and distribution of goods are the keys to war-fighting capability and will remains firmly planted as a cornerstone of Air Force thinking.

Air power was ineffective throughout the Johnson era of the Vietnam War because both civilian and military leaders possessed preconceived ideas that affected its application. Much like European political and military leaders in 1914, American officials in Vietnam encountered a war that differed from experience and expectations. Having reached political maturity in the atmosphere of the Cold War and witnessed Chinese intervention in Korea, Johnson and his advisers could not help but take a cautious approach to escalation in Vietnam. In addition, they had seen a Soviet retreat in Cuba that stemmed from the threat of air power, and they believed that a similar threat in Vietnam would ultimately deter Northern aggression. Air leaders thought that air power, applied against an enemy's war-making capability, could make a—if not *the*—key contribution to victory. As a result of these perceptions, Johnson and his advisers never defined a clear military objective for air power, and the objective the air chiefs themselves defined did not mesh with the President's political goals or the nature of the war. That prewar thinking had such a significant impact on Rolling Thunder is in retrospect regrettable, but understandable, given the intensity of the beliefs.

Difficult to fathom is the air chiefs' lingering conviction that their doctrine was right throughout Vietnam—and that it is right for the future. "Airpower can be strategically decisive if its application is intense, continuous, and focused on the enemy's vital systems," Momyer concludes in his analysis of American air operations since 1941.[13] Unlike generals after World War I, post-Vietnam air commanders have advocated no sweeping doctrinal changes. They parade Linebacker II as proof that bombing will work in limited war, and they dismiss the notion that too much force could trigger nuclear devastation. Yet no matter how remote the threat of nuclear war, American political leaders must respect that threat when fighting an enemy with superpower backing. Vietnam's political controls were no anomalies; the atomic bomb has made them a standard feature of war in the modern era. For the Air Force, the guerrilla struggle during most of the Vietnam War was an unacknowledged anomaly that may well reappear. If it does, military controls will again be likely to limit air power's efficacy as a political tool. Bombing doctrine remains geared to a fast-paced conventional war, and the conviction that such doctrine is appropriate for any kind of conflict permeates the service. Until air commanders and civilian officials alike realize that air power is unlikely to provide either "cheapness" or "victory" in a guerrilla war—and that success in such a conflict may well equate to stalemate—the prospect of an aerial Verdun will endure.

VIII

—————•—————

Epilogue

A *symmetric* is the current buzzword used to describe a type of warfare that has been with us much longer than the newfangled term. In its purest sense, asymmetric warfare is about ends, ways, or means—fighting for ends that do not match an opponent's objectives, fighting in ways that differ from an opponent's approach to war, or fighting with means different from an opponent's resources. In the *Quadrennial Defense Review Report* of 2001, however, the term most often describes a weaker power's use of an unanticipated means of striking at the vulnerability of a stronger power—in this case, the United States.[1] Any type of military force can be applied asymmetrically, including air power, as al Qaeda's terrorists demonstrated in devastating fashion on 11 September 2001. Yet, how might air power best be used *against* an asymmetric foe? The answer is not so different from the response to the fundamental question regarding *any* application of air power against *any* enemy—that is, how can it be used as an effective instrument of war?

Gauging air power's effectiveness is not an easy task. One reason for that difficulty is that no universal agreement exists on the meaning of *effectiveness*. Clausewitz offers perhaps the best means of measurement—how much does the military instrument help towards achieving the ultimate aim of winning the war? The author of *On War* equates "winning" to achieving the nation's political objectives, and that criterion guides the following framework for evaluating air power's effectiveness.[2] Like all true frameworks, though, this one does not provide a set of standard answers. Nor does it predict the future or offer a universal guide for success or failure. Instead, it offers a consistent approach for determining the value of air power in any circumstance. This approach includes a distinctive terminology that categorizes various air power applications, and those categories are used in ascertaining how effectively an application supports a political goal. Yet, determining air power's political effectiveness is not a straightforward proposition because political goals are not always straightforward. As the discussion of the framework makes clear, those goals can be either "positive" or "negative"—which in turn affects how well a particular air power application can achieve them.

While the categories of air power applications can be thought of as constants (the essence of how air power is applied in each of the categories does not change), five key variables affect the ability of each application to achieve success. Those variables include the (1) nature of the enemy, (2) type of war waged by the enemy, (3) nature of the combat environment, (4) magnitude of military controls, and (5) nature of the political objectives. The importance of each variable may change in different situations to yield different results. Thus, political and military leaders who would employ air power must understand exactly what the variables are and how they might blend to produce a particular outcome. The framework provides a method for analyzing air power applications— one that thoroughly dissects the variables and examines how their integration may affect air power's ability to achieve political success. Hopefully, it also offers practical considerations and cautions for the statesman contemplating the use of air power, as well as for the commander charged with transforming political goals into military objectives.

Air Power and Its Applications

Before this article delves into the framework's particulars, a definition of the elusive term *air power* seems in order. Brigadier General William "Billy" Mitchell specified it as "the ability to do something in the air," a description too vague to be useful.[3] Much better is the definition offered by two Britons—Air Marshal R. J. Armitage and Air Vice Marshal R. A. Mason—in their classic work *Air Power in the Nuclear Age*: "The ability to project military force through a platform in the third dimension above the surface of the earth."[4] Although Armitage and Mason admit that their definition contains gray areas (e.g., whether or not air power includes ballistic missiles or surface-to-air weapons), it suffices to guide the proffered framework. Indeed, their definition recognizes qualities of air power "that are sometimes overlooked"—specifically, its latent impact and its ability to apply force directly or to distribute it.[5] These characteristics form the basic distinctions used in the framework to categorize air power missions.

Air power's modes of application—the ways in which it can be used— are key components of the framework. For instance, air power poised for use but not actually engaged in an operation is a latent application— a potential impact—that corresponds to its deterrent value. In this case, air power is not directly used in a contingency; rather, its use is threatened. Examples of latent application abound: Adolf Hitler's references to the Luftwaffe during the reoccupation of the Rhineland in 1936 or the Munich crisis of 1938; President Harry Truman's deployment of B-29s to England during the Berlin airlift of 1948; President Dwight Eisenhower's warning of an atomic air attack against North Korea and Manchuria during the closing stages of the Korean War; and President John Kennedy's reliance on Strategic Air Command's B-52s and missile force during the Cuban missile crisis of 1962, among others.

Although the framework acknowledges such latent applications, it primarily concerns itself with the actual use of air power during a contingency. In a crisis, the application of air power is twofold, based upon the purpose of the mission: it is either *direct* or *indirect*, and it is either *auxiliary* or *independent*. The direct application of air power is the intended, lethal application—designed to expend ordnance. Dropping bombs, shooting missiles, and firing guns fall into this category of employment. Conversely, the indirect application of air power is the intended, nonlethal use—such as airlift, reconnaissance, electronic jamming, and aerial refueling.

Besides being direct or indirect, the use of air power is also either auxiliary or independent. Auxiliary air power supports ground or sea forces on a specific battlefield, whereas independent air power aims to achieve objectives apart from those sought by armies or navies at a specific location. The auxiliary form includes both close air support (CAS) and air attack against enemy forces on the battlefield that are not in contact with friendly troops.[6] So-called strategic bombing—aimed at an enemy's war-making potential before he can bring it to bear on the battlefield—exemplifies the independent application. Yet, the terms *strategic* and *tactical* often overlap and frequently blur. Many air attacks during the last half century's limited wars not only have affected the ebb and flow of a particular engagement, but also have had significant "strategic" consequences. For instance, American air strikes on mobile Scud launchers during the Persian Gulf War of 1991 aimed to wreck Iraq's tactical capability to launch ballistic missiles and to achieve the strategic goal of placating the Israelis, thus keeping them out of the conflict.

Because of such blurred distinctions, the terms *auxiliary* and *independent* seem better suited than *tactical* and *strategic* to delineate various air power applications. The former pair, however, is not completely pristine because the distinction between the two depends upon how the user defines the word *battlefield*. In modern war, a specific battlefield may extend for many hundreds of miles; in an insurgent conflict like Vietnam, the battlefield may be even larger. General William Westmoreland, commander of U.S. Military Assistance Command, Vietnam from 1964 to 1968, described his battlefield as "the whole country of South Vietnam."[7] Such a parameter may seem extreme, but it illustrates the fact that the definition of the battlefield depends to a large extent on the type of war being fought.[8] In a "conventional" conflict waged to seize or preserve territory, a battlefield's boundaries are likely to be much more distinct than those in a guerrilla war—especially one like Vietnam, in which insurgent forces fought infrequently.

According to the framework's terminology, each application of air power has two designations: direct or indirect, auxiliary or independent. For example, the American bombing of the ball-bearing factories in Schweinfurt, Germany during World War II was a direct/independent application; the Berlin airlift of 1948–49 was an indirect/independent application; the B-52 strikes around Khe Sanh, North Vietnam, during the siege of 1968 were a direct/auxiliary application; and the C-130 airlift of supplies into the beleaguered Marine base there was an indirect/auxiliary application. The dual designators describe the purpose of individual air power missions more clearly than the amorphous terms *tactical* and *strategic*. In addition, the framework's focus on the intent of the mission highlights air power's inherent flexibility by showing that one type of aircraft—whether designated bomber, fighter, airlift, and so forth—can participate in different applications.

But what about the air superiority mission? Where does it fit in the framework? The air control mission is *either* auxiliary *or* independent, *depending upon* the use made of the airspace. For instance, obtaining air superiority over Kuwait to enable allied ground forces to attack Iraqi troops represents a direct/auxiliary application. Achieving air superiority over Baghdad to enable aircraft to strike the city's key communication and electric power facilities constitutes a direct/independent application. On occasion, gaining air superiority can be *both* an auxiliary *and* an independent application. The achievement of daylight air superiority over the European continent as a result of the "Big Week" operations in February 1944 is one such example. The resultant air control guaranteed that American bomber operations would continue against German industry and provided the prerequisite protection for the Normandy invasion.

Some might contend that air superiority should be a separate category in the framework, in much the same way that "counterair" is a distinctive "air and space power function" in the current edition of the Air Force's basic doctrine manual.[9] The framework does not list air superiority separately because air superiority is not an end in itself. Air control—which

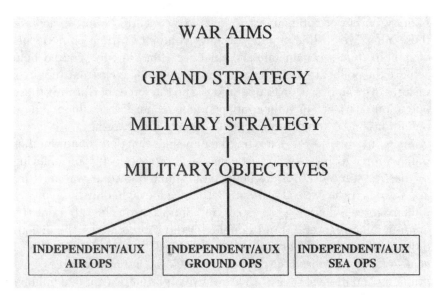

Figure 1. War Aims and the Application of Airpower

employs both direct and indirect methods—allows the direct, indirect, auxiliary, and independent applications to occur. In much the same fashion, the categorization of such indirect applications as aerial refueling, airlift, and reconnaissance depends upon the type of mission that they facilitate. For example, refueling fighters that provide CAS for ground forces would constitute an indirect/auxiliary application. Airlifting smart bombs for F-117 operations against targets in Belgrade, Yugoslavia during Operation Allied Force would be an indirect/independent application. And obtaining reconnaissance photographs of Iraqi frontline positions in Kuwait would be an indirect/auxiliary application.

However, achieving air superiority that facilitates a cross-channel invasion or securing reconnaissance photographs that lead to a breakthrough of Iraqi defenses does not necessarily imply a successful application of air power. Only one true criterion exists for evaluating the success of air power, regardless of whether it was direct, indirect, auxiliary, or independent. That criterion is the ultimate bottom line: *how well did the application contribute to achieving the desired political objective*? Did it, in fact, help win the war? Answering that question first requires a determination of what is meant by *winning*. The war aims must be defined, and the application of air power must be linked to accomplishing those objectives (fig. 1).

War aims—the political goals of a nation or organization at war—can range from limited to total. Grand strategy blends diplomatic, economic, military, and informational instruments in a concerted effort to achieve those aims. Meanwhile, military strategy combines various components of military force to gain military objectives that, in turn, should help achieve the political goals. Attaining the military objectives may require a mixture of ground, sea, or air operations, and the forces performing those operations may act in either independent or auxiliary fashion. These definitions and connections are relatively straightforward.

Such linkages, however, are not the only ones that determine whether military force—air power in particular—will prove effective in achieving the desired war aims. Besides being either limited or total, war aims are also *positive* or *negative*. *Positive* goals are achievable only by *applying* military force, while negative goals, in contrast, are achievable only by *limiting* military force.[10] For example, for the United States, the unconditional surrender of Germany in World War II was a positive political goal—one that required the destruction of Germany's armed forces, government, and the National Socialist way of life. America applied military force to achieve this goal, and few negative objectives limited its use of the military instrument. By comparison, in Kosovo the United States had both the positive objective of removing Serb forces and the negative objective of preserving the North Atlantic Treaty Organization, the latter goal restraining the amount of force that America could apply. A similar example comes from the Persian Gulf War of 1991, although in that conflict the American aim of preserving the alliance was both a positive and a negative goal. That is, President George H. W. Bush had to commit American military force against Iraqi Scuds to keep the Israelis out of the war, but if he applied too much force in the air campaign, he risked dissolving the coalition.

While some critics might equate the notion of negative objectives to constraints, to do so would be a mistake because such objectives have more significance than that. In fact, they have the same importance as positive goals. Failure to secure *either* the positive *or* the negative goals results in defeat; to achieve victory, *both* must be obtained. The United States would not have succeeded during either the Persian Gulf War or Kosovo had the coalitions that backed those enterprises collapsed. Of course, the contradictory nature of positive and negative goals creates a dilemma—what helps achieve a positive objective works against a negative one. In a limited war, negative objectives always exist; the more limited the war, the greater the number of negative objectives. As President Lyndon Johnson tragically found out in Vietnam, once his negative objectives eclipsed his positive goals, he lost the ability to achieve success with any military force—especially air power.

How do positive and negative objectives affect the application of air

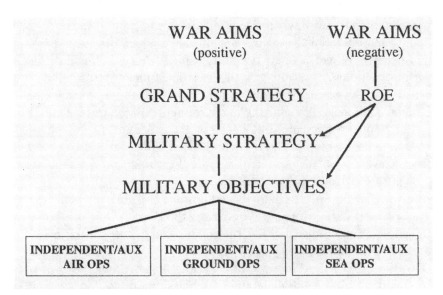

Figure 2. Effect of Negative Objectives on the Application of Airpower

power? On the one hand, the absence of negative goals encourages the design of an air campaign with few restrictions, such as World War II's Combined Bomber Offensive against Germany or Twentieth Air Force's assault on Japan. A preponderance of negative goals, on the other hand, limits the application of air power. Negative objectives have restrained American air campaigns in every major conflict since World War II— Korea, Vietnam, the Persian Gulf, Bosnia, Kosovo, and, most recently, Afghanistan. The restrictions typically appear in the form of rules of engagement, "directives issued by competent military authority that delineate the circumstances and limitations under which United States forces will initiate and/or continue combat engagement with other forces encountered."[11] The impetus for these directives comes from political leaders and their negative goals (fig. 2).

The greater the number of negative objectives—and the greater the significance attached to them by political leaders—the more difficult it becomes for air power to attain success in achieving the positive goals. This assessment is especially true of the direct, independent application of air power. If negative objectives outweigh positive goals, they will likely curtail—perhaps even prohibit—air power's ability to strike at the heart of an enemy state or organization. Yet, before a user of the framework points to this statement as a basic truth, he or she should realize that the measuring of positive versus negative objectives remains an inherently *subjective* activity. Typically, positive and negative goals are not quantifiable; even when they are, comparing numerical results will likely equate to comparing apples and orange juice. Moreover, positive and negative objectives may be stated explicitly or only implied, which further muddies the water in terms of evaluating results. Spelling out the objectives does not guarantee clarity, however, and the lack of clearly defined goals makes gauging their achievement particularly difficult. For instance, in the Persian Gulf War, the stated American positive goals of "immediate, complete, and unconditional withdrawal of Iraqi forces from Kuwait" and "restoration of Kuwait's legitimate government" were straightforward, and success in achieving them was easy to determine. In contrast, gauging success in the stated positive objective of obtaining the "security and stability of Saudi Arabia and the Persian Gulf" proved anything but straightforward during the conflict and has remained uncertain in the aftermath of the war.[12]

In the case of the Persian Gulf War, the negative objectives of preserving the coalition and maintaining public support, both in the United States and worldwide, did not prevent air power from helping remove Iraqi troops from Kuwait. Likewise, the various applications of air power in that war did not stop President Bush from achieving his negative goals, even though the direct, independent application that hit the Al Firdos bunker in Baghdad and the direct, auxiliary applications that produced deaths from friendly fire in Kuwait made achieving the negative objectives more difficult. Ultimately, that is how air power's effectiveness must be measured—in terms of *how well it supports the positive goals without jeopardizing the negative objectives.*

Key Variables

In determining when air power is most likely to help achieve the positive goals, five main variables, mentioned earlier, come into play.[13] These variables are complex factors that cannot be easily dissected; nor can one variable be considered in isolation from the others because the variables' effects are often complementary. Each has questions associated with it, and the questions provided are not all-inclusive—others will certainly come to mind. Answering the questions differently for one variable may cause the other variables to assume greater or lesser importance. No formula determines what variable may be the most important in any particular situation or how their combined effect may contribute to— or hinder—the achievement of the positive goals. If *all* five variables argue against a particular application of air power, however, that application is unlikely to be beneficial. The assumptions made in answering the questions for each variable are also of critical importance. If those assumptions are flawed, the assessment of the variables is likely to be flawed as well.

Nature of the Enemy

What military capabilities does the enemy possess? What is the nature of his military establishment? Is it a conscript force, volunteer military, or blend? Is the enemy population socially, ethnically, and ideologically unified? Where is the bulk of the populace located? Is the populace primarily urban or agrarian? What type of government or central leadership apparatus does the enemy have? What about the individuals who lead it? Are they strong or weak, supported by the populace or despised? Or is the populace ambivalent? What is its relationship with the military and its commanders? How resolute is the political leadership? The military? The populace? How does the enemy state or organization make its money? Is it self-sufficient in any area? How important is trade? What allies does the enemy have, and how much support do they provide? If more than one enemy is involved, these questions must be asked about each enemy and a determination made about which one poses the greatest threat.

Type of War Waged by the Enemy

This variable also affects air power's ability to achieve a positive political objective. Is the conflict a conventional war to seize or hold territory? Is it an unconventional guerrilla struggle? Is it an insurgency supported by a third party? Is the conflict a war of movement or a stagnant fight from fixed positions? How often does the fighting occur? In general, the direct application of air power, whether applied independently or as an auxiliary function, works best against an enemy waging a fast-paced, conventional war of movement. For example, the combination of independent and auxiliary attacks during the "dynamic" first year of the Korean War had a telling effect on the ability of the North Koreans and Chinese to fight. During the final two years of the conflict, when the North Koreans and Chinese fought sluggishly in a confined area along the 38th parallel, the direct application of air power made little headway in achieving President Truman's goal of a negotiated settlement that preserved a non-Communist South Korea.

Nature of the Combat Environment

What are the climate, weather, terrain, and vegetation in the hostile area? How might they affect applications of air power? Are adequate bases available? What are the distances involved in applying air power, and can those distances be overcome? What type of support is required?

Magnitude of Military Controls

This variable involves constraints placed on air power applications by military rather than political leaders. Ideally, no military controls exist, but that may or may not be the case—such controls can stem from many sources. Is there unity of command? What are the administrative arrangements for controlling air power, and do those arrangements conflict with operational control? The "route package" system that segregated Air Force from Navy airspace over North Vietnam and helped trigger competition between the two services for sorties stands as perhaps the most egregious example of how the lack of command unity can disrupt an air campaign. Doctrine can also lead to military controls. Is the doctrine that guides the various applications of air power adaptable to different circumstances? What are the personal beliefs of commanders regarding how best to apply air power? Personal convictions can play a significant role in limiting air power applications—witness the Korean War. During that conflict, the Army's General Matthew Ridgway, United Nations commander, prohibited the bombing of North Korean hydroelectric plants even though he had the authority to conduct the raids and had been encouraged to do so by the Joint Chiefs of Staff. Ridgway believed that such attacks might expand the scope of the war, but his successor, General Mark Clark, had no such misgivings.[14] One month after Clark took command, Air Force, Navy, and Marine aircraft attacked these facilities.

Nature of the Political Objectives

Often, this variable is the most important. Are the positive goals truly achievable through the application of military force? Is the application of air power necessary to obtain the positive objectives? How committed is the leadership that is applying air power to achieving the positive goals? How committed is its populace? Can leadership attain the positive goals without denying the negative objectives? How do the negative objectives limit air power's ability to help achieve the positive goals? The direct, independent application of air power seems to work best for a belligerent with no negative objectives—*provided a suitable type of enemy wages a suitable type of war in a suitable type of environment free of significant military restrictions.* For the United States in World War II, the suitable conditions existed. Few negative objectives or military controls limited the application of military force. Americans had a decent understanding of both enemies—the Germans and the Japanese—who fought as expected in environments that ultimately proved conducive to the direct, independent application of air power. However, since World War II, negative objectives have played prominent roles in guiding American war efforts. For the United States in the foreseeable future, the prospect of a war without them is remote indeed.

The Current Conflicts

In the on-going conflicts in Afghanistan and Iraq, the multi-faceted nature both of American political objectives and the conflicts themselves have made the effectiveness of air power applications difficult to gauge. In Afghanistan, those political goals might be listed as: (1) the destruction of Al Qaeda's ability to conduct global terrorism, which included denying Al Qaeda sanctuaries for launching attacks; (2) exacting retribution for the 11 September attacks ("bringing those responsible to justice"); (3) preventing the expansion/future development of global terrorism; and (4) maintaining maximum support for American actions from the rest of the world, especially the Islamic world.

In Iraq, distinct political goals guided the initial phase of America's war there: (1) the removal of Saddam Hussein from power to eliminate his perceived capability to engage in terrorist activities on a global scale, particularly with weapons of mass destruction, and (2) maintaining maximum support for American actions from the rest of the world, especially the Islamic world. Since removing Hussein from power, the United States has pursued two key goals in Iraq: (1) creating the conditions necessary to foster a democratic government; and (2) maintaining maximum support for American actions from the rest of the world, especially the Islamic world.

At first glance, the first three goals in Afghanistan, and the first goals in both phases of the war in Iraq, could be deemed positive, while the last goal, to "maintain maximum support for American actions from the rest of the world" could be labeled negative. Yet, while the third objective in Afghanistan has required lethal military force to destroy terrorist cells and prevent them from expanding, applying too much force could produce collateral damage or the perception of indiscriminate destruction, either of which could serve as an Al Qaeda recruiting vehicle and achieve the opposite of the desired results. Thus, this third goal must be categorized as *both* positive *and* negative.

In Iraq, during the initial phase of Operation Iraqi Freedom, the goal to remove Saddam Hussein from power demanded the use of lethal military force and was hence a positive objective. Since Saddam's defeat, however, the goal of creating the conditions necessary to foster democracy has emerged as a thorny objective. On the one hand, lethal military force is necessary to prevent widespread unrest and terrorist activities that threaten the nascent government. On the other hand, applying too much force could exacerbate tensions and lead to additional violence and turmoil, undercutting the prospect for a democratic Iraq. Accordingly, this goal must also be labeled as *both* positive *and* negative.

In both conflicts, the other variables have had, and will continue to have, a significant impact on air power effectiveness. In Afghanistan, the Al Qaeda and the Taliban were not the same enemies, and wrecking the Taliban did not equate to eliminating Al Qaeda. They also did not wage the same type of war. For the first four months of the conflict, the Taliban provided the bulk of the forces in Afghanistan and fought a "conventional" war against Northern Alliance and allied forces. Air power contributed enormously to wrecking Taliban strength during that span. Since that time, however, the fighting has resembled the guerrilla conflict that plagued Soviet forces for much of their eight-year ordeal. Both Afghanistan's terrain and its climate have proven less than ideal for air operations, although technology has helped to overcome some of those difficulties. Military controls have also affected the air effort in the form of legal reviews of potential targets.

During the initial, "conventional" phase of combat in Iraq, air power was devastatingly effective in stopping the movement of Saddam's troops and annihilating them once they were isolated. Against the insurgent forces that have appeared since Saddam's defeat, air power's impact has been less certain. Like in Afghanistan, the guerrilla conflict in Iraq has created problematic conditions for applying air power successfully. Technology has again helped to eliminate some of the difficulties, but military controls also exist in Iraq, and there too legal reviews of potential targets are commonplace.

Yet such reviews must occur if air power is to help achieve the negative as well as the positive goals in the current conflicts. In both wars, which are in many respects global struggles for "hearts and minds," perceptions are often more potent than reality, and enemies that rely on asymmetric means will be quick to use favorable perceptions to their own ends. Defeating those foes will require a careful employment of air power—whether its application is direct/independent against isolated leadership targets, direct/auxiliary in support of ground operations, or indirect/independent in humanitarian relief efforts. Regardless of how it is applied, a key to success will be assuring that *all* concerned view its use in the best possible light.

In the final analysis, the effectiveness of air power against any type of enemy depends on how well it supports the positive political goals without risking the achievement of the negative ones. The framework presented here offers no guarantee of success or failure—nor is it a predictor of the future. But it does charge those leaders who might apply air power to think carefully before making that decision. Clausewitz warns that "no one starts a war—or rather, no one in his senses ought to do so—without first being clear in his mind what he intends to achieve by that war and how he intends to conduct it."[15] That admonishment, delivered almost two centuries ago to readers who had fought against Napoleon with muskets and sabers, remains apt in the age of air warfare.

Notes

———— • ————

Note: Full citations are given for works at their first appearance in a chapter. When a short form occurs more than ten numbers beyond the last previous citation, the note number of the full citation is given in parenthesis.

Chapter I
FROM UNCONDITIONAL SURRENDER TO FLEXIBLE RESPONSE

1. Carl von Clausewitz, *On War,* ed. and trans. Michael Howard and Peter J. Paret (Princeton, N.J.: Princeton University Press, 1976), p. 87.

2. Air Force Manual 1-2, 1 December 1959, p. 5.

3. Its graduates included, among others, future generals Carl A. Spaatz, Frank M. Andrews, Ira C. Eaker, Curtis E. LeMay, George E. Stratemeyer, Otto P. Weyland, and Hoyt S. Vandenberg.

4. See "The Aim in War," in the Haywood S. Hansell Papers, Box 20, USAF Academy Library. Hansell was most influential in the formation of Army Air Forces bombing doctrine as one of four officers who developed AWPD-1, the plan that guided the American air campaign against Germany. On the idea of destroying will through attacks on war-making capability, see Michael S. Sherry, *The Rise of American Air Power: The Creation of Armageddon* (New Haven: Yale University Press, 1987), pp. 54-8.

5. Robert T. Finney, *History of the Air Corps Tactical School* (Maxwell AFB, Ala.: Air University, 1955), p. 32. See pp. 26–39 for a discussion of ACTS doctrinal development, as well as Thomas H. Greer, *The Development of Air Doctrine in the Army Air Arm 1917–1941* (Maxwell AFB, Ala.: Air University, 1955), pp. 14–122; Wesley F. Craven and James L. Cate, *The Army Air Forces in World War II,* 7 vols. (Chicago: University of Chicago Press, 1948–58), I: 17–71; I. B. Holley, Jr., *Ideas and Weapons* (New Haven: Yale University Press, 1953; reprint ed., Washington, D.C.: Office of Air Force History, 1983), pp. 157–74; and Robert F. Futrell,

Ideas, Concepts, Doctrine: A History of Basic Thinking in the United States Air Force, 1907–1964 (Maxwell AFB, Ala.: Air University, 1971), pp. 69–85.

6. In 1931, after a battle with the Navy, the Air Corps received control of all land-based aviation involved in coastal defense.

7. U.S. Army Training Regulation 440-15, "Employment of the Air Forces of the Army," 15 October 1935, quoted in Finney, *History of ACTS*, p. 34.

8. Quoted in DeWitt S. Copp, *A Few Great Captains* (Garden City, N.Y.: Doubleday, 1980), p. xv. For an analysis of the Air Corps's emphasis on strategic bombing to achieve autonomy, see pp. 318–32.

9. Raymond G. O'Connor, *Diplomacy for Victory: FDR and Unconditional Surrender* (New York: W. W. Norton, 1971), p. 5, and Bernard Brodie, *War and Politics* (New York: Macmillan, 1973), p. 39.

10. O'Connor, *Diplomacy for Victory*, pp. 49–50; Robert Dallek, *Franklin D. Roosevelt and American Foreign Policy, 1932–1945* (Oxford: Oxford University Press, 1979); Gaddis Smith, *American Diplomacy During the Second World War* (New York: John Wiley, 1965), p. 55; and Herbert Feis, *Churchill, Roosevelt, Stalin: The War They Waged and the Peace They Sought* (Princeton, N.J.: Princeton University Press, 1957, 1967), p. 357.

11. For a discussion of positive and negative objectives, see the preface to this volume.

12. See William Emerson, "Franklin Roosevelt as Commander-in-Chief in World War II," *Military Affairs* 12 (Winter 1958–59): 204–7; David MacIsaac, *Strategic Bombing in World War II* (New York: Garland Publishing, 1976), p. 107; R. J. Overy, *The Air War 1939–1945* (New York: Stein & Day, 1980), pp. 134–35; and David MacIsaac, gen. ed., *The United States Strategic Bombing Survey* (hereafter referred to as *USSBS*), 10 vols. (New York: Garland Publishing, 1976), I: x–xi. The acronym "AWPD" resulted from the name of the office that developed the document, the Air War Plans Division of the Army Air Staff. For a thorough look at AWPD-1's evolution, see Haywood Hansell, *The Air Plan That Defeated Hitler* (Atlanta: Higgins-McArthur/Longino & Porter, 1972), and James C. Gaston, *Planning the American Air War: Four Men and Nine Days in 1941* (Washington, D.C.: National Defense University Press, 1982).

13. MacIsaac, *Strategic Bombing*, pp. 12–15; MacIsaac, *USSBS*, I: x; DeWitt S. Copp, "The Pioneer Plan for Air War," *Air Force*, October 1982, pp. 76–77; Barry D. Watts, *The Foundations of U.S. Air Doctrine* (Maxwell AFB, Ala.: Air University, 1984), pp. 17–26; Craven and Cate, *Army Air Forces*, I: 131–50, 597–611; Futrell, *Ideas, Concepts, Doctrine*, and Robert L. Gallucci, *Neither Peace nor Honor: The Politics of Ameri-*

can Military Policy in Viet-Nam (Baltimore: Johns Hopkins Press, 1975), pp. 74–75.

14. MacIsaac, *Strategic Bombing,* p. 15.

15. The receipt of a German message via ULTRA on 13 May 1944, the day following the first large-scale raid by the 8th Air Force on German oil production centers, influenced Spaatz's decision to make oil the highest-priority target. The message noted that the Luftwaffe operations staff had ordered a massive transfer of flak batteries from the defenses of both the Eastern Front and aircraft production plants to the emplacements surrounding the refineries attacked. See U. S. Army Air Forces, *ULTRA and the History of the United States Strategic Air Force in Europe vs. the German Air Force,* ed. Paul L. Kesaris (Frederick, Md.: University Publications of America, 1980), p. 89.

16. Craven and Cate, *Army Air Forces,* III: 725.

17. Message, Doolittle to Spaatz, 1 February 1945, in Carl A. Spaatz Papers, Box 23, Library of Congress, Washington, D.C.

18. *Ibid.* At the bottom of Doolittle's message, Spaatz typed: "Replied by telephone conversation and told Doolittle to hit oil if visual assured; otherwise, Berlin—center of City. C. S."

19. For an examination of the Dresden attacks, see Mark A. Clodfelter, "Culmination Dresden: 1945" *Aerospace Historian* 26 (Fall 1979): 134–47.

20. Ira C. Eaker and Arthur G. B. Metcalf, "Conversations with Albert Speer," *Air Force,* April 1977, p. 57.

21. MacIsaac, *USSBS,* IV, *Summary Report (Pacific War):* 18.

22. John W. Dower, *War Without Mercy: Race and Power in the Pacific War* (New York: Pantheon Books, 1986), pp. 38–41.

23. Brodie, *War and Politics* (note 9 above), p. 55. In contrast to this "accepted" view, Rufus Miles makes a strong case that Roosevelt's 1942 decision to develop the atomic bomb "carried with it the implicit intent to use it as soon as it became available if it would shorten the war. There was no need to take into account other considerations." The premise that Hiroshima and Nagasaki averted hundreds of thousands of American deaths is, Miles contends, false. See Rufus E. Miles, Jr., "Hiroshima," *International Security* 10 (Fall 1985): 139–40.

24. H. H. Arnold, *Global Mission* (New York: Harper & Brothers, 1949), pp. 278, 333, 496, and Craven and Cate, *Army Air Forces,* V: 624.

25. Melden E. Smith, Jr., "The Strategic Bombing Debate: The Second World War and Vietnam," *Journal of Contemporary History* 12 (1977): 180.

26. MacIsaac, *USSBS,* I, *The Effects of Strategic Bombing on German Morale:* 7, and I, *Overall Report (Europe):* 37.

27. *Ibid.*, VII, *Summary Report (Pacific War)*: 16, 18–19; Craven and Cate, *Army Air Forces*, V: 754–75; and Overy, *Air War* (note 12 above), p. 125.

28. MacIsaac, *USSBS*, IV, *The Effects of Strategic Bombing on German Morale*: 1.

29. *Ibid.*, I, *Overall Report (Europe)*: 108.

30. *Ibid.*, VII, *Summary Report (Pacific War)*: 21. The Survey obtained these figures by interviewing a cross-section of the Japanese civilian populace, including both urban and rural sectors and various economic and social classes.

31. *Ibid.*, VII, *Japan's Struggle to End the War*: 12.

32. *Ibid.*, I, *Overall Report (Europe)*: 38.

33. *Ibid.*, VII, *Summary Report (Pacific War)*: 26.

34. Office of Statistical Control, *Army Air Forces Statistical Digest: World War II* (December 1945), p. 51. Casualties among the Army Air Forces in the Far East totaled 17,237 men.

35. USAF Oral History interview of General Carl A. Spaatz by Arthur Goldberg, 19 May 1965, on file at the Air Force Historical Research Center (hereafter referred to as AFHRC), Maxwell AFB, Alabama, file number K239.0512-755, p. 13.

36. Curtis E. LeMay with MacKinlay Kantor, *Mission with LeMay* (Garden City, N.Y.: Doubleday, 1965), p. 388.

37. Report, "Strategic Implications," 3 February 1947, quoted in John T. Greenwood, "The Emergence of the Postwar Strategic Air Force, 1945–1953," in Alfred F. Hurley and Robert C. Ehrhart, eds., *Air Power and Warfare: Proceedings of the Eighth Military History Symposium at the U.S. Air Force Academy* (Washington, D.C.: Office of Air Force History, 1979), p. 223. For an analysis of Air Force organizational and doctrinal developments during the postwar era, see Perry McCoy Smith, *The Air Force Plans for Peace 1943–1945* (Baltimore: Johns Hopkins Press, 1970); Herman S. Wolk, *Planning and Organizing the Postwar Air Force* (Washington, D.C.: Office of Air Force History, 1984); and Futrell, *Ideas, Concepts, Doctrine* (note 5 above), pp. 193–262.

38. Robert F. Futrell, "The Influence of the Air Power Concept on Air Force Planning, 1945–1962," in Harry R. Borowski, ed., *Military Planning in the Twentieth Century: Proceedings of the Eleventh Military History Symposium at the U.S. Air Force Academy* (Washington, D.C.: Office of Air Force History, 1986), p. 257.

39. Greenwood, "Emergence of Postwar Strategic Air Force," pp. 228, 237.

40. *Ibid.*, pp. 228–29. For a thorough examination of the Air Force's deficiencies as an atomic attack force during the early postwar period, see

Harry R. Borowski, *A Hollow Threat: Strategic Air Power and Containment Before Korea* (Westport, Conn.: Greenwood Press, 1982).

41. MacIsaac, *USSBS*, VII, *Summary Report (Pacific War)*: 28.

42. Harry S Truman, *Memoirs*, II, *Years of Trial and Hope* (Garden City, N.Y.: Doubleday, 1956): 339.

43. *Ibid.*, II: 337.

44. The Army mobilized 2,834,000 men and twenty divisions during the war. Eight Army divisions and one Marine division served in Korea; the remainder served as a reserve pool and guarded against the expected Soviet thrust in Europe. See Russell F. Weigley, *History of the United States Army* (New York: MacMillan, 1967), p. 508.

45. Interview of Dean Acheson by Hillman, Noyes, and Heller, 18 February 1955, Kansas City, Mo., in Post-Presidential Files—"Memoirs" File, Harry S Truman Library, Independence, Mo., Box 1.

46. Memorandum, Secretary of Defense George C. Marshall to President Truman, 27 September 1950, in Department of State, *Foreign Relations of the United States: 1950* (hereafter cited as *FR*) (Washington: U.S. Government Printing Office, 1982), VII, *Korea:* 792–93.

47. UN Resolution 376, 7 October 1950, *ibid.*, VII: 904.

48. Truman, *Memoirs*, II: 455–56.

49. Interview of Dean Rusk by the author, Athens, Georgia, 15 July 1985.

50. Truman wrote regarding the May 1952 proposal at Panmunjom to repatriate only those prisoners who desired the exchange: "I had made it very clear that I would not agree to any trade of prisoners that might result in forcibly returning non-Communists to Communist control. To have agreed would have been not only inhumane and tragic but dishonorable as well." See Truman, *Memoirs*, II: 462.

51. Dwight D. Eisenhower, *The White House Years*, I, *Mandate for Change* (Garden City, N.Y.: Doubleday, 1963): 179–80. The President stated in a 6 May meeting of the National Security Council that "we have got to consider the atomic bomb as simply another weapon in our arsenal." See *FR, 1952–54*, XV, *Korea*, pt. 1: 977.

52. Edward C. Keefer, "President Dwight D. Eisenhower and the End of the Korean War," *Diplomatic History* 10 (Summer 1986): 280. In 1965, Eisenhower told Army General Andrew Goodpaster that "he had passed the word secretly to the Chinese at the time of Korea that if they failed to stop the war they were liable to direct attack by us, including nuclear weapon attack." See "Meeting with General Eisenhower, 12 May 1965," memorandum, Goodpaster to President Johnson, National Security Files, Name File: President Eisenhower, Lyndon Baines Johnson Library, Austin, Texas, Box 3.

53. "Air Attack on German Civilian Morale," 7 August 1944, White House Central Files, Confidential Files—Subject Series, Dwight D. Eisenhower Library, Abilene, Kansas, Folder: "Operation Alert (1)," Box 47.

54. Eisenhower, *White House Years*, I: 180.

55. *Ibid.*, I: 145.

56. USAF Historical Study No. 127: *The United States Air Force Operations in the Korean Conflict 1 July 1952–27 July 1953* (1 July 1956), AFHRC, file number 101-127, p. 9.

57. "Statement to the Press by Lt. Gen. George E. Stratemeyer, 3 October 1950," Frank E. Lowe File, Harry S Truman Library, Independence, Mo., Box 247.

58. USAF Oral History interview of Thomas K. Finletter by Colonel Marvin Stanley, February 1967, AFHRC, file number K239.0512-760, p. 27. Finletter was Secretary of the Air Force during the Truman era of the Korean War. In his interview with Stanley, he emphasized that MacArthur's statement had appeared in a telegram to Washington following Inchon.

59. George E. Stratemeyer diary, entries for 23 and 31 December 1950, AFHRC, file number 168.7018-16, Vol. 3.

60. USAF Study No. 127, p. 5.

61. Hoyt S. Vandenberg, "Air Power in the Korean War," in *The Impact of Air Power*, ed. Eugene M. Emme (Princeton, N.J.: Van Nostrand, 1959), p. 403. Otto P. Weyland, "The Air Campaign in Korea," also in the Emme volume, concurs with this explanation of Strangle II's purpose. See p. 395.

62. Headquarters FEAF, *FEAF Operations Policy Korea Mid-1952: An Addendum to the FEAF Histories for that Year* (March 1955), AFHRC, file number K720.01, p. 4.

63. Quoted in Robert F. Futrell, *The United States Air Force in Korea 1950–1953* (New York: Duell, Sloan & Pearce, 1961), p. 481.

64. *Ibid.*, p. 482.

65. "Annex to Minutes of the FEAF Formal Target Committee Meeting, 24 March 1953," *FEAF Formal Target Committee Minutes, 30 December 1952–24 March 1953*, AFHRC, file number K720.151A.

66. "Minutes of the FEAF Formal Target Committee Meeting, 7 April 1953," *FEAF Formal Target Committee Minutes, 4 November 1952–7 April 1953*, AFHRC, file number K720.151A.

67. Message, Clark to JCS, 14 May 1953, FR, *1952–54*, XV, *Korea*, pt. 1: 1022.

68. "Minutes of the FEAF Formal Target Committee Meeting, 12 May 1953," *FEAF Formal Target Committee Minutes, 12 May 1953*, AFHRC, file number K720.151A.

69. USAF Oral History interview of General O. P. Weyland by Dr. James Hasdorff and Brigadier General Noel Parrish, San Antonio, Texas, 19 November 1974, AFHRC, file number K239.0512-813, p. 114.

70. "Minutes of the FEAF Formal Target Committee Meeting, 26 May 1953," *FEAF Formal Target Committee Minutes, 26 May 1953*, AFHRC, file number K720.151A.

71. "Destruction of North Korean Irrigation Dams," letter from Brigadier General Don Z. Zimmerman to Director of Intelligence/HQ USAF, 8 July 1953, in *FEAF Command Report, June 1953, Vol. IIA*, AFHRC, file number K720.02.

72. Gregory A. Carter, *Some Historical Notes on Air Interdiction in Korea*, RAND Corporation Paper No. 3452, September 1966, p. 6.

73. USAF Study No. 127 (note 56 above), p. 4. On 8 October 1950, two F-80s attacked a Soviet airfield near Vladivostok by mistake and caused heavy damage. The Soviets protested loudly, and Truman and Eisenhower both gave assurances that no such incidents would happen again.

74. Department of State memo, John M. Allison to Mr. Matthews, 28 August 1952, in Korean War Files—Department of State, Harry S Truman Library, Folder 49: Bombing of North Korean Power Plants, Box 13.

75. Stratemeyer diary (note 59 above), entry for 23 December 1950.

76. USAF Study No. 127, p. 5.

77. Admiral C. Turner Joy, *How Communists Negotiate* (Santa Monica, Calif.: Fidelis Publications, 1955, 1970), p. 176.

78. Oral History interview of Nathan F. Twining by John T. Mason, Jr., 12 September 1967, Arlington, Va., Eisenhower Library, p. 196.

79. JCS message to CINCFE, 99713, 26 December 1950; CINCFE message to JCS, 52125, 27 December 1950, in Korean War File—Department of Defense, Harry S Truman Library, Folder: Pertinent Papers on Korean Situation (Vol. II), Box 15.

80. Futrell, *USAF in Korea* (note 63 above), p. 447. Weyland recalled: "I don't know why Ridgway wouldn't let me do it [bomb the electric plants]. He said, 'Oh, that would be politically unacceptable.' I said, 'Oh crap,' or words to that effect. Anyhow, we didn't. He was my boss, and he wouldn't let me do it. I said, 'Well, the JCS has cleared it.' He said, 'Well, the time isn't right,' or something. So Ridgway left and Mark Clark cam in. . . . He [Clark] said, 'Why, those are juicy targets. Why haven't you done it?' I said, 'Ridgway wouldn't let me.' He said, 'Well, let's get about it.' So we clobbered them in very quick order." Weyland interview, 19 November 1974 (note 69 above), pp. 107, 113.

81. USAF Study No. 127, p. 5.

82. Weyland interview, 19 November 1974, p. 112.

83. Futrell, *USAF in Korea*, p. 115.

84. "Minutes of the FEAF Formal Target Committee Meeting, 22 July 1953," *FEAF Formal Target Committee Minutes, 22 July 1953*, AFHRC, file number K720.151A.

85. Futrell, *USAF in Korea*, p. 645.

86. Carter, *Air Interdiction* (note 72 above), p. 6.

87. *Ibid.*, pp. 5–18. Carter's study provides an excellent synthesis on the difficulties of carrying out interdiction in Korea.

88. *Ibid.*, p. 2; Futrell, *USAF in Korea*, pp. 452, 482, 626, 645; and Weyland, "Air Campaign in Korea" (note 61 above), pp. 396, 398.

89. Joy, *How Communists Negotiate* (note 77 above), pp. 165–66.

90. On 17 April 1951, two months *before* the front stabilized, Stratemeyer noted that Communist forces *required* 3,120 tons of supply per day, and that North Korean lines of communication had the *capacity* to provide up to 5,125 tons daily. See Stratemeyer diary (note 59 above), entry for 17 April 1951.

91. NSC 147, 2 April 1953, *FR, 1952–54, Vol. 15: Korea*, pt. 1, p. 842.

92. Keefer, "Eisenhower and End of Korean War" (note 52 above), pp. 282, 287, 289. Keefer's analysis of Eisenhower's "atomic ultimatum" is the most thorough to date, evaluating contentions in many secondary works in the light of documents recently reproduced in *The Foreign Relations of the United States* and others maintained in presidential libraries. He concludes that "Eisenhower ended the war by accepting the possibility of atomic warfare and even global conflict."

93. "Minutes of FEAF Formal Target Committee Meeting, 24 March 1953," (note 65 above).

94. "The Attack on the Irrigation Dams in North Korea," *Air University Quarterly Review* 6 (Winter 1953–54): 55.

95. Rusk interview, 15 July 1985 (note 49 above).

96. Nikita Khrushchev, *Khrushchev Remembers*, trans. and ed. Strobe Talbott (Boston: Little, Brown, 1970), pp. 367–72.

97. William W. Momyer, *Air Power in Three Wars* (Washington, D.C.: U.S. Government Printing Office, 1978), p. 172.

98. HQ FEAF, *FEAF Operations Policy Korea Mid-1952: An Addendum* (note 62 above), p. 65.

99. U.S. Congress, Senate, *The Korean War and Related Matters; Report of the Sumcommittee to Investigate the Administration of the Internal Security Act and Other Security Laws to the Committee on the Judiciary*, 84th Cong., 1st sess., 1955, p. 10.

100. *Ibid.*, p. 23.

101. LeMay with Kantor, *Mission* (note 36 above), p. 464.

102. *Ibid.*, p. 459.

103. Weyland, p. 397.

104. "Attack on Irrigation Dams in North Korea," p. 60.

105. Paul Nitze, "The Relationship of the Political End to the Military Objective," Air War College lecture, October 1954, AFHRC file number K239.716254-55, p. 12. Nitze was president of the Foreign Service Educational Foundation at the time of his address.

106. Futrell, "Influence" (note 38 above), p. 266.

107. David Alan Rosenberg, "The Origins of Overkill: Nuclear Weapons and American Strategy, 1945–1960," *International Security* 7 (Spring 1983): 66.

108. Futrell, "Influence," p. 269.

109. Air Force Manual 1-2, 1 April 1955, p. 3, and Air Force Manual 1-2, 1 December 1959, p. 5; emphasis added. Air Force Manual 1-1 replaced 1-2 on 13 August 1964. It stated: "Of utmost importance . . . is that we maintain superior capabilities for the higher intensities of war. Such a posture makes it evident to an enemy that if conflict escalates the advantage will become more and more clearly ours." See p. 1–3

110. Air Force Manual 1-8, 1 May 1954, p. 6.

111. *Ibid.*, p. 2.

112. *Ibid.*, p. 4.

113. *Ibid.*, pp. 5, 8.

114. U.S. Congress, Senate, *Airpower: Report of the Subcommittee on the Air Force of the Committee on Armed Services, January 25, 1957*, 85th Cong., 1st sess., 1957, p. 71.

115. Futrell, "Influence," p. 266.

116. Thomas K. Finletter, "Air Power and Foreign Policy, Especially in the Far East," *The Annals of the American Academy of Political and Social Science* 299 (May 1955): 84–5.

117. Bernard Brodie, *Strategy in the Missile Age* (Princeton, N.J.: Princeton University Press, 1959), p. 358.

118. LeMay with Kantor, *Mission* (note 36 above), p. 6.

119. Rosenberg, "Origins of Overkill" (note 107 above), p. 42, and Futrell, "Influence," p. 266.

120. Rosenberg, "Origins of Overkill," p. 37.

121. *Ibid.*, p. 68.

122. USAF Oral History interview of Brigadier General Noel F. Parrish by Dr. James C. Hasdorff, 10–14 June 1974, San Antonio, Texas, AFHRC file number K239.0512-744, pp. 203–4.

123. *Ibid.*, p. 204. Parrish examined an organizational chart of Air Force offices in the Pentagon to obtain this information.

124. Air Force Manual 1-2, 1 December 1959, p. 4.

125. Air Force Manual 1-2, 1 April 1955, p. 5.

126. Air Force Manual 1-2, 1 December 1959, p. 11.

127. *Ibid.*, p. 13.

128. Air Force Manual 1-7, 1 March 1954, p. 1; Air Force Manual 1-8, 1 May 1954, p. 2.

129. Air Force Manual 1-7, 1 March 1954, pp. 2, 15.

130. Air Force Manual 1-2, 1 December 1959, p. 4. The 1961 edition of Pacific Air Forces (PACAF) Training Manual F-100 stated: "Nuclear training will in every instance take precedence over nonnuclear familiarization and qualification. It is emphasized that conventional training will not be accomplished at the expense of the higher priority nuclear training required by this manual." Quoted in David MacIsaac, "The Evolution of Air Power since 1945: The American Experience," in *War in the Third Dimension: Essays in Contemporary Air Power*, ed. R. A. Mason (London: Brassey's Defense Publishers, 1986).

131. Edward J. Timberlake, "Air Power Implications," Speech to Aviation Writers' Association Convention, San Francisco, California, 30 May 1956, in *Speeches by Major General Timberlake, 1956–57*, AFHRC file number K533.309-1, p. 5.

132. *Ibid.*, p. 9.

133. *Ibid.*, p. 5.

134. Futrell, "Influence" (note 38 above), p. 266.

135. Air Force Manual 1-2, 1 December 1959, p. 7.

136. Parrish Oral History interview, 10–14 June 1974 (note 122 above), p. 201.

137. U.S. Congress, Senate, *Airpower* (note 114 above), p. 72.

138. Timberlake, "Air Power Implications," p. 9.

139. Robert B. Johnson, "RAND Studies of Air Power in Limited Wars," 21 May 1957, AFHRC file number K720.3102-7, pp. 1–10.

140. Colonel Ephraim M. Hampton, "The USAF in Limited War," 14 March 1957, *Project File No. Au-1-57-ESAWAC*, AFHRC file number K239.042957-1, pp. 1–9.

141. Bernard Brodie, *The USAF in Limited War*, AFHRC file number K239.042957-1, p. 7.

142. *Ibid.*, p. 20.

143. *Ibid.*, p. 22.

144. *Ibid.*, p. 56.

145. Brodie, *Strategy* (note 117 above), p. 330. Italics in original.

146. Memo, Robert Cutler to President Eisenhower, "Limited War in the Nuclear Age," 7 August 1957, National Security Adviser Files, NSC

Series, Briefing Notes Subseries, Eisenhower Library, Folder: Limited War (2), Box 12.

147. Much as its counterpart guiding strategic operations, Air Force Manual 1-7, dated 1 March 1954, remained current until 14 June 1965.

148. Hoyt Vandenberg, "Lecture to the Air War College," 6 May 1953, AFHRC file number K239.716253-126, pp. 6–7.

149. *Ibid.*, pp. 4–5.

150. Air Force Manual 1-8, 1 May 1954, p. 4.

Chapter II
THE GENESIS OF GRADUATED THUNDER

1. Memorandum, Robert S. McNamara to the President, "U.S. Policy Towards Viet Nam," 16 March 1964, National Security Files, NSC Meetings File, Vol. 1, Tab 5, Lyndon Baines Johnson Library, Austin, Texas, Box 1, p. 7. This memorandum became NSAM 288 on 17 March.

2. The assertion that Vietnam, from 1964 to 1968, was "primarily a guerrilla struggle" contradicts Harry Summers's contention in *On Strategy* (Novato, Calif.: Presidio Press, 1982) and will be explained fully in Chapter IV.

3. NSAM 273, 26 November 1963, National Security Files, National Security Action Memorandums, Johnson Library, Boxes 1–9, p. 1.

4. Neil Sheehan *et al.*, *The Pentagon Papers* (New York: Bantam Books, Inc., 1971), p. 283.

5. Quoted in Townsend Hoopes, *The Limits of Intervention* (New York: David McKay, 1969), p. 19.

6. *The Pentagon Papers: The Defense Department History of United States Decisionmaking in Vietnam*, Senator Gravel edition (Boston: Beacon Press, 1971), III: 172.

7. Lyndon Baines Johnson, *The Vantage Point* (New York: Holt, Rinehart & Winston, 1971), p. 152.

8. Sheehan, *et al.*, *Pentagon Papers*, p. 284. See also Johnson, *Vantage Point*, p. 120.

9. McNamara memorandum, "U.S. Policy Towards Viet Nam," p. 8.

10. "It became increasingly clear that Ho Chi Minh's military campaign against South Vietnam was part of a larger, much more ambitious strategy being conducted by the Communists. . . . Peking was promising Hanoi full support and was urging 'wars of national liberation' as the solution to all the problems of non-Communist underdeveloped nations," Johnson wrote of the 1964–65 period. See Johnson, *Vantage Point*, p. 134.

11. Walt W. Rostow, *The Diffusion of Power* (New York: MacMillan, 1972), p. 435; Maxwell Taylor, *Swords and Plowshares* (New York: W. W.

Norton, 1972), pp. 399–401; Chester L. Cooper, *The Lost Crusade: America in Vietnam* (New York: Dodd, Mead, 1970), pp. 417–20; Henry Graff, *The Tuesday Cabinet* (Englewood Cliffs, N.J.: Prentice Hall, 1970), p. 149; Doris Kearns, *Lyndon Johnson and the American Dream* (New York: Signet, 1976), p. 264. See also Bernard Brodie, *War and Politics* (New York: MacMillan, 1973), pp. 116–17; Larry Berman, *Planning a Tragedy: The Americanization of the War in Vietnam* (New York: W. W. Norton, 1982), pp. 130–31; and George C. Herring, *America's Longest War: The United States and Vietnam 1950–1975* (New York: Wiley, 1979), pp. 142–43.

12. Johnson, *Vantage Point*, p. 153.

13. CIA Special Memorandum No. 11-65, "Future Soviet Moves in Vietnam," 27 April 1965, National Security Files, NSC History: "Deployment of Major U.S. Forces to Vietnam, July 1965," Vol. 3, Johnson Library, Box 41, and CIA Special Memorandum No. 18-65, "Soviet Tactics Concerning Vietnam," 15 July 1965, National Security Files, NSC History: "Deployment of Major U.S. Forces to Vietnam, July 1965," Vol. 6, Johnson Library, Box 43.

14. *Ibid.*

15. Johnson, pp. 66–67.

16. Interview of Dean Rusk by the author, Athens, Georgia, 15 July 1985.

17. "Cabinet Room Meeting Notes, 22 July 1965," Meeting Notes File, 21–27 July 1965, Meetings on Vietnam, Johnson Library," Box 1, p. 22.

18. Rusk interview, 15 July 1985. Walt W. Rostow, Chief of the State Department's Policy Planning Council and later Special Assistant to the President for National Security Affairs, offers a contrasting opinion. There was "no way you could've got the Chinese involved, unless you went to the Red River Delta [with ground troops] and I'm not sure about that." Interview of Rostow by the author, Austin, Texas, 23 May 1986.

19. "Summary of the President's Breakfast with Boys on Carrier *Constellation*," 19 February 1968, Tom Johnson's notes of meetings, Lyndon Baines Johnson Library, Box 2.

20. Two examples of this message relay occurred in the winter of 1965. On 24 February, the American Ambassador to Poland informed his Chinese counterpart that "the United States had no designs on the territory of North Vietnam, nor any desire to destroy the DRV [Democratic Republic of (North) Vietnam]." Canadian emissary Blair Seaborn communicated the same message to Hanoi officials the next month. See *Pentagon Papers*, Gravel edition (note 6 above), III: 330.

21. Kearns, *Johnson and American Dream*, p. 263.

22. Douglas Kinnard, *The War Managers* (Hanover, N.H.: University Press of New England, 1977), pp. 24–25. Kinnard's work presents perceptions of the war from 111 Army generals who commanded in Vietnam.

23. *Pentagon Papers*, Gravel edition, III: 154.

24. McNamara memorandum, "U.S. Policy Towards Viet Nam" (note 1 above), p. 7.

25. Guenter Lewy, *America in Vietnam* (New York: Oxford University Press, 1978), p. 374; Rostow interview, 23 May 1986; Robert S. McNamara, memorandum to the President, "Program of Expanded Military and Political Moves with Respect to Vietnam," 26 June 1965, National Security Files, NSC Meetings File, Vol. 3, Johnson Library, Box 1, p. 1; and McGeorge Bundy, memorandum to the President, "A Policy of Sustained Reprisal," 7 February 1965, *Pentagon Papers*, Gravel edition, III: 311.

26. *Pentagon Papers*, Gravel edition, III: 176.

27. McNamara memorandum, "U.S. Policy Towards Viet Nam," p. 7.

28. *Pentagon Papers*, Gravel edition, III: 165. The start of a North Vietnamese–backed Communist offensive against Souvanna Phouma's Loatian government on 17 May caused the JCS to tailor their plans to supporting non-Communist forces in Laos as well as South Vietnam.

29. *Ibid.*, III: 166.

30. *Ibid.*, III: 168.

31. Cable from the Chairman, JCS to CINCPAC and CINCMACV, 30 May 1964, *Pentagon Papers*, Gravel edition, III: 74–75.

32. JCSM-471-64, 2 June 1964, *Pentagon Papers*, Gravel edition, III: 144, 172.

33. U.S. Congress, Senate, Committee on Armed Services, Preparedness Investigating Subcommittee, *Air War Against North Vietnam*, 90th Cong., 1st sess., part 3, 22–25 August 1967, p. 212.

34. *Pentagon Papers*, Gravel edition, III: 179.

35. *Ibid.*, III: 172–73, and Wallace J. Thies, *When Governments Collide: Coercion and Diplomacy in the Vietnam Conflict 1964–1968* (Berkeley: University of California Press, 1980), pp. 35–36.

36. Oral History interview of William Bundy by Paige E. Mulhollan, 26 May 1969, Tape 1, Johnson Library, p. 23; SNIE 50-2-64, 25 May 1964, *Pentagon Papers*, Gravel edition, III: 125; Rusk interview, 15 July 1985 (note 16 above); Rostow interview, 23 May 1986 (note 18 above); and George W. Ball, "How Valid Are the Assumptions Underlying Our Viet-Nam Policies?" 5 October 1964, *Atlantic Monthly* 230 (July 1972): 46; emphasis added.

37. Lewy, *America in Vietnam* (note 25 above), p. 29; and William Bundy interview, 26 May 1969, Tape 1, p. 23. The first regular North

Vietnamese infantry regiment did not depart North Vietnam for the South until October 1964. See Thies, *When Governments Collide*, p. 51.

38. *Pentagon Papers*, Gravel edition, III: 173.

39. *Ibid.*, III: 127.

40. *Ibid.*, III: 181.

41. While the North Vietnamese apparently attacked the destroyer *Maddox* on the morning of 1 August, considerable doubt remains whether they attacked the *Maddox* and the *C. Turner Joy* on 4 August. See Herring, *America's Longest War* (note 11 above), pp. 119–22.

42. *Pentagon Papers*, Gravel edition, III: 180.

43. Letter, Lyndon Johnson to Maxwell Taylor, undated, *Pentagon Papers*, Gravel edition, III: 79, and cable, Taylor to State Department, 18 August 1964, *Pentagon Papers*, Gravel edition, III: 545–48.

44. William Bundy interview, 26 May 1969, Tape 2, pp. 1–2.

45. Cable, State Department to Maxwell Taylor, 14 August 1964, *Pentagon Papers*, Gravel edition, III: 533–37.

46. Rostow interview, 23 May 1986.

47. *Pentagon Papers*, Gravel edition, III: 109–10.

48. *Ibid.*, III: 109–10 and 201–2; emphasis in original.

49. JCSM-729-64, 24 August 1964, *Pentagon Papers*, Gravel edition, III: 145; memorandum, McNamara to the Chairman, Joint Chiefs of Staff, 31 August 1964, *Pentagon Papers*, Gravel edition, III: 555–56; John T. McNaughton, "Plan of Action for South Vietnam," 3 September 1964 (second draft), *Pentagon Papers*, Gravel edition, III: 557.

50. *Pentagon Papers*, Gravel edition, III: 110, 145, 193–94, 204, and McGeorge Bundy, "Memorandum for Record," 14 September 1964, Meeting Notes File, Johnson Library, Box 1.

51. McGeorge Bundy, "Memorandum for Record," 14 September 1964; emphasis added.

52. William Bundy interview, 26 May 1969, Tape 1, p. 35.

53. Herbert Y. Schandler, *The Unmaking of a President: Lyndon Johnson and Vietnam* (Princeton, N.J.: Princeton University Press, 1977), p. 6.

54. *Pentagon Papers*, Gravel edition, III: 204–5.

55. Ball, "How Valid" (note 36 above), pp. 37–38.

56. William Bundy interview, 26 May 1969 (note 36 above), Tape 2, pp. 2–6, 23, and *Pentagon Papers*, Gravel edition, III: 209.

57. NSC Working Group draft memorandum, 17 November 1964, *Pentagon Papers*, Gravel edition, III: 215.

58. *Pentagon Papers*, Gravel edition, III: 226.

59. JCS draft memorandum, 8 November 1964, *Pentagon Papers*, Gravel Edition, III: 218.

60. *Pentagon Papers*, Gravel edition, III: 226.

61. William P. Bundy and John T. McNaughton, "Courses of Action in Southeast Asia," 21 November 1964, *Pentagon Papers*, Gravel edition, III: 663, 665.

62. William Bundy interview, 26 May 1969, Tape 2, p. 6.

63. John T. McNaughton, "Action for South Vietnam," 7 November 1964, *Pentagon Papers*, Gravel edition, III: 602, 604.

64. Text of briefing by Maxwell Taylor, 27 November 1964, *Pentagon Papers*, Gravel edition, III: 666–72.

65. Taylor briefing text, Annex I, 27 November 1964, *Pentagon Papers*, Gravel edition, III: 673.

66. McGeorge Bundy, "Cabinet Room Meeting Notes," 1 December 1964, Meeting Notes File, Johnson Library, Box 1, and draft instructions, Johnson to Taylor, 2 December 1964, *Pentagon Papers*, Gravel edition, III: 91.

67. Message, Johnson to Taylor, 7 January 1965, National Security Files, NSC History: "Deployment of Major U.S. Forces to Vietnam, July 1965," Vol. 1, Johnson Library, Box 40.

68. Message, McNaughton to McNamara and Vance, 7 February 1965, National Security Files, NSC History: "Deployment of Major U.S. Forces to Vietnam, July 1965," Vol. 1, Johnson Library, Box 40; emphasis added. The message, sent at 1300 Saigon time, contained a notation to guarantee delivery prior to the 0800 NSC meeting on the 7th. Thirteen hours separated Washington and Saigon.

69. McGeorge Bundy, "A Policy of Sustained Reprisal," 7 February 1965, *Pentagon Papers*, Gravel edition, III: 309–15.

70. "Summary Notes of the 545th NSC Meeting," 6 February 1965, Meeting Notes File, Johnson Library, Box 1, p. 2; Johnson, *Vantage Point* (note 7 above), p. 125; William Bundy interview, 26 May 1969, Tape 2, p. 12.

71. William Bundy interview, 26 May 1969, Tape 2, p. 14; memorandum, Taylor to the President, 10 February 1965, National Security Files, NSC History: "Deployment of Major U.S. Forces to Vietnam, July 1965," Vol. 1, Johnson Library, Box 40; and *Pentagon Papers*, Gravel edition, III: 306.

72. By mid-February, the North Vietnamese had deployed three regiments of their regular army to South Vietnam; U.S. intelligence sources estimated they had 5,800 regular troops in the South by 1 March 1965. See Lewy, pp. 39–40.

73. Oral History interview of Maxwell Taylor by Ted Gittinger, Washington, D.C., 14 September 1981, Johnson Library, Tape 3, pp. 7–8, and cable, Taylor to the President, 12 February 1965, *Pentagon Papers*, Gravel edition, III: 315–17.

74. William Bundy, "Memorandum to the Secretary," 6 January 1965, *Pentagon Papers*, Gravel edition, III: 684; "National Security Council Meeting," 18 February 1965, National Security Files, NSC Meeting Files, Vols. 1–3, Johnson Library, Box 1; and *Pentagon Papers*, Gravel edition, III: 331.

75. McGeorge Bundy, "A Policy of Sustained Reprisal," p. 312; John T. McNaughton, "Observations re South Vietnam after Khanh's Re-Coup," 27 January 1965, *Pentagon Papers*, Gravel edition, III: 686–87; and McNaughton, "Action for South Vietnam," 10 March 1965, National Security Files, NSC History: "Deployment of Major U.S. Forces to Vietnam, July 1965," Vol. 2, Johnson Library, Box 40.

76. William E. Simons, "The Vietnam Intervention, 1964–65," in Alexander L. George, David K. Hall, and William E. Simons, *The Limits of Coercive Diplomacy: Laos, Cuba, and Vietnam* (Boston: Little, Brown, 1971), p. 163; memorandum, McNamara to the Chairman, JCS, 17 February 1965, *Pentagon Papers*, Gravel edition, III: 333; and "Memorandum of Meeting with the President," 17 February 1965, Meeting Notes File, Johnson Library, Box 1, p. 8.

77. "Memorandum of Meeting with the President," 17 February 1965, p. 9. Johnson later commented regarding the decision to begin Rolling Thunder: "I now concluded that political life in the South would collapse unless the people there knew that the North was paying a price in its own territory for its aggression." See Johnson, *Vantage Point*, p. 132.

78. Johnson, *Vantage Point*, p. 132.

79. *Pentagon Papers*, Gravel edition, III: 307.

80. McGeorge Bundy, "Vietnam—Telegrams from the Public," 9 February 1965, National Security Files, NSC History: "Deployment of Major U.S. Forces to Vietnam, July 1965," Vol. 1, Johnson Library, Box 40.

81. "National Security Council Meeting," 18 February 1965.

82. *Pentagon Papers*, Gravel edition, III: 303, 307–8.

83. McGeorge Bundy, draft memorandum for Maxwell Taylor, 16 February 1965, National Security Files, NSC History: "Deployment of Major U.S. Forces to Vietnam, July 1965," Vol. 1, Johnson Library, Box 40. Emphasis added.

84. McGeorge Bundy, memorandum to the President, "Vietnam Decisions," 16 February 1965, National Security Files, NSC History: "Deployment of Major U.S. Forces to Vietnam, July 1965," Vol. 1, Johnson Library, Box 40.

85. *Ibid.*

86. Cable, Johnson to U.S. ambassadors, 18 February 1965, *Pentagon Papers*, Gravel edition, III: 324.

87. William Bundy interview, 26 May 1969 (note 36 above), Tape 2, pp. 14–17.

88. *Pentagon Papers*, Gravel edition, III: 272, 329.

89. Cables from Taylor to the President, 8 March 1965, *Pentagon Papers*, Gravel edition, III: 335.

90. Cable, Foy Kohler to Rusk, 2 March 1965, National Security Files, NSC History: "Deployment of Major U.S. Forces to Vietnam, July 1965," Vol. 2, Johnson Library, Box 40.

91. *Pentagon Papers*, Gravel edition, III: 332.

92. "Agenda for (White House) Luncheon," 30 March 1965," National Security Files, files of McGeorge Bundy, folder: "Luncheons with the President," Vol. 1, part 1, Johnson Library, Box 19.

93. Cable, Rusk to Taylor, 15 March 1965. *Pentagon Papers*, Gravel edition, III: 339.

94. Thies, *When Governments Collide* (note 35 above), p. 87.

95. John T. McNaughton, "Plan of Action for South Vietnam," 24 March 1965, National Security Files, NSC History: "Deployment of Major U.S. Forces to Vietnam, July 1965," Vol. 2, Johnson Library, Box 40, and McGeorge Bundy, draft for 1 April 1965 meeting with the President, n. d., *Pentagon Papers*, Gravel edition, III: 346.

96. *Pentagon Papers*, Gravel edition, III: 247.

97. Cooper, *Lost Crusade* (note 11 above), p. 224.

98. Simons, "Vietnam Intervention" (note 76 above), pp. 147–50.

99. NSAM 328, 6 April 1965, National Security Files, National Security Action Memorandums, Johnson Library, Boxes 1–9.

100. *Ibid.*

101. Memorandum by Walt. W. Rostow, 1 April 1965, *Pentagon Papers*, Gravel edition, III: 382.

102. John McCone, letter and memorandum to the President, 2 April 1965, National Security Files, NSC History: "Deployment of Major U.S. Forces to Vietnam, July 1965," Vol. 2, Johnson Library, Box 40.

103. General Andrew Goodpaster to the President, "Meeting with General Eisenhower, 12 May 1965," National Security Files, Name File: President Eisenhower, Johnson Library, Box 3.

104. Lewy, *America in Vietnam* (note 25 above), p. 47. Support troops, rather than combat units, composed the largest percentage of this total.

105. Cable, Ball to Taylor and Alexis Johnson, 1 June 1965, National

Security Files, NSC History: "Deployment of Major U.S. Forces to Vietnam, July 1965," Vol. 4, Johnson Library, Box 41.

106. Cable, Taylor and Alexis Johnson to Ball, 3 June 1965, National Security Files, NSC History: "Deployment of Major U.S. Forces to Vietnam, July 1965," Vol. 4, Johnson Library, Box 41.

107. Memorandum, McGeorge Bundy to the President, 5 June 1965, National Security Files, NSC History: "Deployment of Major U.S. Forces to Vietnam, July 1965," Vol. 4, Johnson Library, Box 41.

108. Berman, *Planning a Tragedy* (note 11 above), pp. 67–68.

109. Memorandum, McNamara to the President, 26 June 1965 (Revised 1 July), National Security Files, NSC Meeting File, Vol. 3, Johnson Library, Box 1.

110. Memorandum, McGeorge Bundy to McNamara, 30 June 1965, National Security Files, NSC History, "Deployment of Major U.S. Forces to Vietnam, July 1965," Vol. 6, Johnson Library, Box 43; State Department Memorandum to McNamara, 30 June 1965, National Security Files, NSC History: "Deployment of Major U.S. Forces to Vietnam, July 1965," Vol. 6, Johnson Library, Box 43; and memorandum, Ball to the President, 29 June 1965, National Security Files, NSC History: "Deployment of Major U.S. Forces to Vietnam, July 1965," Vol. 6, Johnson Library, Box 43.

111. Memorandum, McNamara to the President, 20 July 1965, NSF Country File: Vietnam, Folder 2E, Johnson Library, Box 74.

112. Memorandum, McNamara to the President, 28 July 1965, National Security Files, NSC History: "Deployment of Major U.S. Forces to Vietnam, July 1965," Vol. 1, Johnson Library, Box 40.

113. Memorandum, McNamara for the President, 30 July 1965, *Pentagon Papers*, Gravel edition, III: 388; emphasis in original.

114. Rostow letter to Rusk, "Hitting Hanoi Targets," 26 July 1965, National Security Files, NSC History: "Deployment of Major U.S. Forces to Vietnam, July 1965," Vol. 7, Johnson Library, Box 43, and memorandum, Ball to the President, 29 June 1965.

115. Johnson's questions to his advisers during the July deliberations "were not intended to make a difference in option selection. Rather, their purpose was to legitimize a previously selected option by creating the illusion that other views were being considered." See Berman, *Planning a Tragedy*, p. 112. Cooper writes: "It is my belief that the issue of additional deployments was already resolved when the NSC met in late July." Cooper, *Lost Crusade* (note 11 above), p. 285.

116. William Bundy interview, 26 May 1969 (note 36 above), Tape 2, pp. 36–37.

117. Johnson commented in February 1967: "Hanoi is trying to force us to give up the bombing of North Vietnam. We will keep on until we

get something from the North Vietnamese." A year later, in response to the Tet Offensive, he approved attacks on fourteen targets near the center of Hanoi. See "Summary Notes of the 568th NSC Meeting," 8 February 1967, National Security Files, NSC Meetings, Vol. 4, Johnson Library, Box 2; "Notes of the President's Tuesday Luncheon Meeting," 6 February 1968, President's appointment file, "February 6, 1968," Johnson Library, Box 89.

Chapter III
AN EXTENDED APPLICATION OF FORCE

1. Curtis E. LeMay with MacKinlay Kantor, *Mission with LeMay* (Garden City, N.Y.: Doubleday, 1965), p. 564; emphasis in original.

2. Chief among these self-imposed restrictions were prohibitions against terror raids on civilians. Chapter IV discusses this issue more fully.

3. Joint Chiefs of Staff Memorandum (hereafter JCSM) 652-65, 27 August 1965, National Security Files, Country File: Vietnam, JCS Memorandums, Vol. 1, Johnson Library, Box 193, p. 1. At the end of May 1967, the Joint Chiefs criticized Secretary of Defense Robert S. McNamara for suggesting a course of action in Vietnam that was not consistent with NSAM 288's objectives. See *The Pentagon Papers: The Defense Department History of United States Decisionmaking in Vietnam*, Senator Gravel edition (Boston: Beacon Press, 1971), IV: 178–80.

4. Herbert Y. Schandler, *The Unmaking of a President: Lyndon Johnson and Vietnam* (Princeton, N.J.: Princeton University Press, 1977), p. 50. See also William C. Westmoreland, *A Soldier Reports* (Garden City, N.Y.: Doubleday, 1976), p. 69, and Oral History interview of General John P. McConnell by Dorothy Pierce McSweeny, Washington, D.C., 14 and 28 August 1969, Lyndon Baines Johnson Library, Austin, Texas, Tape 1, p. 24.

5. JCSM 652-25, 27 August 1965, p. 1.

6. See, for example, Admiral U. S. Grant Sharp, *Strategy for Defeat: Vietnam in Retrospect* (San Rafael, Calif.: Presidio Press, 1978), p. 4, and USAF Oral History interview of Lieutenant General Glen W. Martin by Lieutenant Colonel Vaughn H. Gallagher, 6–10 February 1978, Air Force Historical Research Center (hereafter AFHRC), Maxwell Air Force Base, Alabama, File Number K239.0512-982, p. 480. As Commander-in-Chief, Pacific Command (CINCPAC), Sharp was the ranking air commander in the Pacific; Martin was Air Force Deputy Chief of Staff from 1965 to 1967.

7. Interview of Lieutenant Colonel William H. Greenhalgh by the author, Maxwell Air Force Base, Alabama, 15 May 1985.

8. USAF Oral History interview of Major General Robert N. Gins-

burgh by Colonel John E. Van Duyn and Major Richard B. Clement, 26 May 1971, AFHRC, file number K239.0512-477, p. 25.

9. Quoted in Sharp, *Strategy for Defeat*, p. 99.

10. U.S. Congress, Senate, Committee on Armed Services, Preparedness Investigating Subcommittee, *Air War Against North Vietnam*, 90th Cong., 1st sess., part 3, 22–23 August 1967, p. 201.

11. Martin interview, 6–10 February 1978, p. 491.

12. JCSM 471-64, 2 June 1964, *Pentagon Papers*, Gravel edition, III: 172.

13. Letter from Lieutenant General Joseph H. Moore (ret.) to the author, 1 October 1986. The 2d Air Division comprised Air Force fighter units in Southeast Asia. It became the 7th Air Force in 1966.

14. One example is Message 222325Z June 1965, CINCPAC to CINC-PACFLET, CINCPACAF, and COMUSMACV, in *Commander-in-Chief, PACOM Outgoing Messages, 22 January–28 June 1965*, AFHRC, file number K712.1623-2.

15. On 18 November 1964, after the JCS had completed months of detailed planning for an air campaign, Wheeler wrote McNamara: "It is desirable that a clear set of military objectives be agreed upon before further military involvement in Southeast Asia is undertaken." See memorandum, the Chairman, JCS, to Secretary of Defense, 18 November 1964. *Pentagon Papers*, Gravel edition, III: 640.

16. Senate Preparedness Subcommittee, *Air War Against North Vietnam*, part 3, 22–23 August 1967, p. 201.

17. Message 110735Z February 1965, CINCPAC to JCS, in *Commander-in-Chief, PACOM Outgoing Messages, 22 January–28 June 1965*.

18. LeMay remained Air Force Chief of Staff until 1 February 1965, when McConnell became the service head.

19. Quoted in Colonel Dennis M. Drew, *Rolling Thunder 1965: Anatomy of a Failure* (Maxwell AFB, Ala.: Air University Press, 1986), p. 29.

20. JCS briefing text, "Air Operations Against North Vietnam and Laos," January 1967, *Target Study—North Vietnam*, AFHRC, file number K178.2-34.

21. Senate Preparedness Subcommittee, *Air War Against North Vietnam*, p. 212.

22. JCSM 746-64, LeMay to the Secretary of Defense, 26 August 1964, *Pentagon Papers*, Gravel edition, III: 551.

23. LeMay with Kantor, *Mission* (note 1 above), p. 565.

24. Air planners persisted in this belief despite the Sigma II War Games conducted 8–11 September 1964 by the Joint War Games Agency, Cold War Division of the Joint Chiefs of Staff. According to Under Secretary of State George Ball, the games revealed that destroying the ninety-

four targets "would not cripple Hanoi's capability for increasing its support to the Viet Cong, much less force suspension of present support levels on purely logistical grounds." George W. Ball, "How Valid Are the Assumptions Underlying Our Viet-Nam Policies?" 5 October 1964, *Atlantic Monthly* 230 (July 1972), p. 39.

25. Wheeler commented in 1967 about Rolling Thunder's origins: "From the start, we have sought to obstruct, reduce, and harass the flow of war-supporting matériel within North Vietnam, and from North Vietnam to South Vietnam, and to destroy the war-supporting facilities of the enemy." See Senate Preparedness Subcommittee, *Air War Against North Vietnam*, part 2, 16 August 1967, p. 126.

26. *Pentagon Papers*, Gravel edition, III: 209.

27. Memorandum, Wheeler to Secretary of Defense, 18 November 1964, *Pentagon Papers*, Gravel edition, III: 639–40.

28. Quoted in *Pentagon Papers*, Gravel edition, III: 233–34. The other JCS options were: (1) to withdraw from Vietnam; (2) to continue with present policies, and (4) to implement the 18 November JCS proposal.

29. Quoted in *Pentagon Papers*, Gravel edition, III: 213-14; emphasis in original.

30. Memorandum, Chairman, JCS, to Secretary of Defense, 11 February 1965, *Pentagon Papers*, Gravel edition, III: 320.

31. Memorandum, Chairman, JCS, to Secretary of Defense, 13 February 1965, *Pentagon Papers*, Gravel edition, III: 340.

32. McConnell added twelve extra days to the original plan because of the winter moonsoon weather in Vietnam.

33. *Pentagon Papers*. Gravel edition, III: 320.

34. Message 271945Z February 1965, CINCPAC to JCS, in *Commander-in-Chief, PACOM Outgoing Messages, 22 January–28 June 1965* (see note 14 above).

35. JCSM 221-65, Chairman, JCS, to Secretary of Defense, 27 March 1965, National Security Files, NSC History: "Deployment of Major U.S. Forces to Vietnam, July 1965," Vol. 2, Johnson Library, Box 40.

36. Message 040304Z April 1965, CINCPAC to JCS, in *Commander-in-Chief, PACOM, Outgoing Messages, 22 January–28 June 1965*; emphasis added.

37. CM 534-65, Chairman, JCS, to Secretary of Defense, 6 April 1965, National Security Files, NSC History: "Deployment of Major U.S. Ground Forces to Vietnam, July 1965," Vol. 3, Johnson Library, Box 41.

38. Memorandum, McNamara to the President, 21 April 1965, *Pentagon Papers*, Gravel edition, III: 358–59; emphasis added.

39. *Pentagon Papers*, Gravel edition, III: 359.

40. Sharp, *Strategy for Defeat* (note 6 above), p. 80.

41. Memorandum, McNamara to the President, 26 June 1965 (revised 1 July), National Security Files, NSC Meeting File, Vol. 3, Johnson Library, Box 1.

42. Memorandum, McNamara to the President, 3 November 1965, National Security Files, Country File: Vietnam, Folder 2E, Johnson Library, Box 75.

43. Message 120314Z May 1965, CINCPAC to JCS, in *Commander-in-Chief, PACOM, Outgoing Messages, 22 January–28 June 1965.*

44. *Pentagon Papers*, Gravel edition, III: 384–85.

45. *Ibid.*, IV: 24.

46. See Chapter II, pp. 71–72.

47. Oral History interview of General Earle G. Wheeler by Dorothy Pierce McSweeny, Washington, D.C., 21 August 1969, Johnson Library, Tape 1, p. 30.

48. McConnell commented in 1969: "The interdiction . . . certainly cut down the capability of the North Vietnamese and the Viet Cong to carry on sustained operations." See McConnell interview, 28 August 1969 (note 4 above), Tape 1, p. 22.

49. Memorandum, McNamara for the President, 28 July 1965, National Security Files, NSC History: "Deployment of Major U.S. Forces to Vietnam, July 1965," Vol. 1, Johnson Library, Box 40.

50. David C. Humphrey, "Tuesday Lunch at the Johnson White House: A Preliminary Assessment," *Diplomatic History* 8 (Winter 1984): 90. Humphrey notes that many accounts have listed Wheeler as a member beginning in 1966, but his careful research of primary documents shows that this was not the case.

51. Ginsburgh interview, 26 May 1971 (note 7 above), p. 50.

52. Senate Preparedness Subcommittee, *Air War Against North Vietnam* (note 10 above), part 4, 25 August 1967, p. 333.

53. Ginsburgh interview, 26 May 1971, p. 36.

54. Interview of Dean Rusk by the author, Athens, Georgia, 15 July 1985.

55. Senate Preparedness Subcommittee, *Air War Against North Vietnam*, part 5, 27–29 August 1967, pp. 476–85, and interview of Lieutenant Colonel Charles Ferguson by the author, 17 May 1985, Maxwell Air Force Base, Alabama.

56. USAF Oral History interview of Colonel Henry H. Edelen by Major Samuel E. Riddlebarger and Lieutenant Colonel S. Bissell, 27 January 1970, AFHRC, file number K239.0512-243, pp. 1–6, 15–17, 24–26; emphasis added.

57. *Ibid.*, pp. 6, 24.

58. Senate Preparedness Subcommittee, *Air War Against North Vietnam*, part 2, 16 August 1967, p. 139.

59. Edelen interview, 27 January 1970, p. 28.

60. Rusk interview, 15 July 1985.

61. Edelen interview, 27 January 1970, pp. 13–14.

62. *Ibid.*, pp. 38–39.

63. Telephone interview with Robert S. McNamara by the author, 15 December 1986.

64. JCSM 613-65, memorandum, Chairman, JCS, to Secretary of Defense, 27 August 1965, National Security Files, Country File: Vietnam, Folder 2EE, Johnson Library, Box 75. Hon Gay was North Vietnam's second largest port city.

65. *Ibid.*

66. *Ibid.* and JCSM 652-65, 27 August 1965.

67. "Cumulative Statistics, Southeast Asia," in DJSM 1162-65, 5 October 1965, National Security Files, Name File: Colonel R. C. Bowman, Johnson Library, Box 1; JCS Briefing Text, "Air Operations Against North Vietnam and Laos," January 1967, and *Pentagon Papers*, Gravel edition (note 3 above), IV: 59.

68. The President had ordered Phase I deployments in July 1965 to stymie the Communist advance. Phase II called for 125,000 more men to allow American and South Vietnamese forces to control 65 percent of the South's population and 20–30 percent of its land by the spring of 1967.

69. Memorandum, McNamara to the President, 3 November 1965 (note 42 above).

70. *Ibid.*

71. JCSM 811-65, Chairman, JCS, for Secretary of Defense, 10 November 1965, National Security Files, Country File: Vietnam, JCS Memorandums, Vol. 2, Johnson Library, Box 193.

72. Message 202213Z November 1965, CINCPAC to JCS, in *Commander-in-Chief, PACOM, Outgoing Messages, 25 July–7 December 1965*, AFHRC, file number K712.1623-2.

73. Oral History interview of William Bundy by Paige E. Mulhollan, 26 May 1969, Johnson Library, Tape 3, p. 16.

74. "12:35 P.M. Meeting with Foreign Policy Advisors on Bombing Pause," 18 December 1965. Meeting Notes File, Johnson Library, Box 1.

75. During much of the debate over a bombing halt, Wheeler was away from Washington touring military installations in the Far East. He communicated his opposition to a pause to Army General Andrew J. Goodpaster, Director of the Joint Staff, who reported Wheeler's view to the President. Until 6 January 1966, after Wheeler returned, the Joint Chiefs

were unaware of this backchannel arrangement because of Johnson's requirement that it be kept secret. Nor did they know of the intense deliberation over the pause that occurred during late December and early January. See Wallace M. Greene, "The Bombing 'Pause': Formula for Failure," *Air Force*, April 1976, pp. 36–39. Greene was Commandant of the Marine Corps during the bombing pause discussions.

76. William Bundy interview, 26 May 1969, Tape 3, pp. 16–21; "Meeting with Foreign Policy Advisors on Vietnam," 3 January 1966, Meeting Notes File, Johnson Library, Box 1; "Summary Notes of the 555th NSC Meeting," 5 January 1966, National Security Files, NSC Meeting Notes File, Vols. 3–5, Johnson Library, Box 2; "Meeting with Foreign Policy Advisors on Bombing Pause," 10 January 1966, Meeting Notes File, Johnson Library, Box 1; "Meeting in Cabinet Room," 27 January 1966, Meeting Notes File, Johnson Library, Box 1; "Meeting with Foreign Policy Advisors on Resumption of Bombing," 28 January 1966, Meeting Notes File, Johnson Library, Box 1; Chester L. Cooper, *The Lost Crusade: America in Vietnam* (New York: Dodd, Mead, 1970), p. 294; and "Summary Notes of the 556th NSC Meeting," 29 January 1966, National Security Files, NSC Meeting Notes File, Vols. 3–5, Johnson Library, Box 2.

77. William Bundy interview, 26 May 1969, Tape 3, p. 24.

78. At a 20 January 1966 Cabinet meeting, Johnson told his advisers that he planned "to drive the nail in" with air power if the North Vietnamese did not favorably respond to the pause. Yet he also said that the administration "must be careful and cautious" in renewing Rolling Thunder. See "Cabinet Room Meeting," 20 January 1966, Meeting Notes File, Johnson Library, Box 1.

79. JCS briefing text, "Air Operations Against North Vietnam and Laos," January 1967 (note 20 above).

80. JCSM 810-65, "Air Operations Against the North Vietnam POL System," 10 November 1965, National Security Files, Country File: Vietnam, JCS Memorandums, Vol. 1, Johnson Library, Box 193.

81. Message from Sharp to the JCS, 12 January 1966, *Pentagon Papers*, Gravel edition: IV: 40; emphasis added.

82. *Pentagon Papers*, (note 3 above), Gravel edition, IV: 67. The Defense Intelligence Agency comprised military analysts from the four services.

83. Intelligence assessment by Richard Helms, 28 December 1965, *Pentagon Papers*, Gravel edition, IV: 64–65.

84. *Pentagon Papers*, Gravel edition, IV: 68.

85. John T. McNaughton, "Some Observations About Bombing North Vietnam," 18 January 1966, *Pentagon Papers*, Gravel edition, IV: 42–49.

86. *Ibid.*

87. Memorandum, McNamara to the President, 24 January 1966, *Pentagon Papers*, Gravel edition, IV: 49, 68.

88. *Pentagon Papers*, Gravel edition, IV: 76.

89. In the Secretary's opinion, the attacks against two airfield storage sites recommended by the JCS would cause heavy civilian casualties.

90. *Pentagon Papers*, Gravel edition IV: 77–78.

91. Note, Johnson to Bromley Smith, 19 March 1966, National Security Files, Country File: Vietnam, Folder 2 EE, Johnson Library, Box 75.

92. JCS briefing text, "Air Operations Against North Vietnam and Laos," January 1967 (note 20 above), and *Pentagon Papers*, Gravel edition, IV: 79.

93. Andrew J. Goodpaster, "Telephone Conversations with General Eisenhower," 25 April 1966, National Security Files, Name File: President Eisenhower, Johnson Library, Box 3.

94. *Pentagon Papers*, Gravel edition, IV: 94.

95. Memorandum, Maxwell Taylor to the President, 27 April 1966, *Pentagon Papers*, Gravel edition, IV: 95.

96. Memorandum, William Bundy to Secretary of State, 3 May 1966, *Pentagon Papers*, Gravel edition, IV: 97.

97. Memorandum, Walt Rostow to McNamara and Rusk, 6 May 1966, *Pentagon Papers*, Gravel edition, IV: 100–101.

98. The authors of the *Pentagon Papers* speculate that Johnson gave the order for strikes on major POL storage areas at the end of May. Minutes from 17 and 22 June NSC meetings, not cited in the *Pentagon Papers*, disprove this supposition.

99. "National Security Council Meeting, 17 June 1966," Meeting Notes File, Johnson Library, Box 1. The President stated at the meeting: "A decision on bombing is not being made now and one is not imminent."

100. "National Security Council Meeting, 22 June 1966," Meeting Notes File, Johnson Library, Box 1.

101. Oral History interview of Lyndon Baines Johnson by William J. Jordan, LBJ Ranch, Texas, 12 August 1969, Johnson Library, p. 19.

102. *Pentagon Papers*, Gravel edition, IV: 105–6.

103. *Pentagon Papers*, Gravel edition, IV: 106, 109; Sharp, *Strategy for Defeat*, p. 119; Message 070323Z July 1966, CINCPACAF to 7AF, in *PACAF Outgoing Messages, 15 March–31 December 1966*, AFHRC, file number K717.1623; and Message 080730Z July 1966, CINCPACAF to 7AF, in *PACAF Outgoing Messages, 15 March–31 December 1966*.

104. "Opening the Fourth Front," *Newsweek*, 18 July 1966, p. 18.

105. William Bundy interview, 29 May 1969 (note 73 above), Tape 3, p. 36.

106. *Pentagon Papers,* Gravel edition, IV: 109–10.

107. Jason Summer Study, "The Effects of U.S. Bombing in North Vietnam," *Pentagon Papers,* Gravel edition, IV: 111–20.

108. Memorandum, McNamara to the President, 14 October 1966, *Pentagon Papers,* Gravel edition, IV: 125–26.

109. Memorandum, Ginsburgh to Walt Rostow, 13 September 1966, National Security Files, Country File: Vietnam, Folder: Effects of U.S. Bombing, Johnson Library, Box 192; emphasis added.

110. Quoted in *Pentagon Papers,* Gravel edition, IV: 128.

111. CM 1906-66, memorandum, Chairman, JCS, to Secretary of Defense, 8 November 1966, National Security Files, Country File: Vietnam, Folder 2EE, Johnson Library, Box 75.

112. "National Security Council Meeting," 22 June 1966 (note 100 above).

113. *Pentagon Papers,* Gravel edition, IV: 130–31.

114. Presidential daily diary, November 1966, Johnson Library.

115. Memorandum, McNamara to the President, 8 November 1966, National Security Files, Country File: Vietnam, Folder 2EE, Johnson Library, Box 75.

116. Sharp, *Strategy for Defeat* (note 6 above), p. 122.

117. Johnson returned to Washington on 14 November and entered Bethesda Naval Hospital on the 15th for minor throat and abdominal surgery. He remained at Bethesda until the 19th, when he again departed for Texas.

118. "In other words," William Bundy remembered, "we would give them the idea that the bombing stopped for nothing on the face of things, provided we in fact knew that something was going to happen." See William Bundy interview, 29 May 1969 (note 73 above), Tape 4, p. 24.

119. George C. Herring, *America's Longest War: The United States and Vietnam 1950–1975* (New York: Wiley, 1979), p. 168. Johnson contended that since the North Vietnamese had not required a bombing halt as a prerequisite for negotiations, the Hanoi attacks could not have been responsible for the failure to show in Warsaw. See Lyndon Baines Johnson, *The Vantage Point* (New York: Holt, Rinehart & Winston, 1971), pp. 251–52.

120. Memorandum, Rostow to the President, "Rolling Thunder 53," 23 January 1967, National Security Files, Country File: Vietnam, Folder 2EE, Johnson Library, Box 75.

121. Johnson, *Vantage Point,* p. 252. For an in-depth examination of the Polish initiative, code-named Marigold, see George C. Herring, ed., *The Secret Diplomacy of the Vietnam War: The Negotiating Volumes of*

the Pentagon Papers (Austin: University of Texas Press, 1983), pp. 211–370.

122. Nguyen Duy Trinh's interview with Wilfred Burchett, 28 January 1967, in Herring, *Secret Diplomacy*, p. 424.

123. Letter, Lyndon B. Johnson to Ho Chi Minh, 8 February 1967, in Herring, *Secret Diplomacy*, p. 441.

124. William Bundy interview, 29 May 1969 (note 73 above), Tape 4, pp. 25–27; letter, the President to Prime Minister Wilson, 7 February 1967, in Herring, *Secret Diplomacy*, pp. 436–38. Johnson told Wilson on 7 February that "we are prepared to and plan . . . to inform Hanoi that if they will agree to an assured stoppage of infiltration in South Viet Nam, we will stop the bombing of North Viet Nam." The President was not clear, however, about which side was to act *first*, and Wilson assumed that the Phase A–Phase B plan remained in effect.

125. "Ho Chi Minh's Reply," 15 February 1967, in Johnson, *Vantage Point*, p. 594.

126. Johnson, *Vantage Point*, p. 259.

127. *Pentagon Papers*, Gravel edition, IV: 144. Although a majority of Americans backed Rolling Thunder, opposition to the bombing remained a rallying point in the growing antiwar movement.

128. *Ibid.*, IV: 150.

129. U. S. Grant Sharp and William C. Westmoreland, *Report on the War in Vietnam (as of 30 June 1968)* (Washington, D.C.: U.S. Government Printing Office, 1968), p. 31.

130. Senate Preparedness Subcommittee, *Air War Against North Vietnam* (note 10 above), part 4, 25 August 1967, p. 293.

131. "Summary Notes of the 568th NSC Meeting," 8 February 1967, National Security Files, NSC Meetings, Vol. 4, Johnson Library, Box 2.

132. *Pentagon Papers*, Gravel edition, IV: 149.

133. CM 1906-66, 8 November 1966.

134. Memorandum, Chairman, JCS, to the President, 5 May 1967, *Pentagon Papers*, Gravel edition, IV: 152.

135. *Pentagon Papers*, Gravel edition, IV: 154, 161–76.

136. Memorandum, William Bundy to the President, 9 May 1967, National Security Files, Country File: Vietnam, Folder 2EE, Johnson Library, Box 75.

137. Memorandum, McNamara to the President, 19 May 1967, National Security Files, Country File: Vietnam, Folder 2EE, Johnson Library, Box 75.

138. At Glassboro, Johnson gave Kosygin the same terms to pass on to

Hanoi that he had earlier offered in his letter to Ho. The North Vietnamese did not respond.

139. *Pentagon Papers*, Gravel edition, IV: 196.

140. The Joint Chiefs' list contained 242 fixed targets prior to the addition of Sharp's targets.

141. CM 2650-67, memorandum, Chairman, JCS, to Secretary of Defense, 15 September 1967, in *Target Study—North Vietnam*, AFHRC, file number, K178.2-34.

142. USAF Oral History interview of Lieutenant Colonel William H. Greenhalgh by Lieutenant Colonel Robert Eckert, 11 October 1967, AFHRC, file number K239.0512-40, p. 21.

143. *Pentagon Papers*, Gravel edition, IV: 198.

144. Johnson, *Vantage Point* (note 119 above), p. 266.

145. *Pentagon Papers*, Gravel edition, IV: 234.

146. Quoted in *ibid.*, IV: 206.

147. Johnson, *Vantage Point*, p. 268.

148. "President's Meeting with Robin Olds," 2 October 1967, Tom Johnson's Notes of Meetings, Johnson Library, Box 1, and Herring, *America's Longest War* (note 119 above), p. 173.

149. JCSM 555-67, memorandum, Chairman, JCS, to Secretary of Defense, 17 October 1967, *Pentagon Papers*, Gravel edition, IV: 210–11.

150. *Pentagon Papers*, Gravel edition, IV: 215.

151. Senate Preparedness Subcommittee, *Air War Against North Vietnam* (note 10 above), 22–23 August 1967, part 3, p. 213.

152. Oral History interview of Clark M. Clifford by Joe B. Frantz, Bethesda, Maryland, 2–14 July 1969, Johnson Library, Tape 2, pp. 24–25, and Tape 3, pp. 4–5.

153. Clark Clifford replaced McNamara as Secretary of Defense at the end of February 1968.

154. Jason Summer Study Report, December 1967, *Pentagon Papers*, Gravel edition, IV: 222–25.

155. "1967 Progress Report," message from CINCPAC to JCS, in Sharp, *Strategy for Defeat* (note 6 above), p. 302.

156. Ginsburgh interview, 26 May 1971 (note 8 above), pp. 10–14. Rostow established a White House intelligence evaluation group that first predicted an enemy offensive; the CIA and DIA soon confirmed the Rostow group's assessment.

157. *Pentagon Papers*, Gravel edition, IV: 233.

158. Rusk interview, 15 July 1985 (note 54 above).

159. Dave Richard Palmer, *Summons of the Trumpet* (Novato, Calif.: Presidio Press, 1978), pp. 186–87.

160. "Notes of the President's Tuesday Luncheon Meeting," 6 February 1968, President's Appointment File, Johnson Library, Box 89.

161. *Pentagon Papers,* Gravel edition, IV: 268.

162. Clifford interview, 2 July 1969, Tape 2, pp. 25–26.

163. Clifford Working Group memorandum, 3 March 1968, *Pentagon Papers,* Gravel edition, IV: 250–52.

164. Clifford interview, 14 July 1969, Tape 3, p. 5. Those "wise men" recommending disengagement were Dean Acheson, McGeorge Bundy, Arthur Dean, Douglas Dillon, George Ball, and Cyrus Vance. See Johnson, *The Vantage Point* (note 119 above), pp. 416–18.

165. Townsend Hoopes, Johnson's Under Secretary of the Air Force, maintains that Clifford's dissatisfaction with the war was the key reason for the President's March decision to de-escalate. See Townsend Hoopes, *The Limits of Intervention* (New York: David McKay, 1969).

166. Thomas J. Schoenbaum, *Waging Peace and War: Dean Rusk in the Truman, Kennedy, and Johnson Years* (New York: Simon & Schuster, 1988), pp. 470–79, and Johnson, *Vantage Point,* p. 419. Schoenbaum insists that Rusk "played the decisive role" in persuading Johnson to decrease Rolling Thunder.

167. Herring, *America's Longest War* (note 119 above), p. 205. In March 1968, before the President's speech, a Gallup poll reported that 40 percent of the American public thought the United States should stop bombing the North, while 51 percent disagreed. In April, those numbers had changed to 64 percent in favor of a bombing halt and 26 percent opposed. See Philip E. Converse and Howard Schuman, "'Silent Majorities' and the Vietnam War," *Scientific American* 222 (June 1970): 21.

168. Johnson, *Vantage Point,* p. 422.

169. Louis Harris, *The Anguish of Change* (New York: W. W. Norton, 1973), p. 64.

170. Quoted in *Pentagon Papers,* Gravel edition, IV: 275.

Chapter IV
RESTRAINTS AND RESULTS, 1965–68

1. George W. Ball, "How Valid Are the Assumptions Underlying Our Viet-Nam Policies?" 5 October 1964, *Atlantic Monthly* 230 (July 1972), p. 38.

2. Memorandum, McGeorge Bundy to Secretary of Defense, 30 June 1965, National Security Files, NSC History: "Deployment of Major U.S. Forces to Vietnam, July 1965," Vol. 6, Lyndon Baines Johnson Library, Austin, Texas, Box 43.

3. *The Pentagon Papers: The Defense Department History of United*

States Decisionmaking in Vietnam, Senator Gravel edition (Boston: Beacon Press, 1971) III: 209, 333–34.

4. Memorandum, General Andrew Goodpaster to the President, "Meeting with General Eisenhower," 12 October 1965, National Security Files, Name File: President Eisenhower, Johnson Library, Box 3.

5. Raphael Littauer and Norman Uphoff, eds., *The Air War in Indochina* (Boston: Beacon Press, 1972), p. 44.

6. *Pentagon Papers,* Gravel edition, IV: 233.

7. In an 18 December 1965 meeting with Johnson and his principal civilian advisers, Secretary of Defense Robert S. McNamara stated that the May pause "was a propaganda effort—not for the Soviets to help [negotiate]." No one challenged this explanation. See "12:35 P.M. Meeting with Foreign Policy Advisors on Bombing Pause," 18 December 1965, Meeting Notes File, Johnson Library, Box 1.

8. Message, Maxwell Taylor to George Ball, 3 June 1965, National Security Files, NSC History: "Deployment of Major U.S. Forces to Vietnam, July 1965," Vol. 4, Johnson Library, Box 41.

9. Oral History interview of William Bundy by Paige E. Mulhollan, 29 May 1969, Johnson Library, Tape 2, p. 27.

10. David C. Humphrey, "Tuesday Lunch at the Johnson White House: A Preliminary Assessment," *Diplomatic History* 8 (Winter 1984): 82–89.

11. Interview of Dean Rusk by the author, Athens, Georgia, 15 July 1985.

12. Chester L. Cooper, *The Lost Crusade: America in Vietnam* (New York: Dodd, Mead, 1970), p. 414.

13. William Bundy interview, 2 June 1969, Tape 5, pp. 12–13.

14. Quoted in Humphrey, "Tuesday Lunch," p. 98.

15. Message, Secretary of State to CINCPAC and COMUSMACV, 10 May 1965, *Pentagon Papers,* Gravel edition, III: 367.

16. U.S. Congress, Senate, Committee on Armed Services, Preparedness Investigating Subcommittee, *Air War Against North Vietnam,* 90th Cong., 1st sess., part 5, 27–29 August 1967, p. 478.

17. Message, 190935Z May 1965, 41st ADIV ADVON to 2 AD CP, in *PACAF Outgoing Messages, 3 April–24 December 1965,* AFHRC, Maxwell AFB, Alabama, file number K717.1623. "Pending more definitive guidance from headquarters," the wing commander defined a convoy as "three or more internal combustion vehicles going the same direction on not more than a one mile segment of a specified route."

18. Oral History interview of Earle G. Wheeler by Dorothy Pierce McSweeny, Washington, D.C., 21 August 1969, Johnson Library, Tape 1, p. 12.

19. "Meeting with Foreign Policy Advisors on Vietnam," 17 December 1965; "12:35 P.M. Meeting with Foreign Policy Advisors on Bombing Pause," 18 December 1965; and "Meeting with Foreign Policy Advisors," 21 December 1965, in Meeting Notes File, Johnson Library, Box 1.

20. USAF Oral History interview of Major General Robert N. Ginsburgh by Colonel John E. Van Duyn and Major Richard B. Clement, 26 May 1971, AFHRC, file number K239.0512-477, pp. 65–68. The group was known as the "no committee" because of the President's wish to keep the existence of yet another formal committee quiet. Directed by Under Secretary of State Nicholas Katzenbach, its membership included McNamara, Rusk, Rostow, McNaughton, and William Bundy.

21. Senate Preparedness Subcommittee, *Air War Against North Vietnam*, part 5, 27–29 August 1967, p. 478.

22. Letter, Lieutenant Colonel William H. Greenhalgh to the author, 4 April 1987; emphasis added.

23. Senate Preparedness Subcommittee, *Air War Against North Vietnam*, part 5, 27–29 August 1967, p. 478. Poor weather also contributed to the low total of fixed targets struck.

24. Ginsburgh interview, 26 May 1971, pp. 74–75.

25. "Meeting with Foreign Policy Advisors on Vietnam," 17 December 1965, and "12:35 P.M. Meeting with Foreign Policy Advisors on Bombing Pause," 18 December 1965.

26. Oral History interview of General John P. McConnell by Dorothy Pierce McSweeny, Washington, D.C., 14 and 28 August 1969, Johnson Library, Tape 1, p. 38.

27. CM 1906-66, memorandum, Chairman, JCS, to Secretary of Defense, 8 November 1966, National Security Files, Country File: Vietnam, Folder 2EE, Johnson Library, Box 75.

28. Ginsburgh interview, 26 May 1971, p. 74.

29. Interview of Walt W. Rostow by the author, Austin, Texas, 23 May 1986.

30. Cooper, *Lost Crusade* (note 12 above), p. 420.

31. William Bundy interview, 29 May 1969 (note 9 above), Tape 3, p. 24, and Oral History interview of Clark M. Clifford by Joe B. Frantz, Bethesda, Maryland, 2 July 1969, Johnson Library, Tape 2, p. 20.

32. Clifford interview, 15 December 1969, Tape 5, pp. 20–21.

33. William Bundy interview, 29 May 1969, Tape 3, p. 17.

34. *Ibid.*, pp. 13–14; emphasis in transcript.

35. Johnson placed Roosevelt's portrait on the wall across from his chair in the Cabinet Room. See Henry Graff, *The Tuesday Cabinet* (Englewood Cliffs, N.J.: Prentice Hall, 1970), p. 57.

36. Lyndon Baines Johnson, *The Vantage Point: Perspectives of the Presidency 1963–1969* (New York: Holt, Reinhart & Winston, 1971), p. 423.

37. As a rationale for raids on power plants, the Joint Chiefs stated that the attacks would have "significant sociological and psychological effects" on the North Vietnamese populace. See Annex A to Appendix A of JCSM 811-65, memorandum, Chairman, JCS, to Secretary of Defense, 7 December 1965, National Security Files, Country File: Vietnam, JCS Memorandums, Vol. 2, Johnson Library, Box 193.

38. Appendix C to JCSM 613-65, memorandum, Chairman, JCS, to Secretary of Defense, 27 August 1965, National Security Files, Country File: Vietnam, Folder 2EE, Johnson Library, Box 75.

39. *Pentagon Papers*, Gravel edition (note 3 above), IV: 56.

40. CM 1906-66, 8 November 1966 (note 27 above).

41. Ginsburgh interview, 26 May 1971 (note 20 above), and interview of Lieutenant Colonel William H. Greenhalgh by the author, Maxwell AFB, Alabama, 17 May 1985.

42. Jon M. Van Dyke, *North Vietnam's Strategy for Survival* (Palo Alto, Calif.: Pacific Books, 1972), p. 184. A dam burst in 1945, killing between 1.5 million and 2 million people.

43. McConnell interview, 14 and 28 August 1969 (note 26 above), Tape 1, p. 21, and Ginsburgh interview, 26 May 1971, p. 49.

44. Wheeler interview, 21 August 1969 (note 18 above), Tape 1, p. 17.

45. See Chapter I, p. 6.

46. Wheeler interview, 21 August 1969, Tape 1, pp. 24–25.

47. See Chapter III, pp. 102–3.

48. See Chapter III, pp. 106–7.

49. USAF Oral History interview of Colonel Henry Edelen by Major Samuel E. Riddlebarger and Lieutenant Colonel S. Bissell, 27 January 1970, AFHRC, file number K239.0512-243, p. 57.

50. *Ibid.*, pp. 15–26.

51. "Operational" control was the direction of combat activities, while "administrative" control was the direction of personnel. The latter included management of assignments, promotions, leaves and the like.

52. Littauer and Uphoff, *Air War in Indochina* (note 5 above), p. 11, and Carl Berger, ed., *The United States Air Force in Southeast Asia, 1961–1973: An Illustrated Account* (Washington, D.C.: Office of Air Force History, 1984), p. 89.

53. USAF Oral History interview of Lieutenant General Joseph H. Moore by Major Samuel E. Riddlebarger and Lieutenant Colonel Valentino Castellina, 22 November 1969, AFHRC, file number K239.0512-241, pp. 17–18.

54. JCS briefing text, "Air Operations Against North Vietnam and Laos," January 1967, in *Target Study—North Vietnam*, AFHRC, file number K178.2-34.

55. Greenhalgh interview, 17 May 1985 (note 41 above).

56. Robert L. Gallucci, *Neither Peace nor Honor: The Politics of American Military Policy in Viet-Nam* (Baltimore: Johns Hopkins Press, 1975), pp. 80–84, and Littauer and Uphoff, *Air War in Indochina*, p. 38. The shortage of 750-pound "iron" bombs resulted from the Air Force's emphasis on nuclear weapons in the post–World War II era. In February 1966, the Defense Department repurchased five thousand bombs from West Germany at $21.00 apiece. West Germany had originally bought the bombs for scrap at $1.70 each. See John Morrocco, *Thunder from Above* (Boston: Boston Publishing, 1984), pp. 121–22.

57. Quoted in Morrocco, *Thunder from Above*, p. 125. In July 1966, shortly after General William C. Momyer replaced Moore as Seventh Air Force Commander, a period of poor weather obscured targets in the Red River Valley. Momyer ordered his units not to fly and called for ground crews to perform preventive maintenance. A message soon arrived from the Pentagon telling Momyer to fly to prevent the Navy from tallying a higher sortie count. See Greenhalgh interview, 17 May 1985 (note 42 above).

58. Patrick J. McGarvey, "The DIA: Intelligence to Please," *Washington Monthly* 2 (July 1970): 72.

59. "Summary Notes of the 568th NSC Meeting," 8 February 1967, National Security Files, NSC Meetings Files, Vol. 4, Johnson Library, Box 2.

60. Edelen interview, 27 January 1970 (note 49 above), pp. 66–67.

61. Greenhalgh interview, 17 May 1985, and Greenhalgh letter, 4 April 1987 (note 22 above).

62. USAF Oral History interview of Lieutenant Colonel William H. Greenhalgh by Lieutenant Colonel Robert Eckert, 11 October 1967, AFHRC, file number K239.0512-40, pp. 6–7.

63. *Ibid.*, p. 37.

64. U. S. Grant Sharp, *Strategy for Defeat: Vietnam in Retrospect* (San Rafael, Calif.: Presidio Press, 1978), p. 189. Sharp's staff calculated that the North Vietnamese occupied only twenty-five SAM sites at any one time.

65. Jack Broughton, *Thud Ridge* (New York: Bantam Books, 1969), p. 24.

66. Littauer and Uphoff, *Air War in Indochina*, p. 283, and *Pentagon Papers*, Gravel edition (note 3 above), IV: 136. Losses dropped from 3.4 aircraft per 1,000 sorties in 1965 to 2.1 in 1966 and 1.9 in 1967. See *Pentagon Papers*, Gravel edition, IV: 232.

67. Van Tien Dung, "Some Great Experiences of the People's War," in *Visions of Victory: Selected Vietnamese Communist Military Writings, 1964–1968* (Stanford, Calif.: Hoover Institution, 1969), p. 158; Senate Preparedness Subcommittee, *Air War Against North Vietnam* (note 16 above), part 4, 25 August 1967, pp. 324–25; Greenhalgh interview, 11 October 1967, pp. 32–33; Van Dyke, *Strategy for Survival* (note 42 above), p. 49; and Harrison E. Salisbury, *Behind the Lines—Hanoi* (New York: Harper & Row, 1967), pp. 86–91.

68. Quoted in Van Dyke, *Strategy for Survival*, p. 49.

69. Greenhalgh interview, 11 October 1967, pp. 31–32.

70. Van Dyke, *Strategy for Survival*, p. 207; Salisbury, *Behind the Lines*, pp. 90–91; and Greenhalgh interview, 17 May 1985.

71. The Ho Chi Minh "Trail" was actually a series of roadways and paths.

72. *Pentagon Papers*, Gravel edition, IV: 138.

73. Johnson, *Vantage Point* (note 36 above), p. 400.

74. *Air War—Vietnam* (New York: Arno Press, 1978), p. 12.

75. One was finally added in late 1967. Air leaders initially believed that air-to-air missiles sufficed for defensive armament.

76. Peter B. Mersky and Norman Polmar, *The Naval Air War in Vietnam* (Annapolis: Nautical & Aviation Publishing, 1981), p. 19.

77. Quoted in Mersky and Polmar, *Naval Air War*, pp. 180–81.

78. Broughton, *Thud Ridge* (note 65 above), and Jack Broughton, *Going Downtown: The War Against Hanoi and Washington* (New York: Orion Books, 1988), offer numerous examples of the frustrations felt by the Air Force's F-105 pilots. A recipient of the Air Force Cross, Colonel Broughton was court-martialed for his vigorous defense of two pilots accused of strafing a Russian ship in Haiphong harbor. For a Navy pilot's perspective on Rolling Thunder, see John B. Nichols and Barrett Tillman, *On Yankee Station* (Annapolis: Naval Institute Press, 1987).

79. U. S. Grant Sharp and William C. Westmoreland, *Report on the War in Vietnam (as of 30 June 1968)* (Washington, D.C.: U.S. Government Printing Office, 1969), p. 53.

80. *Pentagon Papers*, Gravel edition, IV: 136. The CIA computed Rolling Thunder's cost-effectiveness in early 1967.

81. Headquarters USAF, *Air Operations—North Vietnam*, 27 April 1967, AFHRC, file number K143.0572-90, part 4, p. 6.

82. "Meeting with Foreign Policy Advisors on Vietnam," 18 August 1967, Meeting Notes File, Johnson Library, Box 1. In July 1965, Defense Department analysts estimated that 192,000 Viet Cong and three regiments of the North Vietnamese Army (7,500 men) fought in the South. See memorandum, McNamara to the President, 3 November 1965, National

Security Files, Country File: Vietnam, Folder 2EE, Johnson Library, Box 75.

83. Headquarters USAF, *Analysis of Effectiveness of Interdiction in Southeast Asia, Second Progress Report*, May 1966, AFHRC, file number K168.187-21, p. 7. The study further noted: "The present low requirement of 34 tons/day, though made up largely of ammunition, provides much less than is usually calculated for North Vietnamese forces. Thirty-six percent of the supply support for a soldier in a North Vietnamese light division consists of ammunition. When he is deployed to the south this drops to 18%. Only 6% of the supplies furnished Viet Cong Main Force soldiers is ammunition. Only a 13% firepower utilization rate is presently being experienced by the VC/NVA troops in South Vietnam." McNamara acknowledged in 1967 that Communist forces fought an average of one day in thirty and remarked that they needed 15 tons of supplies daily from external sources. The Joint Chiefs had estimated in August 1965 that the enemy needed 13 tons per day of "external logistical support." See Senate Preparedness Subcommittee, *Air War Against North Vietnam* (note 16 above), 25 August 1967, part 4, p. 299, and Annex A to JCSM 613-65, 27 August 1965, National Security Files, Country File: Vietnam, Folder 2EE, Johnson Library, Box 75. Truong Nhu Tang, *A Viet Cong Memoir* (New York: Vintage Books, 1985), pp. 156–64, details the specific supply requirements of the Viet Cong.

84. The standard military 2½-ton truck could transport 5 tons of goods over roads and 2.5 tons overland.

85. Memorandum, Walt W. Rostow to the President, 6 May 1967, National Security Files, Country File: Vietnam, Folder 2EE, Johnson Library, Box 75, and *Pentagon Papers*, Gravel edition, IV: 146.

86. Appendix A to JCSM 613-65, 27 August 1967.

87. Dung, "Some Great Experiences" (note 67 above), p. 161.

88. Van Dyke, *Strategy for Survival* (note 42 above), p. 51.

89. Jason Summer Study, "Summary and Conclusions," 30 August 1966, *Pentagon Papers*, Gravel edition, IV: 116, and Department of Defense Systems Analysis Report, January 1968, *Pentagon Papers*, Gravel edition, IV: 225–26. The Systems Analysis Report stated: "If economic criteria were the only consideration, North Vietnam would show a substantial net gain from the bombing."

90. CIA Memorandum 11-65, "Future Soviet Moves in Vietnam," 27 April 1965, National Security Files, NSC History: "Deployment of Major U.S. Forces to Vietnam, July 1965," Vol. 3, Johnson Library, Box 41, and CIA Memorandum 18-65, "Soviet Tactics Concerning Vietnam," 15 July 1965, National Security Files, NSC History: "Deployment of Major U.S. Forces to Vietnam, July 1965," Vol. 6, Johnson Library, Box 43.

91. Vo Nguyen Giap,"The Big Victory, The Great Task," in *Visions of Victory* (note 67 above), p. 204.

92. *Pentagon Papers*, Gravel edition, IV: 110–12.

93. Van Dyke, *Strategy for Survival*, p. 210.

94. Edelen interview, 27 January 1970 (note 49 above), pp. 82–83.

95. Oliver Todd, "The Americans Are Not Invincible," *New Left Review* 47 (January–February 1968): 10.

96. CINCPAC, Message to JCS, January 1968, in Sharp, *Strategy for Defeat* (note 64 above), p. 302.

97. *Pentagon Papers*, Gravel edition, IV: 136.

98. See Chapter I, p. 9.

99. Salisbury, *Behind the Lines* (note 67 above), pp. 62–64, and *Pentagon Papers*, Gravel edition, IV: 135.

100. NSSM 1 (February 1969), *Congressional Record 118*, part 13 (10 May 1972): 16833.

101. Salisbury, *Behind the Lines*, pp. 42, 113; Van Dyke, *Strategy for Survival*, pp. 30, 127–33; Todd, "Americans Are Not Invincible," p. 4; and Sharp, *Strategy for Defeat*, p. 161.

102. Van Dyke, *Strategy for Survival*, pp. 28, 160–63; Salisbury, *Behind the Lines*, pp. 120, 182; Department of Defense Systems Analysis Report, January 1968 (note 89 above), p. 227; Giap, "Big Victory," p. 233; and Dung "Some Great Experiences" (note 67 above), p. 165.

103. Salisbury, *Behind the Lines*, p. 196.

104. *Pentagon Papers*, Gravel edition, IV: 330. McNamara announced on 29 June 1966, the day that American aircraft first struck the North's major oil storage facilities: "Our objectives are not to destroy the Communist government of North Vietnam." Quoted in Oleg Hoeffding, *Bombing North Vietnam: An Appraisal of Economic and Political Effects* (December 1966), RAND Corporation Memorandum RM-5213, p. 22.

105. Giap, "Big Victory," p. 207.

106. Statement by Major General Edward Lansdale in W. Scott Thompson and Donaldson D. Frizzell, eds., *The Lessons of Vietnam* (New York: Crane, Russak, 1977), p. 127.

107. Hoeffding, *Bombing North Vietnam*, p. 17.

108. Guenter Lewy, *America in Vietnam* (New York: Oxford University Press, 1978), p. 76, and Gabriel Kolko, *Anatomy of a War: Vietnam, the United States and the Modern Historical Experience* (New York: Pantheon Books, 1985), p. 327. Dave Richard Palmer, *Summons of the Trumpet* (Novato, Calif.: Presidio Press, 1978), p. 208, estimates that Communist losses for the first six months of 1968 amounted to more than 100,000 men.

109. George C. Herring, *America's Longest War: The United States in Vietnam 1950–1975* (New York: John Wiley, 1979), p. 187.

110. Douglas Pike, *PAVN: People's Army of Vietnam* (Novato, Calif.: Presidio Press, 1986), p. 47.

111. Kolko, *Anatomy of a War*, pp. 303–4, 329, 333–34, and Pike, *PAVN*, pp. 223–24.

112. Sharp was one, as were some members of the Pentagon's Joint Staff. See Chapter III, pp. 78 and 80–81.

113. Giap, "Big Victory," p. 232.

114. "12:35 P.M. Meeting with Foreign Policy Advisors on Bombing Pause," 18 December 1965 (note 19 above). In a 15 July 1985 interview with the author at Athens, Georgia (note 11 above), Rusk stated that underestimating the tenacity of the North Vietnamese was one of his greatest mistakes regarding Vietnam: "I thought the North Vietnamese would reach a point, like the Chinese and North Koreans in Korea, and Stalin during the Berlin airlift, when they would finally give in."

115. Quoted in *Pentagon Papers*, Gravel edition (note 3 above), IV: 75.

116. Maxwell D. Taylor, *Swords and Plowshares* (New York: W. W. Norton, 1972), p. 401.

117. Memorandum, Ball to the President, 29 June 1965, National Security Files, NSC History: "Deployment of Major U.S. Forces to Vietnam, July 1965," Vol. 6, Johnson Library, Box 43.

118. Dung, "Some Great Experiences" (note 67 above), p. 155.

119. Giap, "Big Victory," p. 234.

120. Palmer, *Summons of Trumpet* (note 108 above), pp. 166–67, and William Bundy interview, 29 May 1969 (note 9 above), Tape 4, p. 32.

121. Kolko, *Anatomy of a War*, p. 305.

122. Memorandum, McNamara to the President, 30 July 1965, *Pentagon Papers*, Gravel edition, III: 387.

123. "We didn't have any simplistic, naïve views that Communism was monolithic," Rostow stated. "But the split only made it worse [for us in Vietnam], because both Russia and China were competing." Rostow interview, 23 May 1986 (note 29 above).

124. In 1972, when President Richard Nixon mined Northern harbors, the Chinese refused to transport Soviet goods for *three months*. Rostow interview, 23 May 1986.

125. Message, Ambassador Thompson to Secretary of State, 1 March 1968, *Pentagon Papers*, Gravel edition, IV: 246–47.

126. "Opening the Fourth Front," *Newsweek*, 18 July 1966, p. 18. Johnson's approval rating on his conduct of the war rose from 42 to 54 percent.

127. "A New Sophistication," *Newsweek*, 10 July 1967, pp. 20–21; 15 percent of the public opposed bombing, while 13 percent remained uncertain of bombing's utility. Regarding American goals in Vietnam, 36 per-

cent wanted more effort at negotiation, 18 percent desired an "all-out" war, and 6 percent wanted withdrawal.

128. Johnson, *Vantage Point* (note 36 above), p. 240.

129. Oral History interview of Lyndon Baines Johnson by William J. Jorden, LBJ Ranch, Texas, 12 August 1969, Johnson Library, pp. 18–19.

130. Rusk interview, 15 July 1985 (note 11 above).

131. Oral History interview of Maxwell D. Taylor by Dorothy Pierce, Washington, D.C., 10 February 1969, Johnson Library, Tape 2, pp. 10–11, and Oral History interview of Maxwell D. Taylor by Ted Gittinger, Washington, D.C., 14 September 1981, Johnson Library, Tape 1, pp. 7–10.

132. Rostow interview, 23 May 1986. "Everybody was dead wrong on the scale of the supply operation," he stated. "They learned it when the Cambodian government was overthrown by the Cambodian military and they turned over to us the tonnages that went into Sihanoukville. The tonnages they put through were astonishing. . . . Al Haig called my attention to this after I had left the government."

133. Senate Preparedness Subcommittee, *Air War Against North Vietnam*, 25 August 1967 (note 16 above), part 4, pp. 275–78.

134. Robert S. McNamara, statement to Congress, 1 February 1968, *Pentagon Papers*, Gravel edition, IV: 232.

135. "Summary Notes of the 556th National Security Council Meeting," 29 January 1966, National Security Files, NSC Meeting Notes File, Vols. 3–5, Johnson Library, Box 2.

136. Ginsburgh interview, 26 May 1971 (note 20 above), p. 22.

137. USAF Oral History interview of Admiral U. S. Grant Sharp by Dr. Robert R. Kritt, 19 May 1971, AFHRC, file number K239.0512-409, p. 18.

138. Sharp, *Strategy for Defeat* (note 64 above), p. 269.

139. Quoted in David Halberstam, *The Best and the Brightest* (New York: Random House, 1969), pp. 646–47.

140. Momyer, letter to McConnell, 3 July 1969, Personal Papers of General John P. McConnell, 1969, AFHRC, file number 168.7102-15.

141. Sharp interview, 19 May 1971, p. 24; Wheeler interview, 21 August 1969 (note 18 above), Tape 1, p. 30; and Moore interview, 22 November 1969 (note 53 above), p. 69.

Chapter v
NIXON TURNS TO AIR POWER

1. Richard M. Nixon, *RN: The Memoirs of Richard Nixon*, 2 vols. (New York: Warner Books, 1978), II: 63.

2. These activities were the movement of men and supplies across the DMZ, attacks on South Vietnam's major cities, and attacks on American reconnaissance aircraft. Johnson wrote: "Before I made my decision [to halt the bombing], I wanted to be absolutely certain that Hanoi understood our position. . . . Our negotiators reported that the North Vietnamese would give no flat guarantees; that was in keeping with their stand that the bombing had to be ended without conditions. But they had told us that if we stopped the bombing, they would 'know what to do.' [American negotiators] were confident Hanoi knew precisely what we meant and would avoid the actions that we had warned them would imperil a bombing halt." See Lyndon Baines Johnson, *The Vantage Point: Perspectives of the Presidency 1963–1969* (New York: Holt, Rinehart & Winston, 1971), p. 518.

3. In 1969, pilots flew 285 sorties against North Vietnamese targets and 144,323 against the Ho Chi Minh Trail. In 1970, they flew 1,113 sorties against the North. See Guenter Lewy, *America in Vietnam* (New York: Oxford University Press, 1970), pp. 406–7.

4. In early 1967, South Vietnam produced a constitution based on French and American models. Thieu became the nation's first President in September 1967 and was reelected in October 1971.

5. Nixon's proposal stated that all armed forces of "the countries of Indochina must remain within their national frontiers." Because Hanoi maintained that Vietnam was one nation with two armies, the President's offer was ambiguous as to whether Northern troops had to withdraw from the South. The issue remained unclear until Kissinger's visit to Moscow in April 1972. See Tad Szulc, "Behind the Vietnam Cease-Fire Agreement," *Foreign Policy* 15 (Summer 1974): 33–34, 37, and Allan E. Goodman, *The Lost Peace: America's Search for a Negotiated Settlement of the Vietnam War* (Stanford, Calif.: Hoover Institution, 1978), pp. 111–17, 120.

6. Nixon, *RN*, I: 506. See also Richard Nixon, *No More Vietnams* (New York: Arbor House, 1985), pp. 106–7.

7. Richard Nixon, "A Plan for Peace in Vietnam: The President's Address to the Nation, 25 January 1972," *Weekly Compilation of Presidential Documents* 8 (31 January 1972): 120–25.

8. Seymour M. Hersh, *The Price of Power: Kissinger in the Nixon White House* (New York: Summit Books, 1983), p. 357.

9. Henry A. Kissinger, *White House Years* (Boston: Little, Brown, 1979), p. 721.

10. *Ibid.*, p. 1134; Daniel S. Papp, *Vietnam: The View from Moscow, Peking, Washington* (Jefferson, N.C.: McFarland & Company, 1981), pp. 119–22; and Gabriel Kolko, *Anatomy of a War: Vietnam, the United States and Modern Historical Experience* (New York: Pantheon Books, 1985), pp. 402–5.

11. Quoted in Goodman, *Lost Peace*, p. 122. See also Papp, *Vietnam*, pp. 134–37.

12. Louis Harris, *The Anguish of Change* (New York: W. W. Norton, 1973), p. 74.

13. Nixon, *RN*, II: 201.

14. Headquarters, 7th Air Force, *7 AF History of Linebacker Operations, 10 May 1972–23 October 1972*, n.d., AFHRC, Maxwell Air Force Base, Alabama, file number K740.04-24, p. 1.

15. Kissinger, *White House Years*, p. 1104.

16. Hersh, *Price of Power*, p. 505. Believing that his superiors supported his actions, 7th Air Force Commander General John D. Lavelle launched at least twenty-eight missions against Northern supply areas on his own initiative in late 1971 and early 1972. Lavelle ordered his staff to falsify records of the raids, which they did. In March 1972, a member of 7th Air Force Headquarters reported the unauthorized attacks to his senator, who began an investigation. Lavelle was relieved of command, demoted to major general, and replaced by General John W. Vogt, Jr., in April 1972. For a brief overview of the Lavelle affair, see Lewy, *America in Vietnam* (note 3 above), pp. 407–10; for a thorough examination, see U.S. Senate, Committee on Armed Services, *Nomination of John D. Lavelle, General Creighton W. Abrams, and Admiral John S. McCain*, 92d Cong., 2d sess., 11–29 September 1972.

17. Quoted in Kissinger, *White House Years*, p. 1100.

18. HQ 7th AF, *7 AF History of Linebacker Operations*, p. 3; *Air War—Vietnam* (New York: Arno Press, 1978), p. 125; and James R. McCarthy and George B. Allison, *Linebacker II: A View from the Rock* (Maxwell AFB,, Ala.: Air War College, 1979), p. 11.

19. Kissinger, *White House Years*, p. 1105.

20. *Ibid.*, p. 1109.

21. HQ 7th AF, *7 AF History of Linebacker Operations*, pp. 4–6; Headquarters 7/13th Air Force, *History of 7/13 Air Force, 1 January–31 December 1972, vol. I: Narrative* (5 June 1973), AFHRC, file number K744.01, p. 104; *Air War—Vietnam*, pp. 115–25; interview of Major George Thompson (ret.) by the author, Omaha, Nebraska, 27 October 1982; and Peter B. Mersky and Norman Polmar, *The Naval Air War in Vietnam* (Annapolis: Nautical and Aviation Publishing, 1981), p. 195. The Navy possessed three hundred attack aircraft on four carriers by mid-April. See "The New Air War in Vietnam," *US News and World Report*, 24 April 1972, p. 15.

22. *Uncoordinated Draft: Linebacker Study*, MACV (20 January 1973), AFHRC, file number K712.041-19, chap. 2, p. 2.

23. Nixon, *RN*, II: 64.

24. Kissinger, *White House Years*, p. 1118.

25. *Ibid.*, p. 1116.

26. Szulc, "Behind Vietnam Cease-Fire" (note 5 above), p. 36; Goodman, *Lost Peace* (note 5 above), p. 120; and Hersh, *Price of Power*, pp. 512–13.

27. Kissinger, *White House Years*, pp. 1147. See pages 1118–64 for Kissinger's detailed evaluation of his trip to Moscow. Nixon's thoughts on the trip appear in Nixon, *RN*, II: 61–68.

28. Kissinger, *White House Years*, p. 1168.

29. Nixon, *RN*, II: 70.

30. Kissinger, *White House Years*, p. 1175.

31. Richard Nixon, "The Situation in Southeast Asia: the President's Address to the Nation, 8 May 1972," *Weekly Compilation of Presidential Documents* 8 (15 May 1972): 839.

32. *Ibid.*, p. 840.

33. *Ibid.*, p. 841.

34. Quoted in Nixon, *RN*, II: 86.

35. *Ibid.*, II: 85–86; Henry Kissinger, "News Conference 9 May 1972," *Weekly Compilation of Presidential Documents* 8 (15 May 1972), p. 846; Kissinger, *White House Years*, p. 1181; and Donaldson D. Frizzell, "Air Power and Negotiation in 1972," in *The Lessons of Vietnam*, eds. W. Scott Thompson and Donaldson D. Frizzell (New York: Crane, Russak, 1977), p. 164.

36. Headquarters 8th Air Force, *History of Eighth Air Force, 1 July 1972–30 June 1973, vol. I: Narrative* (23 August 1974), AFHRC, file number K520.01, p. 147; *Uncoordinated Draft: Linebacker Study, MACV* (note 22 above), chap. 2, p. 2; and "How Important Is Airpower in Achieving U.S. Objectives in Southeast Asia?" *Air Force Policy Letter for Commanders*, 1 June 1972, p. 3.

37. Kissinger, *White House Years*, p. 1306.

38. HQ 7th AF, *7 AF History of Linebacker Operations* (note 14 above), pp. 7–10.

39. *Ibid.*, p. 20; Headquarters PACAF, *Linebacker: Overview of the First 120 Days* (27 September 1973), AFHRC, file number K717.0414-42, pp. 35–37; Major General Eugene L. Hudson, *End of Tour Report* (20 April 1973), AFHRC, file number K740.131, p. 15; and *Uncoordinated Draft, Linebacker Study, MACV*, chap. 3, p. 1.

40. HQ 8th AF, *History of Eighth Air Force, I: Narrative*, pp. 148–49.

41. Kissinger, *White House Years*, p. 1309.

42. Richard Nixon, "Turning the Battle Around with Airpower," *Air Force Policy Letters for Commanders*, 15 July 1972, p. 1.

43. Kissinger, *White House Years*, p. 1308; emphasis in original.

44. Szulc, "Behind Vietnam Cease-Fire" (note 5 above), pp. 42–44, 48–49, and Goodman, *Last Peace* (note 5 above), pp. 123–24. Kissinger made the offer on 25 May during the Moscow summit, and Soviet President Nikolai Podgorny conveyed it to the North Vietnamese during a trip to Hanoi in mid-June.

45. Kissinger, *White House Years*, p. 1319; emphasis in original.

46. Message, CINCPAC to COMUSMACV, CINCPACAF, CINCPACFLT, CINCSAC, 090225Z Aug 1972, in *Message Traffic, May–December 1972*, AFHRC, file number K168.06-229.

47. See Chapter IV, pp. 129–30, for a discussion of the route package system.

48. HQ 7th AF, *7 AF History of Linebacker Operations*, pp. 25–32; Hudson, *End of Tour Report*, p. 18; and John Morrocco, *Rain of Fire* (Boston: Boston Publishing Company, 1985), p. 154.

49. Message, CINCPAC to CINCPACAF, CINCPACFLT, 17110Z Oct 1972, in *Message Traffic, May–December 1972*, and "CNA Working Paper: Preliminary Summary of Linebacker Operations" (14 February 1973), pp. 5–6, in *USAF Operations in Southeast Asia, Backup Documentation 1971–1973*, AFHRC, file number K239.031-53.

50. Kissinger, *White House Years*, pp. 1343–44.

51. Szulc, "Behind Vietnam Cease-Fire," pp. 48–57, and Goodman, *Lost Peace*, pp. 128–30.

52. Nixon, *RN*, (note 1 above), II: 192–93, 204–5, and HQ 7th AF, *7 AF History of Linebacker Operations*, p. 32. While the suspension of bombing north of the 20th parallel may have partly resulted from Nixon's "good will," other considerations were of equal importance. Nixon did not wish to approve an accord without Thieu's support, but Hanoi *had* agreed to the demands listed in the President's 8 May speech. Thus, Nixon curtailed, rather than ended, the bombing "as promised." See this chapter, pp. 174–75.

53. Headquarters PACAF, *Corona Harvest: The USAF in Southeast Asia, 1970–1973—Lessons Learned and Recommendations: A Compendium* (16 June 1975), AFHRC, file number K717.0423-11, p. 64; Lewy, *America in Vietnam* (note 3 above), p. 410; Juan M. Vasquez, "Pentagon Confident of Bombing Effect," *New York Times*, 9 June 1972; Frizzell, "Air Power and Negotiation" (note 35 above), p. 165; HQ 7th AF, *7 AF History of Linebacker Operations*, p. 20; Robert N. Ginsburgh, "North Vietnam—Air Power," *Vital Speeches of the Day* 38 (15 September 1972): 734; and USAF Oral History interview of General John W. Vogt, Jr., by

Lieutenant Colonel Arthur W. McCants, Jr., and Dr. James C. Hasdorff, 8–9 August 1978, AFHRC, file number K239.0512-1093, p. 64.

54. HQ 8th AF, *History of Eighth Air Force, vol. I: Narrative*, (note 36 above), p. 149; Hudson, *End of Tour Report* (note 39 above), p. 16; and Vogt interview, 8–9 August 1978, pp. 139, 147.

55. Kissinger, *White House Years*, p. 1112; HQ PACAF, *Corona Harvest*, pp. 116–17; HQ 7th AF, *7 AF History of Linebacker Operations*, p. 23; William W. Momyer, *Air Power in Three Wars* (Washington, D.C.: U.S. Government Printing Office, 1978), pp. 103–5; and Vogt Interview, 8–9 August 1978, pp. 116–22.

56. HQ 7th AF, *7 AF History of Linebacker Operations*, pp. 14, 16; *Air War—Vietnam* (note 18 above), p. 267; Edgar Ulsamer, "Air Power Halts an Invasion," *Air Force*, September 1972, p. 71; and McCarthy and Allison, *Linebacker II* (note 18 above), p. 30.

57. HQ 7th AF, *7 AF History of Linebacker Operations*, pp. 48, 53.

58. *Ibid.*, pp. 21, 65.

59. Joseph Kraft, "Letter from Hanoi," *New Yorker*, 12 August 1972, p. 63; Ulsamer, "Air Power Halts Invasion," p. 66; HQ PACAF, *Corona Harvest*, pp. 82–83; and "Air War Against the North—Tougher than Anyone Realizes," *US News and World Report*, 21 August 1972, p. 32.

60. Lewy, *America in Vietnam*, p. 411; HQ 7th AF, *7 AF History of Linebacker Operations*, p. 75; *Linebacker: Overview of the First 120 Days* (note 39 above), p. 20; U.S. House, Committee on Appropriations, Subcommittee on DOD, *DOD Appropriations: Bombings of North Vietnam*, Hearings, 93d Cong., 1st sess., 9–18 January 1973, p. 43; Ginsburgh, "North Vietnam—Air Power," p. 734; and interview of Walt W. Rostow by the author, Austin, Texas, 23 May 1986.

61. Robert Thompson in Thompson and Frizzell, *Lessons of Vietnam* (note 35 above), pp. 104–5.

62. Kraft, "Letter from Hanoi," pp. 58–65, and Joseph Fromm, "Why Hanoi Came to Realize It Could Not Hope to Win," *US News and World Report*, 6 November 1972, p. 19. Fromm's article is an interview with a British authority on North Vietnam, Patrick J. Honey.

63. Fromm, "Why Hanoi," p. 18; Robert F. Rogers, "Risk-Taking in Hanoi's War Policy: An Analysis of Militancy Versus Manipulation in a Communist Party-State's Behavior in a Conflict," Ph. D. dissertation, Georgetown University, 1974, pp. 73, 189–94; Le Duan, "Analysis of Revolutionary Strategy" (February 1970), in Gareth Porter, ed., *Vietnam: The Definitive Documentation of Human Decisions*, 2 vols. (Stanfordville, N.Y.: Earl M. Coleman, 1979), II: 537–39; and Kolko, *Anatomy of a War* (note 10 above), pp. 368–76.

64. Robert Thompson, *Peace Is Not at Hand* (New York: David

McKay, 1974), pp. 86–89, 95–96; Frizzell, "Air Power and Negotiation" (note 35 above), p. 158; CINCPAC, "Current Situation in North Vietnam" (21 July 1972), point paper in *Pave Aegis and Miscellaneous Messages, June 1971–June 1972*, AFHRC, file number K717.03-219, vol. 5; Kraft, "Letter from Hanoi," p. 66; and Kolko, *Anatomy of a War*, p. 422.

65. Thompson, *Peace Is Not at Hand*, pp. 89–93, and letter, Representative Robert L. Leggett to General John D. Ryan, 10 March 1972, in *General John D. Ryan Congressional Correspondence, February–December 1972*, AFHRC, file number K168.7085-152.

66. Kissinger, *White House Years* (note 9 above), pp. 1156–57.

67. Quoted in Don Tate, "Nixon Seeks to Pound Sense into N. Viets," *Columbus Citizen-Journal*, 30 December 1972.

68. Ulsamer, "Air Power Halts Invasion," p. 60. The other division was in Laos.

69. Truong Nhu Tang, *A Viet Cong Memoir* (New York: Vintage Books, 1985), p. 211.

70. Quoted in Kissinger, *White House Years*, p. 1333.

71. Thompson, *Peace Is Not at Hand*, p. 121.

72. Message, "Comments of Le Duc Tho," 242137Z May 1972, Major General Keegan, Chief of Air Force Intelligence, to Generals Clay and Vogt, in *Pave Aegis and Miscellaneous Messages, SEA, June 1971–June 1972*. The message was a verbatim reproduction of a report from the U.S. Peace Delegation in Paris to the Secretary of State and contained Tho's May remarks to French Communist Party members.

73. Truong, *Viet Cong Memoir*, p. 210.

74. Thompson, *Peace Is Not at Hand*, p. 123, and Joseph Alsop, "Hanoi's Strategy Changed," *Washington Post*, 24 January 1973.

75. Nguyen Cao Ky, *How We Lost the Vietnam War* (New York: Scarborough Books, 1976), pp. 186–87.

76. Message, "Comments of Le Duc Tho," 242137Z May 1972.

77. Kissinger, *White House Years*, pp. 1365–66.

78. Nixon, *RN* (note 1 above), II: 195.

79. *Nhan Dan* editorial, 17 August 1972, in Porter, *Vietnam: Definitive Documentation* (note 63 above), II: 568.

80. Nixon, *RN*, II: 78.

81. Kissinger, *White House Years*, p. 1393; emphasis in original.

82. *Ibid.*, p. 1397.

83. Henry Kissinger, "Vietnam Negotiations: News Conference 26 October 1972," *Weekly Compilation of Presidential Documents* 8 (30 October 1973): 1565–66, 1568.

84. HQ PACAF, *Corona Harvest* (note 53 above), p. 65.

85. William C. Westmoreland in Thompson and Frizzell, *Lessons of Vietnam* (note 35 above), p. 61.

86. Vogt interview, 8–9 August 1978 (note 53 above), pp. 87–88.

Chapter VI
PERSUADING ENEMY AND ALLY: THE CHRISTMAS BOMBINGS

1. U.S. House, Committee on Appropriations, Subcommittee on DOD, *DOD Appropriations: Bombings of North Vietnam*, Hearings, 93d Cong., 1st sess., 9–18 January 1973, p. 44.

2. Henry A. Kissinger, *White House Years* (Boston: Little, Brown, 1979), p. 1429.

3. Henry Kissinger, "Vietnam Peace Negotiations: News Conference 16 December 1972," *Weekly Compilation of Presidential Documents* 8 (18 December 1972): 1765.

4. Richard Nixon, *RN: The Memoirs of Richard Nixon*, 2 vols. (New York: Warner Books, 1978), II: 222–23, and Kissinger, *White House Years*, pp. 1411–12.

5. Nixon, *RN*, II: 223–24.

6. *Ibid.*, II: 228.

7. "I put [the sixty-nine changes] forward," Kissinger writes, "in order to avoid the charge that we were less than meticulous in guarding Saigon's concerns—and to ease the task of obtaining Thieu's approval. As often happens when one acts for the record, we achieved neither objective." See Kissinger, *White House Years*, p. 1417. Thieu had ordered his ambassadors in London, Washington, and Paris to attend the November sessions.

8. *Ibid.*, pp. 1417–23.

9. Nixon, *RN*, II: 226–35; Kissinger, *White House Years*, p. 1420; and House Appropriations DOD Subcommittee, *DOD Appropriations: Bombings of North Vietnam*, p. 36. Nixon remarks that *he* favored continued negotiations while Kissinger urged bombing. Kissinger denies Nixon's contention in *White House Years* and claims just the opposite. Given the President's pronouncements and conduct earlier in the year, Kissinger makes the stronger case.

10. Kissinger, *White House Years*, pp. 1428–35, and Nixon, *RN*, II: 237.

11. Kissinger, *White House Years*, p. 1435.

12. Nixon, *RN*, II: 238.

13. Kissinger, *White House Years*, p. 1442. In all their telegrams throughout November and December, Nixon and Kissinger used the terms "strong pressure" and "strong action" to denote bombing.

14. *Ibid.*, pp. 1443.

15. *Ibid.*, p. 1445.

16. Nixon, *RN*, II: 241–42, and Kissinger, *White House Years*, pp. 1447–48.

17. General John C. Meyer, "Speech at Andersen AFB, Guam, 3 January 1973," in *Personal Papers of J. C. Meyer*, AFHRC, Maxwell Air Force Base, Alabama, file number K168.7169, frame 130, reel 23167, and Henry Kissinger, "Agreement on Ending the War and Restoring Peace in Vietnam: News Conference, 24 January 1973," *Weekly Compilation of Presidential Documents* 9 (29 January 1973): 73.

18. Truong Nhu Tang, *A Viet Cong Memoir* (New York: Vintage Books, 1985), p. 168.

19. James R. McCarthy and George B. Allison, *Linebacker II: A View from the Rock* (Maxwell Air Force Base, Ala.: Air War College, 1979), p. 39.

20. Nixon, *RN*, II: 237–38, 245; Kissinger, *White House Years*, pp. 1448–49; and Kissinger, "Vietnam Peace Negotiations" (note 3 above), p. 1768.

21. Nixon, *RN*, II: 245.

22. *Ibid.*, II: 242; House Appropriations DOD Subcommittee, *DOD Appropriations: Bombings of North Vietnam*, pp. 4, 45; McCarthy and Allison, *Linebacker II*, p. 39; and USAF Oral History interview of Lieutenant General Gerald W. Johnson by Mr. Charles K. Hopkins, 3 April 1973, Andersen AFB, Guam, AFHRC, file number K239.0512-831, p. 1.

23. Headquarters PACAF, *Linebacker II USAF Bombing Survey* (April 1973), AFHRC file number K717.64-8, pp. 1, 33; letter, Brigadier General Harry Cordes to Brigadier General James R. McCarthy, n. d., AFHRC, file number K416.04-13, vol. 12, pp. 3, 9 (Cordes was Deputy Chief of Staff for Intelligence at SAC Headquarters during Linebacker II); House Appropriations DOD Subcommittee, *DOD Appropriations: Bombings of North Vietnam*, p. 18; and Nixon, *RN*, II: 244.

24. McCarthy and Allison, *Linebacker II*, p. 26; interview of Major George Thompson (ret.) by the author, Omaha, Nebraska, 27 October 1982; interview of Colonel Clyde E. Bodenheimer by the author, 7 January 1983, Maxwell AFB, Alabama; and Gerald Johnson interview, 3 April 1973, pp. 6–7. Johnson noted: "By the time [word of Linebacker] got to me the decision to go had already been made. The part I played was in terms of *recommendations* concerning the size of the force, the size of individual raids or missions, the tactics to be employed, the utilization of the aircraft, the altitudes to be flown, the defensive techniques and this sort of thing." Emphasis added.

25. Cordes letter to McCarthy, p. 4, and McCarthy and Allison, *Linebacker II*, p. 41.

26. Headquarters 307th Strategic Wing, *History of 307th Strategic Wing, October–December 1972*, AFHRC, file number K-WG-307-HI, I (12 July 1973): 53.

27. Interview of Colonel Robert D. Clark by the author, Robins AFB, Georgia, 6 January 1983.

28. Interview of Major John R. Allen by the author, Osan AB, Korea, 22 September 1981.

29. McCarthy and Allison, *Linebacker II*, pp. 31, 42–43, 47, 65, and HQ PACAF, *Linebacker II USAF Bombing Survey*, p. 25.

30. McCarthy and Allison, *Linebacker II*, pp. 41–44, 77, 89, 96.

31. Nixon, *RN*, II: 246; McCarthy and Allison, *Linebacker II*, p. 81; and "North Vietnam's Statements on the Paris Talks, December 17 and 21, 1972," in Martin F. Herz, *The Prestige Press and the Christmas Bombing, 1972* (Washington, D.C.: Ethics & Public Policy Center, 1980), p. 85. In January 1973 Congressman Daniel P. Flood voiced the perception that Nixon feared: "I was sitting right here when we first started talking about B-52's. That was a concept. Boy that was going to be it. If we ever got B-52's, that would do it. There would be no problems from then on, and here this little backward, these 'gooks' developed [*sic*], and they are knocking down your B-52's like clay pigeons, with all the sophisticated hardware which was beyond our own ken, being run by 'gooks.' This is some kind of lesson." See House Appropriations DOD Subcommittee, *DOD Appropriations: Bombings of North Vietnam*, pp. 30–31.

32. McCarthy and Allison, *Linebacker II*, pp. 91, 97–98, 100, 108, 115. General Meyer asked for 7th Air Force Commander General John Vogt's assistance in destroying SAMs. Meyer had discovered that the primary SAM assembly plant was in the center of Hanoi, but the possibility of civilian casualties prevented B-52s from striking the target. With the approval of Admiral Moorer, Vogt dispatched a flight of sixteen F-4s that bombed the plant through a solid overcast from 20,000 feet using LORAN. The mission was successful. See USAF Oral History interview of General John W. Vogt by Lieutenant Colonel Arthur W. McCants, Jr. and Dr. James C. Hasdorff, 8–9 August 1978, AFHRC, file number K239.0512-1093, p. 92. Andersen contributed twelve B-52s to the raid on 23 December.

33. McCarthy and Allison, *Linebacker II*, pp. 121–39.

34. Nixon received this message on the afternoon of the 26th because of the thirteen-hour time differential.

35. Kissinger, *White House Years*, pp. 1457–58, and Nixon, *RN*, II: 250.

36. McCarthy and Allison, *Linebacker II*, pp. 145–53.

37. Clark interview, 6 January 1983.

38. Allen interview, 22 September 1981.

39. Quoted in Kissinger, *White House Years*, p. 1459.

40. Nixon, *RN*, II: 242, 244; Herz, p. 28; Cordes letter to McCarthy (note 23 above), p. 3; HQ PACAF, *Linebacker II USAF Bombing Survey* (note 29 above), pp. 8, 33; and House Appropriations DOD Subcommittee, *DOD Appropriations: Bombings of North Vietnam*, pp. 9, 38.

41. Howard Silber, "SAC Chief: B-52s Devastated Viet Air Defenses," *Omaha World Herald*, 25 February 1973; McCarthy and Allison, *Linebacker II*, pp. 46–47, 50; Thompson interview, 27 October 1982 (note 24 above); Vogt interview, 8–9 August 1978, pp. 90–91; interview by newsmen of Admiral Moorer, 4 April 1973; Allen interview, 22 September 1981; and cassette tape, Major John R. Allen to the author, June 1982.

42. "Terror Bombing in the Name of Peace," *Washington Post*, 28 December 1972; Tom Wicker, "Shame on Earth," *New York Times*, 26 December 1972; and "Outrage and Relief," *Time*, 8 January 1973, p. 14.

43. House Appropriations DOD Subcommittee, *DOD Appropriations: Bombings of North Vietnam*, p. 51, and Nixon, *RN*, II: 247.

44. Kissinger, *White House Years*, pp. 1453, 1459, and Nixon, *RN*, II: 253–54.

45. Cordes letter to McCarthy, (note 23 above), p. 2; message, 7 AF/CC to CINCSAC, 240725Z Dec 1972, in *Message Traffic, June–December 1972*; McCarthy and Allison, *Linebacker II*, p. 121; and Thompson interview, 27 October 1982.

46. HQ 307th Strategic Wing, *History, October–December 1972* (note 26 above), I: 58; Bodenheimer interview, 7 January 1983 (note 24 above); Headquarters 8th Air Force, *History of Eighth Air Force, 1 July 1972–30 June 1973, Vol. II: Narrative* (23 August 1974), AFHRC, file number K520.01; Allen interview, 22 September 1981 (note 28 above); and Clark interview, 6 January 1983 (note 27 above).

47. Major General Eugene L. Hudson, *End of Tour Report* (20 April 1973), AFHRC, file number K717.1404-42, p. 19; "Staff Meeting Notes," n. d. (probably 27 December 1972), AFHRC, file number K416.04-13, vol. 13; McCarthy and Allison, *Linebacker II*, pp. 68, 129, 171; letter to the author from Major James Rash (Retired), 15 August 1982; Allen interview, 22 September 1981; and "Narrative by Major R. A. Scott, 21 October 1977," AFHRC, file number K416.04-13.

48. McCarthy and Allison, *Linebacker II*, pp. 42, 101, 109, 114, 121, 125, 147, 157, 164; HQ 8th AF, *History, 1 July 1972–30 June 1973, Vol. II: Narrative*, p. 426; and message, 7AF to 7/13 AF Dep CC, 210310Z Dec 1972, in *Message Traffic, June–December 1972*, AFHRC, file number K168.06-229.

49. House Appropriations DOD Subcommittee, *DOD Appropriations: Bombings of North Vietnam*, p. 4; HQ PACAF, *Linebacker II USAF Bombing Survey*, p. 6; *Air War—Vietnam* (New York: Arno Press, 1978),

p. 279; Headquarters PACAF, *Corona Harvest: The USAF in Southeast Asia, 1970–73; Lessons Learned and Recommendations: A Compendium* (16 June 1975), AFHRC, file number K717.0423-11, pp. 80, 95.

50. PACAF Study Group, "Linebacker II Air Operation" (briefing given 18 January 1973) in *Department of Air Force Letters Concerning USAF Air Operations in Southeast Asia, 10 October 1972 to 31 January 1973*, AFHRC, file number K168.06-232; Lieutenant General Gerald W. Johnson, *End of Tour Report* (15 September 1973), AFHRC, file number K416.131, p. 80; House Appropriations DOD Subcommittee, *DOD Appropriations: Bombings of North Vietnam*, pp. 6, 40; HQ PACAF, *Linebacker II USAF bombing Survey*, pp. 12, 18, 34; McCarthy and Allison, *Linebacker II*, p. 171; and Martin M. Ostrow, "The B-52s' Message to Moscow," *Air Force*, April 1973, p. 3.

51. Murray Marder, "North Vietnam: Taking Pride in Punishment," *Washington Post*, 4 February 1973; Herz, *Prestige Press* (note 31 above), p. 54; Tammy Arbuckle, "Bombing Was Pinpointed," *Washington Star*, 1 April 1973; Michael Allen, "Sharing the Agony of Hanoi," *Christian Century*, 24 January 1973, pp. 92–93; HQ PACAF, *Linebacker II USAF Bombing Survey*, p. 37; and address by Rear Admiral James B. Stockdale to the Armed Forces Staff College, 9 April 1975, quoted in U. S. Grant Sharp, *Strategy for Defeat: Vietnam in Retrospect* (San Rafael, Calif.: Presidio Press, 1978), p. 258.

52. Richard Nixon, "Ending the War and Restoring Peace in Vietnam: Address to the Nation, 23 January 1973," *Weekly Compilation of Presidential Documents* 9 (29 January 1973): 44.

53. Truong Nhu Tang, who talked extensively with Northern leaders after the 1975 fall of the South, acknowledges: "The December bombings of Haiphong and Hanoi may indeed have given added credence to Nixon's ability to threaten, but they also exacted a sharp political price." See Truong, *Viet Cong Memoir*, (note 18 above), p. 226; see also Phillip B. Davidson, *Vietnam at War: The History, 1946–1975* (Novato, Calif.: Presidio Press, 1988), p. 728.

54. Quoted in Gabriel Kolko, *Anatomy of a War: Vietnam, the United States, and the Modern Historical Experience* (New York: Pantheon Books, 1985), pp. 444–45.

55. Allan Goodman, *The Lost Peace: America's Search for a Negotiated Settlement of the Vietnam War* (Stanford, Calif.: Hoover Institution, 1978), p. 157; Robert Thompson, *Peace Is Not at Hand* (New York: David McKay, 1974), p. 138; Kissinger quoted in Nixon, *RN*, II: 257–58.

56. "North Viet Bombing Held Critical," *Aviation Week and Space Technology*, 5 March 1973, p. 13; House Appropriations DOD Subcommittee, *DOD Appropriations: Bombings of North Vietnam*, p. 4; Kissinger, *White House Years*, pp. 1417, 1445–46; Nixon, *RN*, II: 231; Cap-

tain (USN) H. E. Rutledge, "A POW View of Linebacker II," *Armed Forces Journal International* 115 (September 1977): 20; Herz, *Prestige Press*, p. 19; and Joseph Alsop, "Hanoi's Strategy Changed," *Washington Post*, 24 January 1973.

57. "North Vietnam's Statements on the Paris Talks, December 17 and 21, 1972," in Herz, *Prestige Press*, p. 84, and Kissinger, *White House Years*, pp. 1457–59.

58. Kissinger, *White House Years*, pp. 1461–65, and Kissinger, "Agreement on Ending War" (note 17 above), p. 69.

59. Kissinger, *White House Years*, pp. 1461, 1463–64.

60. Nixon wrote: "There was no doubt that the Communists had infiltrated the Saigon government." Nixon, *RN*, II: 240.

61. Johnson interview, 3 April 1973 (note 22 above), p. 23.

62. Kissinger, "Agreement on Ending War," p. 71.

63. Nixon, *RN*, II: 245–46, and Kissinger, *White House Years*, pp. 1459–62.

64. Kissinger, *White House Years*, p. 1469.

65. *Ibid.*, p. 1470.

66. Nixon, *RN*, II: 222–23, and Kissinger, *White House Years*, pp. 1467–70.

67. Nixon, *RN*, II: 259; Kissinger, *White House Years*, p. 1461; Barry Goldwater, "Air Power in Southeast Asia," *Congressional Record—Senate*, 119, part 5 (26 February 1973): 5346; "What Admiral Moorer Really Said About Airpower's Effectiveness in SEA," *Air Force*, November 1973, p. 25; Howard Silber, "SAC Chief: B-52s Devastated Viet Air Defenses," *Omaha World Herald*, 25 February 1973; Johnson interview, 3 April 1973, pp. 11–13; Vogt interview, 8–9 August 1978 (note 32 above), p. 69; Sharp, *Strategy For Defeat* (note 51 above), pp. 252, 255, 272; and William W. Momyer, *Air Power in Three Wars* (Washington, D.C.: U.S. Government Printing Office, 1978), p. 339.

68. "Recommendation for Award of the Presidential Unit Citation to the 474th Tactical Fighter Wing, 30 June 1973," *Department of Air Force Letters Concerning USAF Air Operations in SEA, 30 September 1972 to 28 August 1974*, AFHRC, file number K168.06-227; Bodenheimer interview, 7 January 1983 (note 24 above); and Clark interview, 6 January 1983 (note 27 above).

69. Richard Nixon, *No More Vietnams* (New York: Arbor House, 1985), pp. 166–67.

70. "United States Foreign Policy for the 1970s: Shaping a Durable Peace," President's Report to Congress, 3 May 1973, *Weekly Compiliation of Presidential Documents* 9 (14 May 1973): 455–653.

Chapter VII
ASSESSMENT

1. Carl von Clausewitz, *On War*, trans. and ed. Michael Howard and Peter J. Paret (Princeton, N.J.: Princeton University Press, 1976), pp. 88–89.

2. Air Force Manual 1-1, 16 March 1984, p. 3–2.

3. Ronald Schaffer, *Wings of Judgment: American Bombing in World War II* (New York: Oxford University Press, 1985), p. xi. I disagree, however, with Schaffer's contention that "moral constraints almost invariably bowed to what people described as military necessity" (p. xii). See Conrad C. Crane's rebuttal to Schaffer, "Evolution of U.S. Strategic Bombing of Urban Areas," *The Historian* 50 (November 1987): 14–39.

4. Interview of Curtis LeMay by Mary-Ann Bendel, printed in *USA Today*, 23 July 1986, p. 9A.

5. U. S. Grant Sharp, *Strategy for Defeat: Vietnam in Retrospect* (San Rafael, Calif.: Presidio Press, 1978), and William W. Momyer, *Air Power in Three Wars* (Washington, D.C.: U.S. Government Printing Office, 1978).

6. Harry G. Summers, Jr., *On Strategy: A Critical Analysis of the Vietnam War* (Novato, Calif.: Presidio Press, 1982).

7. John L. Frisbee, "Practice of Professionalism," *Air Force*, August 1986, p. 113.

8. Sharp, *Strategy for Defeat*, p. xvii.

9. LeMay interview.

10. Air Force Manual 1-1, 16 March 1984, p. 2-1.

11. *Ibid.*, p. 2-5.

12. *Ibid.*, p. 3-2.

13. Momyer, *Air Power in Three Wars*, p. 339.

Chapter VIII
EPILOGUE

For comments and suggestions, both heeded and unheeded, the author gratefully acknowledges Dr. Ilana Kass, Col James Callard, Col Robert Eskridge, Dr. David MacIsaac, and the students of National War College Elective Class 5855, Air Power and Modern War. The views expressed herein are the author's alone and do not necessarily reflect those of the National War College, National Defense University, or Department of Defense.

1. *Quadrennial Defense Review Report* (Washington, D.C.: Department of Defense, 30 September 2001).

2. Carl von Clausewitz, *On War*, ed. and trans. Michael Howard and Peter Paret (Princeton, N.J.: Princeton University Press, 1976), 87.

3. William Mitchell, *Winged Defense: The Development and Possibilities of Modern Air Power* (1925; reprint, New York: Dover Publications, Inc., 1988), xii.

4. M. J. Armitage and R. A. Mason, *Air Power in the Nuclear Age* (Urbana, Ill.: University of Illinois Press, 1983), 2.

5. *Ibid.*, 3.

6. The largely discarded term *battlefield air interdiction* (BAI) describes this auxiliary function.

7. Quoted in John Schlight, *The War in South Vietnam: The Years of the Offensive, 1965–1968*, United States Air Force in Southeast Asia (Washington, D.C.: Office of Air Force History, 1988), 216.

8. Other factors may help define the battlefield as well. These include the ranges of weapons possessed by deployed ground or sea forces, or the location of such demarcations as the forward line of troops (FLOT) and the fire support coordination line (FSCL). Admiral William Owens, former vice chairman of the Joint Chiefs of Staff, contended that a battlefield would consist of the 40,000 square miles in a 200-by-200-mile area. Although Admiral Owens's precise delineation may be appropriate in a conventional war, it may not suit other types of conflict. See Lieutenant Colonel Terry L. New, "Where to Draw the Line between Air and Land Battle," *Airpower Journal* 10, no. 3 (Fall 1996): 34–49, on how the battlefield is affected by the relationship between the FLOT and the FSCL. For Admiral Owens's notion of the battlefield, see Alan D. Zimm, "Human-Centric Warfare," U.S. Naval Institute *Proceedings* 125 (May 1999): 28.

9. Air Force Doctrine Document (AFDD) 1, *Air Force Basic Doctrine*, 1 September 1997, 46.

10. These terms should not be confused with Clausewitz's concept of positive and negative objectives, which he uses in regard to attacking and defending.

11. Joint Publication 1-02, *Department of Defense Dictionary of Military and Associated Terms*, 12 April 2001, 380, on-line, Internet, 14 September 2002, available from http://www.dtic.mil/doctrine/jel/new_pubs/jp1_02.pdf.

12. See Bard E. O'Neill and Ilana Kass, "The Persian Gulf War: A Political-Military Assessment," *Comparative Strategy* 11 (April–June 1992): 219, for a thorough discussion of American war aims in the Persian Gulf War of 1991.

13. The Clausewitzian notion of friction also affects air power's ability to achieve positive (and negative) political goals, but, unlike the five variables, friction is a constant that cannot be specified according to assumptions and analyses.

14. Robert F. Futrell, *The United States Air Force in Korea, 1950–1953*, rev. ed. (Washington, D.C.: Office of Air Force History, 1983), 480–85; and General O. P. Weyland, transcript of oral history interview by Dr. James Hasdorff and Brigadier General Noel Parrish, San Antonio, Tex., 19 November 1974, Air Force Historical Research Agency, Maxwell AFB, Ala., file no. K239.0512-813, 107, 113.

15. Clausewitz, 579.

Bibliography

———•———

Note: Materials maintained at the Air Force Historical Research Center (AFHRC), Maxwell Air Force Base, Alabama, are referenced with their respective file numbers.

A. PRIMARY SOURCES

1. Manuscript Sources

a. Air Force Studies

BRODIE, BERNARD. *The USAF in Limited War.* February 1958. AFHRC file number K239.042957-1.

HAMPTON, COLONEL EPHRAIM M. *The USAF Limited War.* Project No. AU-1-57-ESAWAC. 14 March 1957. AFHRC file number K239.042957-1.

Headquarters PACAF. *Corona Harvest: The USAF in Southeast Asia, 1970–1973; Lessons Learned and Recommendations: A Compendium.* 16 June 1975. AFHRC file number K717.0423-11.

———. *Linebacker: Overview of the First 120 Days.* 27 September 1973. AFHRC file number K717.0414-42.

———. *Linebacker II USAF Bombing Survey.* April 1973. AFHRC file number K717.64-8.

Headquarters USAF. *Air Operations—North Vietnam.* 27 April 1967. AFHRC file number K143.0572-90.

———. *Analysis of Effectiveness of Interdiction in Southeast Asia, Second Progress Report.* May 1966. AFHRC file number K168.187-21.

———. *Capability of Truck Logistic System—Air Interdiction Study.* 20 January 1967. AFHRC file number K168.187-16.

———. *Command and Control of Southeast Asia Air Operations, 1 January 1965–31 March 1968.* July 1973. AFHRC file number K239.034-4.

———. *Comparative Analysis: AF/USN Route Packages VIA and B.* December 1967. AFHRC file number K712.041-9.

———. *Highway Campaign in North Vietnam.* December 1967. AFHRC file number K712.041-10.

———. *Out-Country Air Operations, Southeast Asia, 1 January 1965–31 March 1968.* July 1973. AFHRC file number K239.034-10.

———. *Project CHECO Report: Rolling Thunder July 1965–December 1966.* 15 July 1967. AFHRC file number K717.0414-12.

JOHNSON, ROBERT B. *RAND Studies of Air Power in Limited Wars.* Headquarters PACAF/FEAF, 21 May 1957. AFHRC file number K720.3102-7.

Operations Analysis Branch, Office of the Vice Chief of Staff, HQ USAF. *Analysis of Effectiveness of Interdiction in SEA, Second Progress Report.* May 1966. AFHRC file number K168.187-21.

SIMONS, LIEUTENANT COLONEL W. E. *Fundamental Considerations of Strategy for the War in Southeast Asia.* 3 November 1966. AFHRC file number K146.003-21.

Uncoordinated Draft: Linebacker Study, MACV. 20 January 1973. AFHRC file number K712.041-19.

USAF Historical Study No. 127: *United States Air Force Operations in the Korean Conflict 1 July 1952–27 July 1953.* 1 July 1956. AFHRC file number 101-127.

b. Unit Histories

Headquarters 8th Air Force. *History of Eighth Air Force, 1 July 1972–30 June 1973, Narrative.* 2 vols. 23 August 1974. AFHRC file number K520.01.

Headquarters, FEAF. *FEAF Command Report June 1953, Vol. IIA.* n. d. AFHRC file number K720.02.

———. *History of the Far East Air Forces, 1 June 1951–31 December 1951.* n. d. AFHRC file number K720.01.

———. *FEAF Operations Policy Korea Mid-1952: An Addendum to the FEAF Histories for that Year.* March 1955. AFHRC file number K720.01.

Headquarters 7th Air Force. *History of Linebacker Operations, 10 May 1972–23 October 1972.* n. d. AFHRC file number K740.04-24.

———. *Seventh Air Force History: Vol. I: Narrative 1 January 1966 to 30 June 1967.* n. d. AFHRC file number K740.01-25.

Headquarters 7th/13th Air Force. *History of 7/13th Air Force, 1 January–31 December 1972, Vol. I: Narrative.* 5 June 1973. AFHRC file number K744.01.

Headquarters 307th Strategic Wing. *History of 307th Strategic Wing October–December 1972, Vol. I.* 12 July 1973. AFHRC file number K-WG-307-HI.

c. Message Traffic/Unit Correspondence

Commander-in-Chief, Pacific Command Outgoing Messages, 22 January 1965–28 June 1965. AFHRC file number K712.1623-2.

Commander-in-Chief, Pacific Command Outgoing Messages, 25 July 1965–7 December 1965. AFHRC file number K712.1623-2.

Department of Air Force Letters Concerning USAF Air Operations in Southeast Asia, 30 September 1972–28 August 1974. AFHRC file number K168.06-227.

Department of Air Force Letters Concerning USAF Air Operations in Southeast Asia, 20 October 1972–31 January 1973. AFHRC file number K168.06-232.

MACV Outgoing Messages, April 1965–November 1966. AFHRC file number K712.1622-3.

Message Traffic, May–December 1972. AFHRC file number K168.06-229.

PACAF Outgoing Messages, 1 March 1965–31 March 1965. AFHRC file number K717.1623.

PACAF Outgoing Messages, 3 April 1965–24 December 1965. AFHRC file number K717.1623.

PACAF Outgoing Messages, 15 March 1966–31 December 1966. AFHRC file number K717.1623.

Pave Aegis and other Miscellaneous Messages, Southeast Asia, June 1971–June 1972. AFHRC file number K717.03-219, vol. 5.

USAF Operations in Southeast Asia, Backup Documentation, 1971–1973. AFHRC file number K239.031-53.

d. End of Tour Reports

FOWLER, COLONEL FREDERICK W. (Chief, Air Intelligence Division, MACV J2). *End of Tour Report.* 17 October 1973. AFHRC file number K712.131.

HUDSON, MAJOR GENERAL EUGENE L. (operational assistant to HQ 7th AF; deputy director of Intelligence, MACV). *End of Tour Report.* 20 April 1973. AFHRC file number K740.131.

JOHNSON, LIEUTENANT GENERAL GERALD W. (8th Air Force Commander). *End of Tour Report.* 15 September 1973. AFHRC file number K416.131.

MORROW, COLONEL JAMES H. (Chief, Linebacker Operations Branch, HQ MACV). *End of Tour Report.* 10 October 1973. AFHRC file number K712.131.

PHILPOTT, BRIGADIER GENERAL JAMMIE M. (deputy chief of staff/intelligence, HQ 7th AF). *End of Tour Report.* 6 December 1967. AFHRC file number K740.131.

e. Personal Correspondence

MCCARTHY, BRIGADIER GENERAL JAMES R. 1977 correspondence concerning *Linebacker II: A View from the Rock.* AFHRC file number K416.04-13, vol. 12.

MCCONNELL, GENERAL JOHN P. Personal papers of, 1969. AFHRC file number 168.7102-15.

MEYER, GENERAL JOHN C. Personal papers of, 1972–74. AFHRC file number K168.7169, reel #23167.

MOMYER, GENERAL WILLIAM W. Letter to Lieutenant General Glen W. Martin concerning command and control. 12 January 1970. AFHRC file number K168.7041-24.

———. Memorandum for General Ellis concerning *Corona Harvest Report: USAF Operations Against North Vietnam, 1 July 1971–30 June 1972.* AFHRC file number K239.031-133.

RYAN, GENERAL JOHN D. Congressional Correspondence, February–December 1972. AFHRC file number K168.7085-152.

STRATEMEYER, LIEUTENANT GENERAL GEORGE E. Diary: 17 December 1950–16 May 1951. AFHRC file number 168.7018-16, vol. 3.

f. USAF Oral History Interviews

EDELEN, COLONEL HENRY H. Interviewed by Major Samuel E. Riddlebarger and Lieutenant Colonel S. Bissell. 27 January 1970. AFHRC file number K239.0512-243.

ESTES, GENERAL HOWELL M., JR. Interviewed by Lieutenant Colonel Robert G. Zimmerman and Lieutenant Colonel Lyn R. Officer, Oakland, California, 27–30 August 1973.

FINLETTER, THOMAS K. Interviewed by Colonel Marvin Stanley. February 1967. AFHRC file number K239.0512-760.

GINSBURGH, MAJOR GENERAL ROBERT N. Interviewed by Colonel John E. Van Duyn and Major Richard B. Clement. 26 May 1971. AFHRC file number K239.0512-477.

GREENHALGH, LIEUTENANT COLONEL WILLIAM H., JR. Interviewed by Lieutenant Colonel Robert Eckert. 11 October 1967. AFHRC file number K239.0512-40.

JOHNSON, LIEUTENANT GENERAL GERALD W. Interviewed by Mr. Charles Hopkins. Andersen AFB, Guam, 3 April 1973. AFHRC file number K239.0512-831.

McKee, General Seth J. Interviewed by Dr. James C. Hasdorff. Litchfield, Arizona, 13–15 February 1978. AFHRC file number K239.0512-983.

Martin, Lieutenant General Glen W. Interviewed by Lieutenant Colonel Vaughn H. Gallacher, San Antonio, Texas, 6–10 February 1978. AFHRC file number K239.0512-982.

Moore, Lieutenant General Joseph H. Interviewed by Major Samuel E. Riddlebarger and Lieutenant Colonel Valentino Castellina. 22 November 1969. AFHRC file number K239.0512-241.

Parrish, Brigadier General Noel F. Interviewed by Dr. James C. Hasdorff. San Antonio, Texas, 10–14 June 1974. AFHRC file number K239.0512-744.

Ryan, General John D. Interviewed by Colonel John E. Van Duyn and Major Richard B. Clement. 20 May 1971. AFHRC file number K239.0512-476.

Sharp, Admiral U. S. Grant. Interviewed by Dr. Robert Kritt. 19 February 1971. AFHRC file number K239.0512-409.

———. Interviewed by Dr. Robert Kritt. 19 May 1971. AFHRC file number K239.0512-755.

Spaatz, General Carl A. Interviewed by Mr. Arthur Goldberg. 19 May 1965. AFHRC file number K239.0512-755.

Taylor, General Maxwell D. Interviewed by Major Richard B. Clement and Jacob Van Staaveren. Washington, D.C., 11 January 1972. AFHRC file number K239.0512-501.

Vogt, General John W., Jr. Interviewed by Lieutenant Colonel Arthur W. McCants and Dr. James C. Hasdorff. 8–9 August 1978. AFHRC file number K239.0512-1093.

Weyland, General O. P. Interviewed by Dr. James C. Hasdorff and Brigadier General Noel F. Parrish. San Antonio, Texas, 19 November 1974. AFHRC file number K239.0512-813.

g. Lectures/Speeches (Texts)

Bundy, McGeorge. "Political Conflict." Presented to the Air War College, 16 August 1951. AFHRC file number K239.716251-32.

Finletter, Thomas K. "Evaluation of the Air Weapon as Reflected in Its Assigned Role." Presented to the Air War College, 17 November 1953. K239.716253-26.

Nitze, Paul. "The Relationship of the Political End to the Military Objective." Presented to the Air War College, October 1954. AFHRC file number K239.716254-55.

TIMBERLAKE, MAJOR GENERAL E. J. "Air Power Implications." Presented to Aviation Writers' Association Convention, San Francisco, California, 30 May 1956. In *Speeches by Major General Timberlake, 1956–57.* AFHRC file number K533.309-1.

VANDENBERG, GENERAL HOYT S. "Remarks." Presented to the Air War College, 6 May 1953. AFHRC file number K239.716253-126.

h. Miscellaneous Documents

CIA/DIA. *An Appraisal of the Bombing of North Vietnam (Through 31 December 1967).* n. d. AFHRC file number K193.56-1.

———. *An Appraisal of the Bombing of North Vietnam (Through 29 February 1968).* n. d. K193.56-1.

FEAF Formal Target Committee. *Minutes, 22 July 1952–22 July 1953.* AFHRC file number K720.151A.

Joint Chiefs of Staff. *Target Study—North Vietnam.* Working papers, n. d. AFHRC file number K178.2-34.

i. Library Manuscripts

Abilene, Kansas. Dwight David Eisenhower Library. Declassified and sanitized documents from: Ann Whitman File, Office of the Special Adviser for National Security Affairs (OSANSA) File, White House Central File—Confidential Files. Oral History interviews of: Walter S. Robertson, General Nathan F. Twining.

Austin, Texas. Lyndon Baines Johnson Library. Declassified and sanitized documents from: Meeting Notes File; National Security File—Country File, Vietnam; National Security File—Memos to the President; National Security File—Name File; National Security File—NSC History Files, Vietnam; National Security File—NSC Meeting File; National Security File—National Security Action Memorandums; National Security File—Files of McGeorge Bundy; President's Appointment File; Presidential Daily Diary; Tom Johnson's Notes of Meetings. Oral History interviews of: William P. Bundy, Clark M. Clifford, Lyndon Baines Johnson, General John P. McConnell, Maxwell D. Taylor, General Earle G. Wheeler.

Independence, Missouri. Harry S Truman Library. Declassified and sanitized documents from: Korean War File—Department of Defense; Korean War File—Department of State; Post-Presidential File—Memoirs Files; Dean Acheson File; Frank E. Lowe File; President's Secretary's File—Cabinet; President's Secretary's File—Korean War; President's Secretary's File—Intelligence. Oral History interview of Dean Acheson.

United States Air Force Academy, Colorado. Air Force Academy Library. Haywood S. Hansell Papers.

Washington, D.C. Library of Congress. Carl A. Spaatz Papers.

2. Official Documents/Studies

Air Force Policy Letters for Commanders. June 1972–March 1973.

DEWS, EDMUND. *A Note on Tactical vs. Strategic Air Interdiction.* RAND Corporation Memorandum RM-6239-PR, April 1970.

Foreign Relations of the United States: 1950. Vol. 7: *Korea.* Washington: U.S. Government Printing Office, 1982.

Foreign Relations of the United States: 1951. Vol. 10: *Korea.* Washington: U.S. Government Printing Office, 1982.

Foreign Relations of the United States: 1952–54. Vol. 15: *Korea.* Washington: U.S. Government Printing Office, 1984.

HERRING, GEORGE C., ed. *The Secret Diplomacy of the Vietnam War: The Negotiating Volumes of the Pentagon Papers.* Austin: University of Texas Press, 1983.

HOEFFDING, OLEG. *Bombing North Vietnam: An Appraisal of Economic and Political Effects.* RAND Corporation Memorandum RM-5213, December 1966.

MACISAAC, DAVID, gen. ed. *The United States Strategic Bombing Survey.* 10 vols. New York: Garland Publishing, 1976.

NSSM 1 (February 1969). *Congressional Record* 118 (10 May 1972): 16780–16834.

The Pentagon Papers: the Defense Department History of United States Decision-making in Vietnam. Senator Gravel Edition. 5 vols. Boston: Beacon Press, 1971.

PORTER, GARETH, ed. *Vietnam: The Definitive Documentation of Human Decisions.* 2 vols. Stanfordville, N.Y.: Earl M. Coleman Enterprises, 1979.

ROSENMAN, SAMUEL I., comp. *The Public Papers and Addresses of Franklin D. Roosevelt.* 10 vols. New York: Harper & Brothers, 1950. Vol. 9: *The Tide Turns (1943).*

SHARP, U. S. GRANT, and WILLIAM C. WESTMORELAND. *Report on the War in Vietnam (as of 30 June 1968).* Washington: U.S. Government Printing Office, 1969.

SHEEHAN, NEIL; HEDRICK SMITH; E. W. KENWORTHY; and FOX BUTTERFIELD, eds. *The Pentagon Papers.* New York: Bantam Books, Inc., 1971.

U.S. Congress, House, Committee on Appropriations, Subcommittee on DOD. *DOD Appropriations: Bombings of North Vietnam.* Hearings, 93d Cong., 1st sess., 9–18 January 1973.

U.S. Congress, Senate. *The Korean War and Related Matters; Report of the Subcommittee to Investigate the Administration of the Internal Security Act and other Security Laws to the Committee on the Judiciary.* 84th Cong., 1st sess., 1955.

U.S. Congress, Senate, Committee on Armed Services. *Nomination of John D. Lavelle, General Creighton Abrams, and Admiral John S. McCain.* 92d Cong., 2d sess., 11–29 September 1972.

U.S. Congress, Senate, Committee on Armed Services, Preparedness Investigating Subcommittee. *Air War Against North Vietnam.* 90th Cong., 1st sess., parts 1–5, 9–29 August 1967.

U.S. Congress, Senate, Subcommittee on the Air Force of the Committee on Armed Services. *Airpower.* 85th Cong., 1st sess., 25 January 1957.

U.S. President. *Public Papers of the Presidents of the United States: Richard Nixon (1972).* Washington: U.S. Government Printing Office, 1974.

U.S. President. *Weekly Compilation of Presidential Documents* (Richard Nixon). vols. 8–9. Washington: U.S. Government Printing Office, 1973–74.

3. Air Force Doctrinal Manuals

Air Force Manual 1-2, United States Air Force Basic Doctrine, 1 April 1955.

Air Force Manual 1-2, United States Air Force Basic Doctrine, 1 December 1959.

Air Force Manual 1-1, United States Air Force Basic Doctrine, 13 August 1964.

Air Force Manual 1-1, United States Air Force Basic Doctrine, 16 March 1984.

Air Force Manual 1-7, Theater Air Forces in Counter Air, Interdiction, and Close Air Support Operations, 1 March 1954.

Air Force Manual 2-1, Tactical Air Operations—Counterair, Interdiction, and Close Air Support, 14 June 1965.

Air Force Manual 1-8, Strategic Air Operations, 1 May 1954.

Air Force Manual 2-11, Strategic Aerospace Operations, 1 December 1965.

4. Books

ACHESON, DEAN. *The Korean War.* New York: W. W. Norton, 1969, 1971.

ARNOLD, H. H. *Global Mission.* New York: Harper & Brothers, 1949.

BRODIE, BERNARD. *Strategy in the Missile Age.* Princeton, N.J.: Princeton University Press, 1959.

BROUGHTON, JACK. *Thud Ridge.* New York: Bantam Books, 1969.

———. *Going Downtown: The War Against Hanoi and Washington.* New York: Orion Books, 1988.

COOPER, CHESTER L. *The Lost Crusade: America in Vietnam*. New York: Dodd, Mead, 1970.

EISENHOWER, DWIGHT D. *The White House Years*. Vol. 1: *Mandate for Change*. Garden City, N.Y.: Doubleday, 1963.

GRAFF, HENRY. *The Tuesday Cabinet*. Englewood Cliffs, N.J.: Prentice Hall, 1970.

HANSELL, HAYWOOD, S. *The Air Plan That Defeated Hitler*. Atlanta: Higgins-McArthur/Logino and Porter, 1972.

———. *Strategic Air War Against Japan*. Washington: U.S. Government Printing Office, 1980.

HOOPES, TOWNSEND. *The Limits of Intervention*. New York: David McKay, 1969.

JOHNSON, LYNDON BAINES. *The Vantage Point: Perspectives of the Presidency 1963–1969*. New York: Holt, Rinehart & Winston, 1971.

JOY, C. TURNER. *How Communists Negotiate*. Santa Monica, Calif.: Fidelis Publishers, 1955, 1970.

KATTENBURG, PAUL M. *The Vietnam Trauma in America Foreign Policy, 1945–1975*. New Brunswick, N.J.: Transaction Books, 1980.

KHRUSHCHEV, NIKITA. *Khrushchev Remembers*. Translated and edited by Strobe Talbott. Boston: Little, Brown, 1970.

KISSINGER, HENRY A. *White House Years*. Boston: Little, Brown, 1979.

KOHN, RICHARD H., and JOSEPH P. HARAHAN, eds. *Air Interdiction in World War II, Korea, and Vietnam: An Interview with Gen. Earle E. Partridge, Gen. Jacob Smart, and Gen. John W. Vogt, Jr.* Washington, D.C.: Office of Air Force History, 1986.

KY, NGUYEN CAO. *How We Lost the Vietnam War*. New York: Scarborough Books, 1976.

LEMAY, CURTIS E., with MACKINLAY KANTOR. *Mission with LeMay*. Garden City, N.Y.: Doubleday, 1965.

NICHOLS, JOHN B., and BARRETT TILLMAN. *On Yankee Station: The Naval Air War over Vietnam*. Annapolis: Naval Institute Press, 1987.

NIXON, RICHARD M. *No More Vietnams*. New York: Arbor House, 1985.

———. *RN: The Memoirs of Richard Nixon*. 2 vols. New York: Warner Books, 1978.

RIDGWAY, MATTHEW B. *The Korean War*. Garden City, Doubleday, N.Y.: 1967.

ROSTOW, WALT W. *The Diffusion of Power*. New York: Macmillan, 1972.

———. *Pre-Invasion Bombing Strategy: General Eisenhower's Decision of March 25, 1944*. Austin: University of Texas Press, 1981.

SALISBURY, HARRISON E. *Behind the Lines—Hanoi.* New York: Harper & Row, 1967.

SHARP, U. S. GRANT. *Strategy for Defeat: Vietnam in Retrospect.* San Rafael, Calif.: Presidio Press, 1978.

SPEER, ALBERT. *Inside the Third Reich.* New York: Avon Books, 1970.

TAYLOR, MAXWELL D. *Swords and Plowshares.* New York: W. W. Norton, 1972.

TRUMAN, HARRY S. *Memoirs.* Vol. 2: *Years of Trial and Hope.* Garden City, N.Y.: Doubleday, 1956.

TRUONG, NHU TANG. *A Viet Cong Memoir.* New York: Vintage Books, 1985.

U.S. Army Air Forces. *ULTRA and the History of the United States Strategic Air Force in Europe vs. the German Air Force.* Edited by Paul L. Kesaris. Frederick, Md.: University Publications of America, 1980.

Visions of Victory: Selected Vietnamese Communist Military Writings, 1964-1968. Stanford, Calif.: Hoover Institution on War, Revolution, and Peace, 1969.

WESTMORELAND, WILLIAM C. *A Soldier Reports.* Garden City, N.Y.: Doubleday, 1976.

5. Articles

"Air Power—What It Is Doing in the Vietnam War." *US News and World Report,* 9 May 1966, pp. 28–29.

"Air War Against the North—'Tougher than Anyone Realizes.'" *US News and World Report,* 21 August 1972, p. 32.

"The Air War: Less than a Success." *Newsweek,* 29 August 1966, p. 21.

ALLEN, MICHAEL. "Sharing the Agony of Hanoi." *The Christian Century,* 24 January 1973, pp. 91–94.

ALSOP, STEWART. "Eternal Damnation?" *Newsweek,* 29 January 1973, p. 78.

"As the Air War Heats Up in Vietnam—." *US News and World Report,* 9 May 1966, p. 27.

"As the Air War Hit a Peak—." *US News and World Report,* 8 January 1973, p. 17.

"The Attack on Electric Power in North Korea." *Air University Quarterly Review* 6 (Summer 1953): 13–30.

"The Attack on the Irrigation Dams in North Korea." *Air University Quarterly Review* 6 (Winter 1953–54): 40–61.

BALL, GEORGE W. "How Valid Are the Assumptions Underlying Our Vietnam Policy?" *Atlantic Monthly,* July 1972, pp. 36–49.

"Bombing: An Admiral's Report." *Newsweek,* 29 May 1967, p. 49.

"Bombing Fallout." *Time*, 22 January 1973, p. 21.

"The Cumulative Effect of Interdiction." *Air University Quarterly Review* 6 (Fall 1953): 74–78.

"A Deal with Hanoi, a Duel with Thieu." *Newsweek*, 30 October 1972, pp. 24–25.

"Diplomacy by Terror: What the Bombing Did." *Newsweek*, 8 January 1973, pp. 10–12.

EAKER, IRA C., and ARTHUR G. B. METCALF. "Conversations with Albert Speer." *Air Force*, April 1977, pp. 53–58.

"Effects of the Bombing." *Time*, 26 June 1972, p. 31.

"Exclusive from Hanoi." *Newsweek*, 30 October 1972, pp. 26–27.

FINLETTER, THOMAS K. "Air Power and Foreign Policy, Especially in the Far East." *The Annals of the American Academy of Political and Social Science* 299 (May 1955): 76–86.

FRISBEE, JOHN L. "The Air War in Vietnam." *Air Force*, September 1972, pp. 48–59.

———. "An Editorial." *Air Force*, March 1973, pp. 2–3.

FROMM, JOSEPH. "Why Hanoi Came to Realize It 'Could Not Hope to Win.'" *US News and World Report*, 6 November 1972, pp. 17–19.

GALBRAITH, JOHN KENNETH. "After the Air Raids." *American Heritage* 32 (April–May 1981): 65–80.

GINSBURGH, ROBERT N. "North Vietnam—Airpower." *Vital Speeches of the Day* 38 (15 September 1972): 732–35.

———. "Strategy and Airpower: The Lessons of Southeast Asia." *Strategic Review* 1 (Summer 1973): 18–24.

GOLDWATER, BARRY. "Air Power in Southeast Asia." *Congressional Record—Senate* 119, part 5 (26 February 1973): 5346.

GREENE, WALLACE M. "The Bombing 'Pause': Formula for Failure," *Air Force*, April 1976, pp. 36–39.

HOTZ, ROBERT. "B-52s over Hanoi." *Aviation Week and Space Technology*, 12 February 1973, p. 7.

———. "Editorial." *Aviation Week and Space Technology*, 30 October 1972, p. 7.

"How Much of the Way with LBJ?" *Newsweek*, 26 September 1966, pp. 25–27.

"Interview with Maxwell Taylor." *US News and World Report*, 27 November 1972, pp. 25–27.

KATZENBACH, NICHOLAS DEB. "Foreign Policy, Public Opinion, and Secrecy." *Foreign Affairs* 52 (October 1973): 1–19.

KISSINGER, HENRY A. "The Viet Nam Negotiations." *Foreign Affairs* 47 (January 1969): 211–34.

KRAFT, JOSEPH. "Letter from Hanoi." *The New Yorker*, 12 August 1972, pp. 58–72.

LEMAY, CURTIS E. "General LeMay Tells How to Win the War in Vietnam." *US News and World Report*, 10 October 1966, pp. 36–43.

"Mr. Nixon Strikes Back." *Newsweek*, 24 April 1972, pp. 21–22.

"The New Air War in Vietnam." *US News and World Report*, 24 April 1972, pp. 15–17.

"A New Sophistication," *Newsweek*, 10 July 1967, pp. 20–22.

"Nixon's Blitz Leads Back to the Table." *Time*, 8 January 1973, pp. 9–14.

"North Viet Bombing Held Critical." *Aviation Week and Space Technology*, 5 (March 1973): 12–13.

"Opening 'The Fourth Front.'" *Newsweek*, 18 July 1966, pp. 18–21.

OSTROW, MARTIN M. "The B-52's Message to Moscow." *Air Force*, April 1973, pp. 2–3.

"Outrage and Relief." *Time*, 8 January 1973, p. 14.

"The Peace of Paris: A Comma Away?" *Newsweek*, 22 January 1973, pp. 17–18.

RUTLEDGE, H. E. "A POW View of Linebacker II." *Armed Forces Journal International* 115 (September 1977): 20.

"Seeing It Through." *Newsweek*, 17 April 1967, p. 52.

"A Tarnished Image Abroad." *Newsweek*, 10 July 1967, pp. 60–61.

TODD, OLIVER. "The Americans Are Not Invincible." *New Left Review* 47 (January–February 1968): 2–19.

TORMOEN, GEORGE E. "Political Air Superiority in the Korean Conflict." *Air University Quarterly Review* 6 (Winter 1953–54): 78–84.

ULSAMER, EDGAR. "Airpower Halts an Invasion." *Air Force*, September 1972, pp. 60–71.

WEYLAND, OTTO P. "The Air Campaign in Korea." In *The Impact of Air Power*, pp. 383–400. Edited by Eugene M. Emme. Princton, N.J.: Van Nostrand, 1959.

"What Admiral Moorer Really Said About Airpower's Effectiveness in SEA." *Air Force*, November 1973, pp. 24–25.

"What the Christmas Bombing Did to North Vietnam." *US News and World Report*, 5 February 1973, p. 18.

"What Went Wrong in Vietnam: The Fallacies in U.S. Policy." *Newsweek*, 15 May 1972, pp. 11–12.

VANDENBERG, HOYT S. "Air Power in the Korean War." In *The Impact of Air Power*, pp. 400–06. Edited by Eugene W. Emme. Princeton, N.J.: Van Nostrand, 1959.

YUDKIN, RICHARD A. "Vietnam: Policy, Strategy, and Airpower." *Air Force*, February 1973, pp. 31–33.

6. Interviews and Correspondence

ALLEN, JOHN R., Major, USAF. Interview, Osan Air Base Korea, 22 September 1981.

———. Cassette Tape to author, June 1982.

BODENHEIMER, CLYDE E., Colonel, USAF. Interview, Maxwell AFB, Alabama, 7 January 1983.

CLARK, ROBERT D., Colonel, USAF. Interview, Robins AFB, Georgia, 6 January 1983.

FERGUSON, CHARLES, Lieutenant Colonel USAF (reserve). Interview, Maxwell AFB, Alabama, 17 May 1985.

GREENHALGH, WILLIAM, Lieutenant Colonel, USAF (ret.). Interview, Maxwell AFB, Alabama, 17 May 1985.

———. Letter to author, 4 April 1987.

KATTENBURG, PAUL M. Interview, Chapel Hill, North Carolina. 10 December 1986.

MCNAMARA, ROBERT S. Telephone interview, 15 December 1986.

MOORE, JOSEPH H., Lieutenant General, USAF (ret.). Letter to author, 1 October 1986.

RASH, JIM, Major, USAF (ret.). Letter to author, 15 August 1982.

ROSTOW, WALT W. Interview, Austin, Texas, 23 May 1986.

RUSK, DEAN. Interview, Athens, Georgia, 15 July 1985.

THOMPSON, GEORGE, Major, USAF (ret.). Interview, Omaha, Nebraska, 27 October 1982.

VOGT, JOHN W., JR., General, USAF (ret.). Interview, Durham, North Carolina, 30 October 1986.

WATTS, FRED, Major, USMC (ret.). Letter to author, 15 April 1985.

7. Newspapers

Columbus (Ohio) *Citizen-Journal*. Selected articles, 1972.

New York Times. Selected articles, 1965–75.

Omaha World-Herald. Selected articles, 1972–73.

USA Today. Selected articles, 1986.

Wall Street Journal. Selected articles, 1972–73.

Washington Post. Selected articles, 1965–73.

Washington Star. Selected articles, 1972–73.

B. SECONDARY SOURCES

1. Books

Air War—Vietnam. New York: Arno Press, 1978.

ARMITAGE, M. J. and R. A. MASON. *Air Power in the Nuclear Age.* Urbana: University of Illinois Press, 1983.

ARMSTRONG, ANNE. *Unconditional Surrender: The Impact of the Casablanca Policy upon World War II.* New Brunswick, N.J.: Rutgers University Press, 1961.

BAILEY, RONALD H. *The Air War in Europe.* Alexandria, Va.: Time-Life Books, 1979.

BATCHELDER, ROBERT C. *The Irreversible Decision 1939–1950.* Boston: Houghton Mifflin, 1962.

BERGER, CARL, ed. *The United States Air Force in Southeast Asia, 1961–1973: An Illustrated Account.* Washington, D.C.: Office of Air Force History, 1984.

BERMAN, LARRY. *Planning a Tragedy: The Americanization of the War in Vietnam.* New York: W. W. Norton, 1982.

BETTS, RICHARD K. *Soldiers, Statesmen, and Cold War Crises.* Cambridge: Harvard University Press, 1977.

BIDINIAN, LARRY J. *The Combined Allied Bombing Offensive Against the German Civilian.* Lawrence, Kan.: Coronado Press, 1976.

BOROWSKI, HARRY R. *A Hollow Threat: Strategic Air Power and Containment Before Korea.* Westport, Conn.: Greenwood Press, 1982.

BRODIE, BERNARD. *War and Politics.* New York: Macmillan, 1973.

BURK, ROBERT F. *Dwight D. Eisenhower: Hero and Politician.* Boston: Twayne Publishers, 1986.

BURNS, JAMES MACGREGOR. *Roosevelt: The Soldier of Freedom 1940–1945.* New York: Harcourt Brace Jovanovich, 1970.

CHANOFF, DAVID, and VAN TOAI DOAN. *Portrait of the Enemy.* New York: Random House, 1986.

CLAUSEWITZ, CARL VON. *On War.* Edited and translated by Michael Howard and Peter J. Paret. Princeton, N.J.: Princeton University Press, 1976.

CRAVEN, WESLEY FRANK, and JAMES LEA CATE. *The Army Air Forces in World War II.* 7 vols. Chicago: University of Chicago Press, 1948–58.

COPP, DEWITT S. *A Few Great Captains.* Garden City, N.Y.: Doubleday, 1980.

———. *Forged in Fire.* Garden City, N.Y.: Doubleday, 1982.

DALLEK, ROBERT. *Franklin D. Roosevelt and American Foreign Policy, 1932–1945.* Oxford: Oxford University Press, 1979.

DAVIDSON, PHILLIP B. *Vietnam at War: The History, 1946–1975.* Novato, Calif.: Presidio Press, 1988.

DONOVAN, ROBERT J. *Eisenhower: The Inside Story.* New York: Harper & Brothers, 1956.

———. *Tumultuous Years: The Presidency of Harry S. Truman, 1949–1953.* New York: W. W. Norton, 1982.

DOWER, JOHN W. *War Without Mercy: Race and Power in the Pacific War.* New York: Pantheon Books, 1986.

FEIS, HERBERT. *Churchill, Roosevelt, Stalin: The War They Waged and the Peace They Sought.* Princeton, N.J.: Princeton University Press, 1957, 1967.

FINNEY, ROBERT T. *History of the Air Corps Tactical School.* Maxwell Air Force Base, Ala.: Air University Press, 1955.

FULLER, J. F. C. *The Second World War: A Strategical and Tactical History.* New York: Duell, Sloan & Pearce, 1949.

FUTRELL, ROBERT F. *Ideas, Concepts, Doctrine: A History of Basic Thinking in the United States Air Force, 1907–1964.* Maxwell Air Force Base, Ala.: Air University Press, 1974.

———. *The United States Air Force in Korea 1950–1953.* New York: Duell, Sloan & Pearce, 1961.

GADDIS, JOHN LEWIS. *Strategies of Containment: A Critical Appraisal of Postwar American National Security Policy.* New York: Oxford University Press, 1982.

GALLUCCI, ROBERT L. *Neither Peacy nor Honor: The Politics of American Military Policy in Viet-Nam.* Baltimore: Johns Hopkins Press, 1975.

GASTON, JAMES C. *Planning the American Air War: Four Men and Nine Days in 1941.* Washington, D.C.: National Defense University Press, 1982.

GEORGE, ALEXANDER L.; DAVID K. HALL; and WILLIAM E. SIMONS. *The Limits of Coercive Diplomacy: Laos, Cuba, and Vietnam.* Boston: Little, Brown, 1971.

GOODMAN, ALLAN E. *The Lost Peace: America's Search for a Negotiated Settlement of the Vietnam War.* Stanford, Calif.: Hoover Institution Press, 1978.

GRANT, ZALIN. *Over the Beach: The Air War in Vietnam.* New York: W. W. Norton, 1986.

GREER, THOMAS H. *The Development of Air Doctrine in the Army Air Arm 1917–1941.* Maxwell Air Force Base, Ala.: Air University Press, 1955.

GREENFIELD, KENT ROBERTS. *American Strategy in World War II: A Reconsideration.* Baltimore: Johns Hopkins Press, 1963.

GRINTER, LAWRENCE E., and PETER M. DUNN, eds. *The American War in Vietnam: Lessons, Legacies, and Implications for Future Conflicts.* New York: Greenwood Press, 1988.

HALBERSTAM, DAVID. *The Best and the Brightest.* New York: Random House, 1969.

HARRIS, LOUIS. *The Anguish of Change.* New York: W. W. Norton, 1973.

HAYES, RICHARD F. *The Awesome Power: Harry S. Truman as Commander in Chief.* Baton Rouge: Louisiana State University Press, 1973.

HERRING, GEORGE C. *America's Longest War: The United States and Vietnam 1950-1975.* New York: John Wiley, 1979.

HERSH, SEYMOUR M. *The Price of Power: Kissinger in the Nixon White House.* New York: Summit Books, 1985.

HERZ, MARTIN F. *The Prestige Press and the Christmas Bombing, 1972: Images and Reality in Vietnam.* Washington, D.C.: Ethics & Public Policy Center, 1980.

HOLLEY, I. B., JR. *Ideas and Weapons.* New Haven: Yale University Press, 1953; reprint edition, Washington, D.C.: Office of Air Force History, 1983.

IKLÉ, FRED CHARLES. *The Social Impact of Bomb Destruction.* Norman: University of Oklahoma Press, 1958.

JANIS, IRVING L. *Air War and Emotional Stress.* New York: McGraw-Hill, 1951.

KAHIN, GEORGE MCTURNAN, and JOHN W. LEWIS. *The United States in Vietnam.* New York: Delta Press, 1967.

KARNOW, STANLEY. *Vietnam: A History.* New York: Viking, 1983.

KEARNS, DORIS. *Lyndon Johnson and the American Dream.* New York: Signet, 1976.

KINNARD, DOUGLAS. *The War Managers.* Hanover, N.H.: University Press of New England, 1977.

KOLKO, GABRIEL. *Anatomy of a War: Vietnam, the United States, and the Modern Historical Experience.* New York: Pantheon Books, 1985.

LEWY, GUENTER. *America in Vietnam.* New York: Oxford University Press, 1978.

LITTAUER, RAPHAEL, and NORMAN UPHOFF, eds. *The Air War in Indochina.* Boston: Beacon Press, 1972.

MCCARTHY, JAMES R., and GEORGE B. ALLISON. *Linebacker II: A View from the Rock.* Maxwell Air Force Base, Ala.: Air War College, 1979.

MACISAAC, DAVID. *Strategic Bombing in World War Two: The Story of the United States Strategic Bombing Survey.* New York: Garland Publishing, 1976.

MERSKY, PETER B., and NORMAN POLMAR. *The Naval Air War in Vietnam.* Annapolis: Nautical & Aviation Publishing Company of America, 1981.

MILLET, ALLEN R. and PETER MASLOWSKI. *For the Common Defense: A Military History of the United States of America.* New York: Free Press, 1984.

MOMYER, WILLIAM W. *Air Power in Three Wars.* Washington, D.C.: U.S. Government Printing Office, 1978.

MORROCCO, JOHN. *Thunder from Above.* Boston: Boston Publishing, 1984.

————. *Rain of Fire.* Boston: Boston Publishing, 1985.

NORDEEN, LON O., JR. *Air Warfare in the Missile Age.* Washington, D.C.: Smithsonian Institution Press, 1985.

O'CONNOR, RAYMOND G. *Diplomacy for Victory: FDR and Unconditional Surrender.* New York: W. W. Norton, 1971.

OVERY, R. J. *The Air War 1939–1945.* London: Europa Publications, 1980.

PALMER, DAVE RICHARD. *Summons of the Trumpet: U.S.–Vietnam in Perspective.* Novato, Calif.: Presidio Press, 1978.

PAPP, DANIEL S. *Vietnam: The View from Moscow, Peking, Washington.* Jefferson, N.C.: McFarland, 1981.

PIKE, DOUGLAS. *PAVN: People's Army of Vietnam.* Novato, Calif.: Presidio Press, 1986.

PORTER, GARETH. *A Peace Denied: The United States, Vietnam, and the Paris Agreement.* Bloomington: Indiana University Press, 1975.

REES, DAVID. *Korea: The Limited War.* Baltimore: Penguin Books, 1964.

RUMPF, HANS. *The Bombing of Germany.* New York: Holt, Rinehart & Winston, 1963.

SAFIRE, WILLIAM. *Before the Fall.* Garden City, N.Y.: Doubleday, 1975.

SCHAFFER, RONALD. *Wings of Judgment: American Bombing in World War II.* New York: Oxford University Press, 1985.

SCHANDLER, HERBERT Y. *The Unmaking of a President: Lyndon Johnson and Vietnam.* Princeton, N.J.: Princeton University Press, 1977.

SCHOENBAUM, THOMAS J. *Waging Peace and War: Dean Rusk in the Truman, Kennedy and Johnson Years.* New York: Simon & Schuster, 1988.

SHERRY, MICHAEL S. *The Rise of American Air Power: The Creation of Armageddon.* New Haven: Yale University Press, 1987.

SMITH, GADDIS. *American Diplomacy During the Second World War 1941–1945.* New York: John Wiley, 1965.

SMITH, PERRY MCCOY. *The Air Force Plans for Peace.* Baltimore: Johns Hopkins Press, 1970.

SUMMERS, HARRY G., JR. *On Strategy: A Critical Analysis of the Vietnam War*. Novato, Calif.: Presidio Press, 1982.

SZULC, TAD. *The Illusion of Peace: Foreign Policy in the Nixon Years*. New York: Viking, 1978.

THIES, WALLACE J. *When Governments Collide: Coercion and Diplomacy in the Vietnam Conflict 1964–1968*. Berkeley: University of California Press, 1980.

THOMPSON, JAMES CLAY. *Rolling Thunder: Understanding Policy and Programming Failure*. Chapel Hill: University of North Carolina Press, 1980.

THOMPSON, ROBERT. *Peace Is Not at Hand*. New York: David McKay, 1974.

THOMPSON, W. SCOTT, and DONALDSON D. FRIZZELL, eds. *The Lessons of Vietnam*. New York: Crane, Russak, 1977.

TURLEY, G. H. *The Easter Offensive*. Novato, Calif.: Presidio Press, 1985.

VAN DYKE, JON M. *North Vietnam's Strategy for Survival*. Palo Alto, Calif.: Pacific Books, 1972.

VERRIER, ANTHONY. *The Bomber Offensive*. London: B. T. Batsford, 1968.

WATTS, BARRY D. *The Foundations of U.S. Air Doctrine*. Maxwell Air Force Base, Ala.: Air University Press, 1984.

WEBSTER, CHARLES, and NOBLE FRANKLAND. *The Strategic Air Offensive Against Germany, 1939–1945*. 4 vols. London: HMSO, 1961.

WEIGLEY, RUSSELL F. *The American Way of War*. New York: Macmillan, 1973.

———. *History of the United States Army*. New York: Macmillan, 1967.

WOLK, HERMAN S. *Planning and Organizing the Postwar Air Force*. Washington, D.C.: Office of Air Force History, 1984.

2. Articles/Studies

APPEL, BERNARD. "Bombing Accuracy in a Combat Environment." *Air University Review* 26 (July–August 1975): 38–52.

BERNSTEIN, BARTON J. "New Light on the Korean War." *International History Review* 3 (April, 1981): 256–77.

BROYLES, WILLIAM, JR. "The Road to Hill 10." *Atlantic Monthly*, April 1985, pp. 90–118.

CARTER, GREGORY A. *Some Historical Notes on Air Interdiction in Korea*. RAND Corporation Paper No. 3452, September 1966.

CLODFELTER, MARK A. "Culmination Dresden: 1945." *Aerospace Historian* 26 (Fall 1979): 134–47.

CONVERSE, PHILIP E., and HOWARD SCHUMAN. "Silent Majorities' and the Vietnam War." *Scientific American* 222 (June 1970): 17–25.

COPP, DEWITT S. "The Pioneer Plan for Air War." *Air Force*, October 1982, pp. 74–78.

CRANE, CONRAD C. "Evolution of U.S. Strategic Bombing of Urban Areas," *The Historian* 50 (November 1987): 14–39.

DAVIDSON, MICHAEL W. "Senior Officers and Vietnam Policymaking." *Parameters*, Spring 1986, pp. 55–62.

DRENKOWSKI, DANA. "The Tragedy of Operation Linebacker II." *Armed Forces Journal International* 114 (July 1977): 24–27.

DREW, DENNIS M. *Rolling Thunder 1965: Anatomy of a Failure.* Report No. AU-ARI-CP-86-3. Maxwell Air Force Base, Ala.: Air University Press, 1986.

———. "Two Decades in the Air Power Wilderness: Do We Know Where We Are?" *Air University Review* 37 (September–October 1986): 2–13.

EMERSON, WILLIAM. "Franklin Roosevelt as Commander-in-Chief in World War II." *Military Affairs* 22 (Winter 1958–59): 181–207.

FRISBEE, JOHN L. "The Practice of Professionalism." *Air Force*, August 1986, p. 113.

FUTRELL, ROBERT F. "The Influence of the Air Power Concept on Air Force Planning, 1945–1962." In *Military Planning in the Twentieth Century: Proceedings of the Eleventh Military History Symposium, USAF Academy, 1984*, pp. 253–74. Edited by Harry R. Borowski. Washington, D.C.: U.S. Government Printing Office, 1986.

GREENWOOD, JOHN L. "The Emergence of the Postwar Strategic Air Force, 1945–1953." In *Air Power and Warfare: Proceedings of the Eighth Military History Symposium at the U.S. Air Force Academy*, pp. 215–44. Edited by Alfred F. Hurley and Robert C. Ehrhart. Washington, D.C.: Office of Air Force History, 1979.

GROPMAN, ALAN L. "Air Power and Low-Intensity Conflict: An Airman's Perspective." *Armed Forces Journal International* 122 (May 1985): 33–42.

HALBERSTAM, DAVID. "The Programming of Robert McNamara." *Harper's*, February, 1971, pp. 37–71.

HOPKINS, CHARLES K. "Linebacker II: A Firsthand View." *Aerospace Historian* 23 (Fall 1976): 128–35.

HUMPHREY, DAVID C. "Tuesday Lunch at the Johnson White House: A Preliminary Assessment." *Diplomatic History* 8 (Winter 1984): 81–101.

HUNTINGTON, SAMUEL P.; ERNEST R. MAY; RICHARD N. NEUSTADT; and THOMAS C. SCHELLING. "Vietnam Reappraised." *International Security* 6 (Summer 1981): 3–26.

KEEFER, EDWARD C. "President Dwight D. Eisenhower and the End of the Korean War." *Diplomatic History* 10 (Summer 1986): 267–89.

KOCH, NOEL C. "Is There a Role for Air Power in a Low-Intensity Conflict?" *Armed Forces Journal International* 122 (May 1985): 32–42.

McGARVEY, PATRICK J. "DIA: Intelligence to Please." *Washington Monthly* 2 (July 1970): 68–75.

MacISAAC, DAVID. "The Evolution of Air Power Since 1945: The American Experience." In *War in the Third Dimension: Essays in Contemporary Air Power*, pp. 11–31. Edited by R. A. Mason. London: Brassey's Defense Publishers, 1986.

————. "Voices from the Central Blue: The Air Power Theorists." In *The Makers of Modern Strategy from Machiavelli to the Nuclear Age*, pp. 624–47. Edited by Peter Paret. Princeton, N.J.: Princeton University Press, 1986.

McCLOUD, BILL. "What Should We Tell Our Children about Vietnam?" *American Heritage* 39 (May–June 1988): 55–77.

MILES, RUFUS E., JR. "Hiroshima." *International Security* 10 (Fall 1985): 121–40.

NICKERSON, HOFFMAN. "The Folly of Strategic Bombing." *Ordnance*, January–February 1949, pp. 245–47.

PARKS, HAYS W. "Linebacker and the Law of War." *Air University Review* 34 (January–February 1983): 2–30.

————. "Rolling Thunder and the Law of War." *Air University Review* 33 (January–February 1982): 2–23.

QUESTER, GEORGE H. "The Impact of Strategic Air Warfare." *Armed Forces and Society* 4 (February 1978): 179–206.

ROSEN, STEPHEN PETER. "Vietnam and the American Theory of Limited War." *International Security* 7 (Fall 1982): 83–113.

ROSENBERG, DAVID ALAN. "The Origins of Overkill: Nuclear Weapons and American Strategy." *International Security* 7 (Spring 1983): 3–71.

SCHLIGHT, JOHN. "Civilian Control of the Military in Southeast Asia." *Air University Review* 31 (November–December 1980): 56–69.

SHY, JOHN. "The American Military Experience." In *A People Numerous and Armed*, pp. 225–54. London: Oxford University Press, 1976.

SMITH, MELDEN E., JR. "The Stretegic Bombing Debate: The Second World War and Vietnam." *Journal of Contemporary History* 12 (1977): 175–91.

SZULC, TAD. "Behind the Vietnam Cease-Fire Agreement." *Foreign Policy* 15 (Summer 1974): 21–68.

"Tragedy of Linebacker II: The USAF Response." *Armed Forces Journal International* 114 (August 1977): 24–25.

3. Unpublished Papers/Dissertations

ROGERS, ROBERT F. "Risk-Taking in Hanoi's War Policy: An Analysis of Militancy Versus Manipulation in a Communist Party-State's Behavior in a Conflict." Ph. D. dissertation, Georgetown University, 1974.

SMITH, RUSSELL H. "Gradualism and the Air War Against North Vietnam." Air War College Research Report Summary No. 4452, Air University, 1971.

WHATLEY, DOUGLAS E. "The Effectiveness of U.S. Airpower in the Air Campaign over North Vietnam." Air War College Research Report Summary No. 4017, Air University, 1971.

Index

——————— • ———————

Acheson, Dean, 13, 19, 111
Agricultural base
  attacks on, 110–11, 126
  Rolling Thunder's efficacy and, 144
Air commanders: *see also* Strategic Air
  Command (SAC); specific
  commanders and bombing programs
  concern for civilian casualties, 127–
  28
  doctrinal and moral beliefs of, 205–6
  misreading of Christmas bombing,
  208
  perception of Vietnam war aims,
  68, 73–76, 82–84, 100–102,
  107–8
  on Rolling Thunder's effectiveness,
  144–46
Air Corps, interwar objectives of, 2–3
Air Corps Tactical School (ACTS), 2,
  11, 36, 73; *see also* Bombing
  doctrine, Air Force
Aircraft types
  A-4 Skyhawk, 133
  A-6 Intruder, 133, 166
  B-29, 9, 12, 21, 26
  B-52 bombers, 118–19, 152, 154,
  159, 166, 182–83, 186–90
  F-105 Thunderchief, 31, 133
  F-111, 161–62, 166
  F-4s, 133, 152, 153, 190
  F-51 Mustang, 21
  F-80, 21
  P-51 Mustang, 5
  in Rolling Thunder air strikes, 133
  XB-17, 2

Air Force: *see also* Air commanders;
  Bombing doctrine, Air Force;
  Doctrinal manuals, Air Force;
  specific air programs and campaigns
  bases, 184, 185, 187
  countermeasures to enemy defenses,
  165
  creation of, 3
  8th, 6, 185
  5th, 21
  perception of Vietnam War, 207–8
  priority on preparing for nuclear
  war, 27, 234*n*.130
  role in Korea, 3
  7/13th, 128
  7th, 109, 192
    attack on missile propellant stor-
    age area (1966), 122–23
    daily mission critiques, 194
    intelligence operations, 130–31
    in Linebacker missions, 161
    Operation Proud Deep Alpha,
    151
    organizational problems in, 128–
    29
    route packages, 129
    unauthorized attacks ordered by
    Lavelle, 264*n*.16
  13th, 128
  20th, 9
Air Force–Navy Coordinating Committee, 129
Air pressure campaign (Korean War),
  16–19, 26
Allen, John R., 186, 189
Andersen Air Force base, 184, 185

Antiwar protest, 91, 109
Arab–Israeli War (1967), 120
Arbuckle, Tammy, 195
Arcadia Conference (1942), 4
"Arc Light" campaign, 119
Army Air Forces, operational restrictions (WW II), 8
Arnold, Henry H. "Hap," 8
Atlee, Clement, 19
Atomic bomb, 7, 10, 11–12, 34, 228n.23
AWPD-1 (WW II), 5, 73

B-29 bombers, 9, 12, 21, 26
B-52 bombers, 152, 166, 179
  in Linebacker missions, 154, 159, 182–83, 186–90
  in Rolling Thunder, 118–19
Ball, George W., 48, 53, 67–69, 71, 91, 117, 141
"Basic Doctrine" (Manual 1-1), 203, 208–9
"Basic Doctrine" (Manual 1-2), 27
  on general vs. limited conflict, 29–31
  on nuclear weapons' priority, 31–32, 234n.130
Beria, Lavrenty, 24
Bien Hoa air base, 53, 77
Bodenheimer, Clyde E., 192, 201
Bomber Command, 21
Bombing, political effectiveness of, xv–xvi
Bombing doctrine, Air Force, xv, xvi, 225n.4
  of Air Corps Tactical School (ACTS), 2–3, 11, 36
  after Korean War, xiv, 3
  under LeMay, 29, 35–36
  Rolling Thunder controls and, 125–127
  World War II, xiv
Bombing pause(s)
  Johnson on, 91
  McNamara's call for, 90, 91
  public opinion on (1968), 253n.167
  during Rolling Thunder, 119, 120, 125
    December–January (1965–66), 90–91, 125

May 1965, 67, 83
  October 1968, 147, 263n.2
Bombs, smart, 159, 164, 167
Bomb tonnage dropped
  in Korean War, 22
  by Linebacker I, 166–67
  by Linebacker II, 194
  by Rolling Thunder, 134
  in World War II, 8
Bradley, Omar N., 15
Brezhnev, Leonid, 155, 157
Brodie, Bernard, 28, 33–34
Broughton, Jack, 131
Buddhist demonstrations (March–May 1965), 95
Bundy, McGeorge, 91, 117
  on McNamara's call for escalation of war, 69
  on Rolling Thunder's efficacy, 65–66
  on sustained bombing, 57–62, 204
  targeting selections, 68, 122
  at Tuesday lunches, 85
Bundy, William, 45, 49–50, 52–56, 62–63, 81, 91
  doubts about sustained bombing, 59
  on Johnson's absences from Washington, 125
  opposition to bombing halt, 96
  opposition to JCS plan to extend war to Laos and Cambodia, 107
  on Rolling Thunder, 52, 108
  on Tuesday luncheons, 121

Casablanca Conference (1943), 4, 5
Casualties: see Civilian casualties
Central Intelligence Agency (CIA), 93–94
Chasan dam, 18
China
  American concern over intervention by, 55, 67–68, 71, 74, 85, 118, 141–42
  border conflicts with Soviet Union, 149–50
  intervention in Korea, 14–16
  Kissinger's visit (1971), 150
  Nixon's isolation of Hanoi government from, 149–50

response to American mining of Northern harbors, 167
response to Flaming Dart, 61
response to Nixon's warning against Northern offensive (1972), 151–52
support of North Vietnam, 42–43, 135, 141–42, 172–73, 196
U.S. fighter planes shot down in (August 1967), 109
Chinh, Truong, 168
Christmas bombings: see Linebacker II (18–29 December 1972)
Churchill, Winston, 4
Civilian casualties
air leaders' concern for, 127–28
as control on Linebacker I, 164
as control on Linebacker II, 190–91
from Linebacker II, 195
from Rolling Thunder, 136–37
Clark, Mark, 16, 17–18
Clark, Robert D., 186, 189, 201–2
Clausewitz, Carl von, xv, xvi, 1, 203 206
Clifford, Clark M., 113–14
Combined Bomber Offensive (CBO), 5, 8–11
Composite Air Strike Force (CASF), 31
Congress, U.S., reactions of
to Linebacker I, 150
to Linebacker II, 178, 191–92
Control, operational vs. administrative, 256n.51
Conventional warfare, Linebacker's efficacy and, 173
Cooper, Chester A., 42, 65, 124
Cordes, Harry, 192
CTF 77, 129
Cuban missile crisis, xiv, 40, 43
Cutler, Robert, 34

Dams: see Irrigation dams
Defense Intelligence Agency (DIA), 93, 94, 99, 130
Democratic Republic of Vietnam: see North Vietnam
Détente, 150, 172–73, 196, 204
Dikes, failure to target, 126–27
Dillon, Douglas, 111

DMZ, Northern military buildup along, 151, 152
Dobrynin, Anatoly, 91, 152, 154, 157
Doctrinal manuals, Air Force
"Basic Doctrine" (Manual 1-1), 203, 208–9
"Basic Doctrine" (Manual 1-2), 27, 29–32, 234n.130
"Strategic Air Operations" (Manual 1-8), 27–28, 29, 36
"Theater Air Forces in Counter Air, Interdiction and Close Air Support Operations" (Manual 1-7), 30
Dominican Republic, 1965 coup attempt in, 120
Dong, Pham Van, 137, 168, 172
Dong Phuong railroad bridge, 81
Doolittle, James H., 6
Dulles, John Foster, 14, 23
Dung, Van Tien, 131–32, 135, 141

Eaker, Ira, 6, 127
Easter Offensive (1972), 151, 152–58, 206
conventional character of, 173
matériel needs arising from, 167
Politburo's commitment to, 168–69
Edelen, Henry H., 86, 128, 130
8th Tactical Fighter Wing, 166
Eisenhower, Dwight D., 5–6, 8, 14–15, 34, 36, 205, 229n.52
Electric power plants, attacks on
efficacy of, 135–36
during Korean War, 17, 19, 20
during Rolling Thunder, 102–7
"Eleven-Day War": see Linebacker II (18–29 December 1972)
Evacuations of Hanoi, 136–37, 195, 197

F-105 Thunderchief, 31, 133
F-111, 161–62, 166
F-4 Phantom, 133, 152, 153, 190
F-51 Mustang, 21
F-80 Shooting Star, 21
Far East Air Forces (FEAF), 15–26
air pressure campaign, 16–19, 26
countermeasures against, 21–22

Far East Air Forces (FEAF) (*cont.*)
  interdiction and air support roles of,
      15–16, 17, 19, 24–25
  political limits on, 19–20, 25–26
Felt, Harry D., 45
Finletter, Thomas K., 28
Firebombing of Japan, 7, 9–10
Flaming Dart operations, 58–59, 61, 79
Fleet, James Van, 22
Flexible response, 29
Flood, Daniel P., 271n.31
"Four-Point Program," 137–38

Gayler, Noel A. M., 162
Geography, as control on Rolling
      Thunder, 132–33
Giap, Vo Nguyen, 138, 141, 152–53,
      155, 168
Ginsburgh, Robert N., 74, 100–101,
      112, 122, 144
Glassboro summit, 120
Goldwater, Barry, 201
Goodpaster, Andrew J., 247n.75
Great Britain, 13, 19, 63
Great Society program, 43, 118, 125,
      142
Greenhalgh, William H., 109, 122–
      23, 126, 131
Ground effort
  Johnson's escalation of, 66–67, 71–
      72, 83, 108
  McNamara's call for escalation of,
      69–70
  Phase II deployments, 89–90
Guerrilla warfare, Rolling Thunder's
      efficacy and, 117–18, 140–41

Haig, Alexander, 156, 178, 182
Haiphong, 88
  attack on thermal power plants of,
      106
  B-52 attacks on, 154
  Christmas bombing of (1972), 187–
      88
  October 1967 bombings of, 110
  oil storage in, 93–94
  POL strikes in, 97–98
  Prohibited Area restrictions on, 119

Rolling Thunder strikes against, 95,
      103
Hampton, Ephraim M., 33
Hanoi
  air attacks on power stations of
      (May 1967), 106–7
  Christmas bombings of (1972), 183,
      185–87, 188
  defenses of, 131
  evacuations of, 136–37, 197
  Linebacker's effect on, 167–68
  October 1967 attacks on, 110
  POL strikes in, 97–98
  Prohibited Area restrictions on, 119
  SAM assembly plant, 190
  Wheeler's call to attack targets in,
      113
Hanoi government: *see also* North
      Vietnam; Peace negotiations
  acceptance of in-place cease-fire,
      170–72
  demand for Thieu's removal, 160,
      170, 171
  détente and, 172–73, 196
  manipulation of negotiations time-
      table for military ends, 152
  Nixon's isolation of, from Chinese
      and Soviets, 149–50
  objectives at bargaining table, 170–
      71
Hanoi Rail Yard, 190
Hansell, Haywood, 2
Harris, Arthur, 6
Hickam, Horace, 3
Ho Chi Minh, 91–92, 104, 105–6
Ho Chi Minh Trail, 129, 133, 147
Hon Gay, 88
Honolulu Conference (1964), 47–48
Honolulu Conference (1965), 81–82
Hudson, Eugene L., 159
Hung, Pham, 168, 170
Huong, Tran Van, 56, 148
Hydroelectric power raids (Korean
      War), 17, 19, 20

Ia Drang Valley, 92
Industry, attacks on, 102–7, 125–26,
      139–40

Intelligence, Rolling Thunder controls from, 130
Interdiction
  accelerated, 88–92
  confusion over targets of, 121–22
  by FEAF, 15–16, 17, 19, 24–25
  by Linebacker I, 162
  McNaughton on, 94
  by Rolling Thunder, 88–92, 99, 134–35
  as tactical function, 30
Irrigation dams
  JCS failure to target, during Rolling Thunder, 126–27
  McNaughton's call to attack, 94
  raids on (Korean War), 17–19, 22, 23–24, 36

Japan in World War II, 7, 9–11
Jason Summer Study (December 1967), 111–12
Jason Summer Study (Fall 1966), 99–101
JCS: *see* Joint Chiefs of Staff (JCS)
Johnson, Alexis, 68
Johnson, Gerald W., 184, 185, 194, 201
Johnson, Harold K., 79
Johnson, Lyndon B.: *see also* Rolling Thunder (2 March 1965–31 October 1968); Tuesday luncheons
  absences from Washington, 125
  approval of POL raids, 95
  backchannel communication with Wheeler, 247n.75
  concern over Communism's spread, 41–42
  concern over Soviet and/or Chinese intervention, 141–42
  decision to use air power, 40
  de-escalation of war, 114
  ego of, 125
  escalations of ground effort, 66–67, 71–72, 83, 108
  on JCS bombing plan, 51–52
  letter to Ho Chi Minh (February 1967), 104, 105–6

  McNamara's call for escalating ground effort and, 69–70
  objectives of, xv, 101, 204
  Phase A–Phase B plan, 104
  preconceived ideas coloring policy, 209
  reliance on civilian advisers, 122–24
  response to Pleiku raid, 58
  San Antonio formula, 112
  uncertainty over POL strikes, 96–97
  view of bombing's utility, xiv, 71–72, 142–43
  war aims of, 40–44
Johnson, Robert, 32, 54
Joint Chiefs of Staff (JCS)
  alternatives to NSC Working group plans, 78
  call for extending war to Laos and Cambodia, 107
  involvement in Linebacker I, 164
  involvement in Linebacker II, 190–91
  involvement in Rolling Thunder
    accelerated interdiction program, 88–92
    call for intensification, 110
    evaluation, 90–91
    failure to target irrigation dams and dikes, 126–27
    focus on targeting industrial base, 126
    ninety-four-target plan, 51, 60, 77, 127, 208
    "Operating Target List," 109
    perceptions of objectives, 73–76
    Rolling Thunder 52 plan, 102–7
    target selection, 86
    12-week bombing campaign (March 1964), 80
  memorandum (2 June 1964) to McNamara, 75
  Operations Plan (OPLAN) 37-64, 45–47
  pre-Rolling Thunder plans for air campaign, 51–52
  rejection of McNamara's view of war, 102
  restraints on Korean air war, 20
Joy, C. Turner, 20, 22, 25

Kennedy, John F., 34
Kennedy, Robert, 114
Kep airfield, 99
Kep Rail Yard, 132
Khanh, Nguyen, 40, 52, 56
Khiem, Tran Thien, 52
Khrushchev, Nikita, 24
Kinh No storage complex, 186
Kissinger, Henry A., 204: see also
        Linebacker I (10 May 1972–23
        October 1972); Linebacker II
        (18–29 December 1972); Peace
        negotiations
    assessment of Easter Offensive, 153
    on escalated aerial assault (1972),
        154
    Moscow visit (April 1972), 155
    negotiations with Le Duc Tho
        August 1969, 147–48
        December 1972, 180–82
        January 1973, 198
        July–August 1972, 160
        May 1972, 155–56
        November 1972, 179–80, 269n.7
        September–October 1972, 162–
        63, 171–72
    Paris negotiations (1967), 109–10
    secret visit to China (1971), 150
    skill as negotiator, 173–74
    on Thieu's demands, 178
    Thieu's demands on, 174–75
Kontum, 155
Korean War, 12–26; see also Far East
        Air Forces (FEAF)
    Air Force role in, 3
    air pressure strategy in, 16–19, 26
    American political resolve and, 37
    bombing doctrine after, xiv, 3, 27–32
    bomb tonnage dropped, 22
    Chinese intervention in, 14–16
    compared with Vietnam War, 39–
        40
    hydroelectric power raids, 17, 19,
        20
    irrigation dam raids, 17–19, 22, 23–
        24, 36
    peace negotiations, 18–19, 22–25
    political objectives during, 12–14

POW issue, 14, 16, 22–23
    target selection during, 21
    war aims, 3, 36–37
Kosygin, Aleksei, 104–5
Kuo-chuan, Wang, 138
Kusong dam, 18
Kuwonga dam, 18
Ky, Nguyen Cao, 68, 95, 171

Lam, Tram Van, 200
Lang Chi Hydroelectric Plant, 164
Lang Dang Rail Yard, 189
Lansdale, Edward, 138
Laos, invasion of (1971), 168
Lavelle, John D., 264n.16
Le Duan, 168, 169
Leggett, Robert L., 169
LeMay, Curtis E., 208
    Air Force bombing doctrine under,
        29, 35–36
    authority delegated to, 8
    on B-29 use in Korean War, 26
    combat experience, 6–7
    firebombing of Japan, 7
    on prospects of winning Vietnam
        war, 206–7
    Rolling Thunder campaign design,
        76
    on SAC, 29
    on strategic bombing's efficacy, 11
    on Vietnam War aims, 73
Lewandowski, Januscz, 104
Libya, April 1986 attack on, xvi
Limited war, 32–34, 118
Linebacker I (10 May 1972–23 Octo-
        ber 1972), xv
    area vs. precision targets, 159
    B-52 strikes in, 159
    campaign overview, 158–63
    Congressional resistance to, 150
    controls on, 163–66
    Easter Offensive (1972) and, 151,
        152–58
    JCS target selection, 164
    May 2 meeting and, 155–56
    October accord and, 175–76
    October 23 cessation of, 162
    public support of, 150
    rationale for, 151–58

results and efficacy, 166–76
  conventional warfare and, 173
  détente and, 172–73
  on Hanoi, 167–68
  "honorable peace" goal and, 174–75
  military's perception of, 176
  negotiations and, 168–76
  Nixon's limited objectives and, 174
  supply line destruction, 167
  tonnage dropped, 166–67
  7th Air Force participation in, 161
  Soviet acquiescence to, 157–58
  war aims, xvi, 148–51, 158, 162
Linebacker II (18–29 December 1972), xiii, xv
  B-52 strikes, 159, 182–83, 186–90
  Congress and, 178, 191–92
  controls on, 188–94
  military perception of, 201–2
  public criticism of, 191
  rationale for, 179–84
  results and efficacy of, 194–202
    civilian casualties, 195
    honorable agreement, 195–96
    resumption of negotiations, 189–90, 197–99
    Thieu's acceptance of January agreement, 199–201
    tonnage dropped, 194
  routing patterns, 185, 186–88
  SAC participation in, 184, 185, 192
  war aims, 177–79

MacArthur, Douglas, 13, 15, 20
McCain, John S., Jr., 161
McCarthy, Eugene, 114
McCarthy, James M., 193
McCone, John, 55, 66–67
McConnell, John P.
  on attacking agricultural base, 110–11, 126
  perception of objectives, 74, 75–76
  on Rolling Thunder, 82–84, 144, 145
McNamara, Robert S., 75
  eight-week air campaign plan (February 1965), 79
  on escalation of war, 68–70, 94–95, 99–100, 107
  at Honolulu Conference (April 1965), 81–82
  involvement in Rolling Thunder assessment, 84, 108, 144
  call for bombing pauses, 90, 91
  call for "evolving" program, 89–90
  opposition to expansion, 111
  targeting process, 80, 85–88, 122, 128
  JCS alienation from, 102
  on Khanh government, 40–42
  on morale-boosting effect of bombing, 48, 141
  opposition to OPLAN, 46
  POL raids and, 98
  resignation of, 111
  on "Rostow thesis," 50–51
  on sustained bombing, 60
  tension with Wheeler, 123–24
  in Tuesday luncheons, 85, 121
  on war aims in Vietnam, 39, 55, 204
McNaughton, John T., 81, 121
  on interdiction, 94
  opposition to extending war, 107
  on Rolling Thunder's efficacy, 64–65
  on sustained bombing, 55, 57, 59–60
Malenkov, Georgyi, 24
Manila Conference (1966), 103
Mansfield, Mike, 192
Martin, Glen W., 74
Massive retaliation, 27, 29, 36; see also Strategic nuclear attack
Mayo, Ben I., 16
Meyer, John C., 184, 186, 187, 190, 201
Meyers, Gilbert L., 86, 98, 122
Michalski, Jerzy, 91
MiG airfields, attacks on, 106–7
MiG fighters, 131, 165, 193
Minh, Duong Van, 52
Mining of Northern harbors, 158, 167
Momyer, William W., 25, 145, 207, 209
Moore, Joseph H., 75, 129
Moorer, Thomas H., 156, 158, 177, 184, 190, 201

Morale
  pilot, 134
  South Vietnamese, 48, 49–50, 141
Moyers, Bill, 85
Murphy, Robert, 111
Mustin, Lloyd, 54, 78

National Council of Reconciliation
    and Concord, 162–63, 172
National Security Action Memoran-
    dums (NSAM)
  273, 40, 42
  288, 40–42, 45, 74, 78
  314, 51–53
  328, 66–67
National Security Council (NSC)
  "Working Group" (1964), 53–
    56, 78
Negative objectives, xv, 4; see also
    Johnson, Lyndon B.; Nixon,
    Richard M.; specific bombing
    campaigns
Negotiations, peace: see Peace negoti-
    ations
Nehru, J., 23
Nitze, Paul, 26–27
Nixon, Richard M.: see also Kissinger,
    Henry A.; Linebacker I (10
    May 1972–23 October 1972);
    Linebacker II (18–29 Decem-
    ber 1972); Peace negotiations
  assessment of Easter Offensive, 153
  bombing policy, xiv–xv
  desire to end war, 150–51
  intent behind Linebacker II, 177
  isolation of Hanoi, 149–50
  negotiations with Hanoi
    ambiguity in October 1971 peace
      proposal, 263n.5
    expansion of air campaigns dur-
      ing, 161, 163
    1971 peace proposal, 148–49
    reelection campaign and, 160
  objectives of, 148, 149, 163–64, 174,
    178, 204–5
  Peking trip (1972), 152
  pledge to support Thieu govern-
    ment, 178–79

  suspension of bombing north of 20th
    parallel, 163, 266n.52
  ultimatum to Thieu, 183–84
  warning to Soviets and Chinese
    against Northern offensive
    (1972), 151–52
  withdrawal of men (1969), 147
North Vietnam: see also Hanoi; Hanoi
    government; Politburo, North
    Vietnamese
  Chinese and Soviet support of, 42–
    43, 135, 141–42, 172–73, 196
  defenses, 131–33, 165–66
  imports, 135
  perceived dependence of Viet Cong
    on, 48
  rice production, 137
  supply needs, 259n.83
NSC 81/1, 13
Nuclear war, priority in preparing for,
    27, 234n.130

Objectives, political: see Negative ob-
    jectives; Positive objectives;
    specific U.S. presidents
October accord (1972), 162–63, 172
  Linebacker I and, 175–76
  Thieu's objections to, 162–63, 175,
    197
  Thieu's proposed changes to, 178
Officers, air: see Air commanders
Oil storage areas: see POL (petroleum,
    oil, and lubricants) raids
On Strategy: A Critical Analysis of the
    Vietnam War (Summers), 207
"Operating Target List," 109
Operational vs. administrative con-
    trol, 128, 256n.51
Operation Barrel Roll, 57, 129
Operation Bullet Shot, 152, 153
Operation Cedar Falls, 105
Operation Constant Guard, 153
Operation Freedom Porch Bravo, 154
Operation Freedom Train, 154
Operation Proud Deep Alpha, 151
Operations Plan (OPLAN) 37-64, 45–
    47
Operation Steel Tiger, 129

Operation Strangle I & II, 16
Operation Thunderclap, 14

P-51 Mustang, 5
Pacific Air Forces (PACAF), 32, 128
Pacific Command (PACOM), 128
Panmunjom, 19, 229n.50
Paris negotiations (1967), 109–10
Paul Doumer Bridge, 158
Parrish, Noel F., 29
Peace negotiations: see also Kissinger,
    Henry A.; Nixon, Richard M.;
    Tho, Le Duc
  Hanoi objectives during, 170–71
  Korean War, 18–19, 22–25
  Linebacker I's effect on, 168–76
  Linebacker II's effect on, 189–90,
    197–99
Pearson, Lester, 96
Peking, Nixon's trip to (1972), 152
Petersen, E. A., 185
Phuc Yen airfield, 77, 99, 110
Pilot(s)
  inexperience of, 165–66, 192–93
  morale of, 134
  operational controls on, 131,
    258n.78
Pleiku, 57, 58
Pocket Money operation, 158
Politburo, North Vietnamese: see also
    Hanoi government
  commitment to Easter Offensive,
    168–69
  motivation for peace settlement,
    198–99
  on prisoner exchange and matériel
    support for South, 172
Political resolve, effectiveness of air
    power and, 37
POL (petroleum, oil, and lubricants)
    raids, 90–91
  delays in, 95–96
  efficacy of, 135–36
  in Hanoi and Haiphong, 97–98
  intelligence information and, 93–
    94, 99
  Johnson and, 95–97
  public opinion on, 98
  during Rolling Thunder, 92–102

  in World War II, 6, 227n.15
Positive objectives, xv, see also John-
    son, Lyndon B.; Nixon, Rich-
    ard M.; specific bombing cam-
    paigns
Power plants: see Electric power
    plants, attacks on
Prisoners of war, 14, 16, 22–23, 172
Prohibited Area restrictions, 119
Protests, antiwar, 91, 109
Public opinion
  on bombing halt (1968), 253n.167
  on Flaming Dart, 61
  on Linebacker I, 150
  on Linebacker II, 191
  on POL attacks, 98
  after Tet Offensive, 114–15
Pueblo incident (1968), 120
Pyongyang, 16, 20

Quang Khe naval base, 63
Quang Tri, 155, 170, 173
Quat, Phan Huy, 63, 64, 68
Qui Nhon attack, 58

Randolph, Richard L., 16
Read, Benjamin, 121
Red River dikes, 126
Retaliation, massive, 27, 29, 36; see
    also Strategic nuclear attack
Rhee, Syngman, 23
Ridgway, Matthew, 16, 20, 231n.80
RIOT SQUAD, 32–33
Rodgers, Turner, C., 11–12
Rogers, William P., 195
Rolling Thunder (2 March 1965–31
    October 1968), xv, 39–72: see
    also Johnson, Lyndon B.; Joint
    Chiefs of Staff (JCS)
  aircraft types performing, 133
  April 1965 raids, 80
  bombing pauses, 119, 120, 125
    December–January (1965–66),
      90–91
    Johnson on, 91
    May 1965, 67, 83
    October 1968, 147, 263n.2
  calls for escalating (1965), 82–83
  campaign designs, 76–84

Rolling Thunder (*cont.*)
    controls on, 118–34
        Air Force bombing doctrine, 125–
            27
        American image overseas, 118
        armament restrictions, 118–19
        concern over Soviet and/or Chi-
            nese intervention, 67–68, 71,
            74, 85, 118
        conditions in South Vietnam,
            119–20
        desire for "sensible" air cam-
            paign, 127
        enemy defenses, 131–32
        geography and weather, 132–33
        Great Society program, 118, 125,
            142
        international events, 120
        interservice competition, 129–30
        Johnson's absences from Wash-
            ington, 125
        Johnson's ego, 125
        Johnson's political objectives and,
            118
        maintenance of Western alli-
            ances, 118
        military intelligence, 130
        military organizational arrange-
            ments, 128–29
        pilot morale, 134
        target restrictions, 119
        target selection conflicts, 122–23
        Tuesday luncheons and, 120–22
        Wheeler–McNamara tension,
            123–24
    disagreement among advisers over,
        44, 60–62
    efficacy of
        agrarian economy and, 144
        guerrilla warfare and, 117–18,
            140–41
        Johnson's controls and, 144–46
        perceptions of, 80–81, 142–46
        Tet Offensive and, 141
        North Vietnamese resolve and,
            140
    escalation of ground effort (1965)
        and, 82
    51, 98–99

52, 102–7
57, 108–15
Honolulu Conference (April 1965)
    on, 81–82
initial raids (Spring, 1965), 63–64
international perceptions of, 142
Jason Summer Studies of, 99–101,
    111–12
Johnson's doubts about, 60–61
Johnson's ordering of, 59, 63–64
lack of immediate success, 65
Linebacker I compared to, 163–64
NSAM 328 and, 66–67
pilot frustration over, 258n.78
public announcement of, 61–63, 64
rationale for, 45–56
    Bien Hoa raid, 53
    enemy provocations, 51–52, 56
    Flaming Dart operations, 58–59
    Honolulu Conference (1964) and,
        47–48
    NSAM 288 and, 45
    NSC Working Group (1964), and
        53–56
    OPLAN 37-64 and, 45–47
    "Rostow thesis" and, 50–51
    South Vietnam's stability and, 49,
        51–53
results of, 134–46
    civilian toll, 136–37
    dollar costs, 134
    on industrial capacity, 139–40
    on Johnson's objectives, 139–42
    on North Vietnamese imports,
        135
    on oil storage areas and electric
        power plants, 135–36
    on Southern war, 140–41
    tonnage dropped, 134
    on Vietnamese resolve, 137–39
second "wise men" meeting and,
    113–14
strikes against Haiphong, 95, 103
target selection, 52, 84–88, 105–6
Tet Offensive and, 112–15
war aims of, xvi, 40–44, 59
    destruction of industry and power
        plants, 102–7

disparity in, 204
ground support, 72
interdiction, 88–92, 99, 134–35
perception of, by air com-
    manders, 68, 73–76, 81–84,
    86, 87, 100–103, 107–8
perception of, by civilian leaders,
    67–71, 84, 108
POL destruction, 92–102
worsening South Vietnam situation
    and, 67–68
Rolling Thunder Alpha, 158; see also
    Linebacker I (10 May 1972–23
    October 1972)
Ronning, Chester, 96
Roosevelt, Franklin D., 3–4, 5, 7–8
Rostow, Walt, 48, 50, 66, 71, 85, 124
opposition to bombing halt, 96
opposition to JCS plan to extend
    war to Laos and Cambodia,
    107
on Rolling Thunder's effectiveness,
    143
support of Swinton theory, 50
Route packages (target zones), 129–
    30, 161, 164
Rusk, Dean, 24, 43, 48–53, 55, 64, 68,
    85, 91, 96, 122, 140, 204
doubts about sustained bombing, 59
on McNamara's call for escalating
    war, 69
on North Vietnamese tenacity,
    261n.114
on Rolling Thunder's effectiveness,
    143
on Tuesday luncheons, 121
Ryan, John D., 98, 123

SAC: see Strategic Air Command
    (SAC)
Salisbury, Harrison, 136
SAMs, 131, 188, 189, 193
SAM sites, 165, 187–90, 194
San Antonio formula, 112
Saxbe, William, 191–92
Schaffer, Ronald, 206
Schoenbrun, David, 132
Seaborn, Blair, 138

2d Air Division, 128; see also Air
    Force: 7th
Seventh Fleet, 21
Sharp, U.S. Grant, 75, 81, 90–91, 121,
    128, 207
call for bombing escalation, 82–83
eight-week pressure program, 79–80
on political controls, 208
on POL targeting, 93
response to second Jason Summer
    Study, 112
on Rolling Thunder, 80–84, 105–6,
    144–45
route package decision, 129
SIERRA, 32–33
Single Integrated Operational Plan
    (SIOP), 29
Smart, Jacob, 17
Smart bombs, 159, 164, 167
Smith, Bromley, 95
South Vietnam
Buddhist demonstrations in
    (March–May 1965), 95
Marines deployed in, 66–67
morale of, 48, 49–50, 141
Rolling Thunder and, 67–68, 119–
    20, 140–41
success against Easter Offensive,
    173
war effort before Tet Offensive, 205
Soviet Union
acquiescence to Linebacker I, 157–
    58
American concern over intervention
    by, 67–68, 71, 74, 85, 118,
    141–42
border conflicts with China, 149–50
Nixon's isolation of Hanoi govern-
    ment from, 149–50
proposal to reopen Geneva Confer-
    ence, 63
response to American air attacks
    (1972), 154–55
response to Flaming Dart, 61
response to Nixon's warning against
    Northern offensive (1972),
    151–52
Rolling Thunder target selection
    and, 85

Soviet Union (*cont.*)
   support of North Vietnam, 42, 135,
      141–42, 172–73, 196
Spaatz, Carl A., 6, 8, 11
Stalin, Joseph, 4, 24
Stennis, John, 106
Stimson, Henry, 5
Stockdale, James B., 74, 195
Strategic air actions, 3, 30–31
Strategic Air Command (SAC)
   LeMay on, 29
   Linebacker II planning, 184, 185,
      192
   mission of, 29
   priority funding for, 28
"Strategic Air Operations" (Manual
   1-8), 27–28, 29, 36
Strategic nuclear attack, 27–32
   criticisms of, 32–34
   post-Korea emphasis on, 29–32
Strategy in the Missile Age (Brodie), 34
Stratemeyer, George E., 15, 16, 19–
   20, 21, 25
Sullivan, William, 198
Summers, Harry G., Jr., 207
Surface-to-air missiles: *see* SAMs
Surrender, unconditional, 4–12, 37
Swinton, Ernest, 50

Tactical Air Command (TAC), 28
Target selection: *see also* Route packages (target zones); Tuesday
   luncheons
   concern over Soviet and/or Chinese
      reaction and, 85
   decision chain in, 86–87
   in Korean War, 21
   Linebacker I, 164
   McNamara and, 80, 86, 87–88, 122,
      128
   package system of, 85–86
   Rolling Thunder, 52, 84–88, 105–6
   changing priorities in, 128
   conflict between civilian and mil-
      itary advisers over, 122–23
Taylor, Maxwell, 40, 42, 47, 49, 51,
   55–56, 58–59, 81, 140, 204
   opposition to bombing halt, 96
   on Rolling Thunder, 63–64, 68, 143

"Teaball" Weapons Control Center,
   165
Tet Offensive (1968), 84, 112–15, 127,
   206
   Rolling Thunder's efficacy and, 141
   Viet Cong's combat effectiveness
      and, 139
Tet truce (February 1967), 104
Thach, Nguyen Co, 197
Thai Nguyen steel complex, 103, 105
Thai Nguyen Thermal Power Plant,
   187
Thanh Hoa railroad bridge, 81
Thant, U, 96
Thao, Pham Ngoc, 63
"Theater Air Forces in Counter Air,
   Interdiction and Close Air
   Support Operations" (Manual
   1-7), 30
Theater (tactical) vs. strategic air ac-
   tions, 30–31
Thi, Nguyen Chanh, 95
Thieu, Nguyen Van, 204
   Hanoi's demand for removal of,
      170, 171
   January agreement and, 199–201
   misreading of Linebacker's success,
      174–75
   Nixon's ultimatum to, 183–84
   October accord and, 148, 162–63,
      175, 178, 197
   rejection of 8 May peace proposal,
      177
Tho, Le Duc, 168, 170; *see also* Peace
   negotiations
   negotiations with Kissinger
      August 1969, 147–48
      December 1972, 180–82
      January 1973, 198
      July–August 1972, 160
      May 1972, 155–56
      November 1972, 179–80, 269n.7
      September–October 1972, 162–
         63, 171–72
   on Thieu, 171
Thompson, George, 190
Thompson, Robert, 167, 168, 170
Thuy, Xuan, 156
Tien, Hguyen Van, 169

Timberlake, Edward J., 31, 32
Todd, Oliver, 136, 137
Toksan dam, 18, 22, 23
Tonkin Gulf, 49, 51, 52, 164
Tozer, Eliot, III, 134
Tra, Tran Van, 196
Trantafellu, Rockly, 131
Trinh, Nguyen Duy, 104, 112
Truman, Harry S, 7–8, 12–13, 14, 19
Truong, Nhu Tang, 170, 182
Tuesday luncheons, 85, 120–22, 124
    disruption of, due to Johnson's ab-
        sences, 125
    lack of military representation in,
        122
    target selection during, 85, 87–88
    Wheeler in, 111
Twining, Nathan F., 20

Unconditional surrender, 4–12, 37
United States Strategic Bombing Sur-
    vey (USSBS), 9–10, 12
"USAF in Limited War, The" (Hamp-
    ton), 33
U-Tapao Air Force base, 184, 185, 187

Vandenberg, Hoyt S., 19, 35
Viet Cong, 207; *see also* North
    Vietnam
    Bien Hoa attack, 77
    combat effectiveness after Tet Of-
        fensive, 139
    perceived dependence on North
        Vietnam (1964), 48
    resupply capacity, 135
    Rolling Thunder and, 56
    supply needs, 134–35, 259*n*.83
Vietnamization, 148, 151
Vogt, John W., Jr., 164–67, 176, 192,
    201
Vy, Nguyen Minh, 187, 197

War aims, xi; *see also* Korean War;
        Linebacker I (10 May 1972–23
        October 1972); Linebacker II
        (18–29 December 1972); Roll-
        ing Thunder (2 March 1965–31
        October 1968); World War II

destruction of enemy's will, 9–10
destruction of war-making capabil-
    ity, 4–9, 11
    LeMay on, 73
    McNamara on, 39, 55, 204
    unconditional surrender, 4–12
    in Vietnam, 40–44
Washington Post, 191
Weather, controlling effect of, 132–
    33, 166, 194
Westmoreland, William C., 68, 81,
    89, 103, 111, 129, 176
Weyland, O. P., 15, 17, 18, 21, 26, 32,
    36, 107
Wheeler, Earle G., 51, 55, 77, 81, 85,
    128, 130
    backchannel communication with
        Johnson, 247*n*.75
    call for POL strikes, 96–97
    concern over civilian casualties, 127
    exclusion from decision-making fo-
        rums, 122
    on failure to attack dikes, 126–27
    response to Tet Offensive, 113
    on Rolling Thunder, 81, 82–84, 103,
        107
    target selection, 86, 87
    tension with McNamara, 123–24
    in Tuesday luncheons, 111
Wicker, Tom, 191
Will, destruction of enemy's, 2, 9–10
Wilson, Charles E., 28
Wilson, Harold, 98, 104–5
Withdrawal from Vietnam, 147–49
World War II, 3–12, 125
    bomb tonnage dropped, 8
    POL targeting in, 6, 227*n*.15
    strategic air campaigns, xiv, 3
    war aims, 3, 37

XB-17, 2
Xom Bay raid, 63

Yalta, joint declaration at, 4
Yalu River hydroelectric plants, 20
Yen Vien Railroad Yard, 159, 186, 187

Zeit, Die, 191
Zimmerman, Don Z., 18